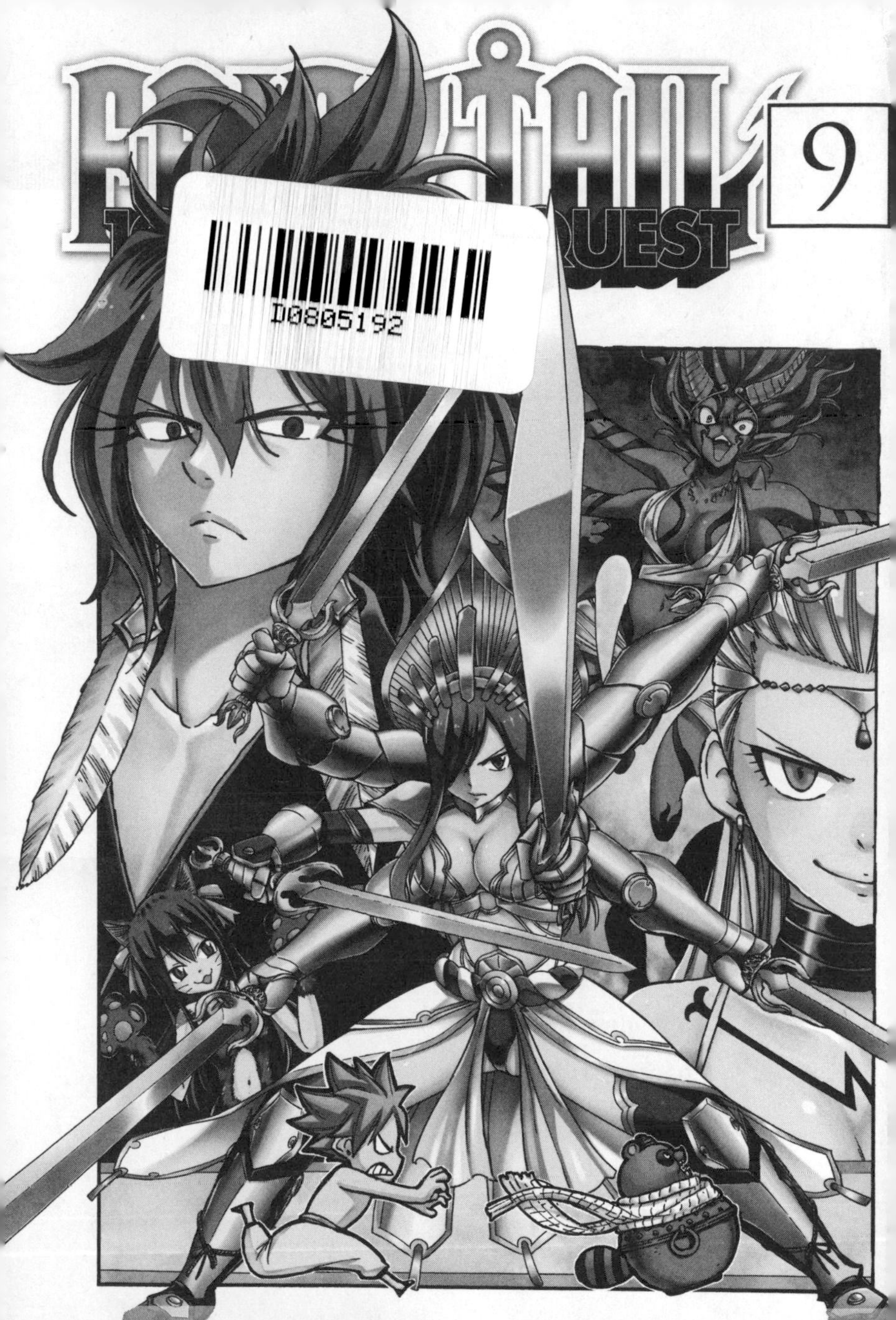
QUEST
9

HIRO MASHIMA ATSUO UEDA

FAIRY TAIL
100 YEARS
QUEST

CONTENTS

FAIRY TAIL
100 YEARS QUEST

Chapter 73: Moonlit Banquet

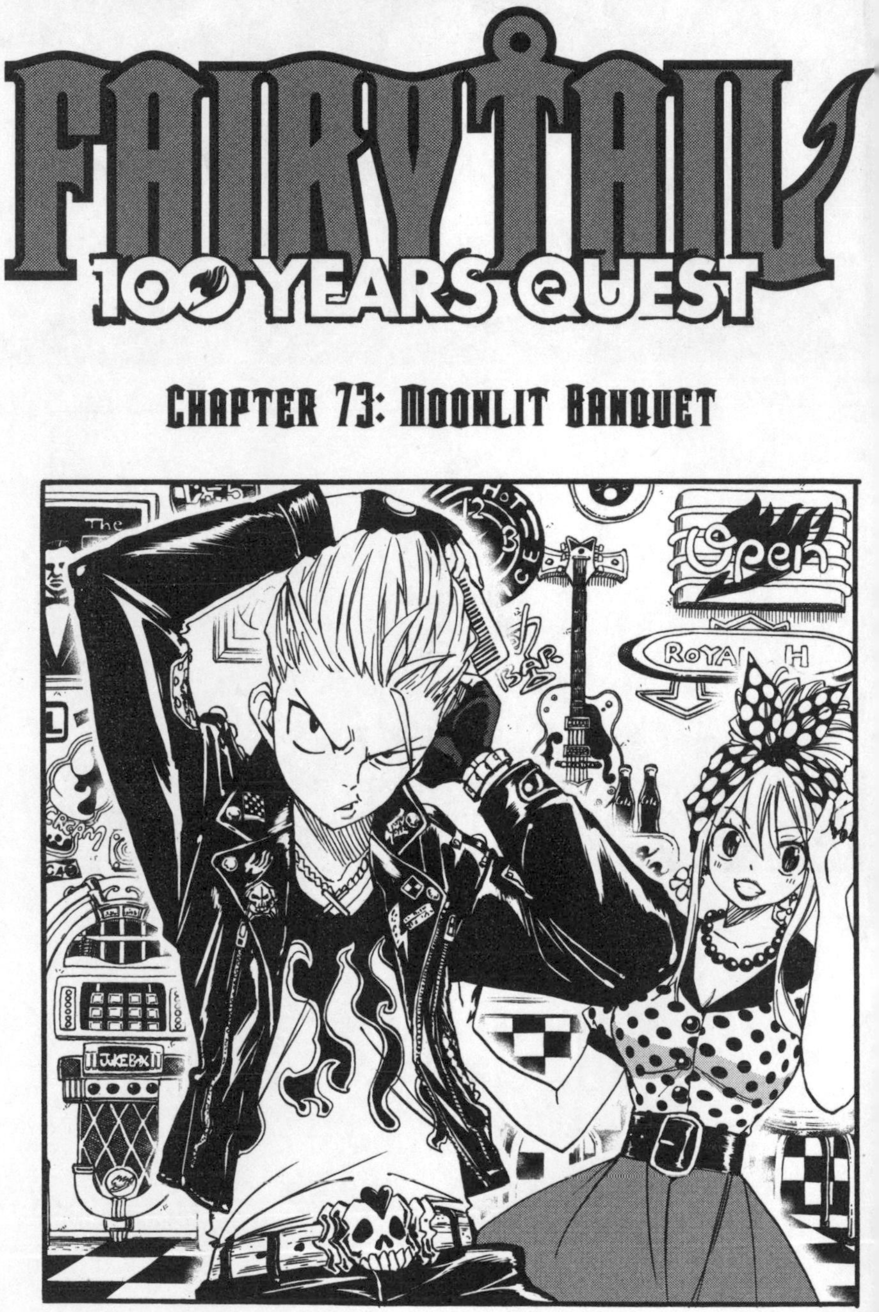

The
Open
BAR
JUKEBOX

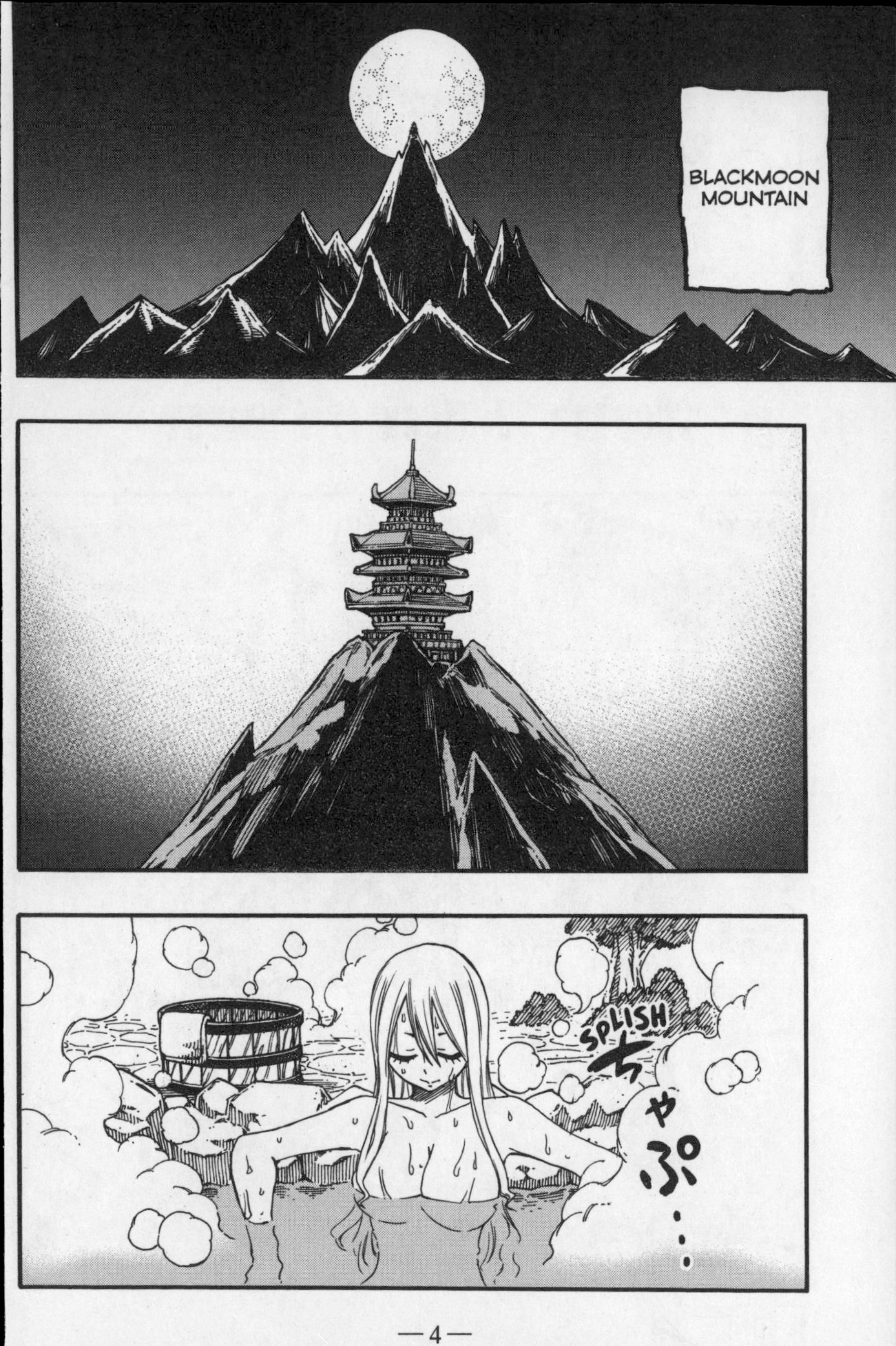
BLACKMOON
MOUNTAIN
SPLISH
ちゃぷ…

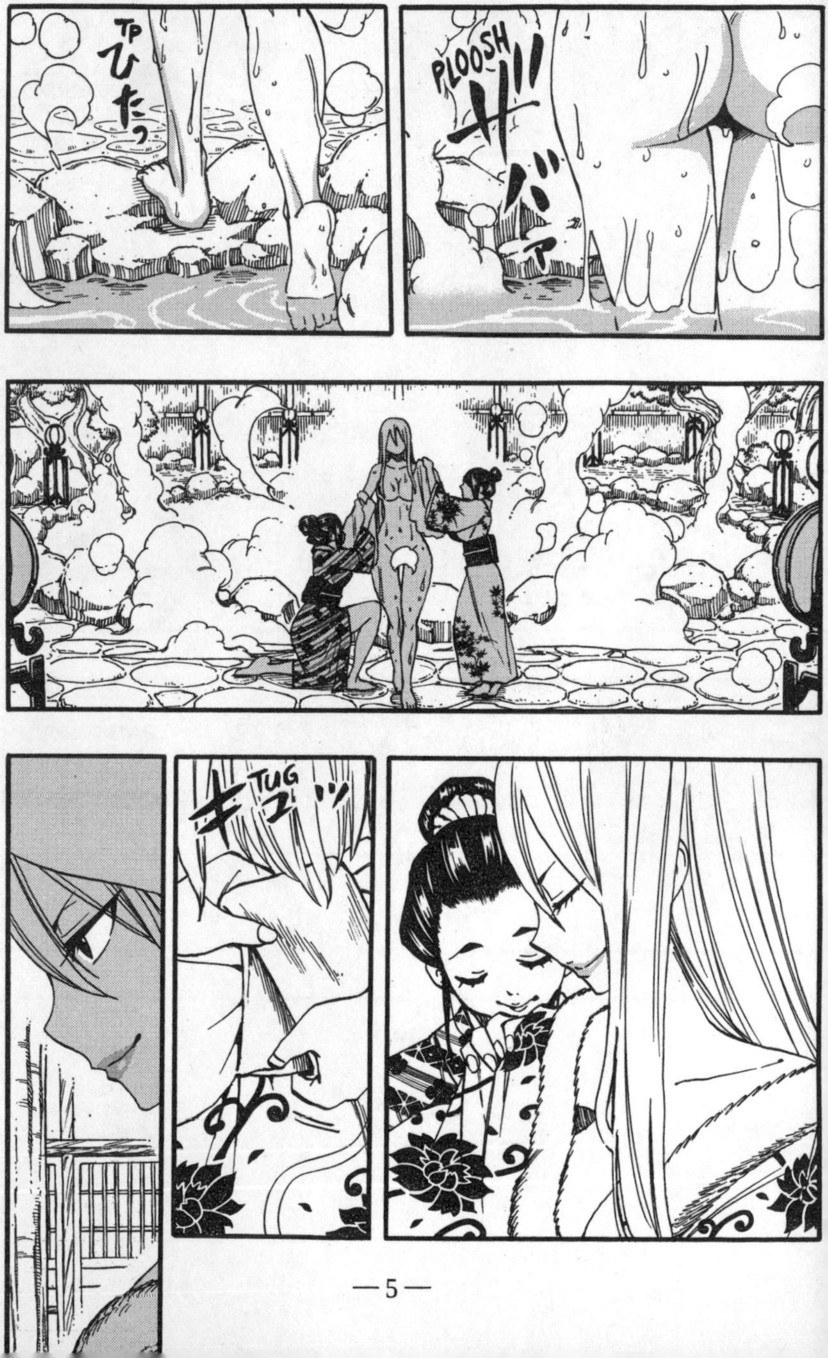
PLOOSH
ザバァ
TP
ひたっ
TUG
ギュッ

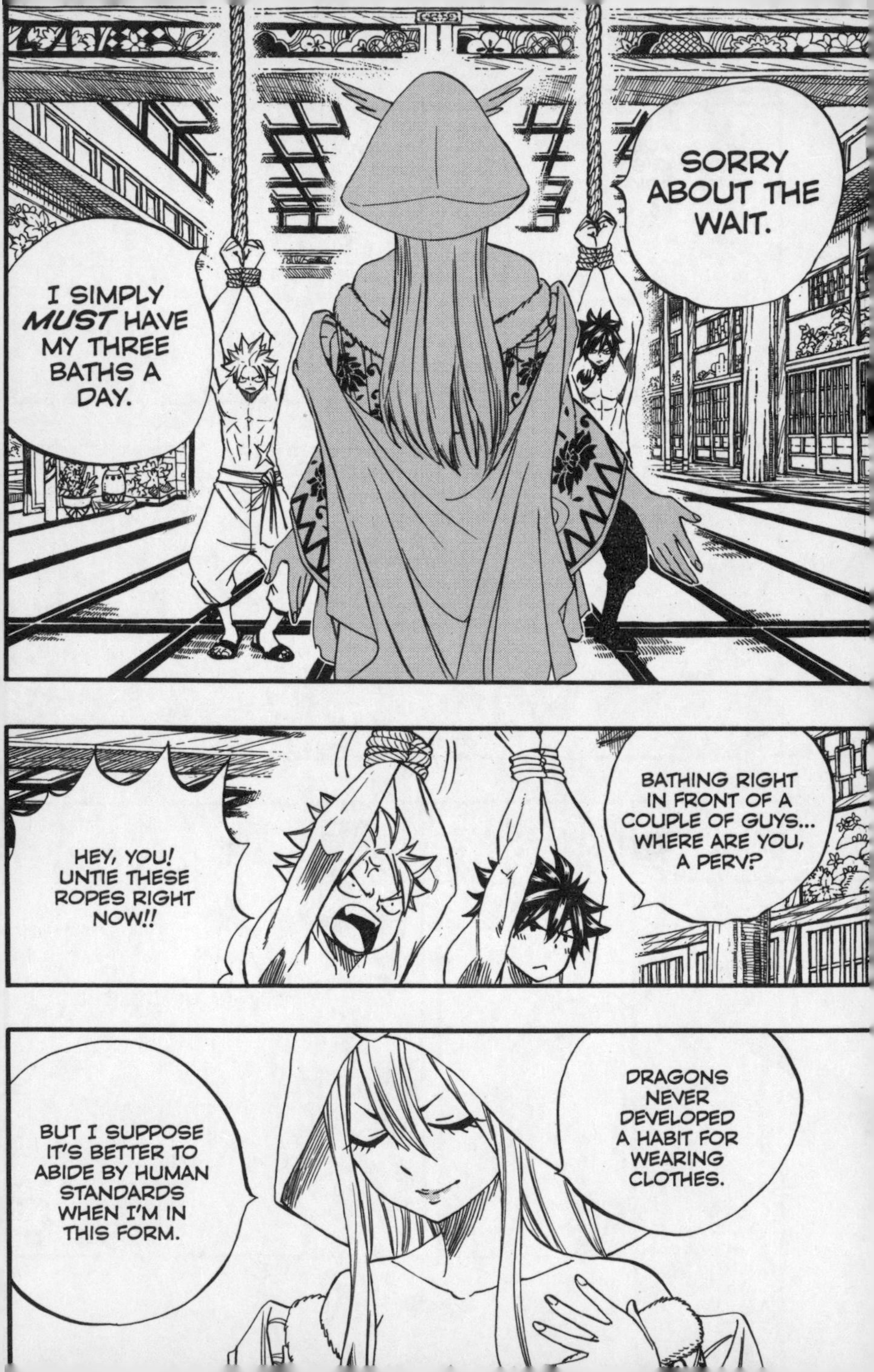
SORRY ABOUT THE WAIT.
I SIMPLY *MUST* HAVE MY THREE BATHS A DAY.
BATHING RIGHT IN FRONT OF A COUPLE OF GUYS... WHERE ARE YOU, A PERV?
HEY, YOU! UNTIE THESE ROPES RIGHT NOW!!
DRAGONS NEVER DEVELOPED A HABIT FOR WEARING CLOTHES.
BUT I SUPPOSE IT'S BETTER TO ABIDE BY HUMAN STANDARDS WHEN I'M IN THIS FORM.

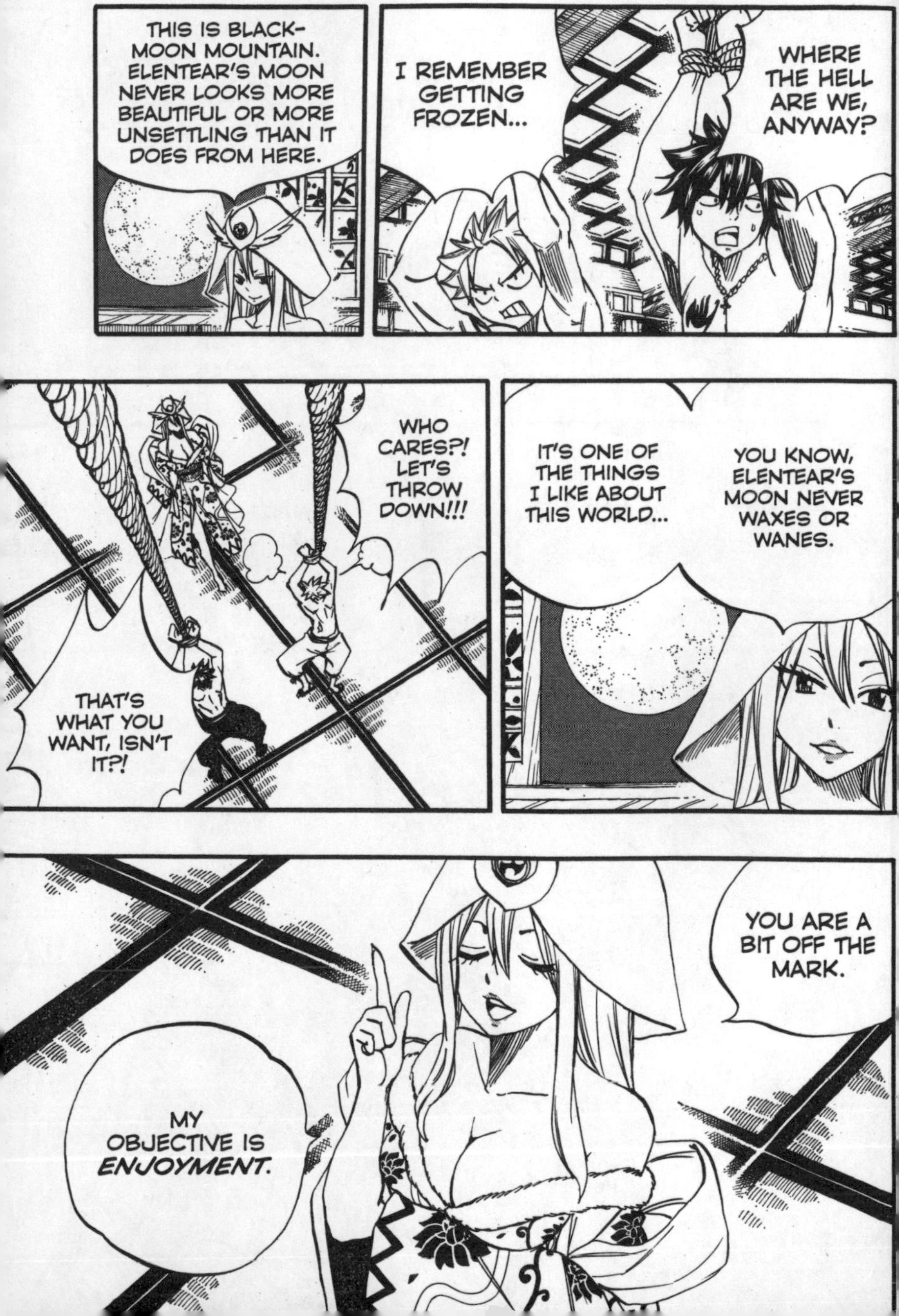
WHERE THE HELL ARE WE, ANYWAY?
I REMEMBER GETTING FROZEN...
THIS IS BLACK-MOON MOUNTAIN. ELENTEAR'S MOON NEVER LOOKS MORE BEAUTIFUL OR MORE UNSETTLING THAN IT DOES FROM HERE.
YOU KNOW, ELENTEAR'S MOON NEVER WAXES OR WANES.
IT'S ONE OF THE THINGS I LIKE ABOUT THIS WORLD...
WHO CARES?! LET'S THROW DOWN!!!
THAT'S WHAT YOU WANT, ISN'T IT?!
YOU ARE A BIT OFF THE MARK.
MY OBJECTIVE IS *ENJOYMENT*.

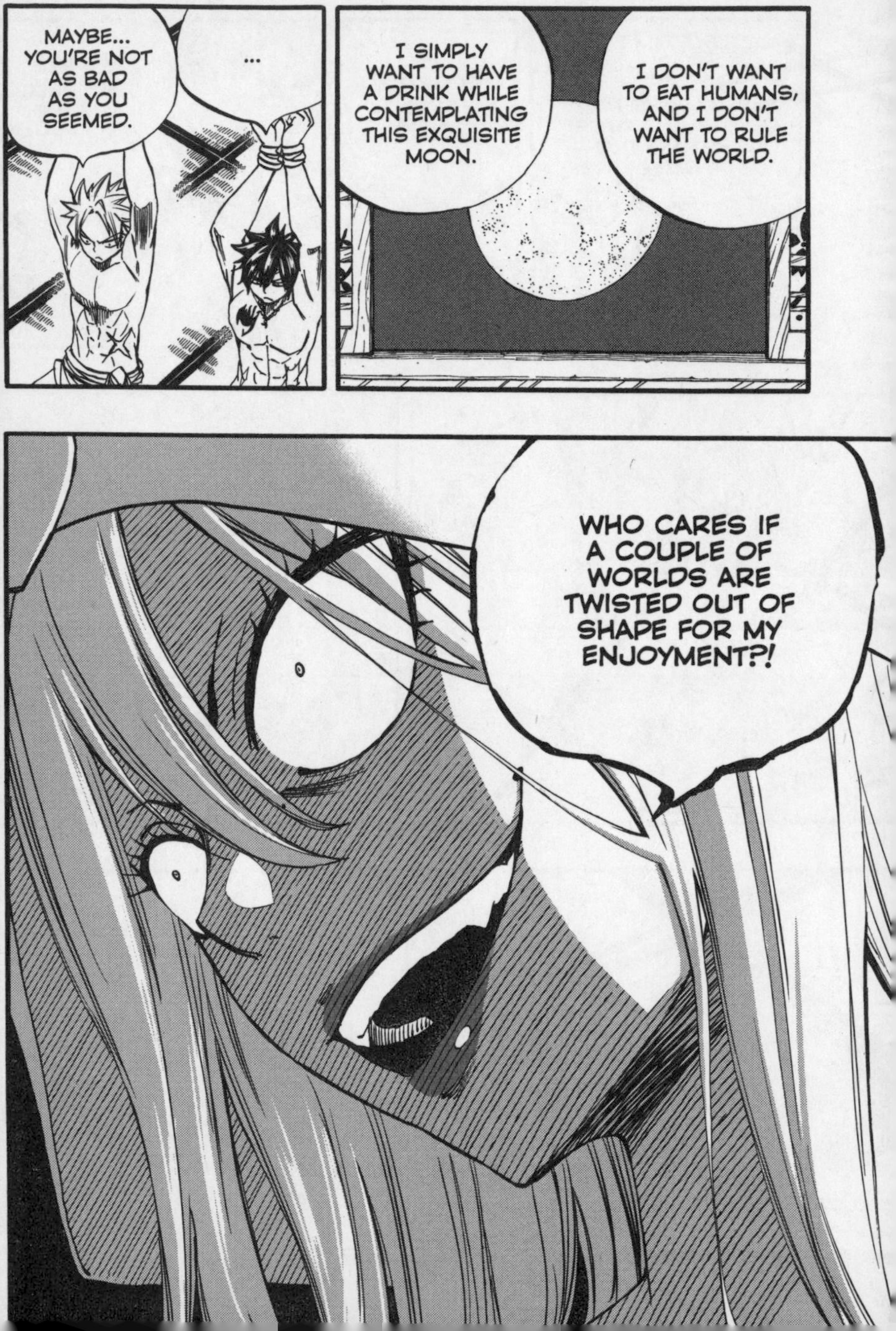
I DON'T WANT TO EAT HUMANS, AND I DON'T WANT TO RULE THE WORLD.
I SIMPLY WANT TO HAVE A DRINK WHILE CONTEMPLATING THIS EXQUISITE MOON.
...
MAYBE... YOU'RE NOT AS BAD AS YOU SEEMED.
WHO CARES IF A COUPLE OF WORLDS ARE TWISTED OUT OF SHAPE FOR MY ENJOYMENT?!

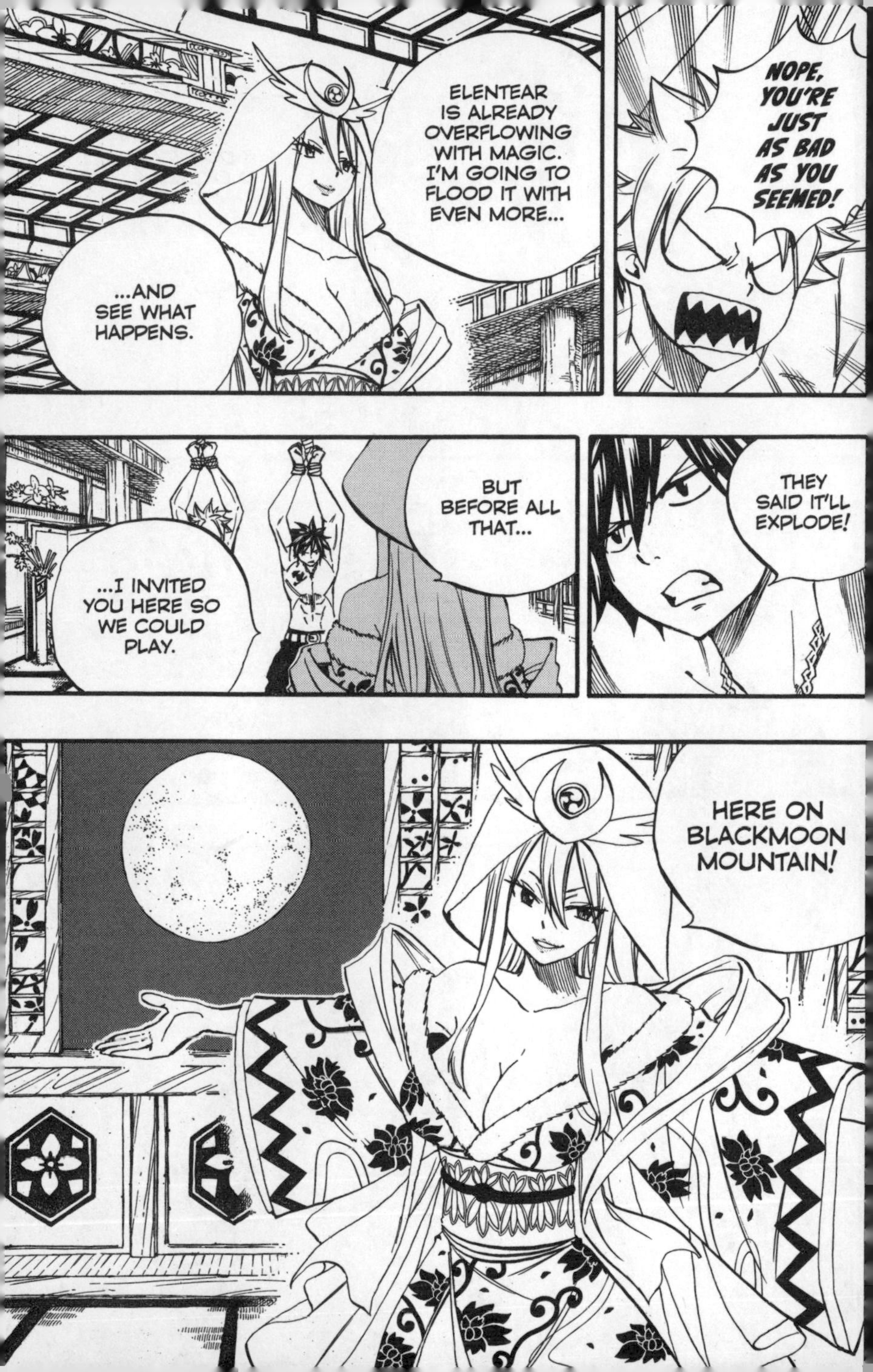
NOPE, YOU'RE JUST AS BAD AS YOU SEEMED!
ELENTEAR IS ALREADY OVERFLOWING WITH MAGIC. I'M GOING TO FLOOD IT WITH EVEN MORE...
...AND SEE WHAT HAPPENS.
THEY SAID IT'LL EXPLODE!
BUT BEFORE ALL THAT...
...I INVITED YOU HERE SO WE COULD PLAY.
HERE ON BLACKMOON MOUNTAIN!

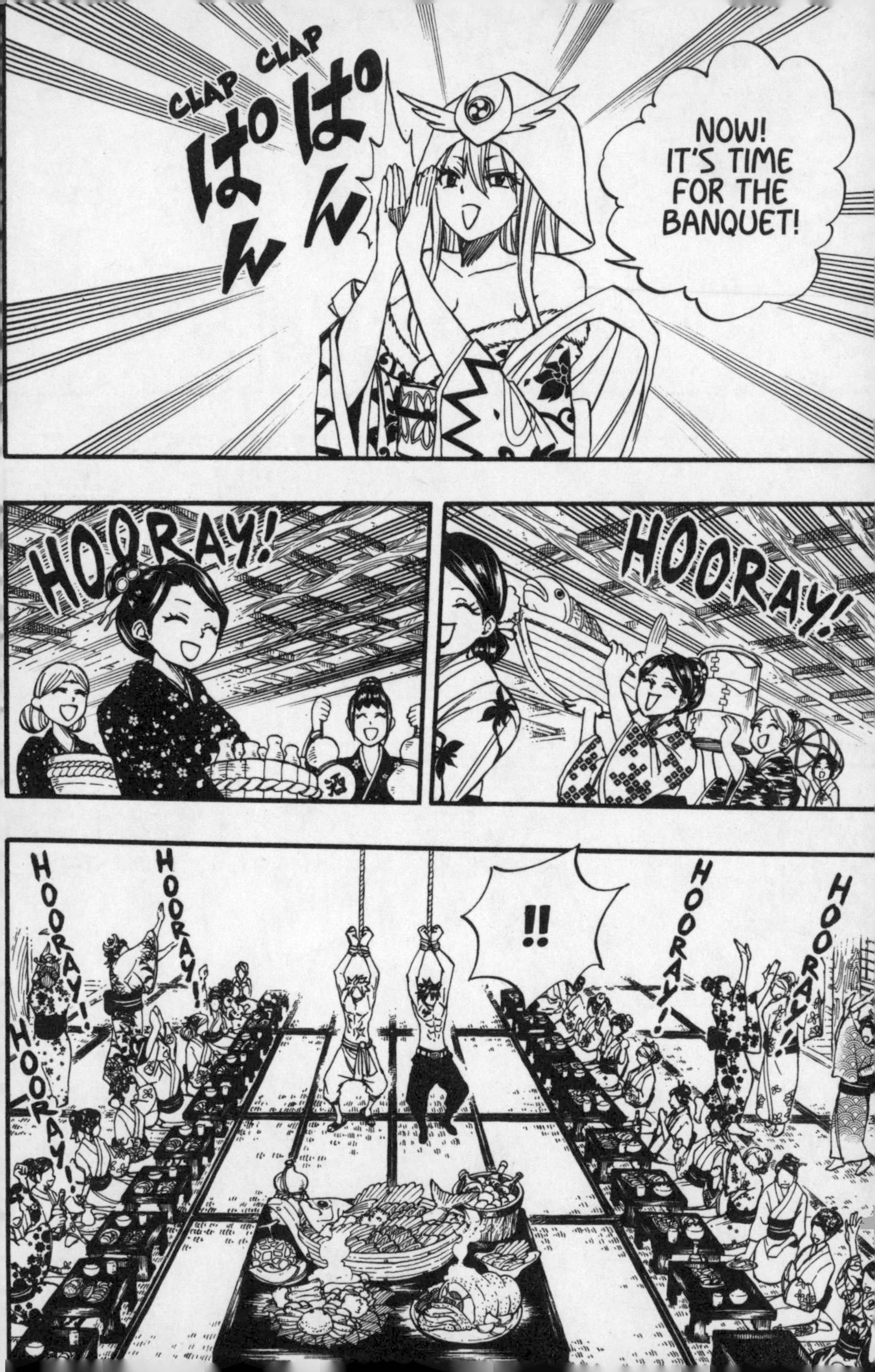
NOW! IT'S TIME FOR THE BANQUET!
CLAP CLAP
ぱんぱん
HOORAY!
HOORAY!
HOORAY!
HOORAY!
!!
HOORAY!
HOORAY!
HOORAY!

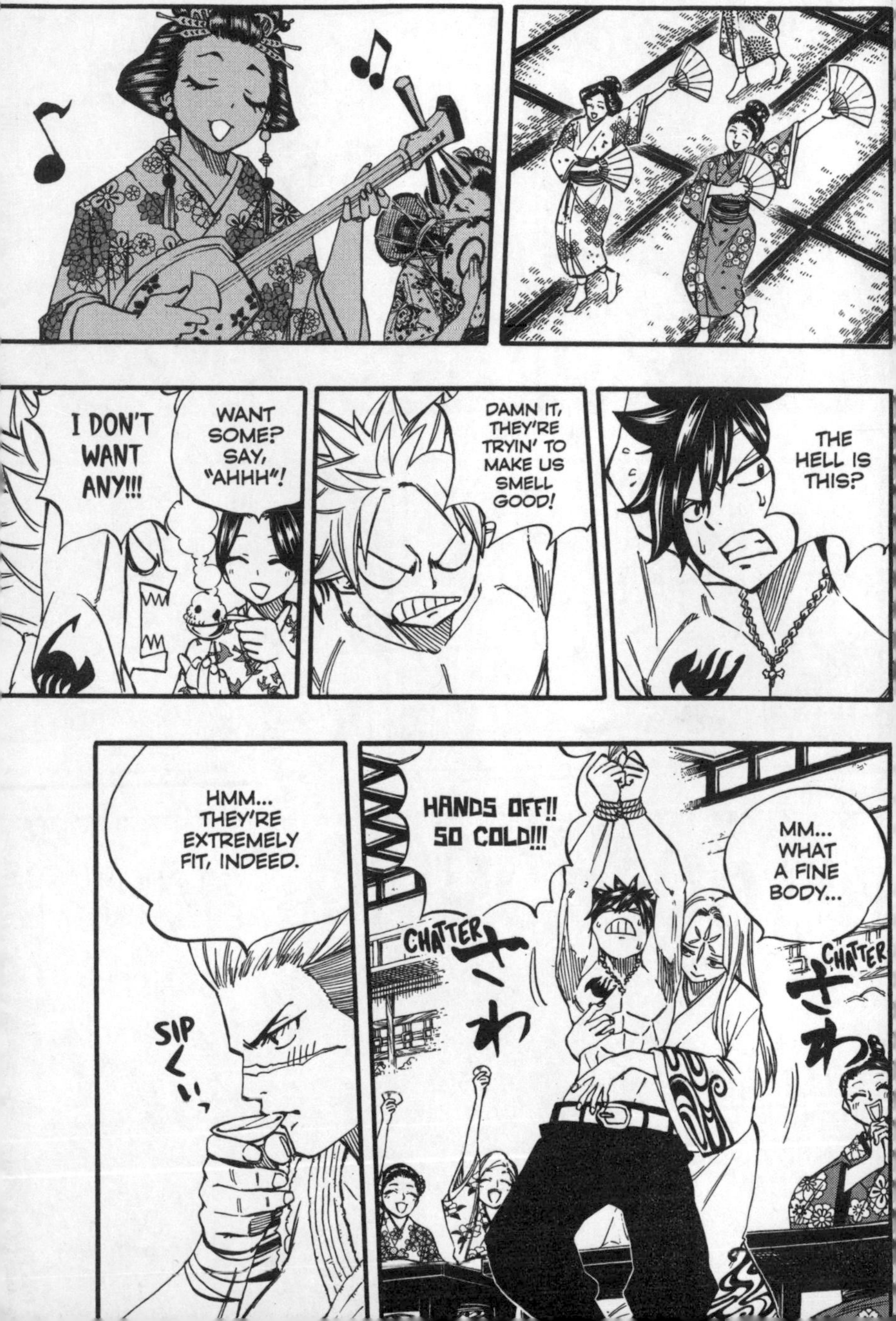
THE HELL IS THIS?
DAMN IT, THEY'RE TRYIN' TO MAKE US SMELL GOOD!
WANT SOME? SAY, "AHHH"!
I DON'T WANT ANY!!!
MM... WHAT A FINE BODY...
HANDS OFF!! SO COLD!!!
CHATTER
さわ
CHATTER
さわ
HMM... THEY'RE EXTREMELY FIT, INDEED.
SIP
くいっ

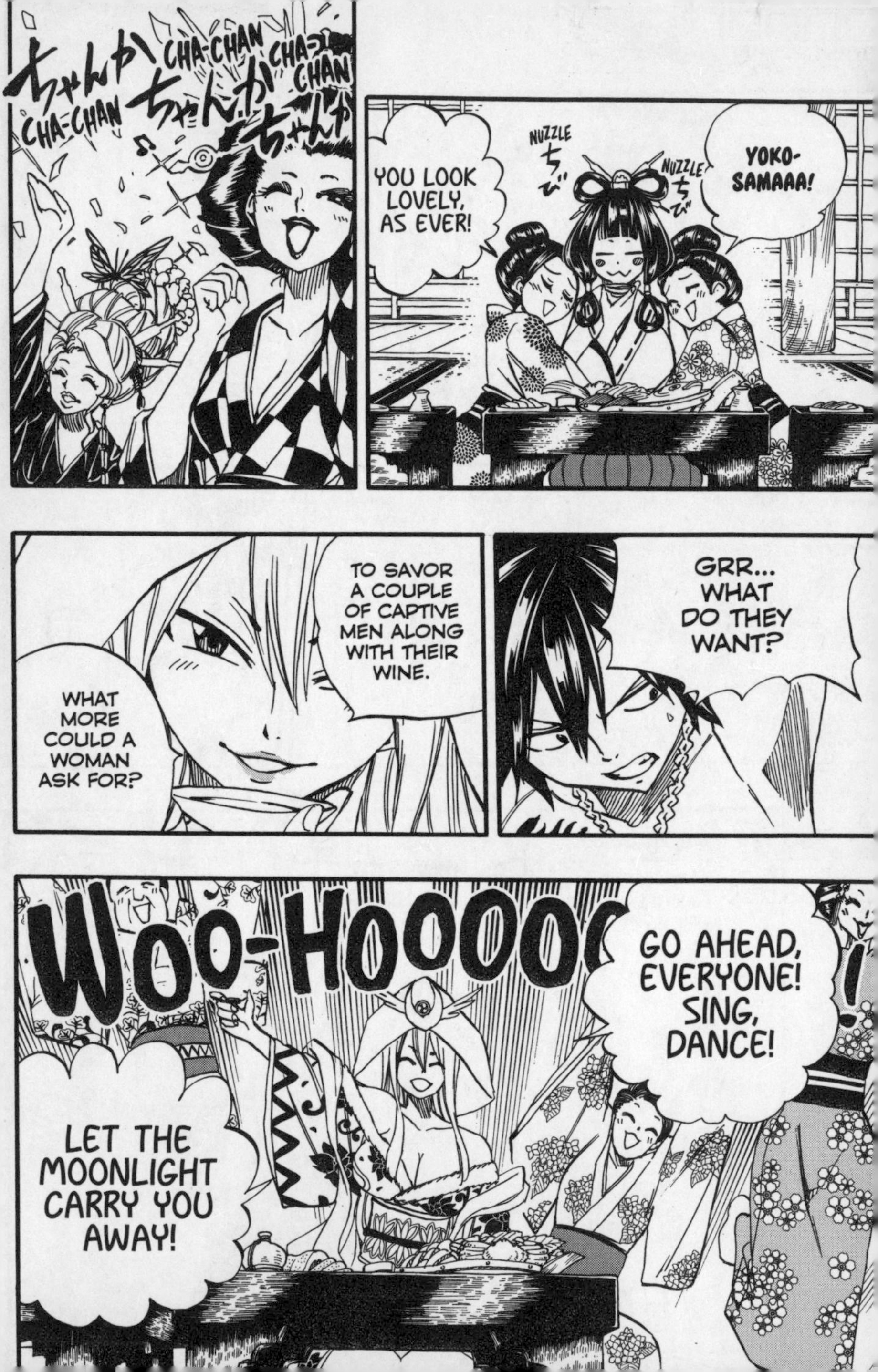
YOKO-SAMAAA!
NUZZLE ちび
NUZZLE ちび
YOU LOOK LOVELY, AS EVER!
CHA-CHAN ちゃんか
CHA-CHAN ちゃんか
CHA-CHAN ちゃんか
GRR... WHAT DO THEY WANT?
TO SAVOR A COUPLE OF CAPTIVE MEN ALONG WITH THEIR WINE.
WHAT MORE COULD A WOMAN ASK FOR?
GO AHEAD, EVERYONE! SING, DANCE!
WOO-HOOOOO!
LET THE MOONLIGHT CARRY YOU AWAY!

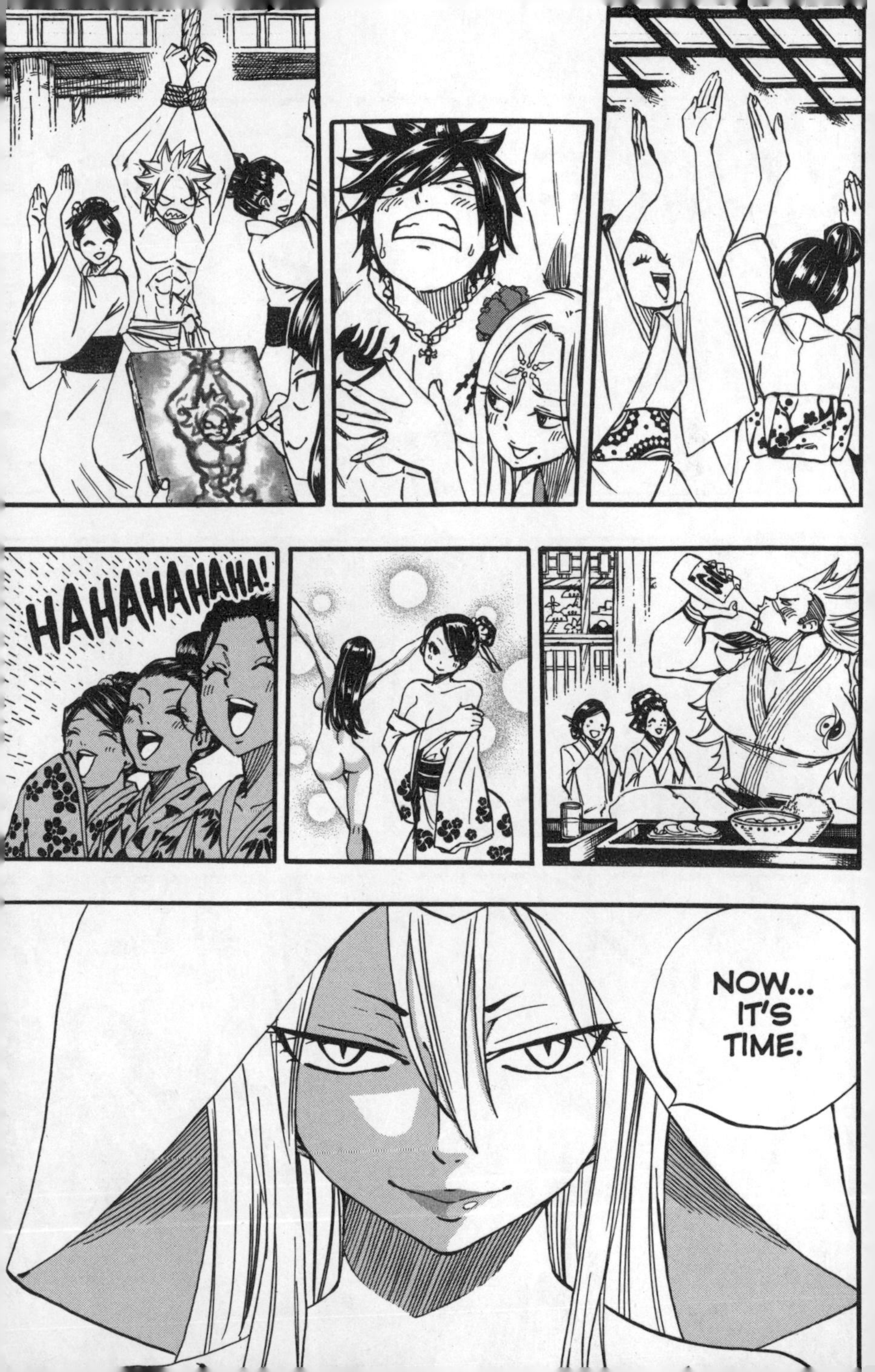
HAHAHAHAHAHA!
NOW... IT'S TIME.

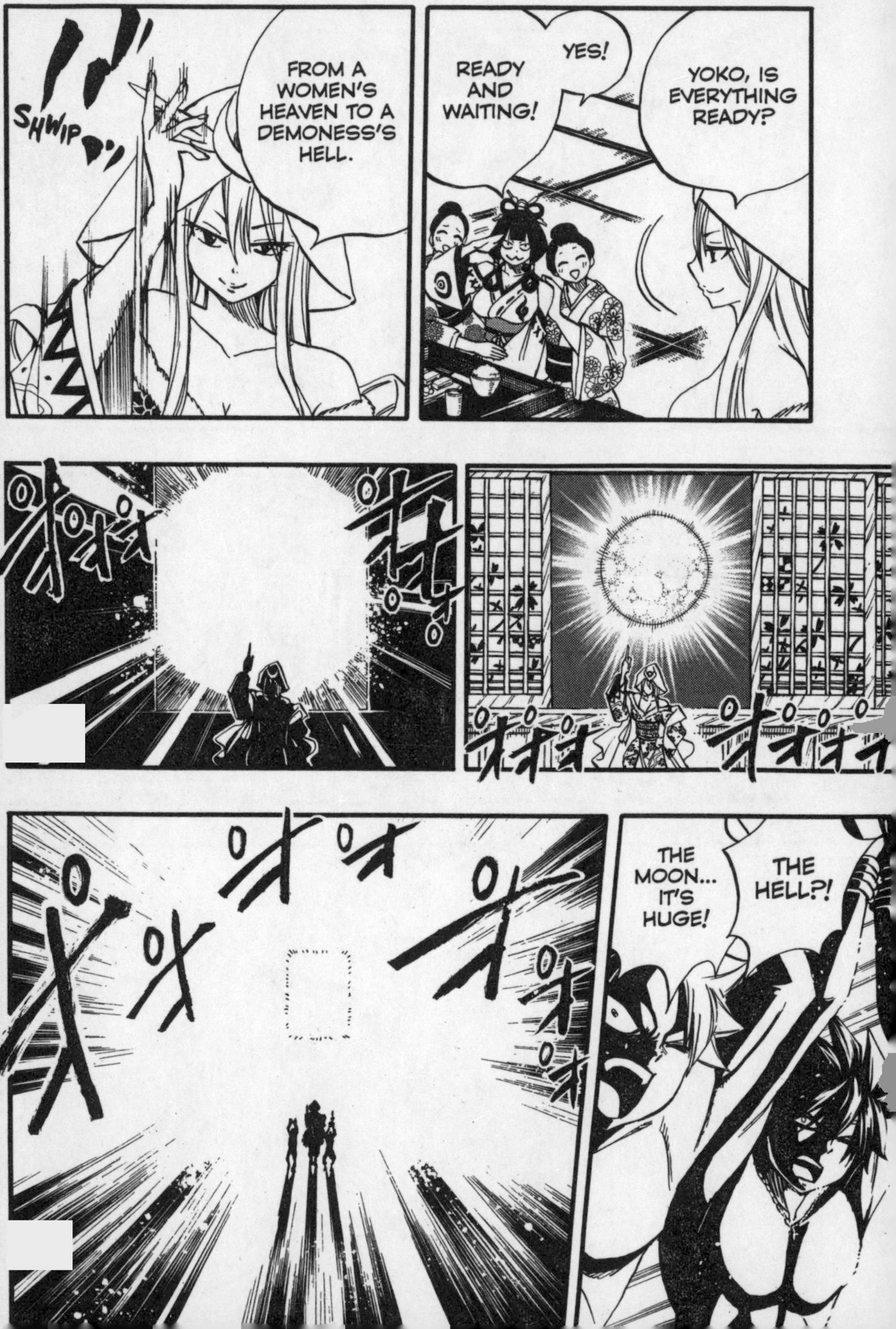
YOKO, IS EVERYTHING READY?
YES!
READY AND WAITING!
FROM A WOMEN'S HEAVEN TO A DEMONESS'S HELL.
SHWIP
THE HELL?!
THE MOON... IT'S HUGE!

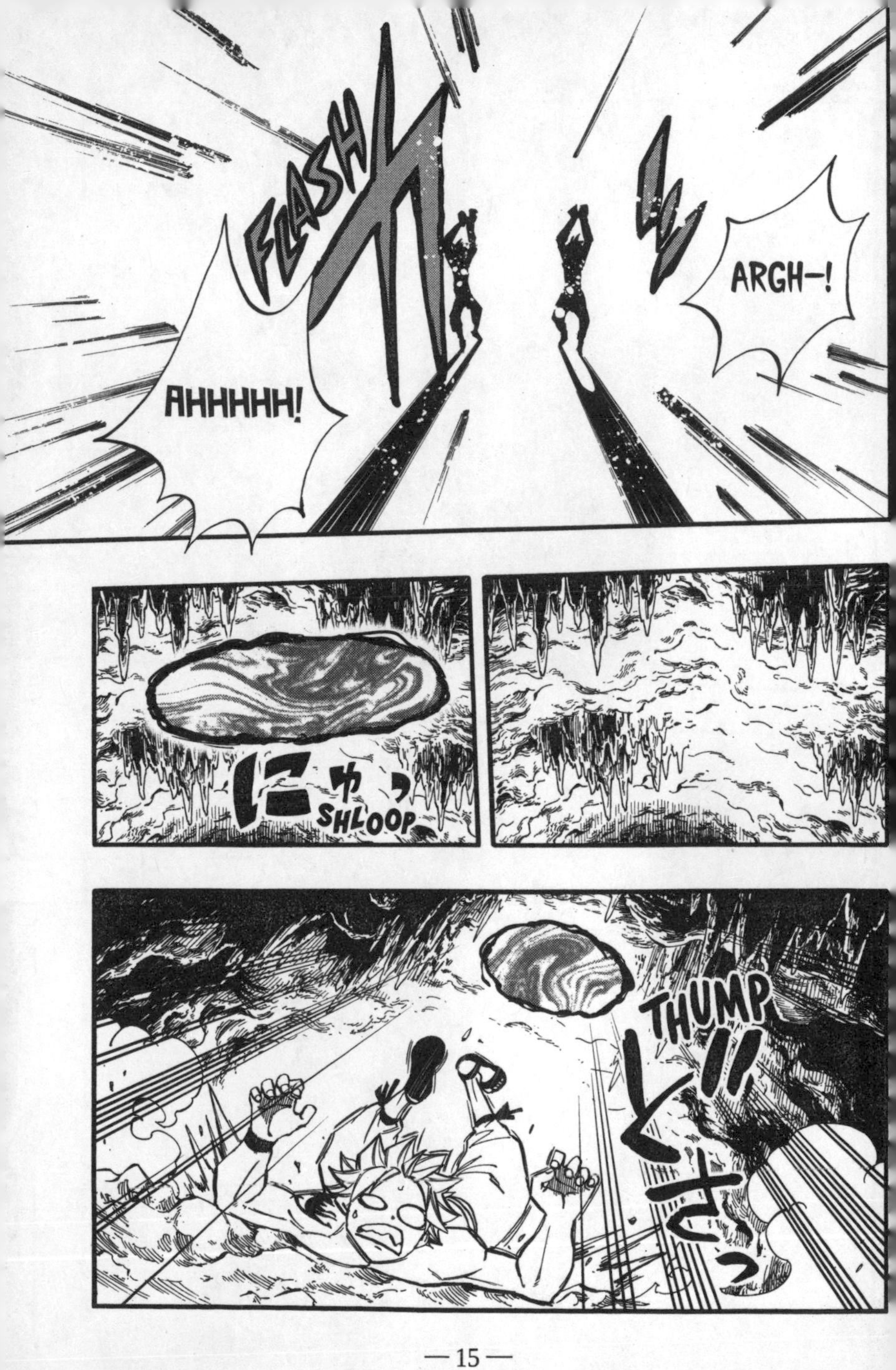
FLASH
ARGH—!
AHHHHH!
にゅっ
SHLOOP
THUMP
どさっ

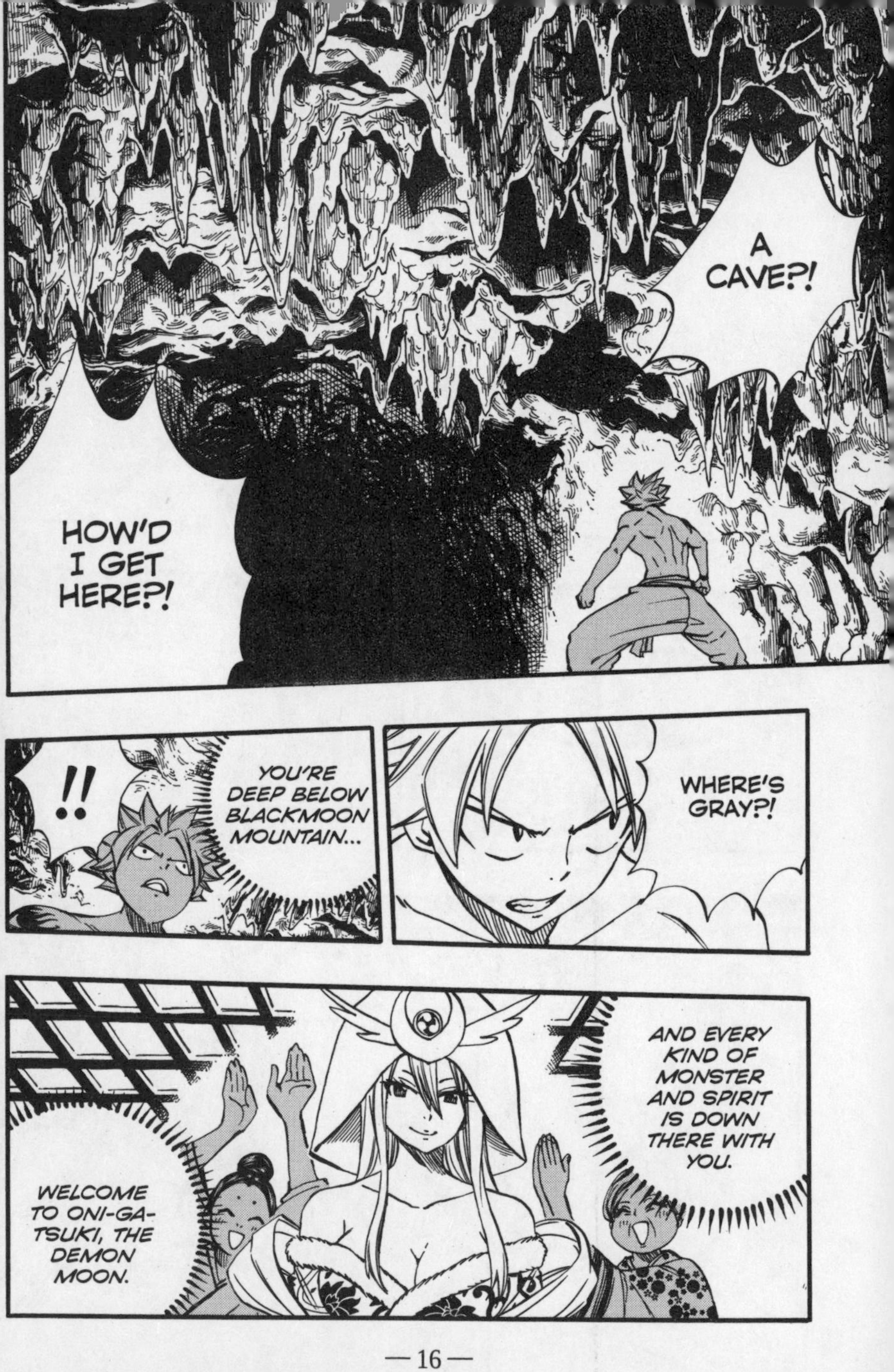

A CAVE?!
HOW'D I GET HERE?!
WHERE'S GRAY?!
YOU'RE DEEP BELOW BLACKMOON MOUNTAIN...
!!
AND EVERY KIND OF MONSTER AND SPIRIT IS DOWN THERE WITH YOU.
WELCOME TO ONI-GA-TSUKI, THE DEMON MOON.

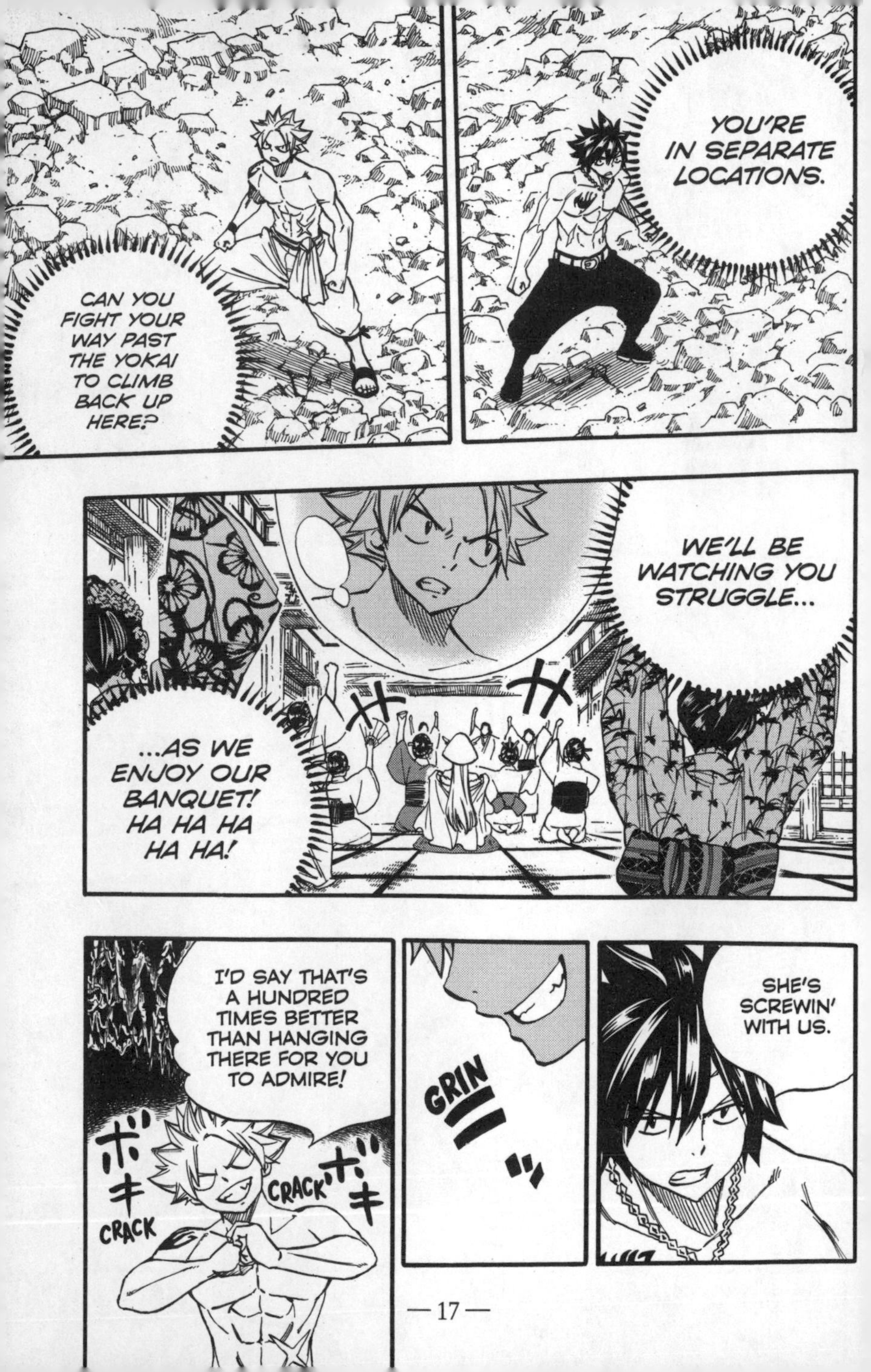
YOU'RE IN SEPARATE LOCATIONS.
CAN YOU FIGHT YOUR WAY PAST THE YOKAI TO CLIMB BACK UP HERE?
WE'LL BE WATCHING YOU STRUGGLE...
...AS WE ENJOY OUR BANQUET! HA HA HA HA HA!
SHE'S SCREWIN' WITH US.
GRIN
I'D SAY THAT'S A HUNDRED TIMES BETTER THAN HANGING THERE FOR YOU TO ADMIRE!
ボキ
CRACK
ボキ
CRACK

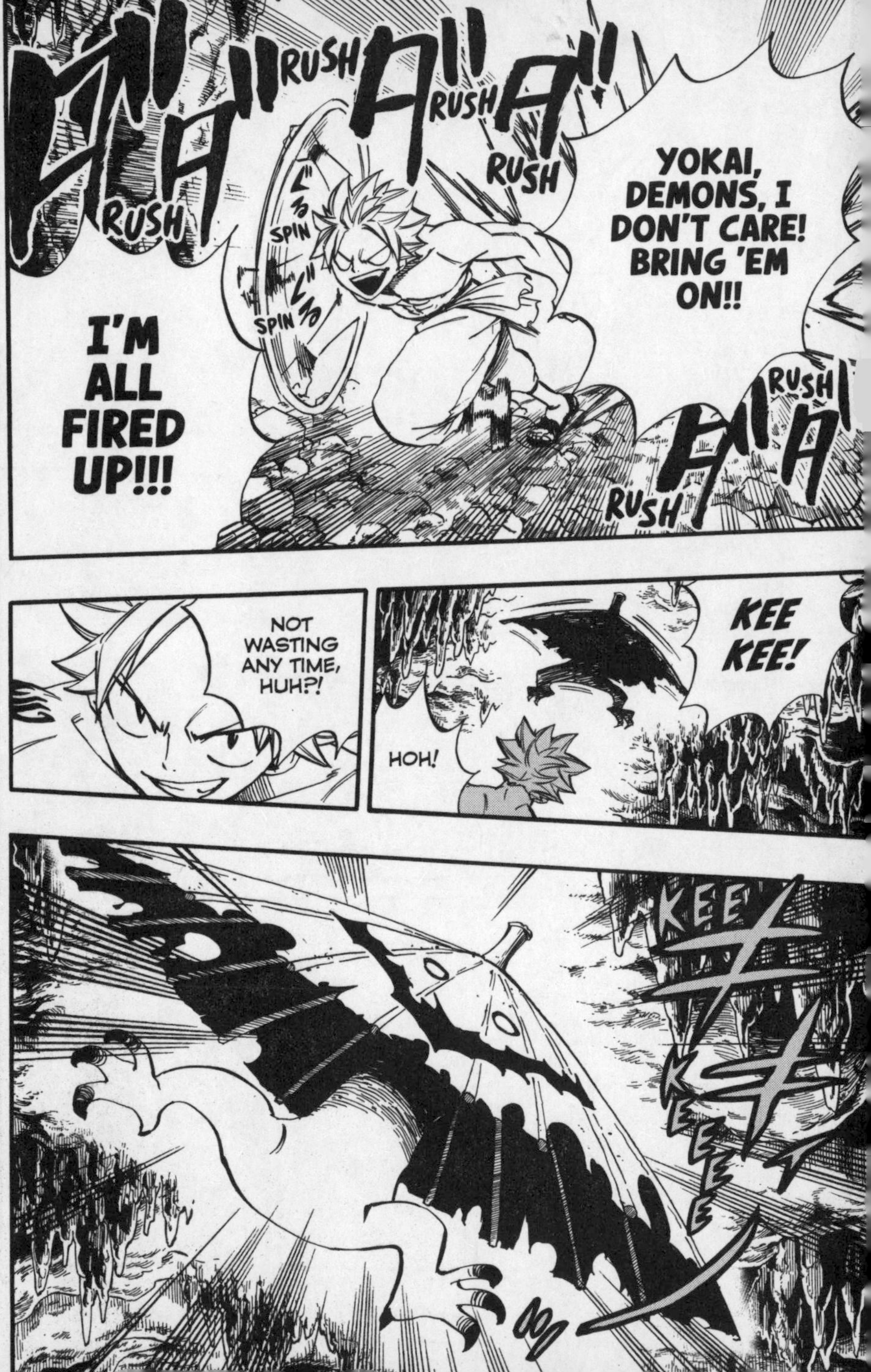
RUSH
YOKAI, DEMONS, I DON'T CARE! BRING 'EM ON!!
RUSH
RUSH
RUSH
SPIN
SPIN
RUSH
I'M ALL FIRED UP!!!
RUSH
RUSH
KEE KEE!
HOH!
NOT WASTING ANY TIME, HUH?!
KEE

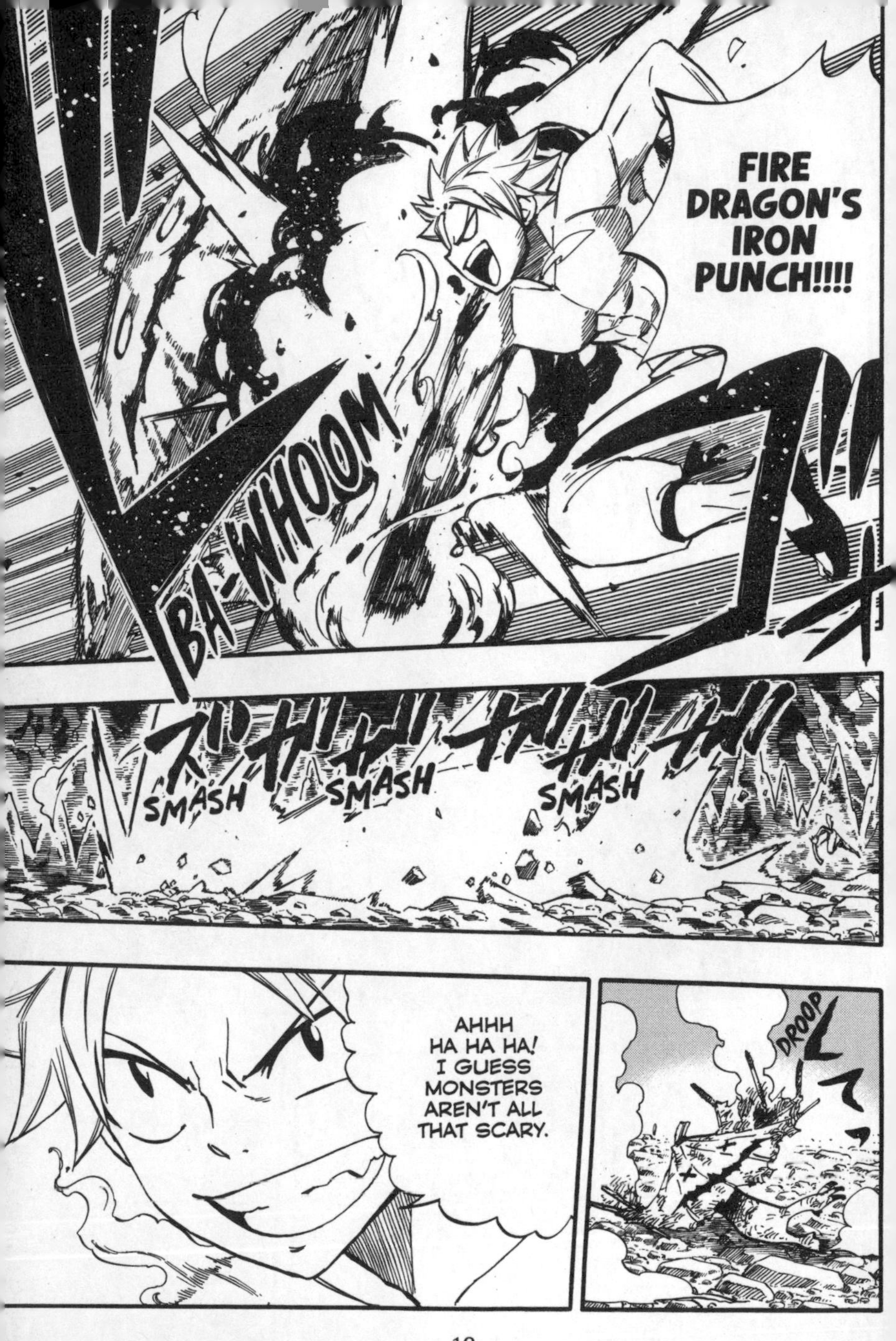
FIRE DRAGON'S IRON PUNCH!!!!
BA-WHOOM
SMASH
SMASH
SMASH
DROOP
AHHH HA HA HA! I GUESS MONSTERS AREN'T ALL THAT SCARY.

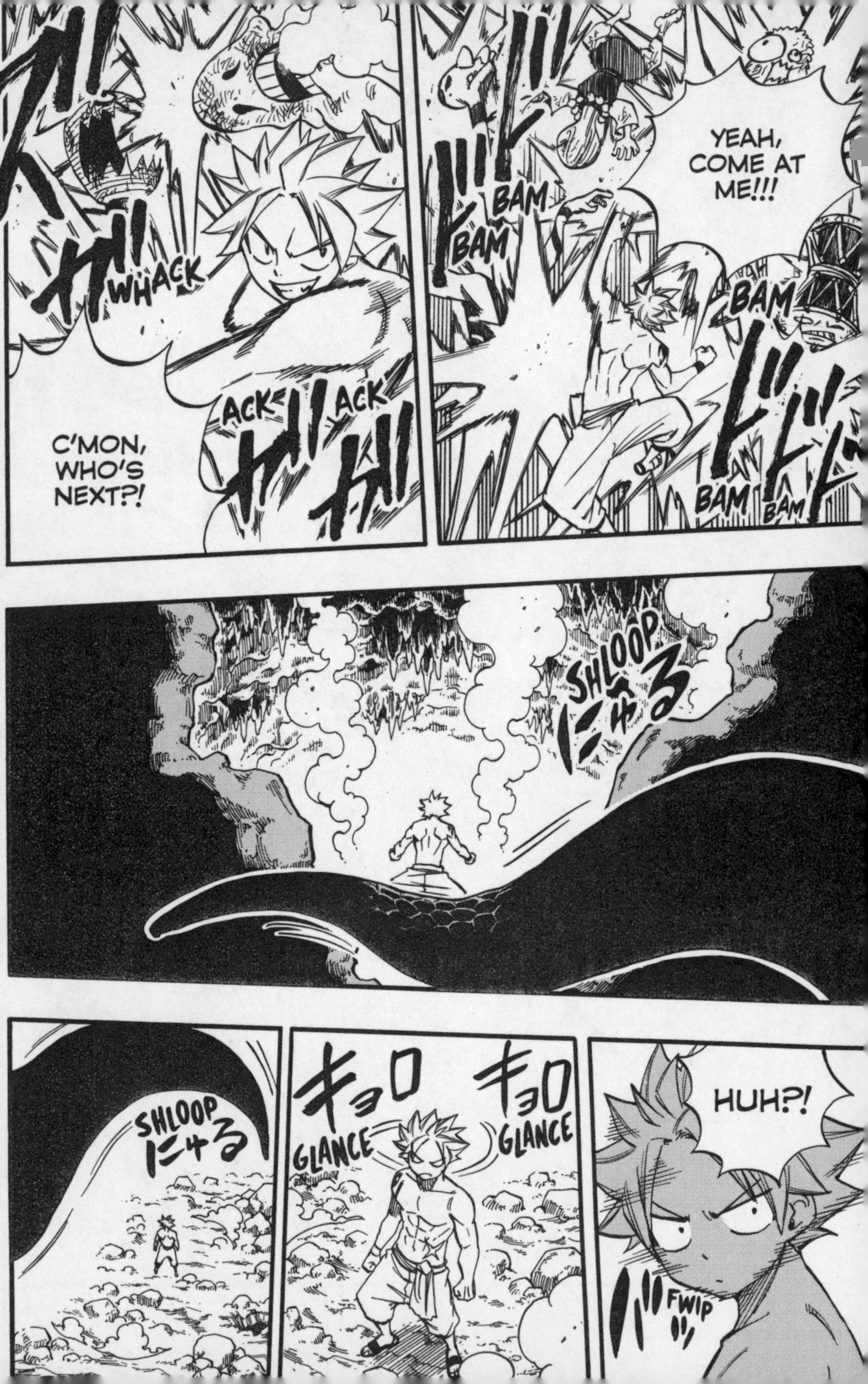
YEAH, COME AT ME!!!
BAM
BAM
BAM
BAM
BAM
BAM
WHACK
ACK
ACK
C'MON, WHO'S NEXT?!
SHLOOP
にゅる
HUH?!
FWIP
キョロ
GLANCE
キョロ
GLANCE
SHLOOP
にゅる

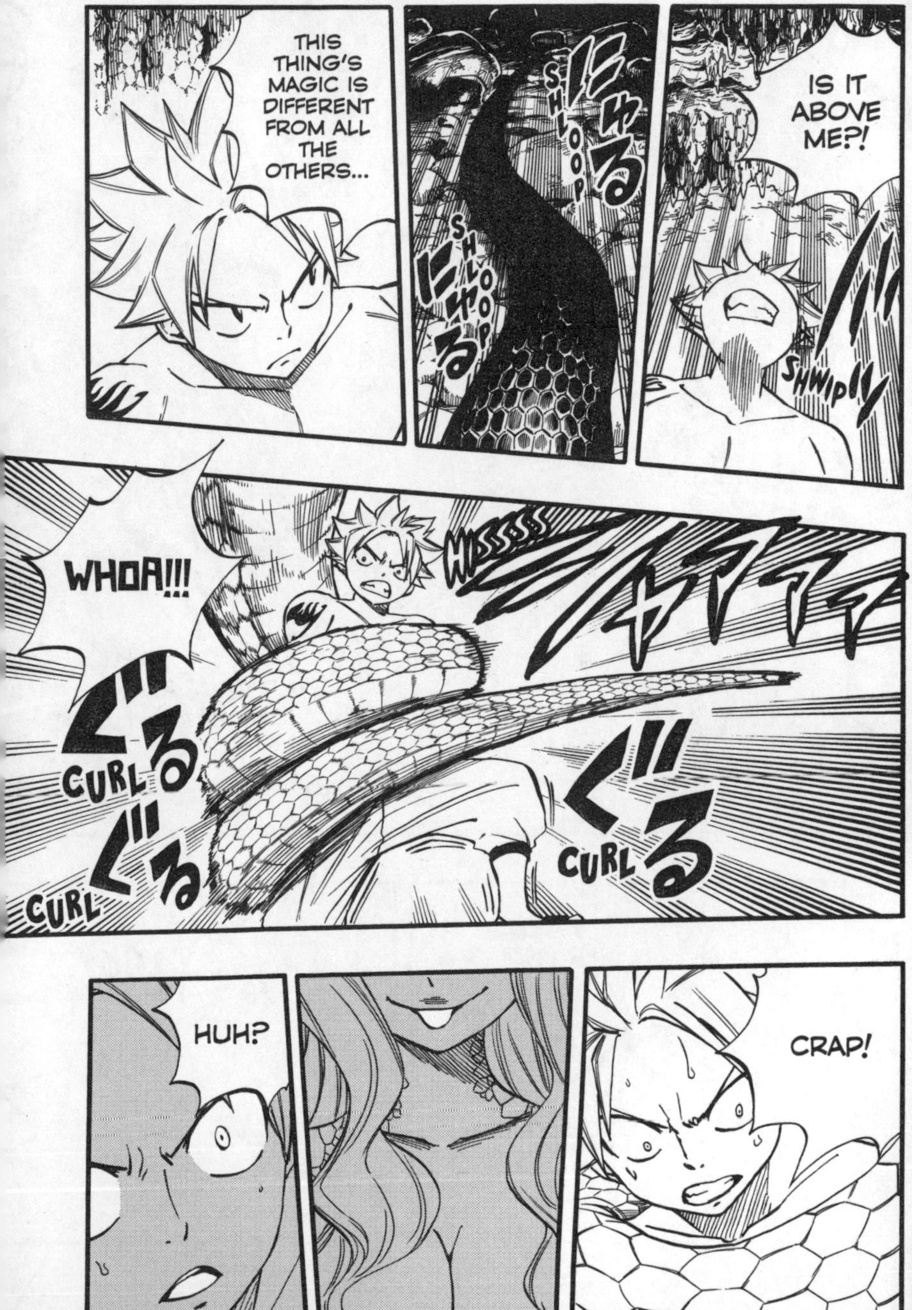

IS IT ABOVE ME?!
SHWIP!!
にゅる
SHLOOP
にゅる
SHLOOP
THIS THING'S MAGIC IS DIFFERENT FROM ALL THE OTHERS...
HISSSS
シャアアア
WHOA!!!
ぐる
CURL
ぐる
CURL
ぐる
CURL
CRAP!
HUH?

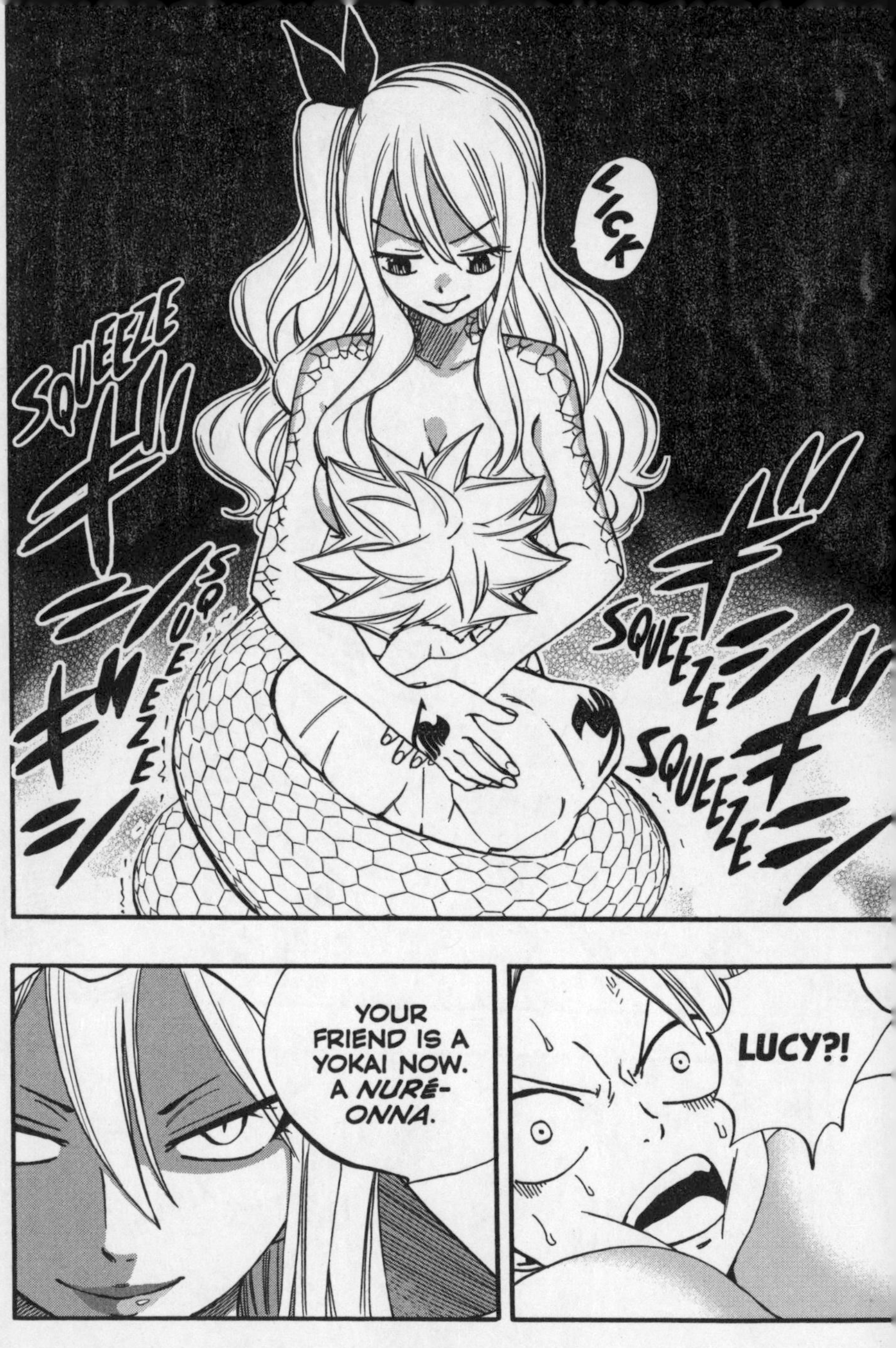
LICK
SQUEEZE
SQUEEZE
SQUEEZE
SQUEEZE
LUCY?!
YOUR FRIEND IS A YOKAI NOW. A *NURÉ-ONNA*.

FAIRY TAIL 100 YEARS QUEST

Chapter 74: Nuré-Onna

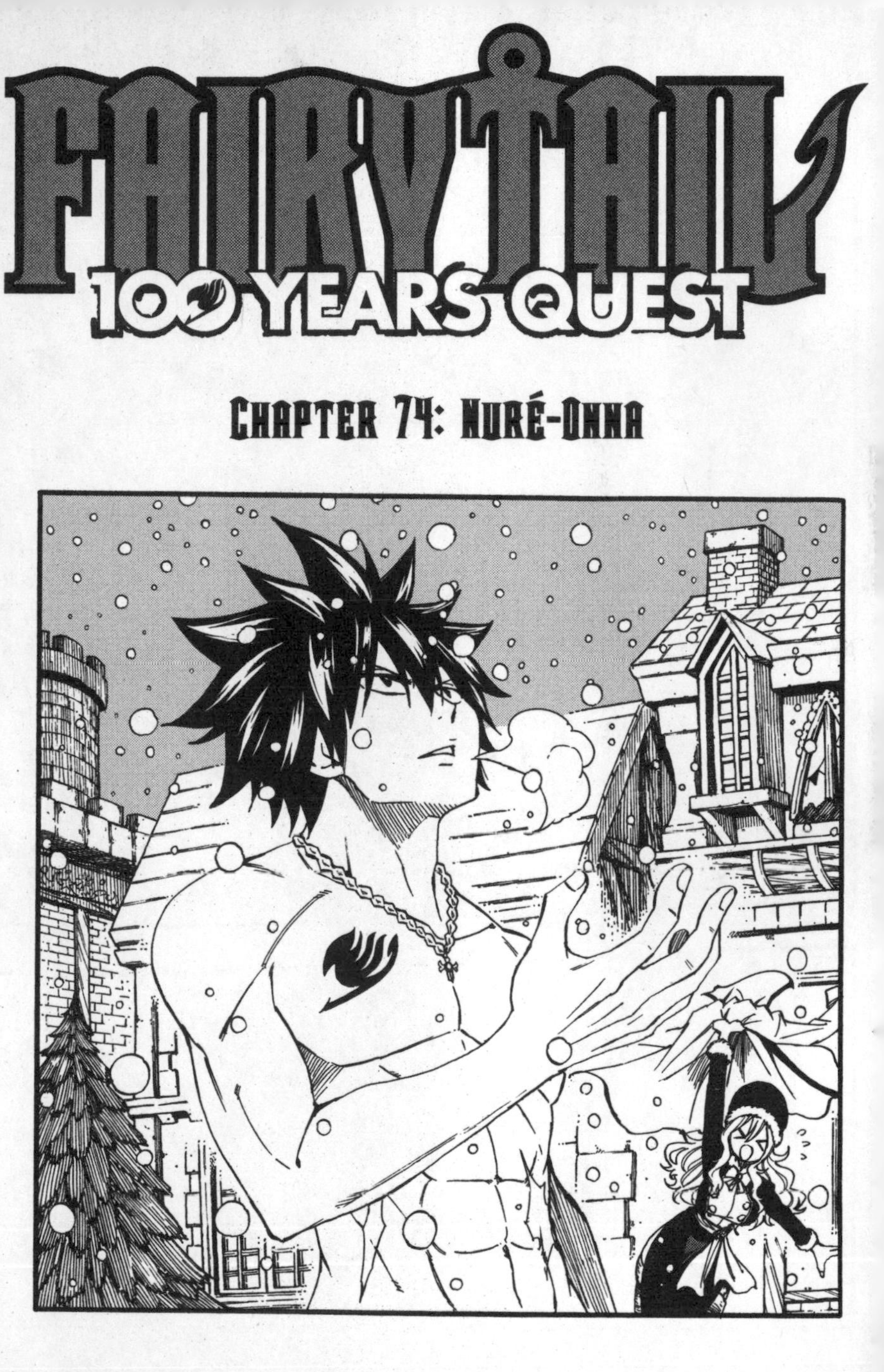

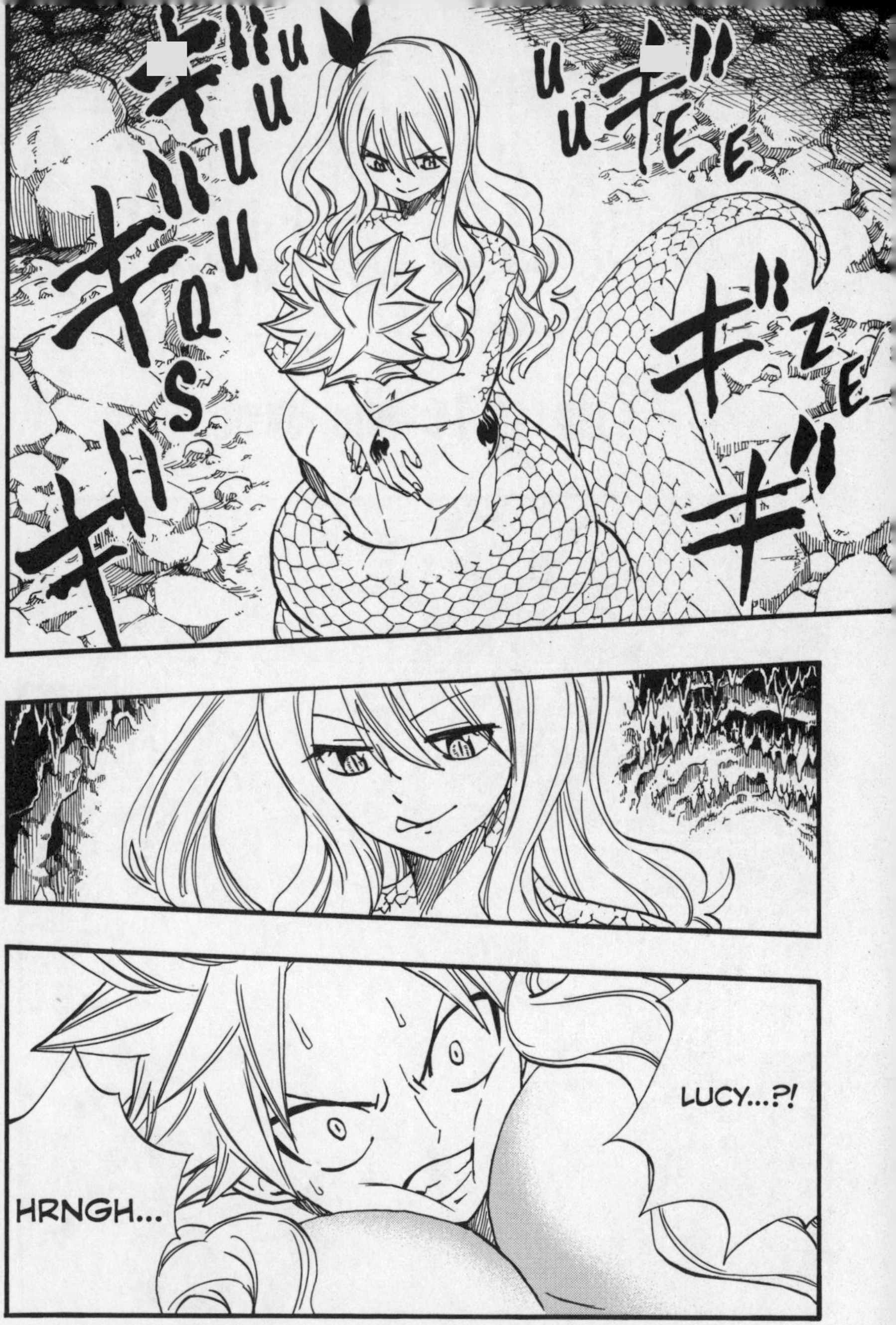
LUCY...?!
HRNGH...

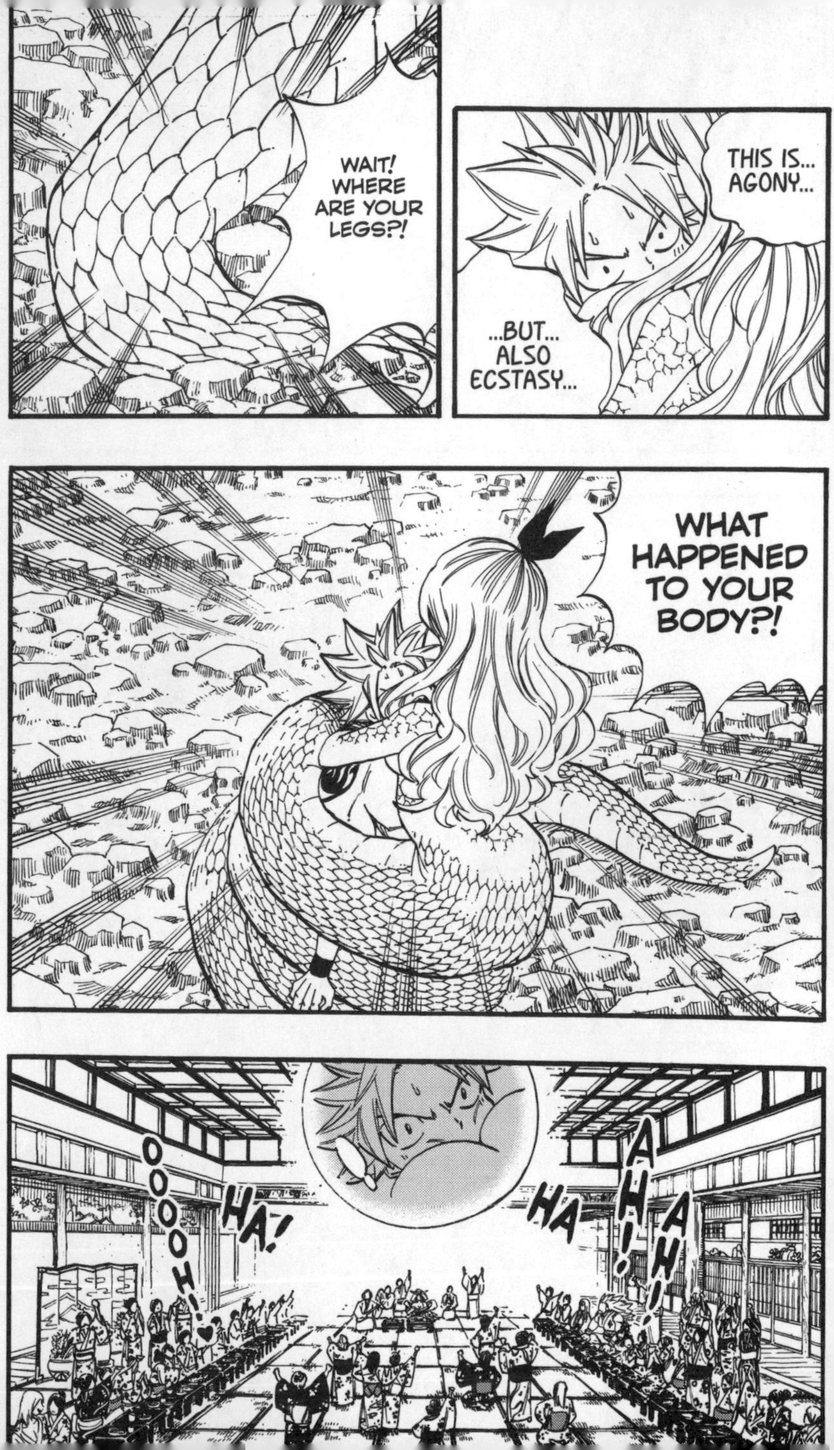
THIS IS... AGONY...
...BUT... ALSO ECSTASY...
WAIT! WHERE ARE YOUR LEGS?!
WHAT HAPPENED TO YOUR BODY?!
AH! AH!
HA
HA!
OOOOH!♥

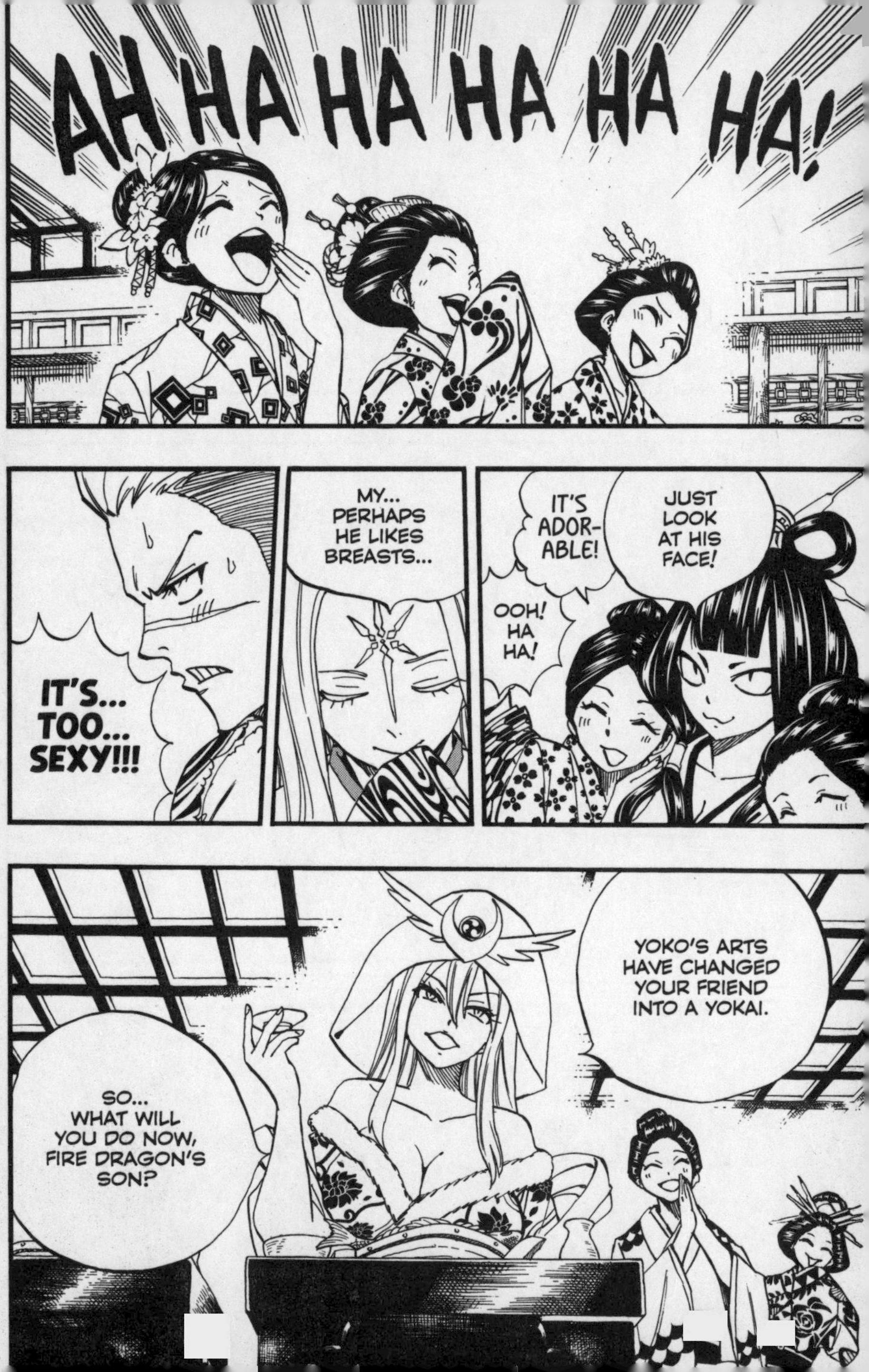
AH HA HA HA HA HA HA!
JUST LOOK AT HIS FACE!
IT'S ADORABLE!
OOH! HA HA!
MY... PERHAPS HE LIKES BREASTS...
IT'S... TOO... SEXY!!!
YOKO'S ARTS HAVE CHANGED YOUR FRIEND INTO A YOKAI.
SO... WHAT WILL YOU DO NOW, FIRE DRAGON'S SON?

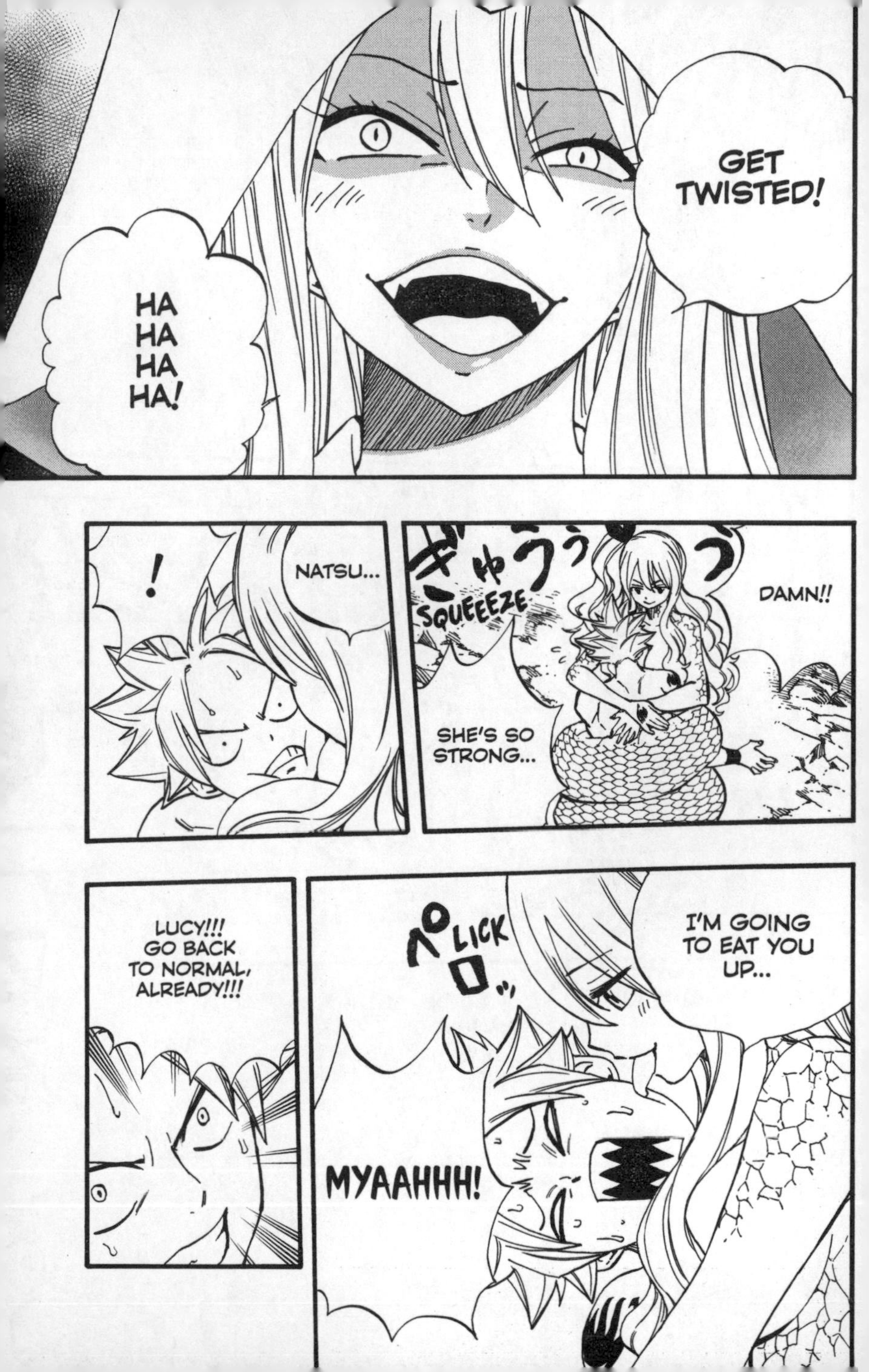
GET TWISTED!
HA HA HA HA!
DAMN!!
ぎゅううう
SQUEEEZE
SHE'S SO STRONG...
NATSU...
!
I'M GOING TO EAT YOU UP...
ペロッ
LICK
MYAAHHH!
LUCY!!! GO BACK TO NORMAL, ALREADY!!!

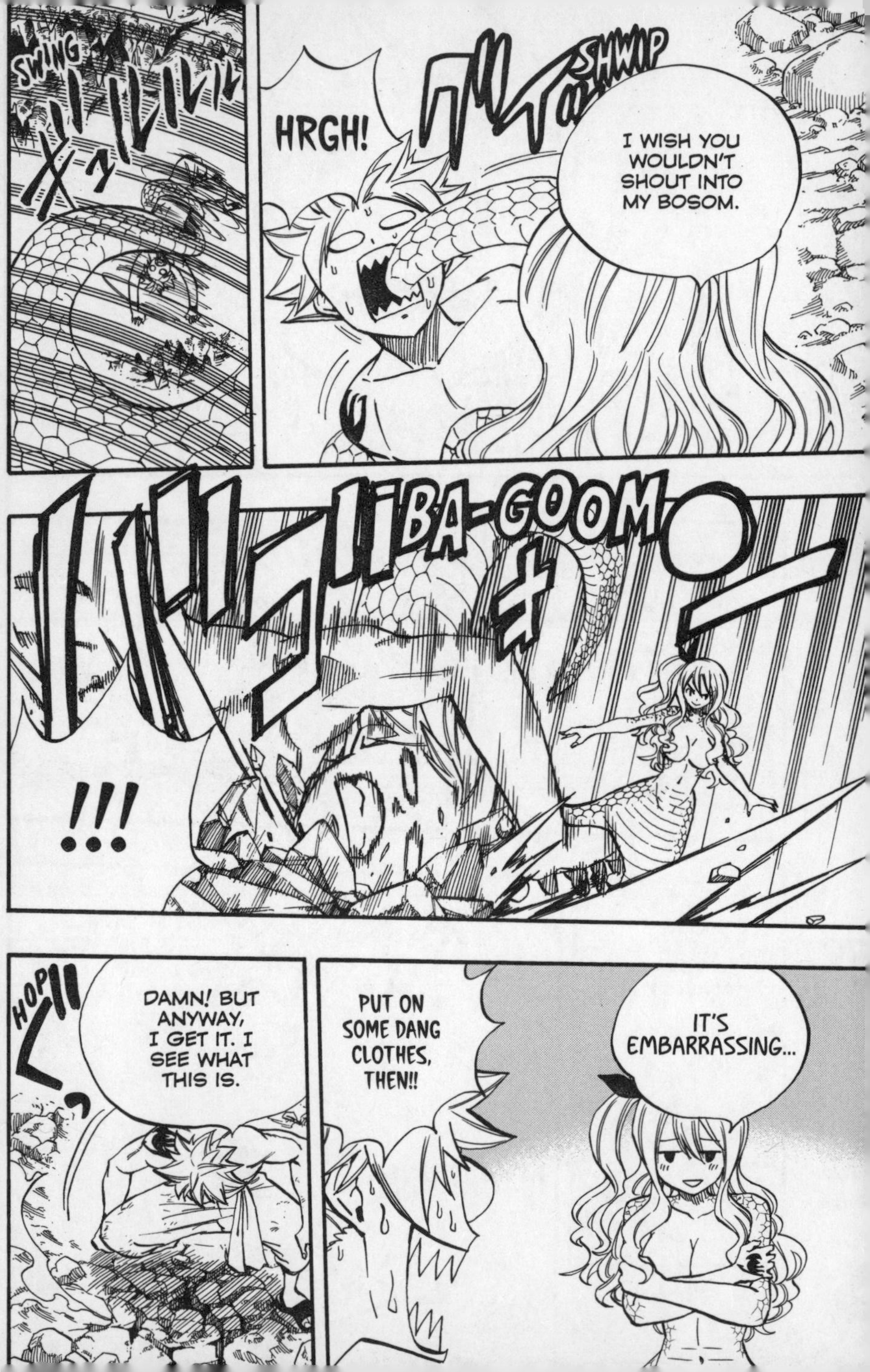

SHWIP
I WISH YOU WOULDN'T SHOUT INTO MY BOSOM.
HRGH!
SWING
BA-GOOM
!!!
IT'S EMBARRASSING...
PUT ON SOME DANG CLOTHES, THEN!!
HOP
DAMN! BUT ANYWAY, I GET IT. I SEE WHAT THIS IS.

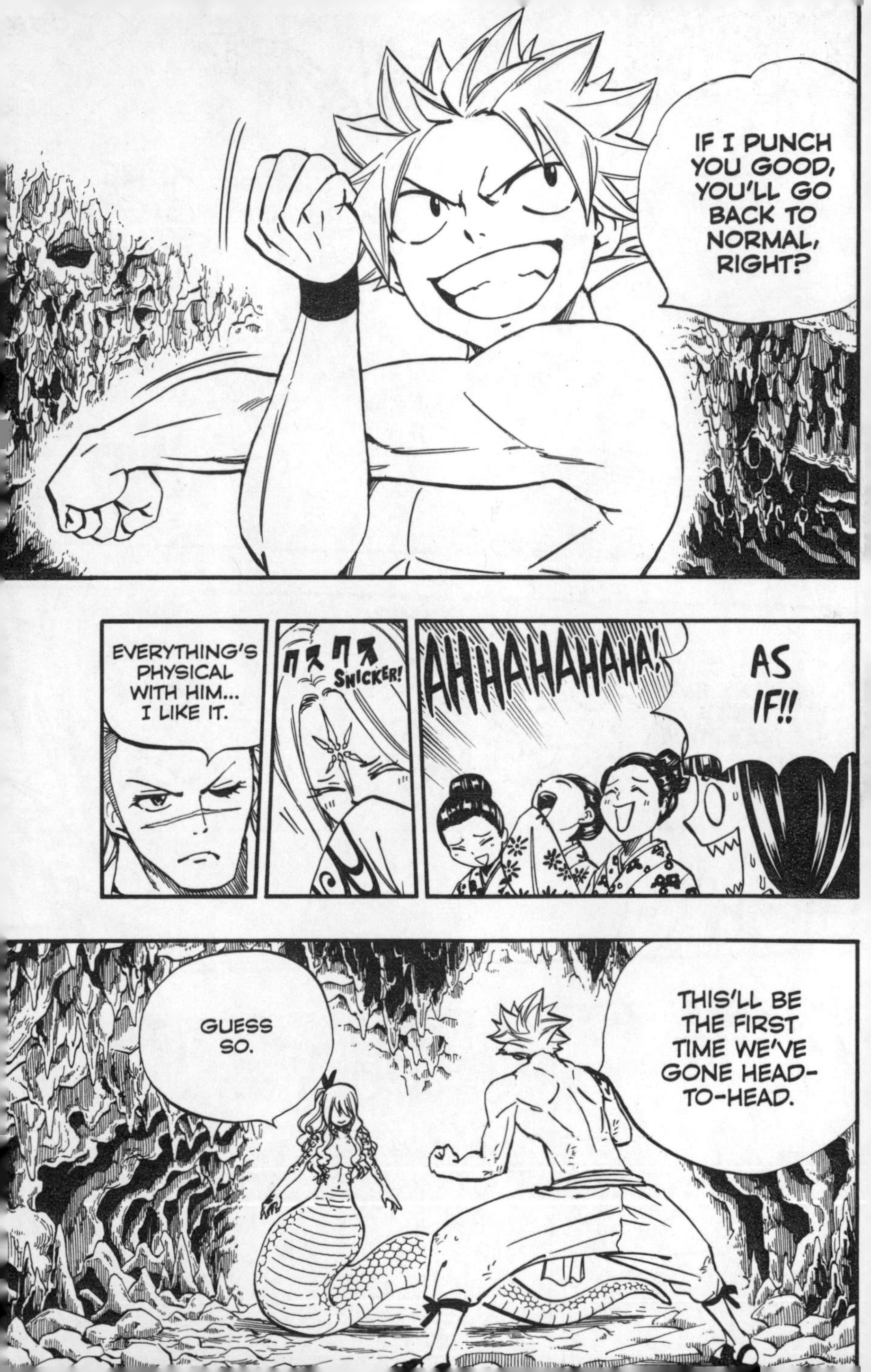
IF I PUNCH YOU GOOD, YOU'LL GO BACK TO NORMAL, RIGHT?
AS IF!!
AHHAHAHAHAHA!
クスクス
SNICKER!
EVERYTHING'S PHYSICAL WITH HIM... I LIKE IT.
THIS'LL BE THE FIRST TIME WE'VE GONE HEAD-TO-HEAD.
GUESS SO.

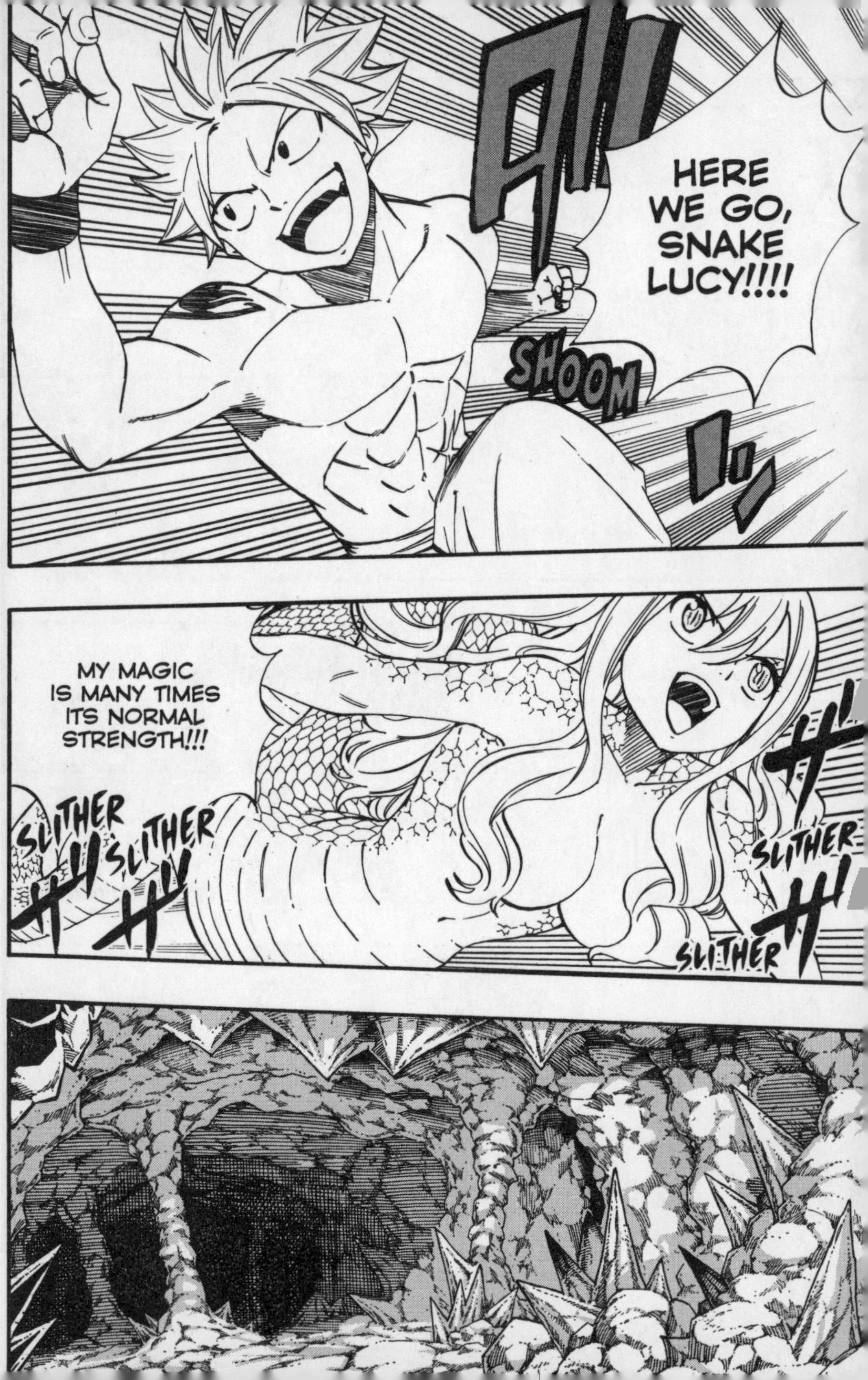
HERE WE GO, SNAKE LUCY!!!!
SHOOM
MY MAGIC IS MANY TIMES ITS NORMAL STRENGTH!!!
SLITHER
SLITHER
SLITHER
SLITHER

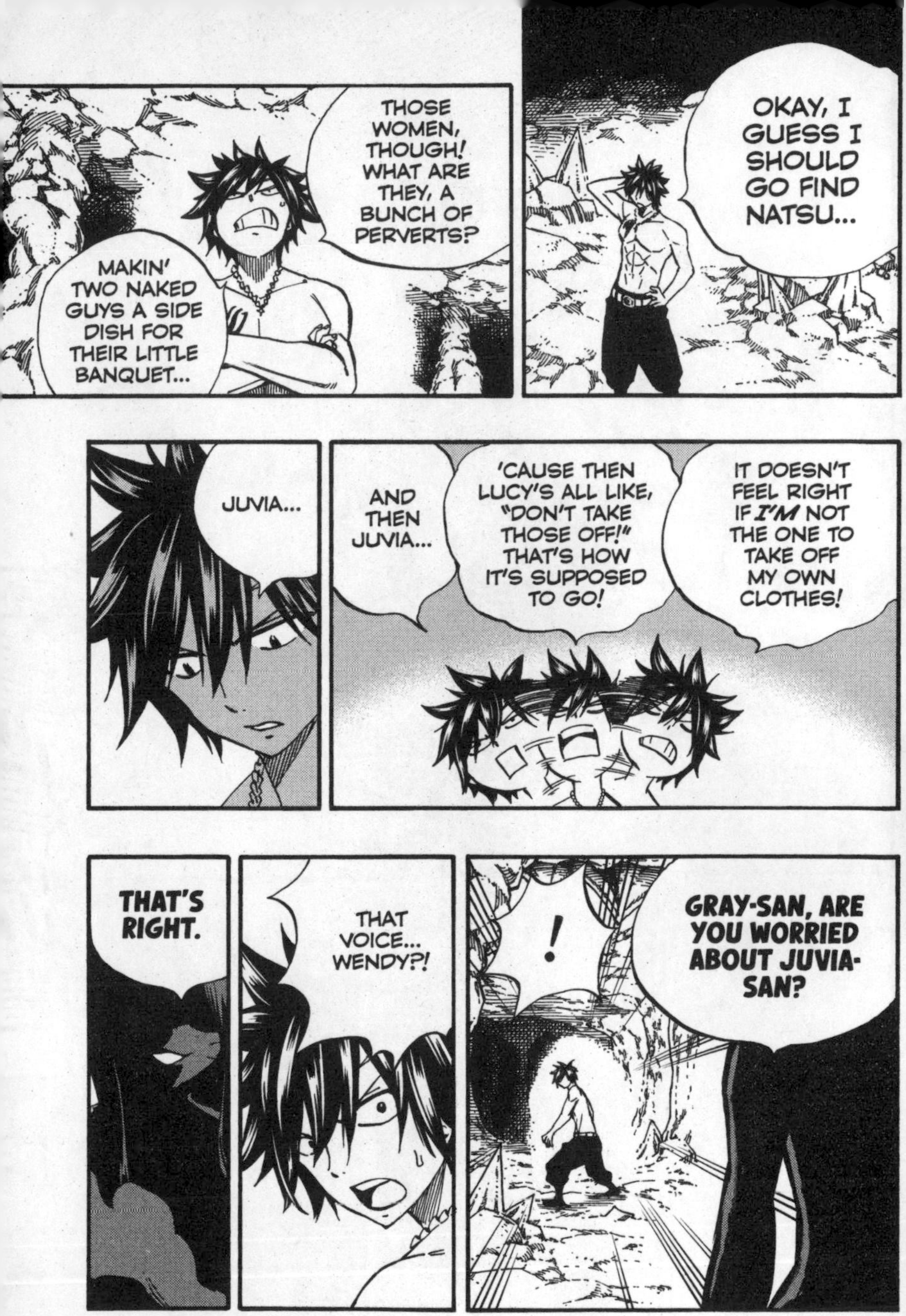
OKAY, I GUESS I SHOULD GO FIND NATSU...
THOSE WOMEN, THOUGH! WHAT ARE THEY, A BUNCH OF PERVERTS?
MAKIN' TWO NAKED GUYS A SIDE DISH FOR THEIR LITTLE BANQUET...
IT DOESN'T FEEL RIGHT IF *I'M* NOT THE ONE TO TAKE OFF MY OWN CLOTHES!
'CAUSE THEN LUCY'S ALL LIKE, "DON'T TAKE THOSE OFF!" THAT'S HOW IT'S SUPPOSED TO GO!
AND THEN JUVIA...
JUVIA...
!
GRAY-SAN, ARE YOU WORRIED ABOUT JUVIA-SAN?
THAT VOICE... WENDY?!
THAT'S RIGHT.

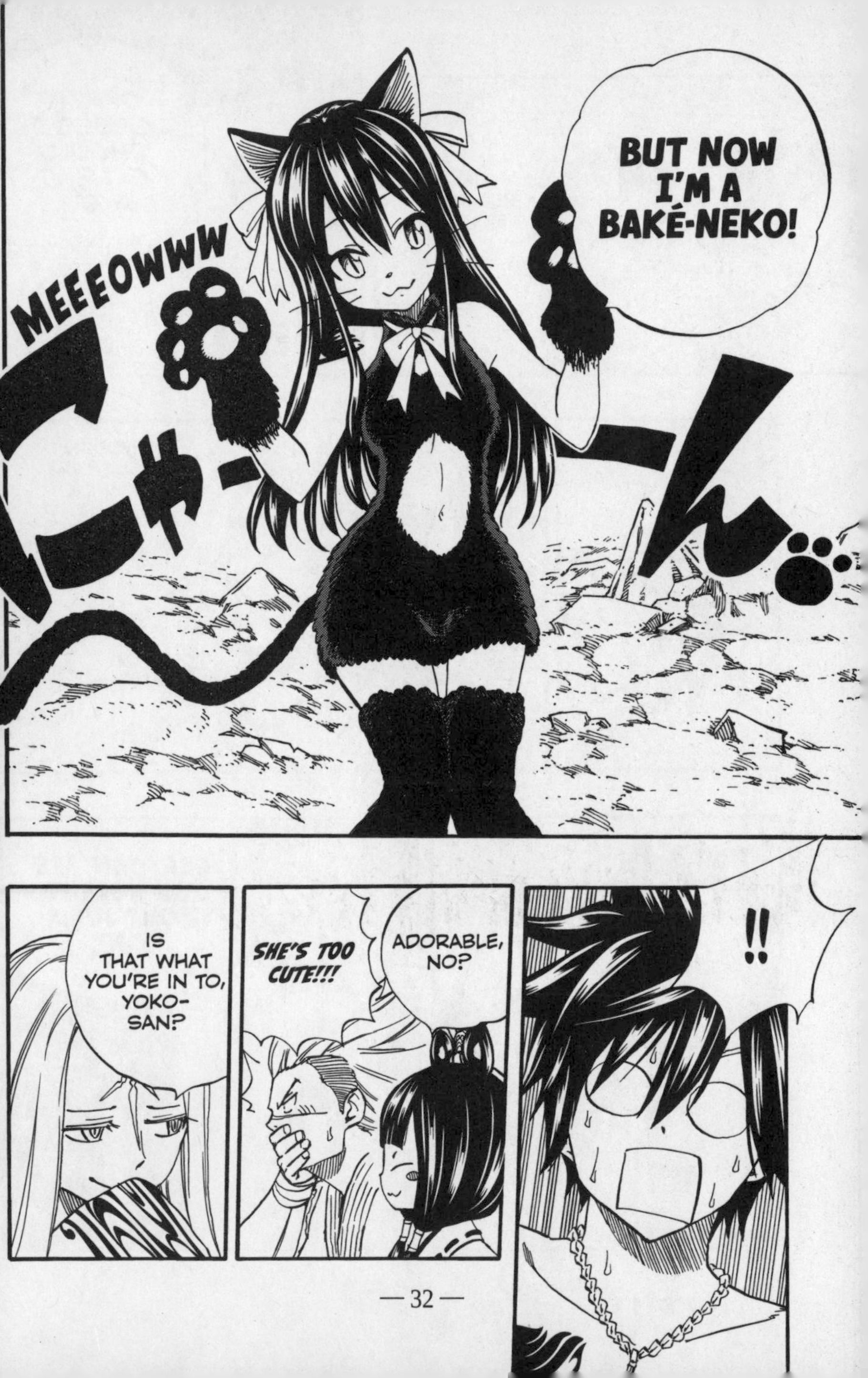
BUT NOW I'M A BAKÉ-NEKO!
MEEEOWWW
にゃーん
!!
ADORABLE, NO?
SHE'S TOO CUTE!!!
IS THAT WHAT YOU'RE IN TO, YOKO-SAN?

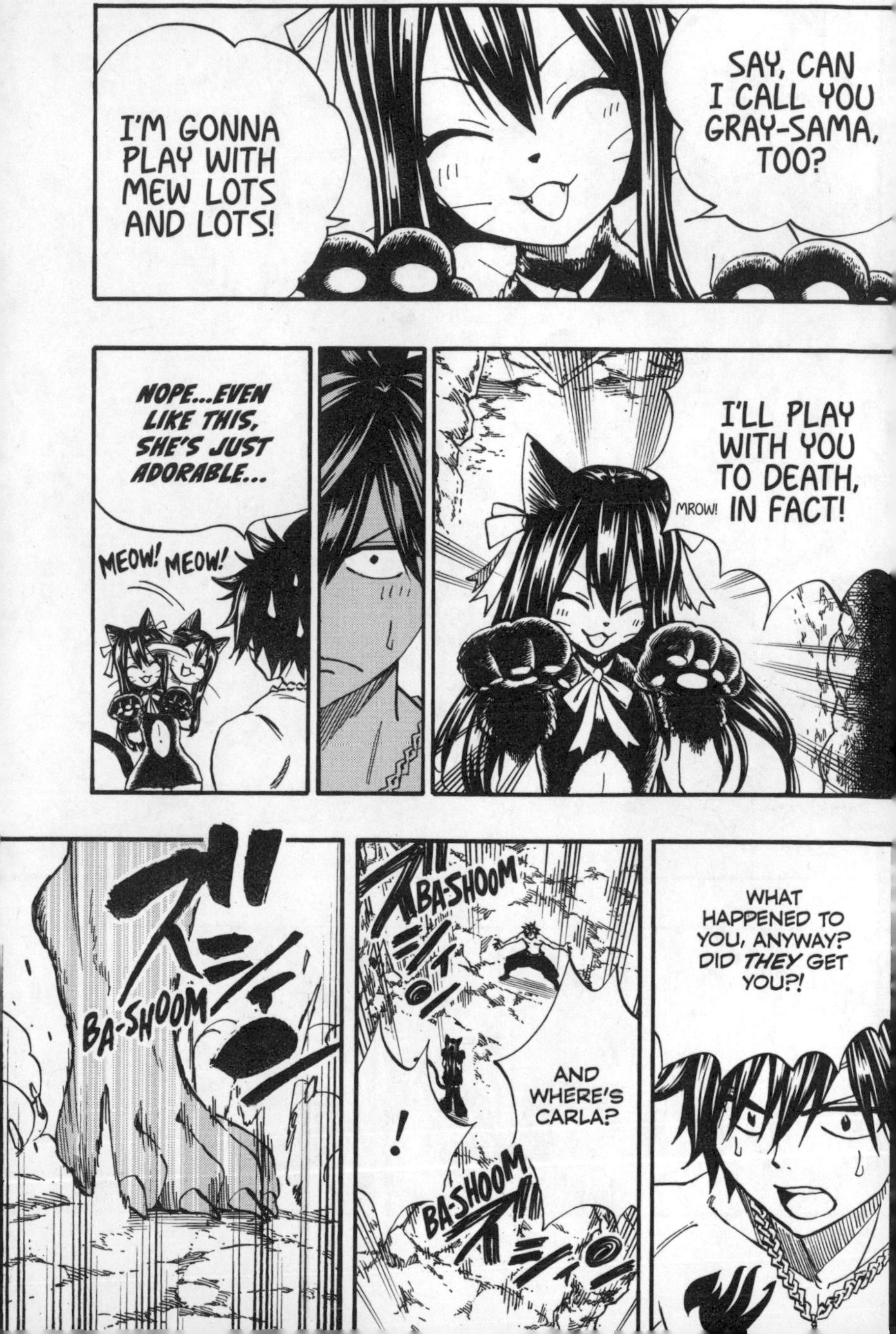
SAY, CAN I CALL YOU GRAY-SAMA, TOO?
I'M GONNA PLAY WITH MEW LOTS AND LOTS!
I'LL PLAY WITH YOU TO DEATH, IN FACT!
MROW!
NOPE...EVEN LIKE THIS, SHE'S JUST ADORABLE...
MEOW! MEOW!
WHAT HAPPENED TO YOU, ANYWAY? DID *THEY* GET YOU?!
BA-SHOOM
AND WHERE'S CARLA?
!
BA-SHOOM
BA-SHOOM

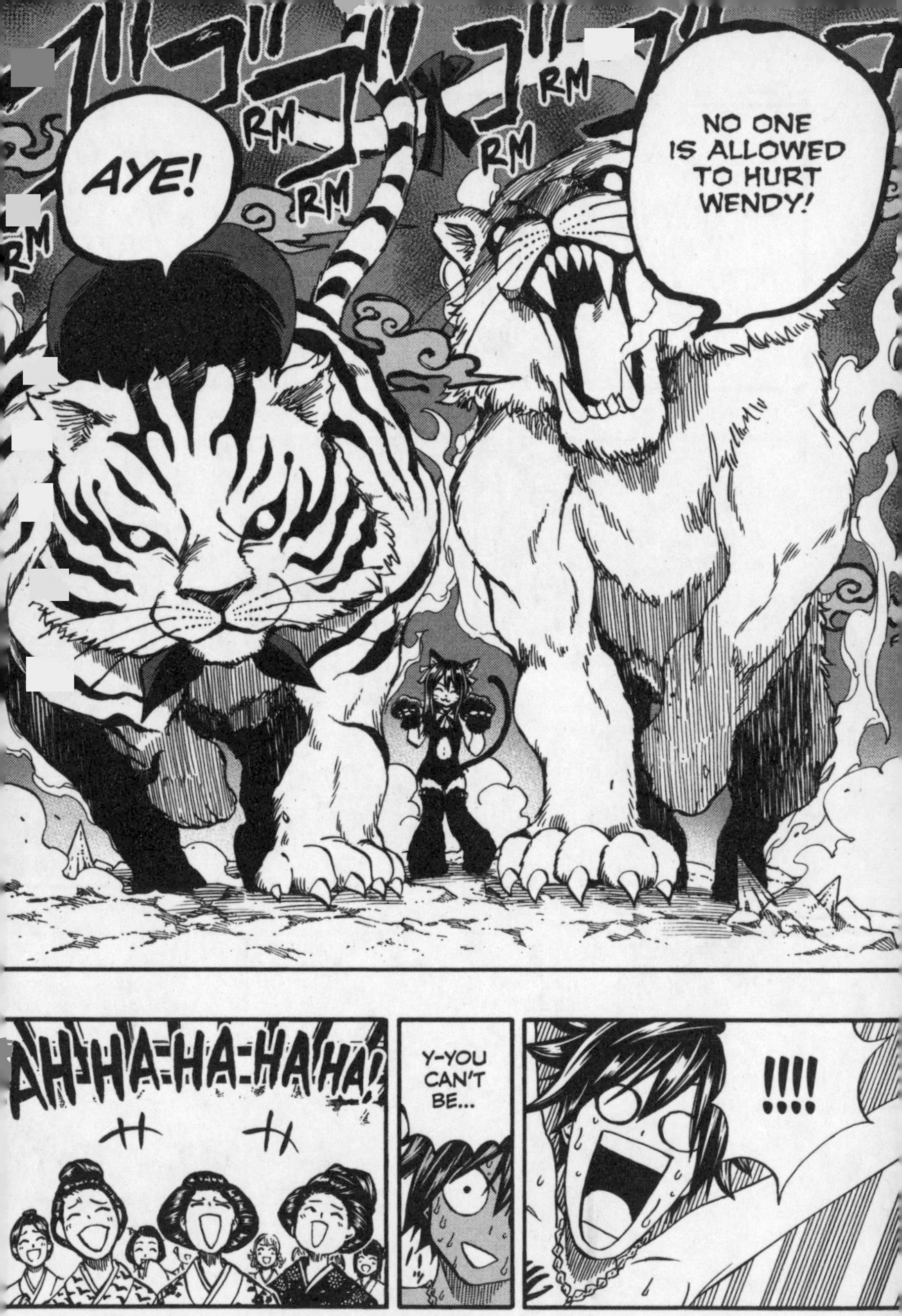
RM
RM
RM
RM
RM
NO ONE IS ALLOWED TO HURT WENDY!
AYE!
!!!!
Y-YOU CAN'T BE...
AH-HA-HA-HA-HA-HA!

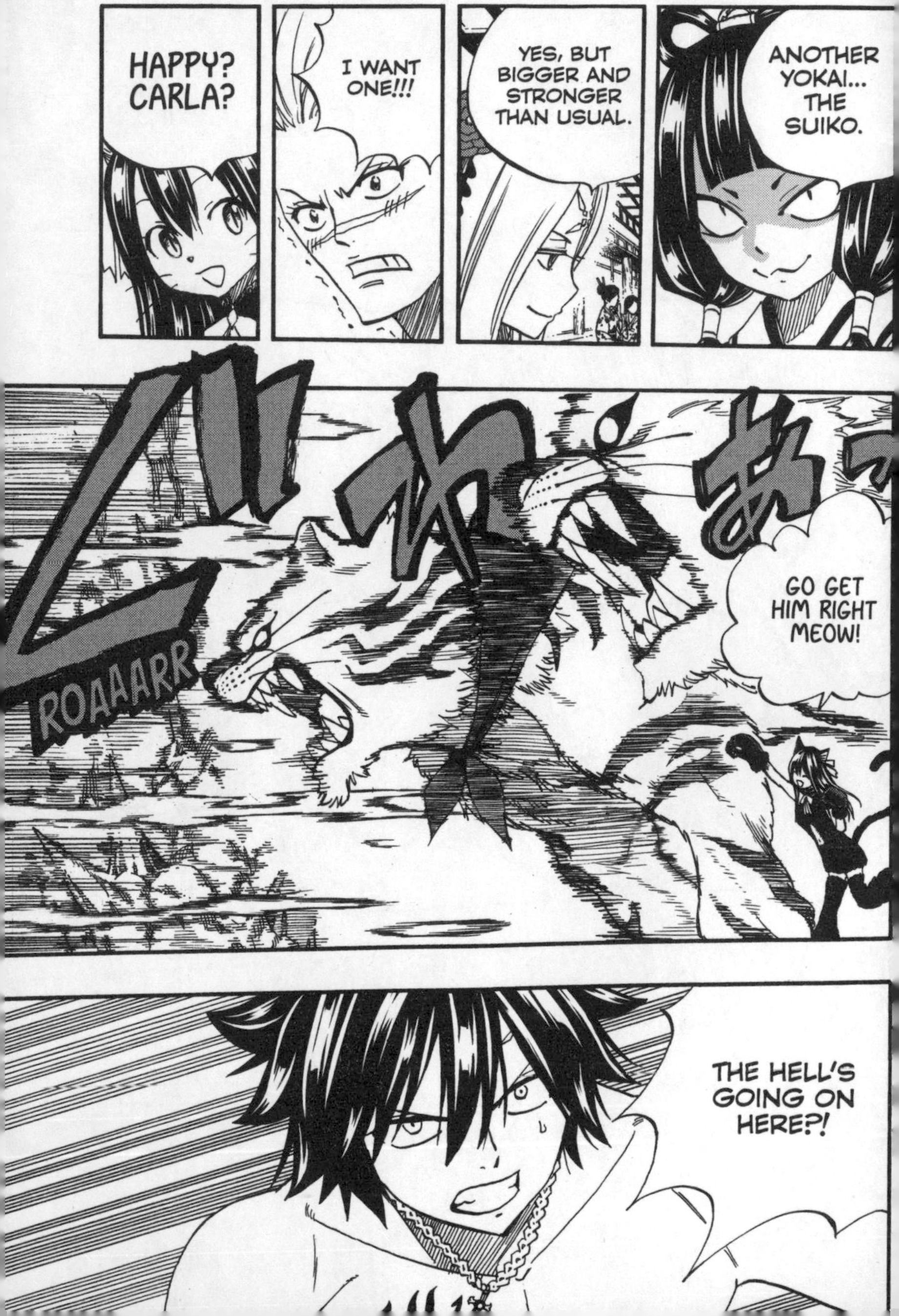
ANOTHER YOKAI... THE SUIKO.
YES, BUT BIGGER AND STRONGER THAN USUAL.
I WANT ONE!!!
HAPPY? CARLA?
GO GET HIM RIGHT MEOW!
ROAAARR
THE HELL'S GOING ON HERE?!

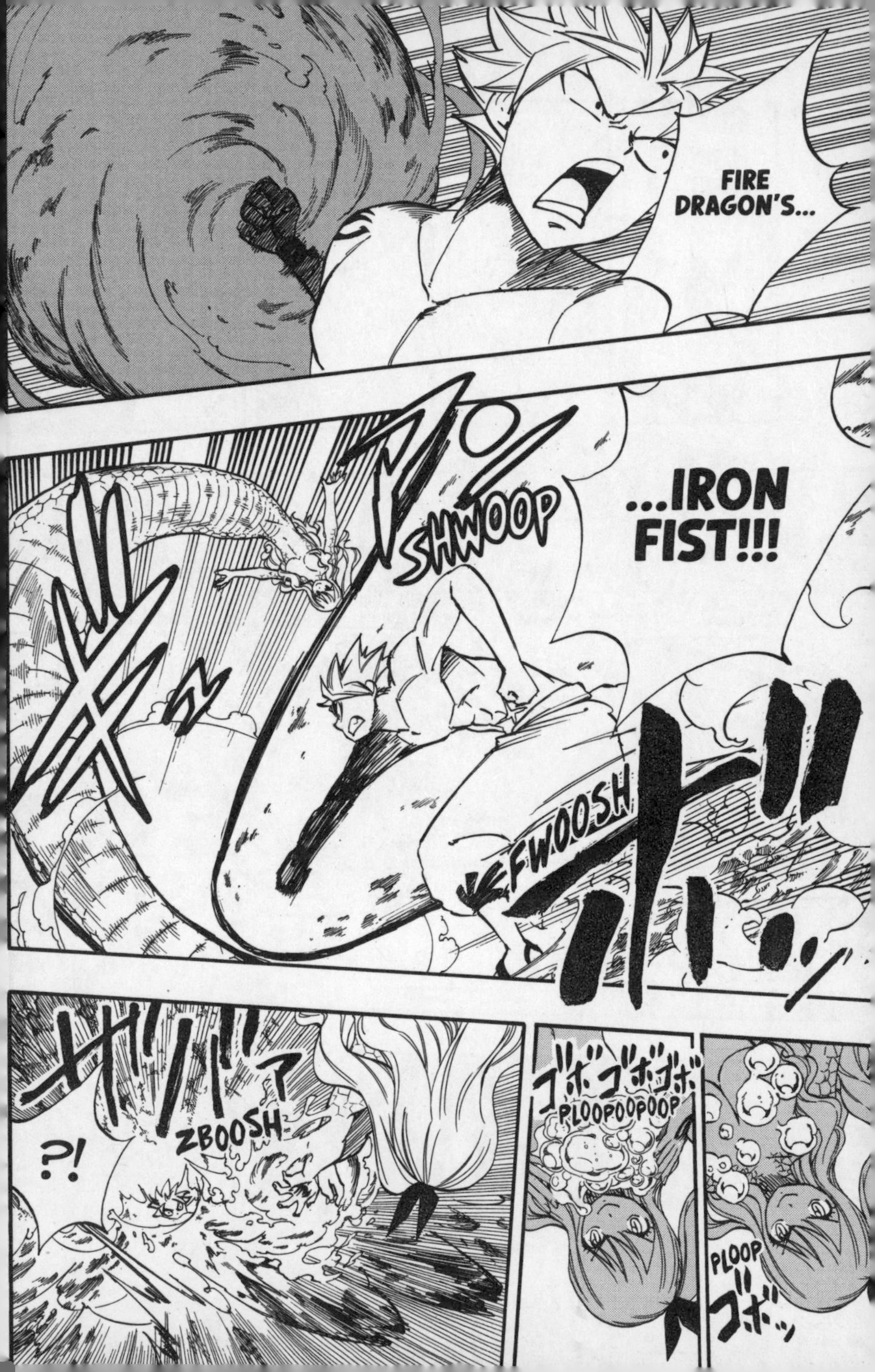
FIRE DRAGON'S...
...IRON FIST!!!
SHWOOP
FWOOSH
PLOOP
PLOOPOOPOOP
ZBOOSH
?!

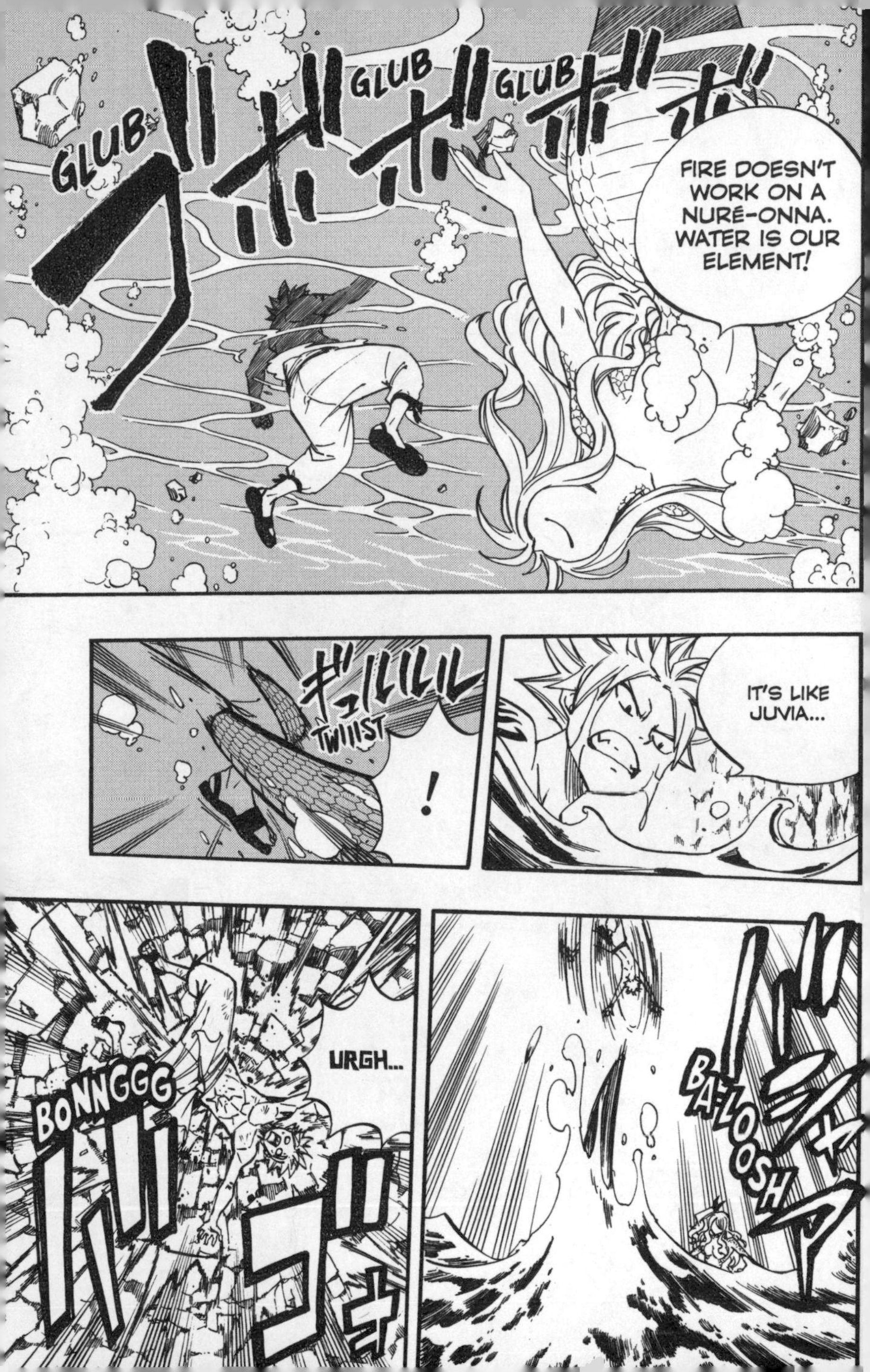
FIRE DOESN'T WORK ON A NURÉ-ONNA. WATER IS OUR ELEMENT!
GLUB
GLUB
GLUB
IT'S LIKE JUVIA...
TWIIIST
!
BA-LOOSH
URGH...
BONNGGG

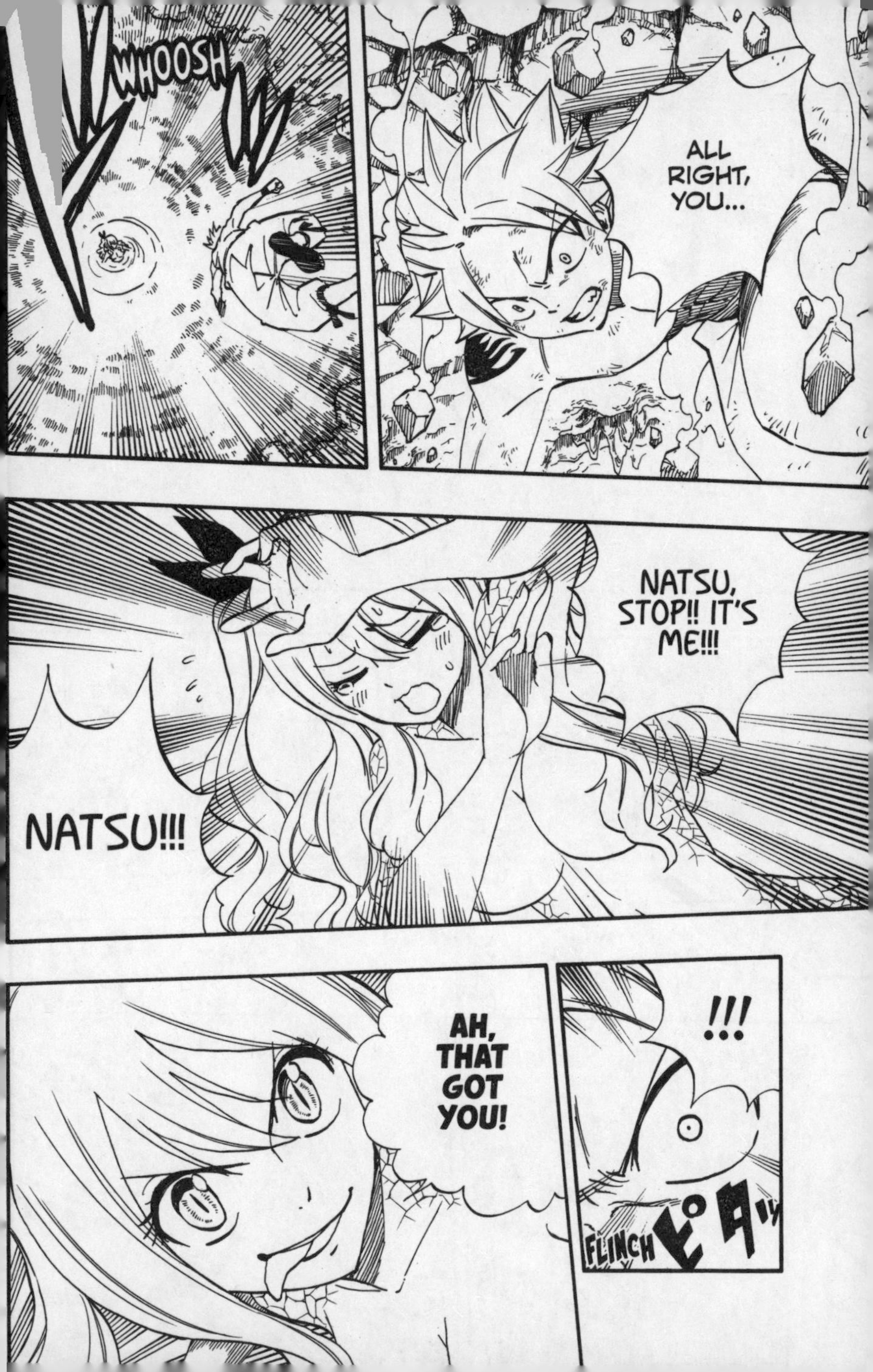
ALL RIGHT, YOU...
WHOOSH
NATSU, STOP!! IT'S ME!!!
NATSU!!!
!!!
FLINCH
AH, THAT GOT YOU!

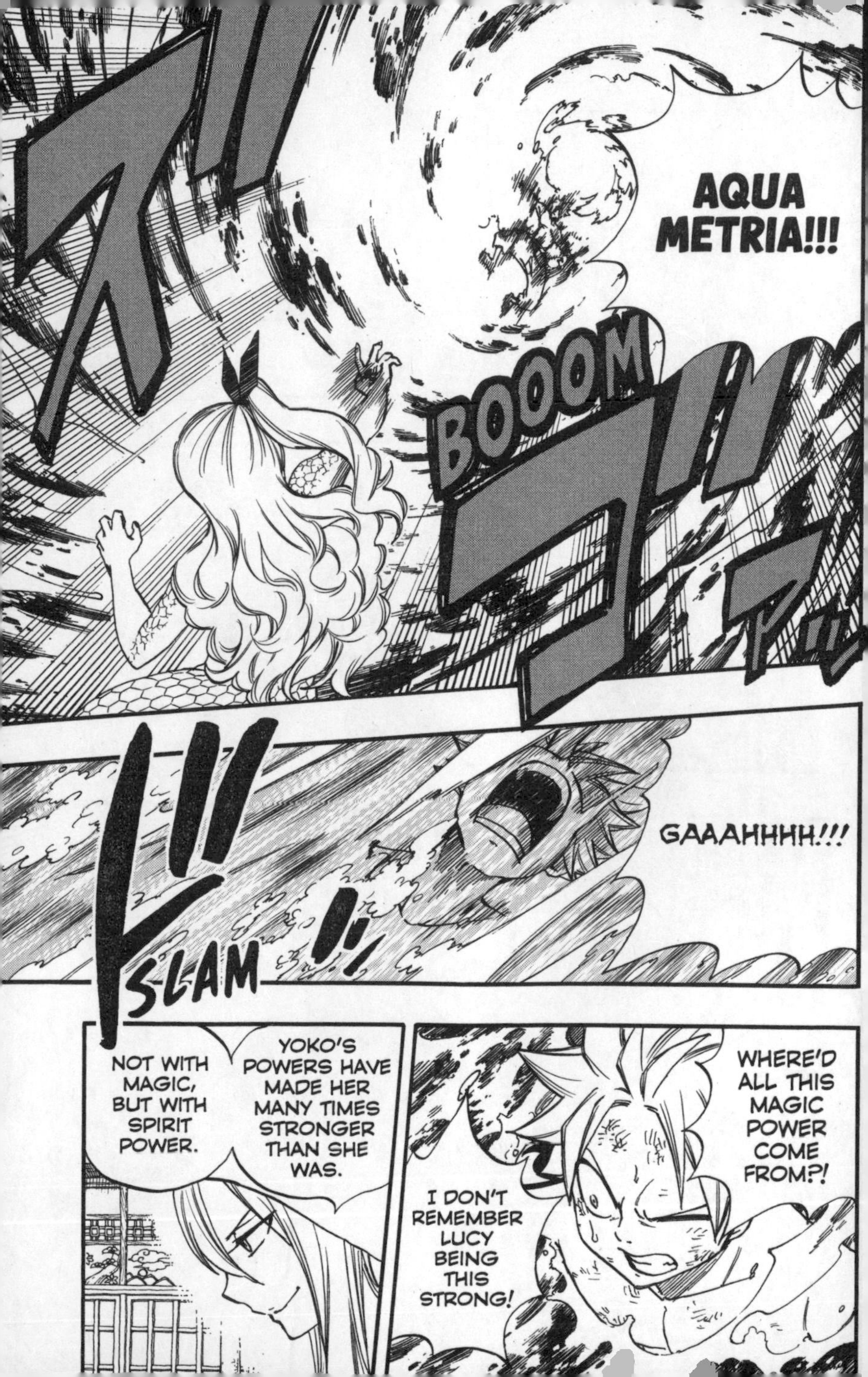
AQUA METRIA!!!
BOOOM
GAAAHHHH!!!
SLAM
WHERE'D ALL THIS MAGIC POWER COME FROM?!
I DON'T REMEMBER LUCY BEING THIS STRONG!
YOKO'S POWERS HAVE MADE HER MANY TIMES STRONGER THAN SHE WAS.
NOT WITH MAGIC, BUT WITH SPIRIT POWER.

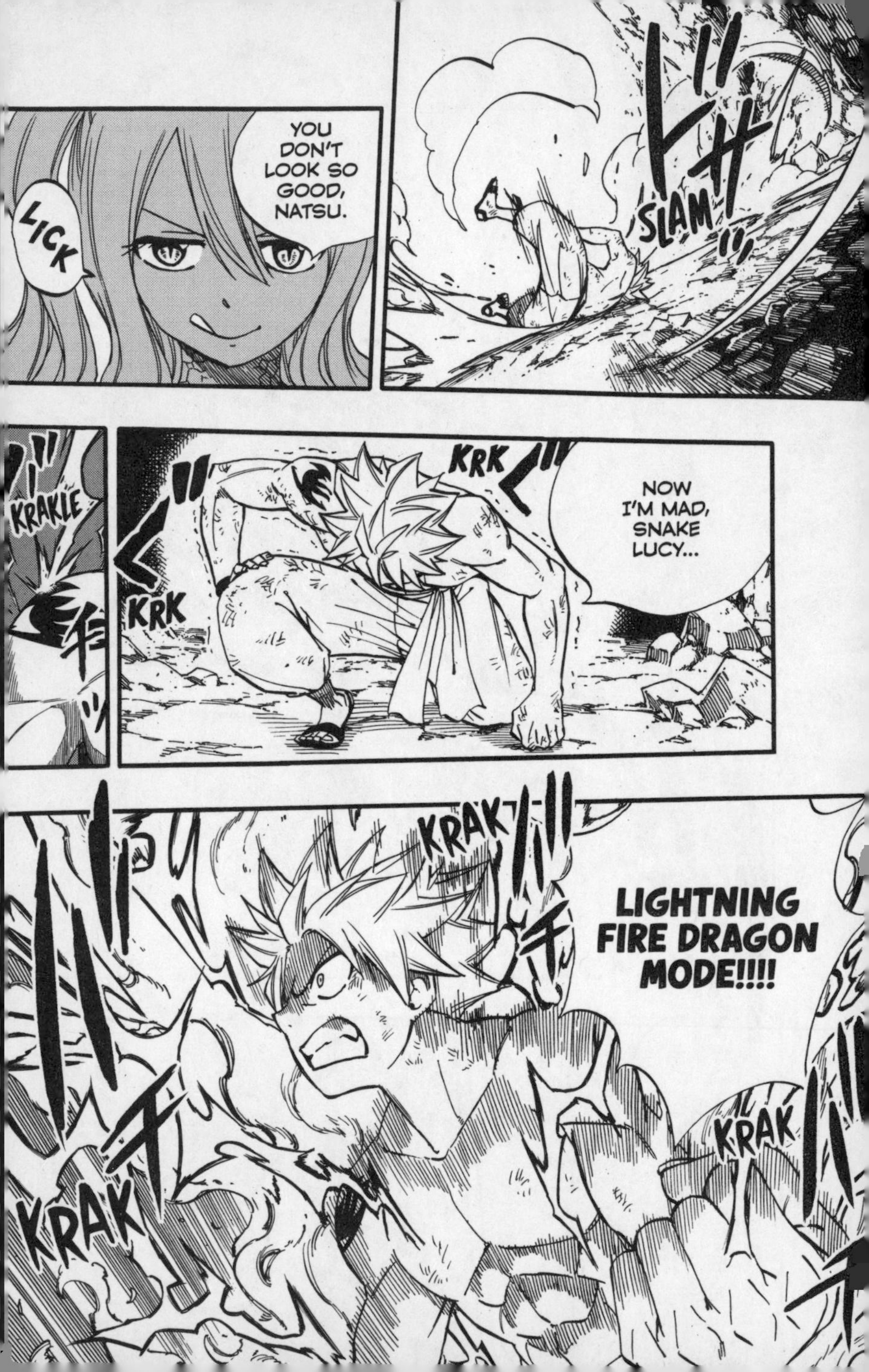
SLAM
YOU DON'T LOOK SO GOOD, NATSU.
LICK
KRK
NOW I'M MAD, SNAKE LUCY...
KRK
KRAKLE
LIGHTNING FIRE DRAGON MODE!!!!
KRAK
KRAK
KRAK

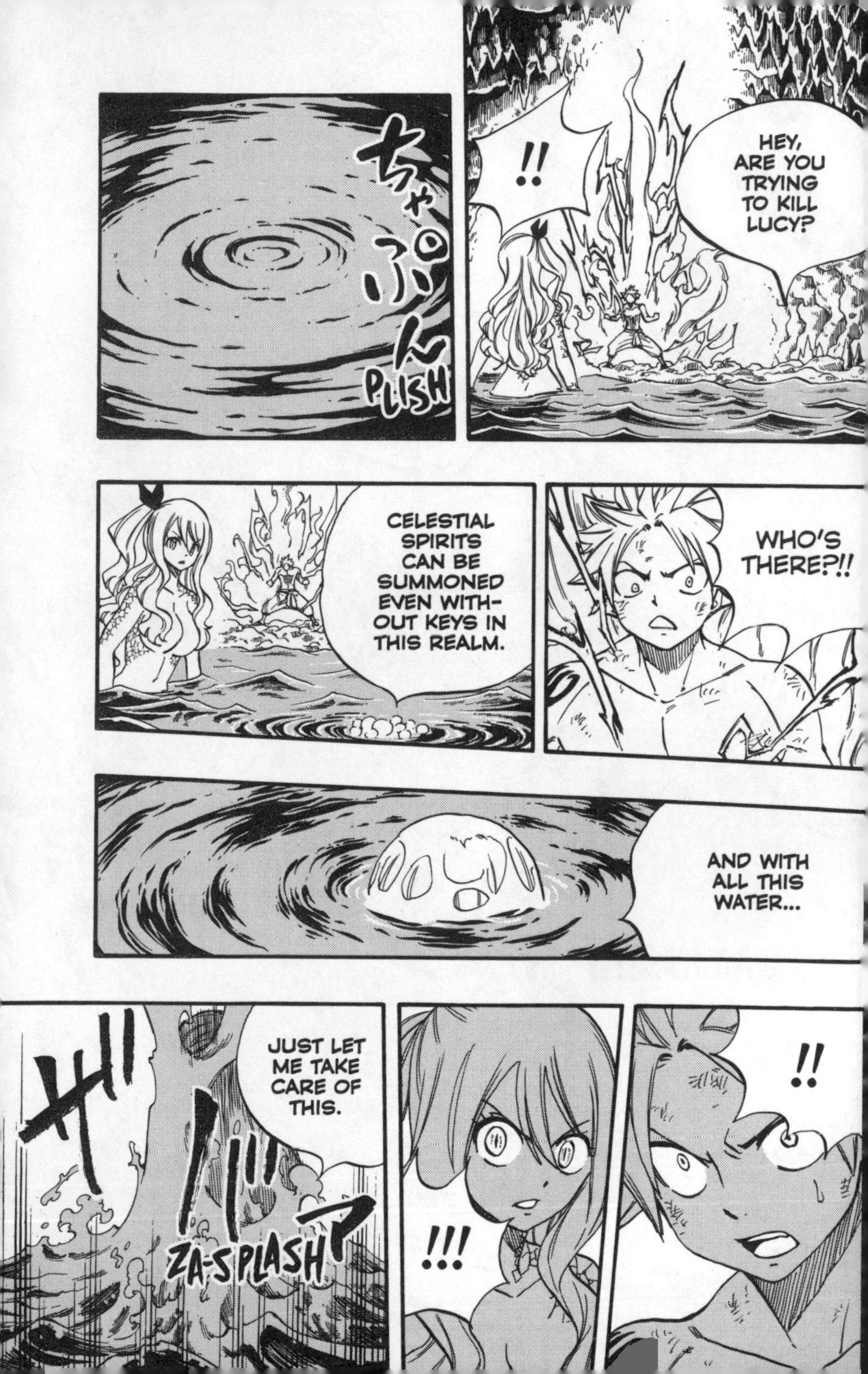
HEY, ARE YOU TRYING TO KILL LUCY?
!!
ちゃぷん
PLISH
WHO'S THERE?!!
CELESTIAL SPIRITS CAN BE SUMMONED EVEN WITH-OUT KEYS IN THIS REALM.
AND WITH ALL THIS WATER...
!!
!!!
JUST LET ME TAKE CARE OF THIS.
ZA-SPLASH

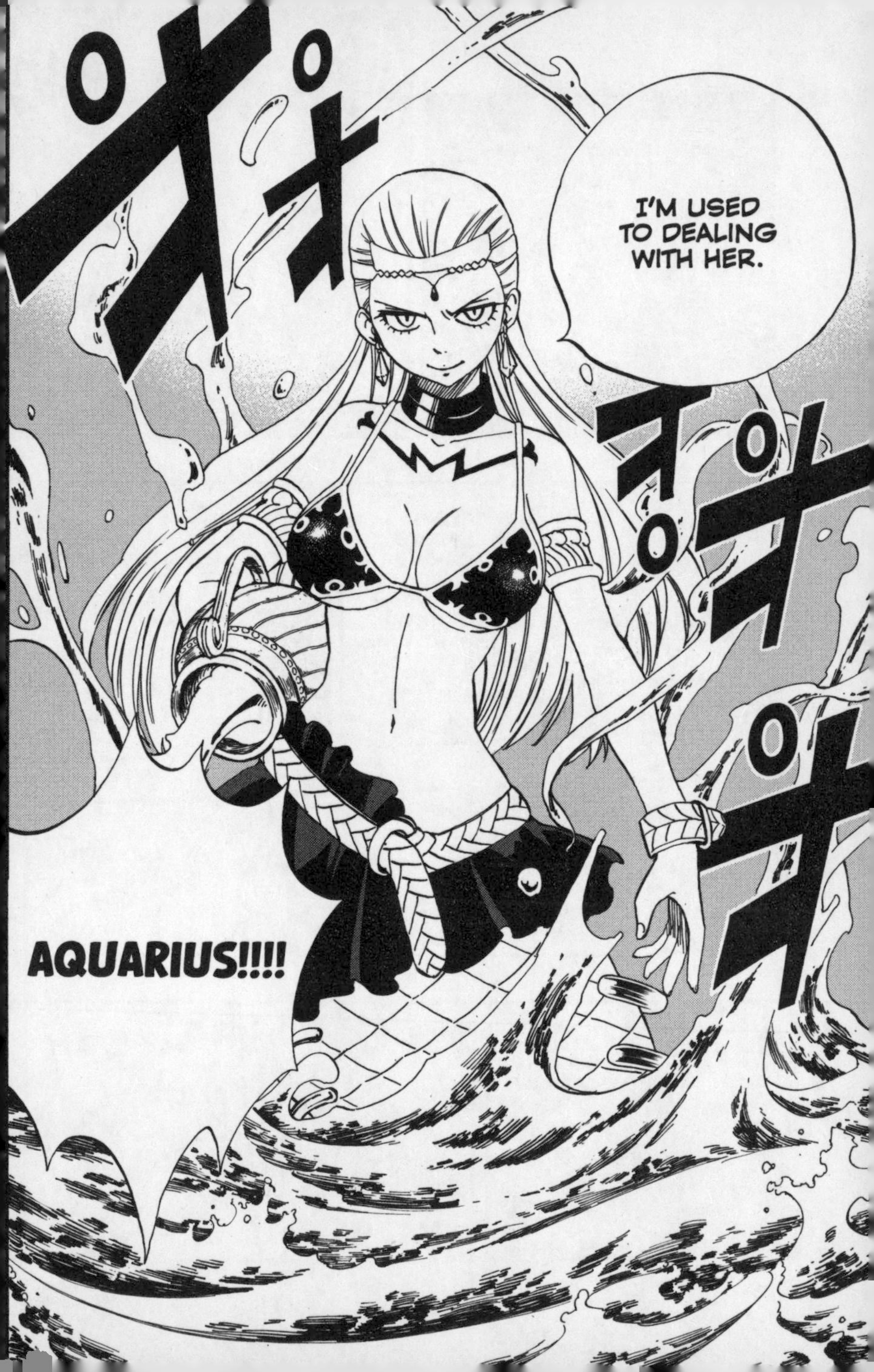
I'M USED TO DEALING WITH HER.
AQUARIUS!!!!

FAIRY TAIL 100 YEARS QUEST

Chapter 75: Memories of Water

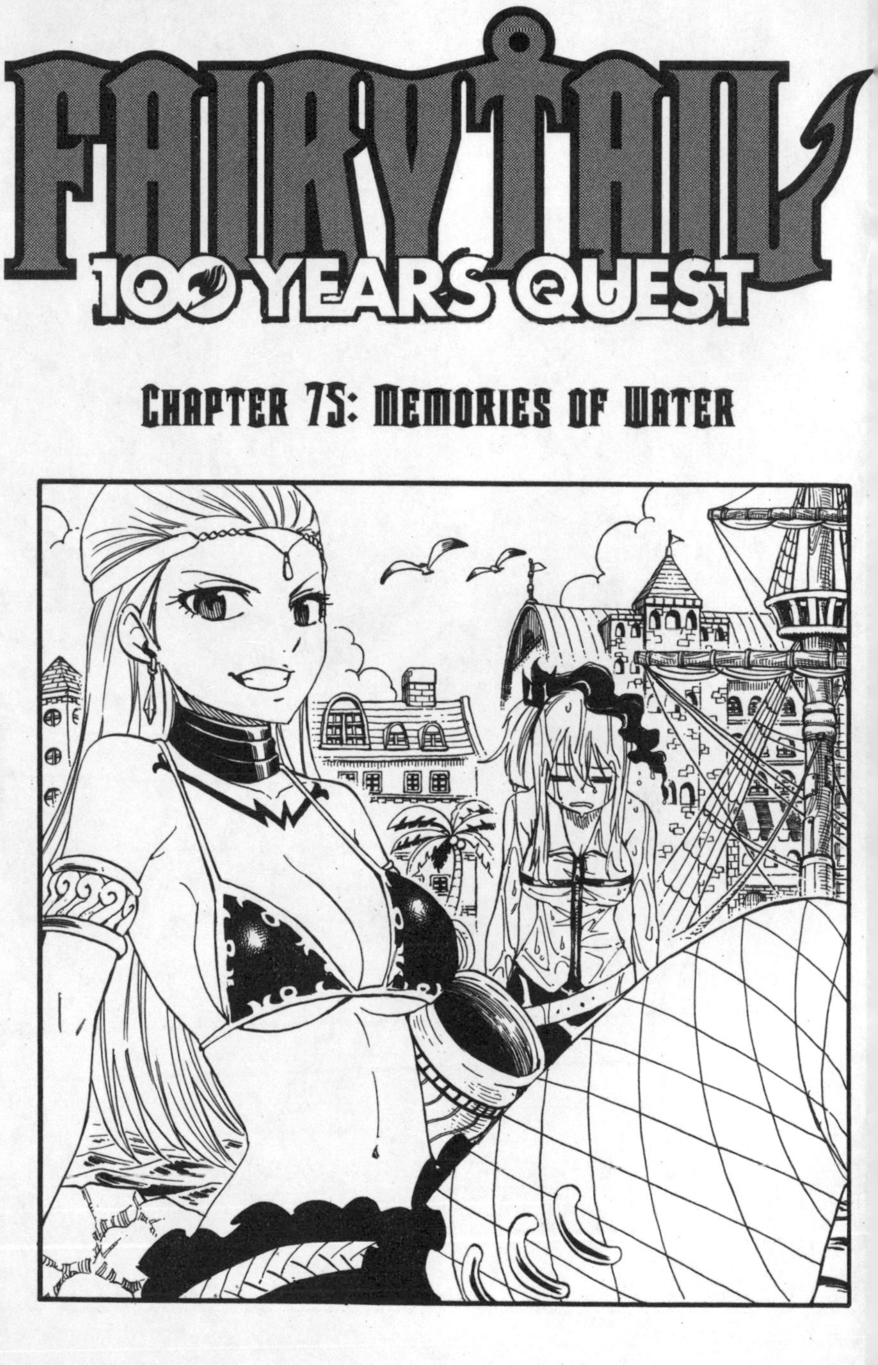

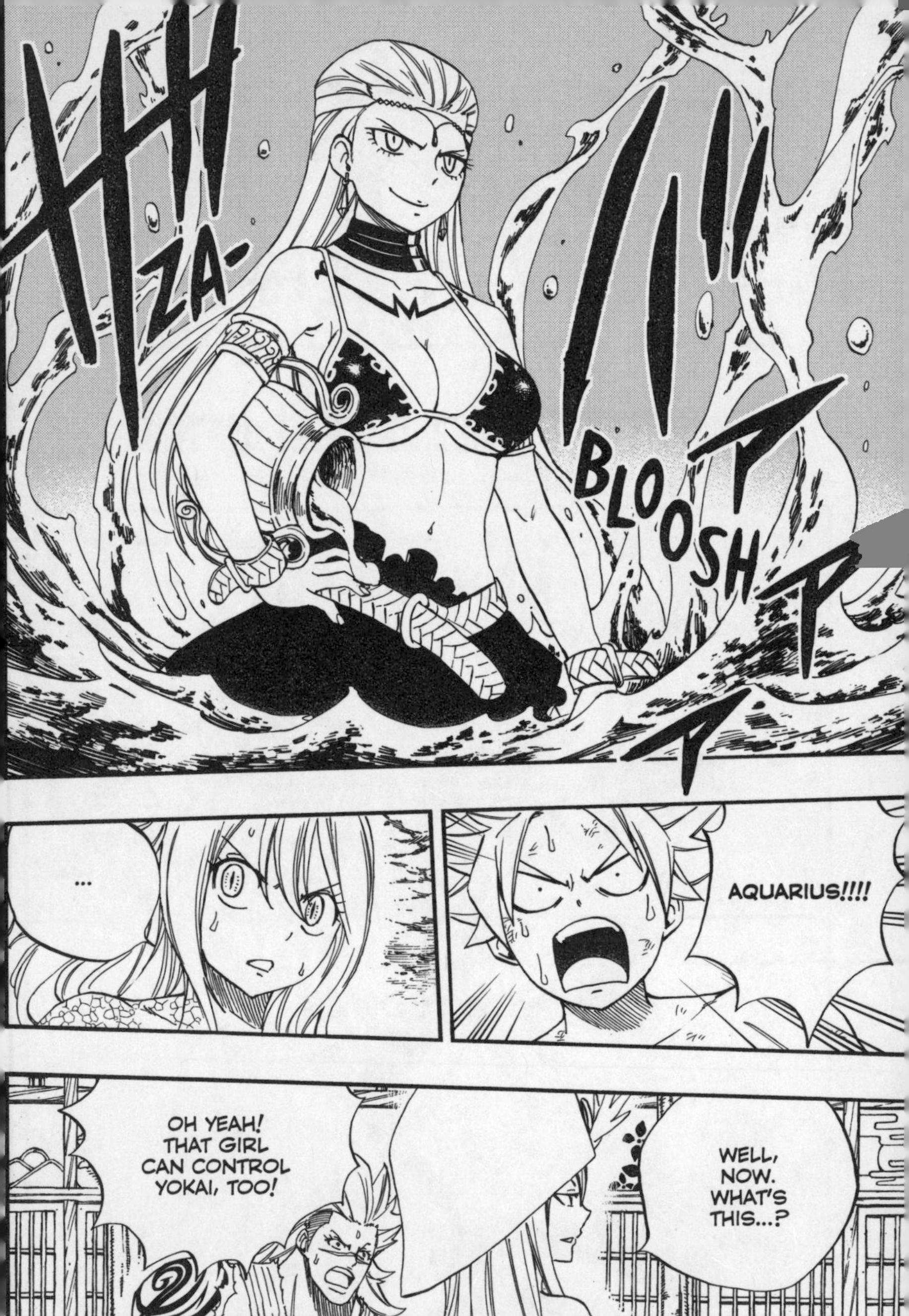
BLOOSH
ZA-
AQUARIUS!!!!
...
WELL, NOW. WHAT'S THIS...?
OH YEAH! THAT GIRL CAN CONTROL YOKAI, TOO!

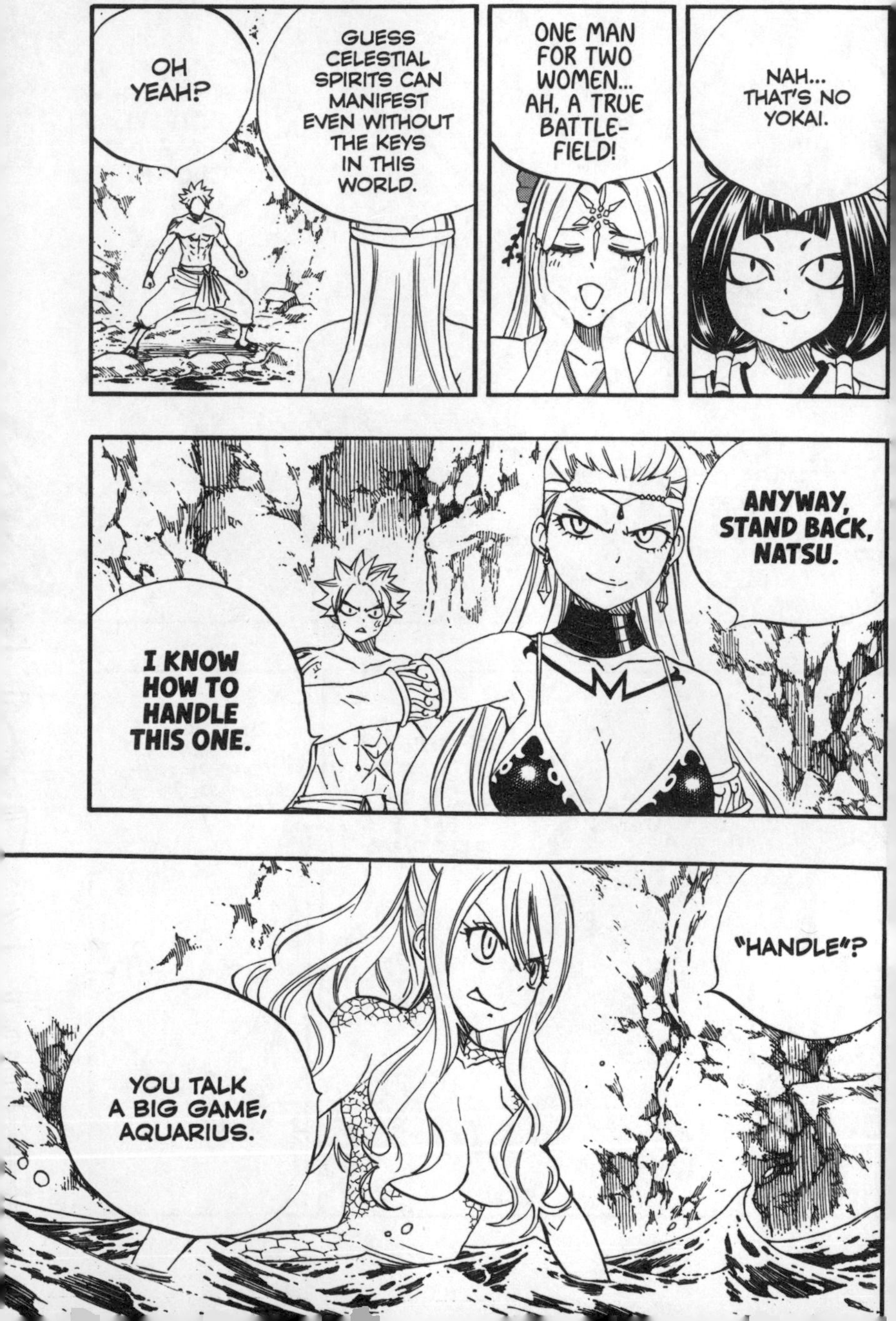
NAH... THAT'S NO YOKAI.
ONE MAN FOR TWO WOMEN... AH, A TRUE BATTLE-FIELD!
GUESS CELESTIAL SPIRITS CAN MANIFEST EVEN WITHOUT THE KEYS IN THIS WORLD.
OH YEAH?
ANYWAY, STAND BACK, NATSU.
I KNOW HOW TO HANDLE THIS ONE.
"HANDLE"?
YOU TALK A BIG GAME, AQUARIUS.

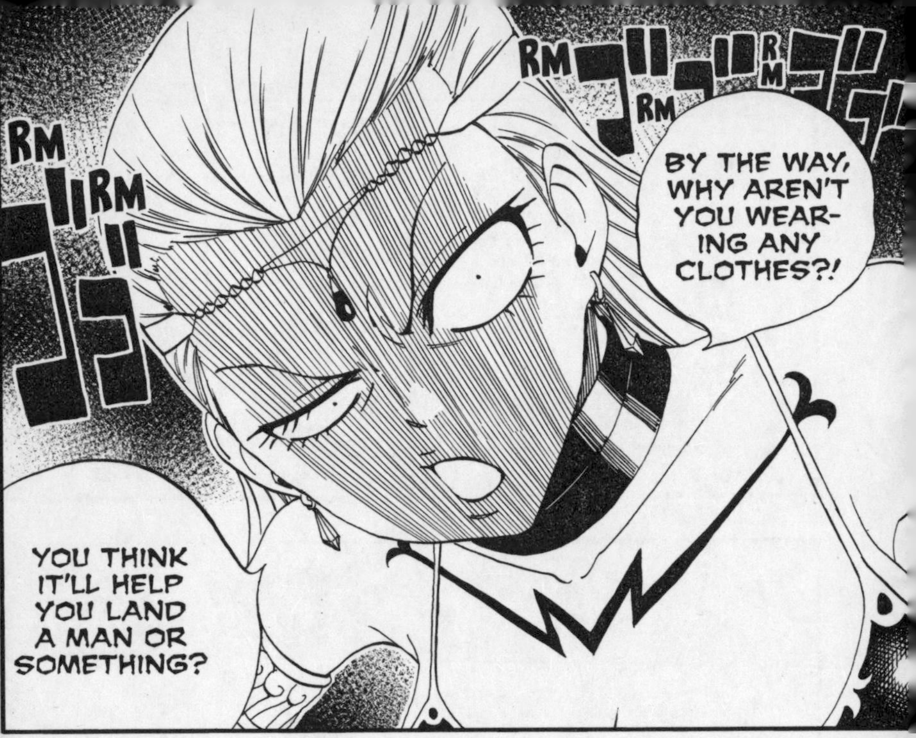
RM RM RM RM
BY THE WAY, WHY AREN'T YOU WEAR-ING ANY CLOTHES?!
RM RM
YOU THINK IT'LL HELP YOU LAND A MAN OR SOMETHING?

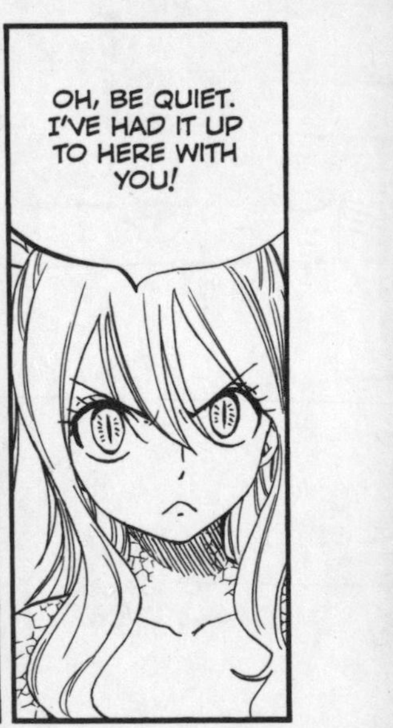
OH, BE QUIET. I'VE HAD IT UP TO HERE WITH YOU!

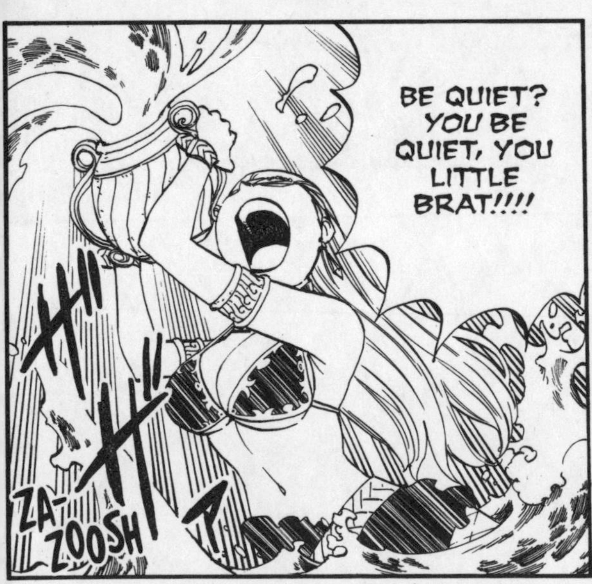
BE QUIET? *YOU* BE QUIET, YOU LITTLE BRAT!!!!
ZA-ZOOSH

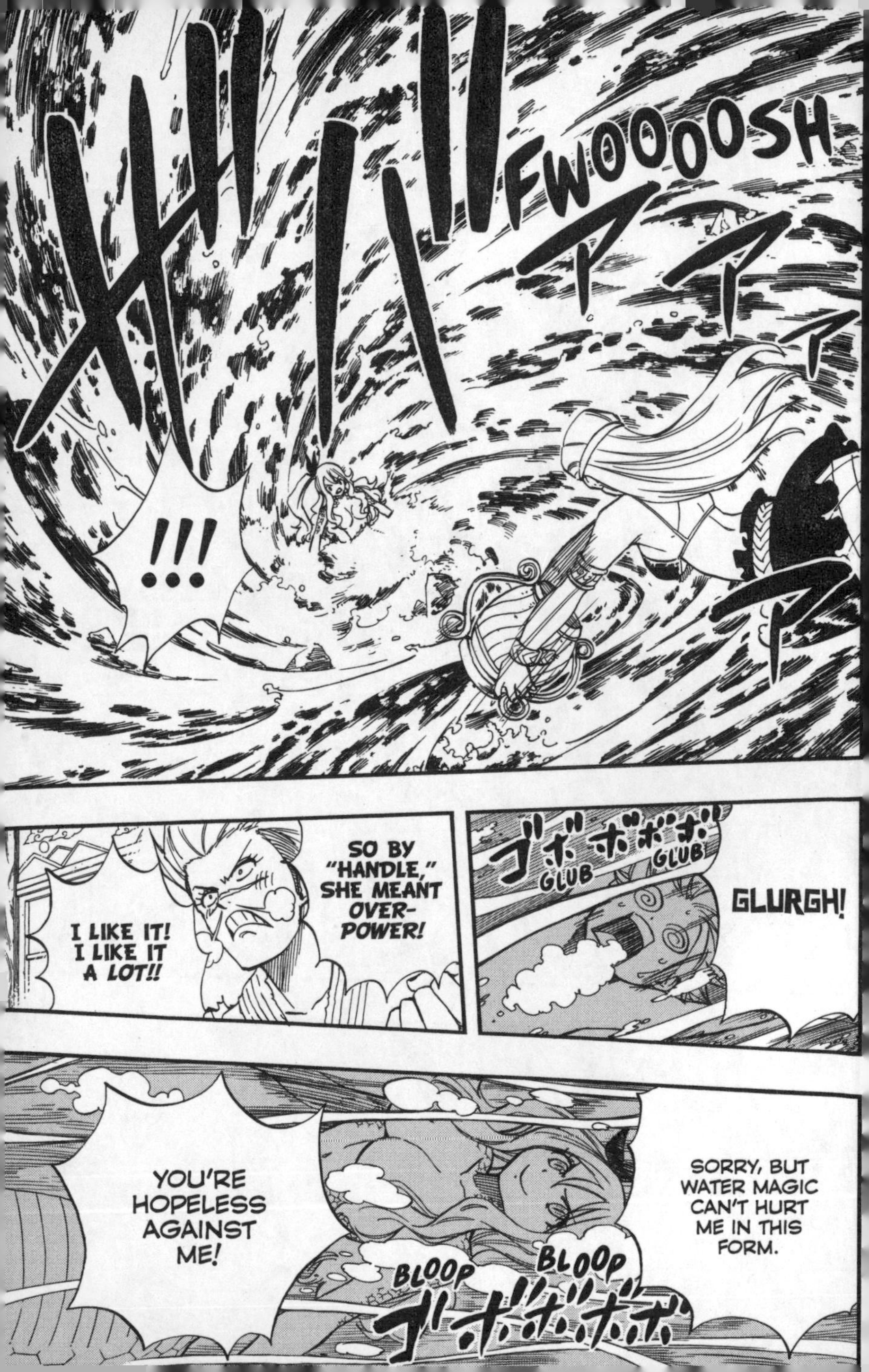
FWOOOOSH
!!!
GLUB
GLUB
GLURGH!
SO BY "HANDLE," SHE MEANT OVER-POWER!
I LIKE IT! I LIKE IT A LOT!!
SORRY, BUT WATER MAGIC CAN'T HURT ME IN THIS FORM.
YOU'RE HOPELESS AGAINST ME!
BLOOP
BLOOP

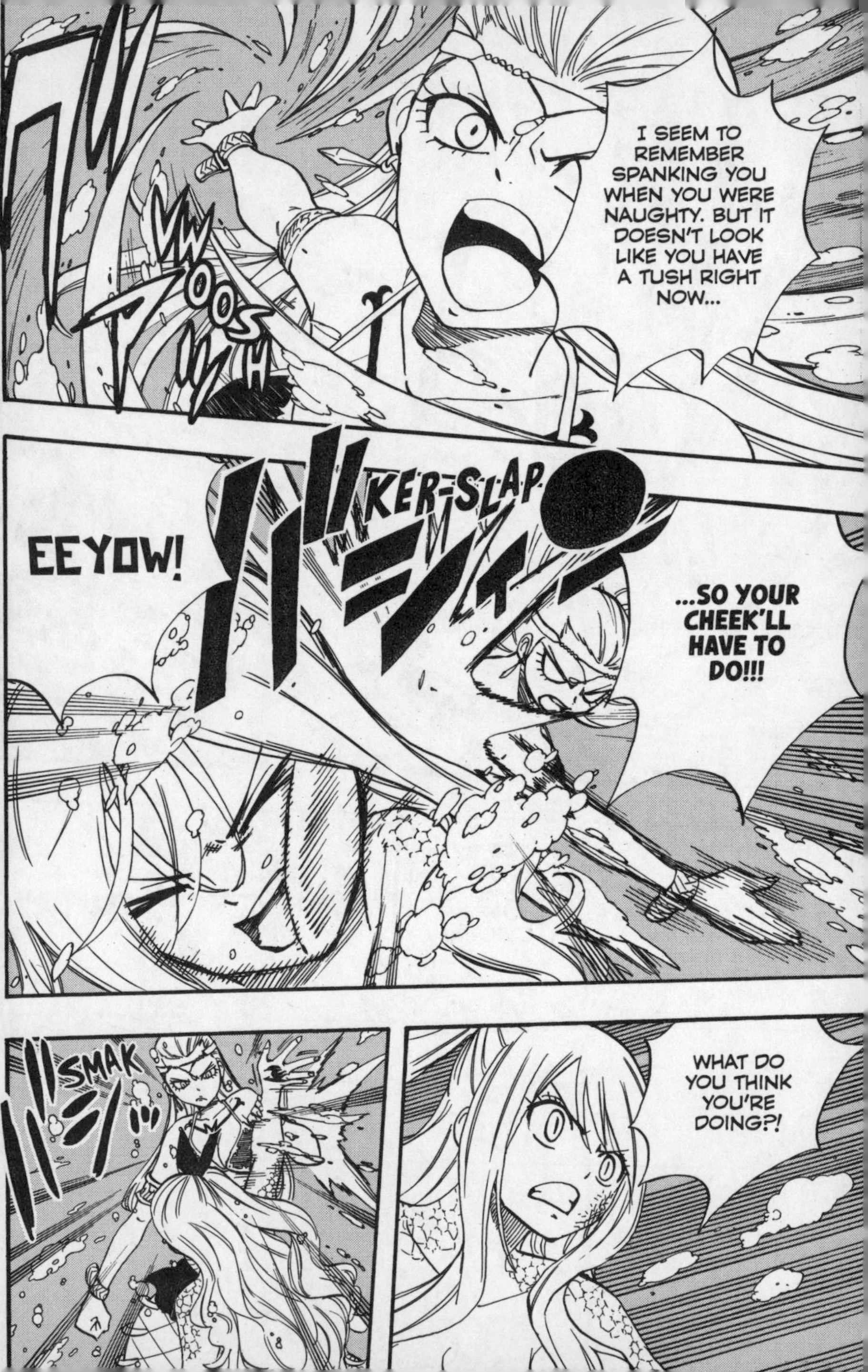
I SEEM TO REMEMBER SPANKING YOU WHEN YOU WERE NAUGHTY. BUT IT DOESN'T LOOK LIKE YOU HAVE A TUSH RIGHT NOW...
WHOOSH
KER-SLAP
...SO YOUR CHEEK'LL HAVE TO DO!!!
EEYOW!
WHAT DO YOU THINK YOU'RE DOING?!
SMAK

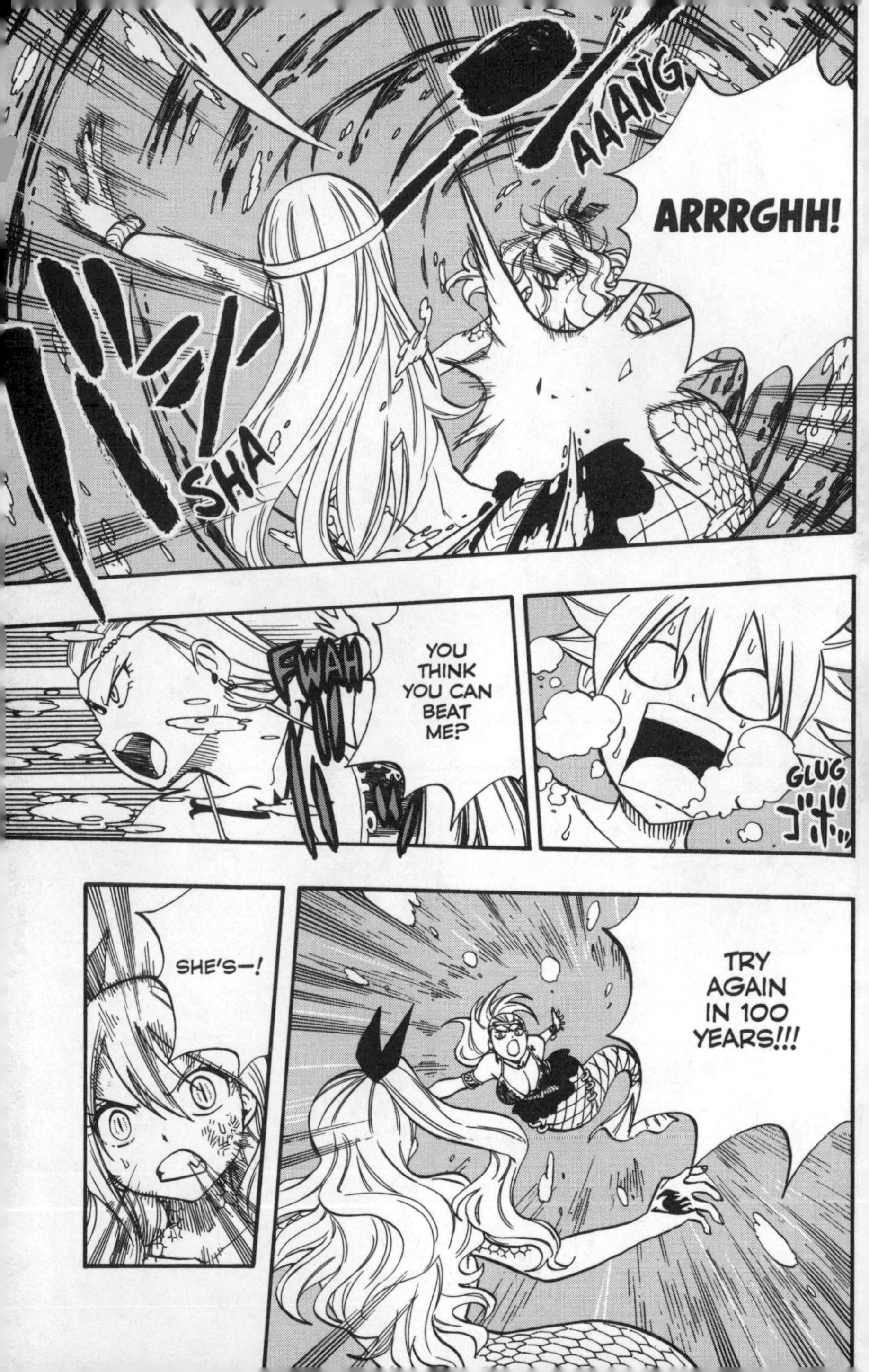
AAANG.
ARRRGHH!
SHA
GLUG
YOU THINK YOU CAN BEAT ME?
FWAH
TRY AGAIN IN 100 YEARS!!!
SHE'S—!

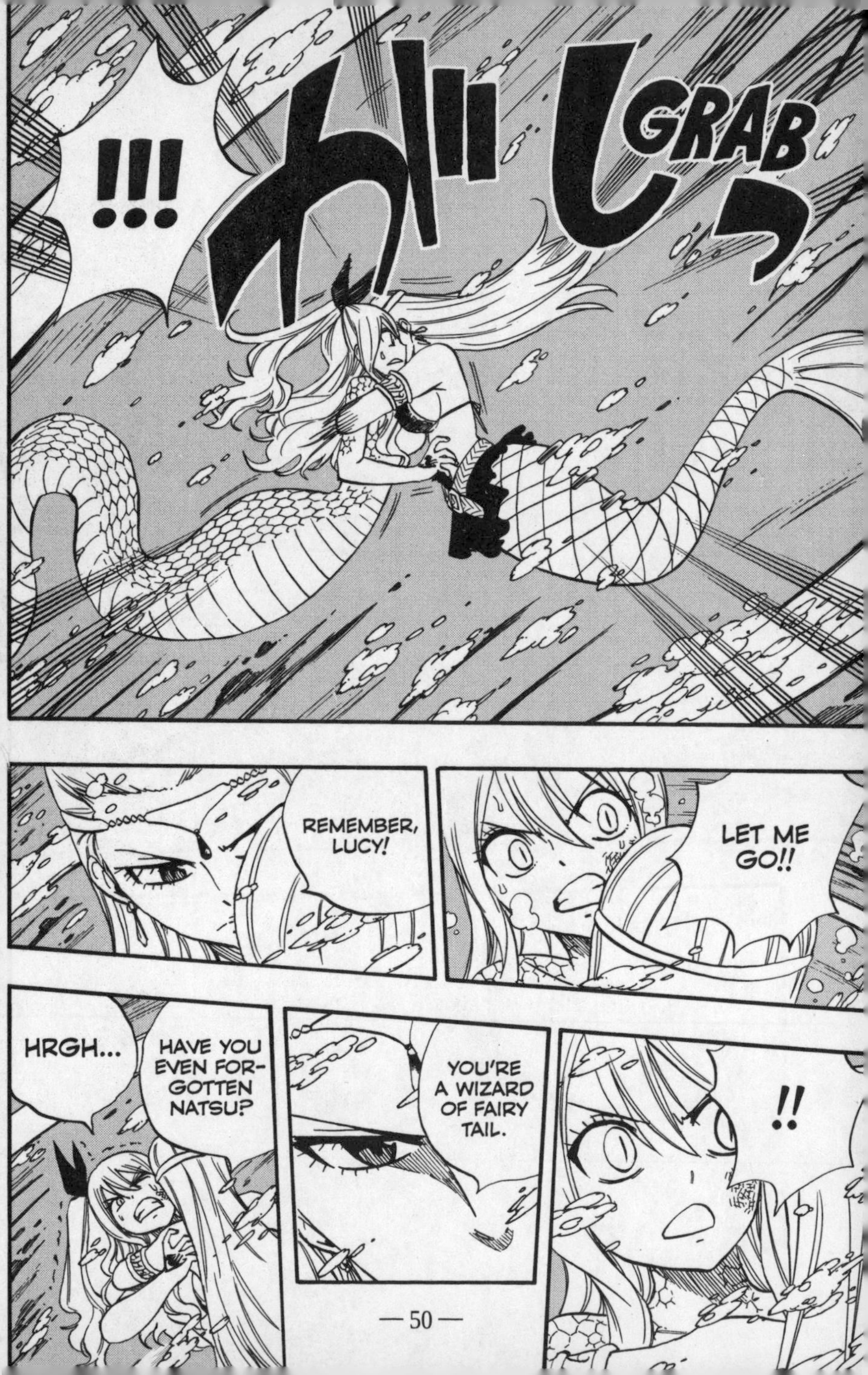
GRAB
!!!
LET ME GO!!
REMEMBER, LUCY!
!!
YOU'RE A WIZARD OF FAIRY TAIL.
HAVE YOU EVEN FOR-GOTTEN NATSU?
HRGH...

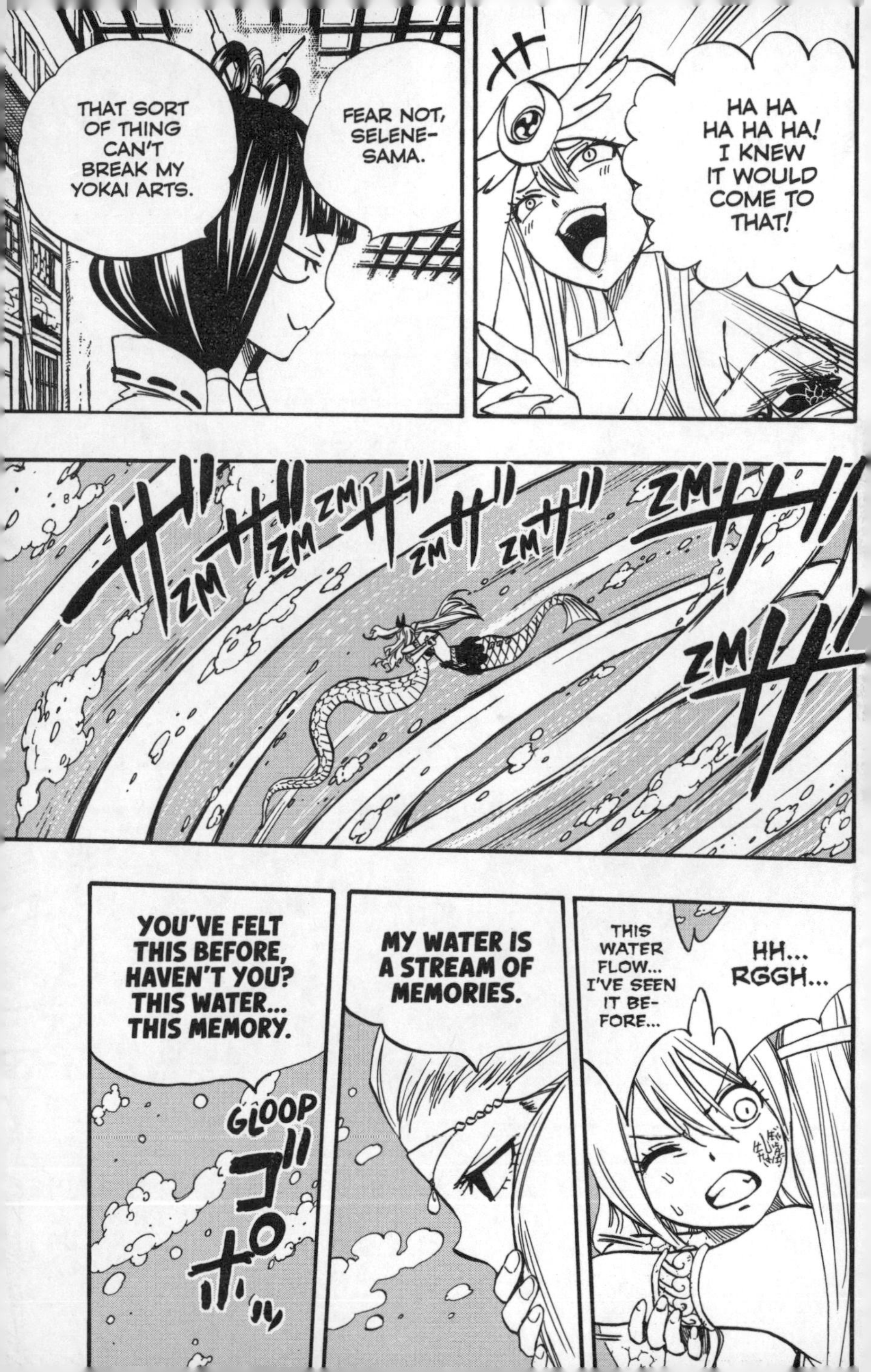
HA HA HA HA HA! I KNEW IT WOULD COME TO THAT!
FEAR NOT, SELENE-SAMA.
THAT SORT OF THING CAN'T BREAK MY YOKAI ARTS.
ZM
ZM
ZM
ZM
ZM
ZM
ZM
HH... RGGH...
THIS WATER FLOW... I'VE SEEN IT BE-FORE...
MY WATER IS A STREAM OF MEMORIES.
YOU'VE FELT THIS BEFORE, HAVEN'T YOU? THIS WATER... THIS MEMORY.
GLOOP
ゴポッ

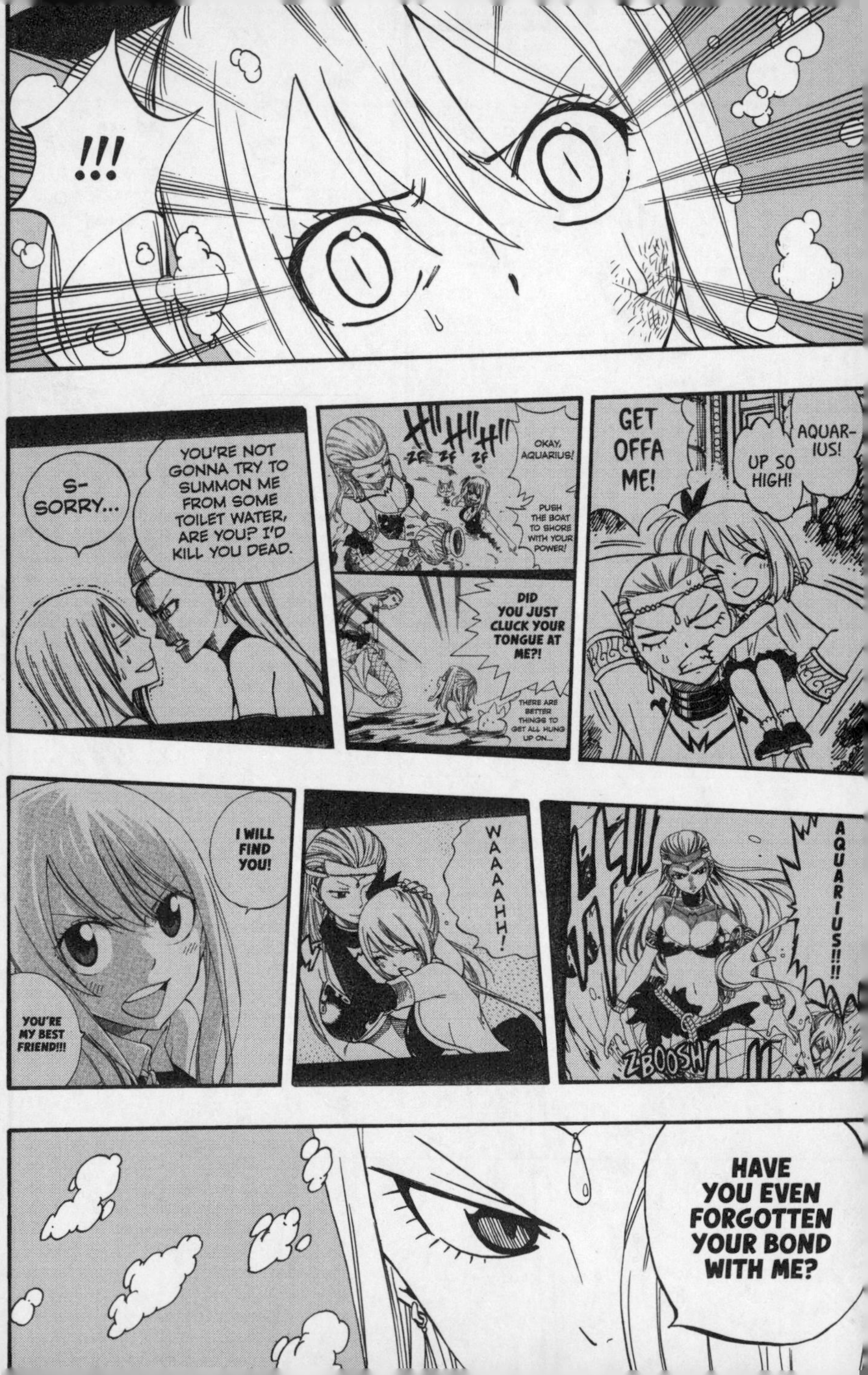
!!!
AQUARIUS!
UP SO HIGH!
GET OFFA ME!
OKAY, AQUARIUS!
PUSH THE BOAT TO SHORE WITH YOUR POWER!
ZF ZF ZF
DID YOU JUST CLUCK YOUR TONGUE AT ME?!
THERE ARE BETTER THINGS TO GET ALL HUNG UP ON...
YOU'RE NOT GONNA TRY TO SUMMON ME FROM SOME TOILET WATER, ARE YOU? I'D KILL YOU DEAD.
S-SORRY...
AQUARIUS!!!
Z-BOOSH
WAAAAHH!
I WILL FIND YOU!
YOU'RE MY BEST FRIEND!!!
HAVE YOU EVEN FORGOTTEN YOUR BOND WITH ME?

HOW LONG DO YOU PLAN TO HIDE BEHIND ME?!
YOU'RE THE ONLY ONE WHO CAN SAVE YOUR FRIENDS NOW!
I DON'T CARE IF YOU HATE ME...
YOU'RE MY BELOVED AQUARIUS...
PLOOP
PLOOP
LUCY...
IMPOS-SIBLE!
CLATTER

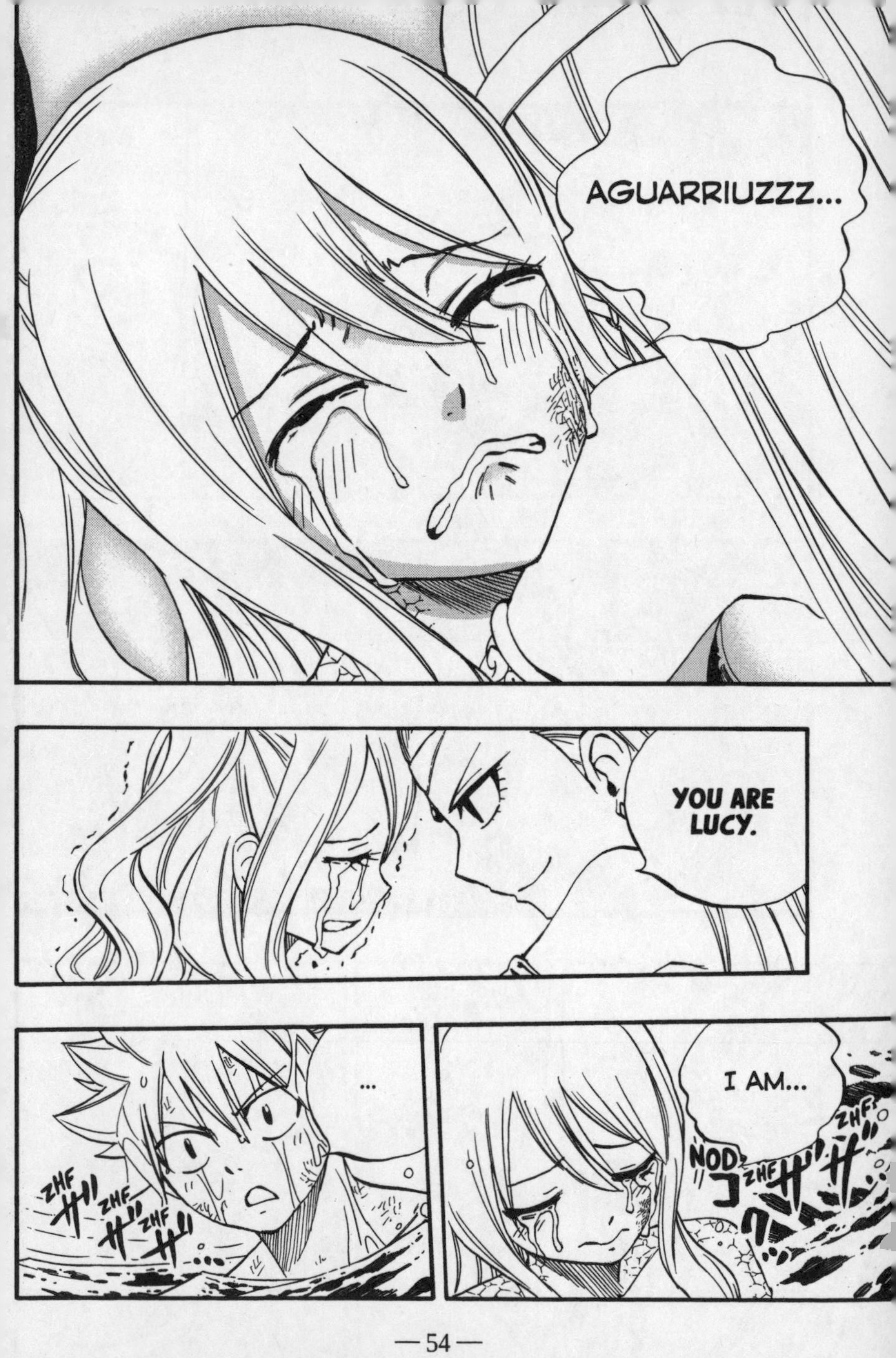
AGUARRIUZZZ...
YOU ARE LUCY.
I AM...
NOD
ZHF
ZHF
...
ZHF
ZHF
ZHF

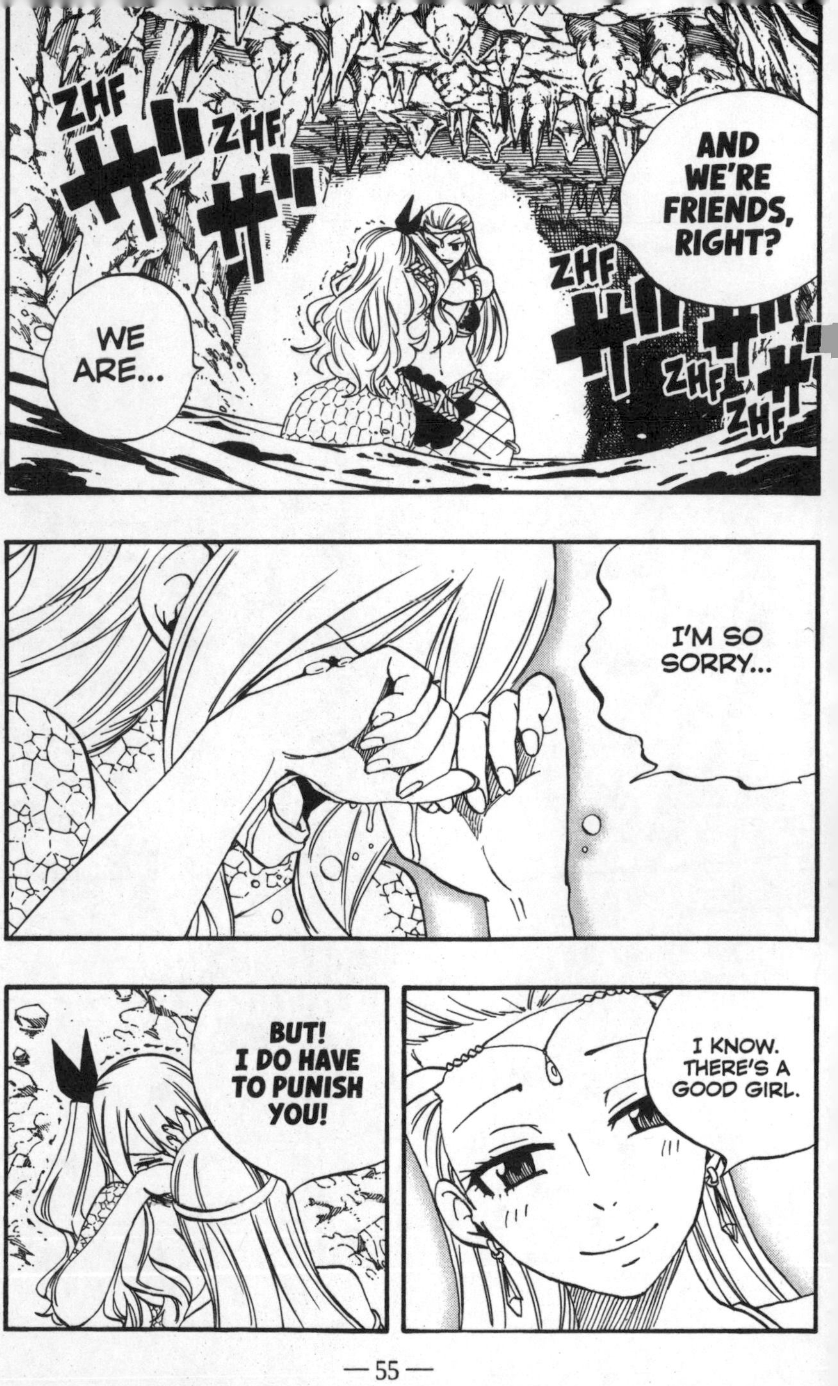
AND WE'RE FRIENDS, RIGHT?
ZHF
ZHF
ZHF
ZHF
ZHF
WE ARE...
I'M SO SORRY...
I KNOW. THERE'S A GOOD GIRL.
BUT! I DO HAVE TO PUNISH YOU!

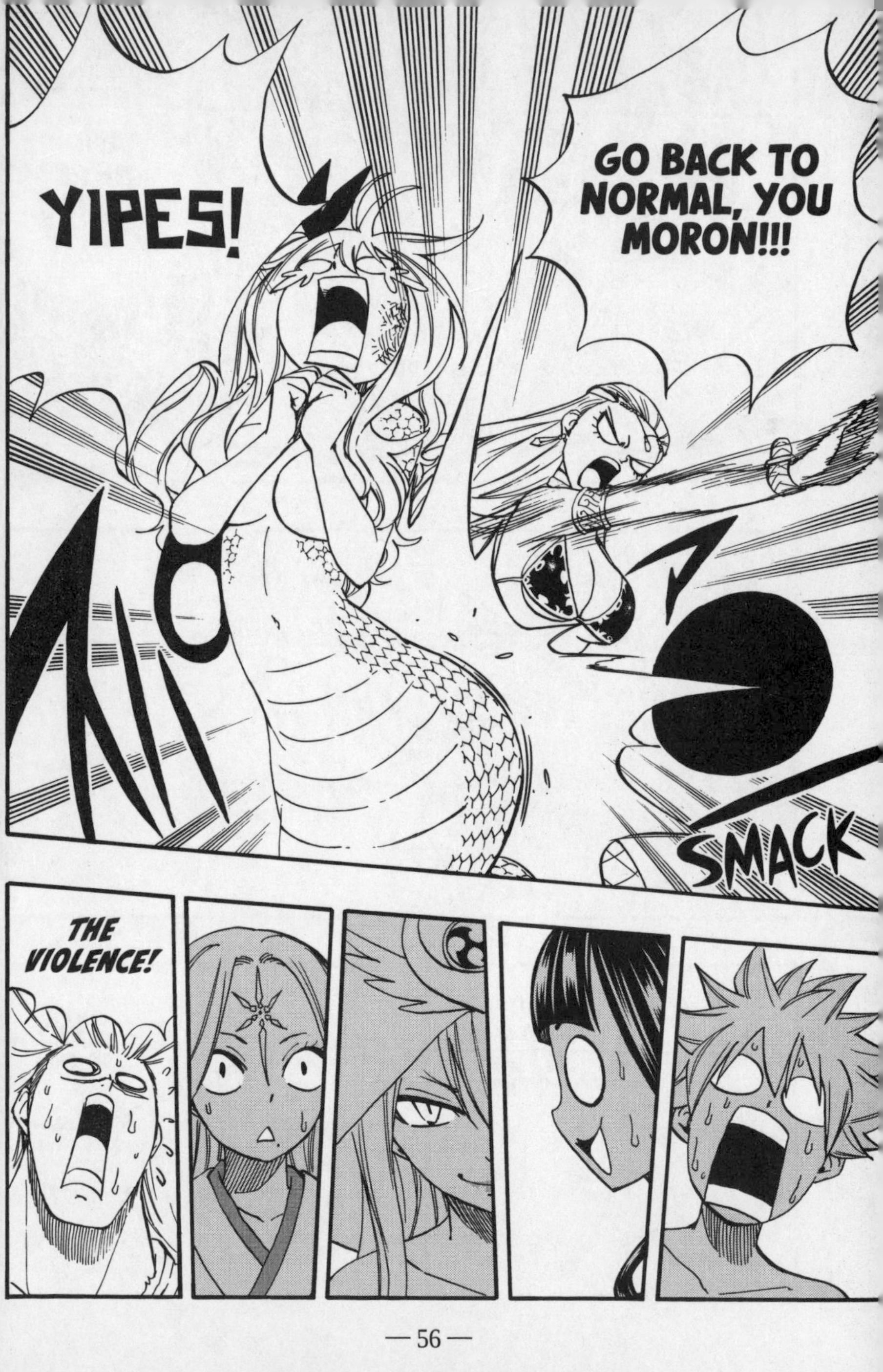
GO BACK TO NORMAL, YOU MORON!!!
YIPES!
SMACK
THE VIOLENCE!

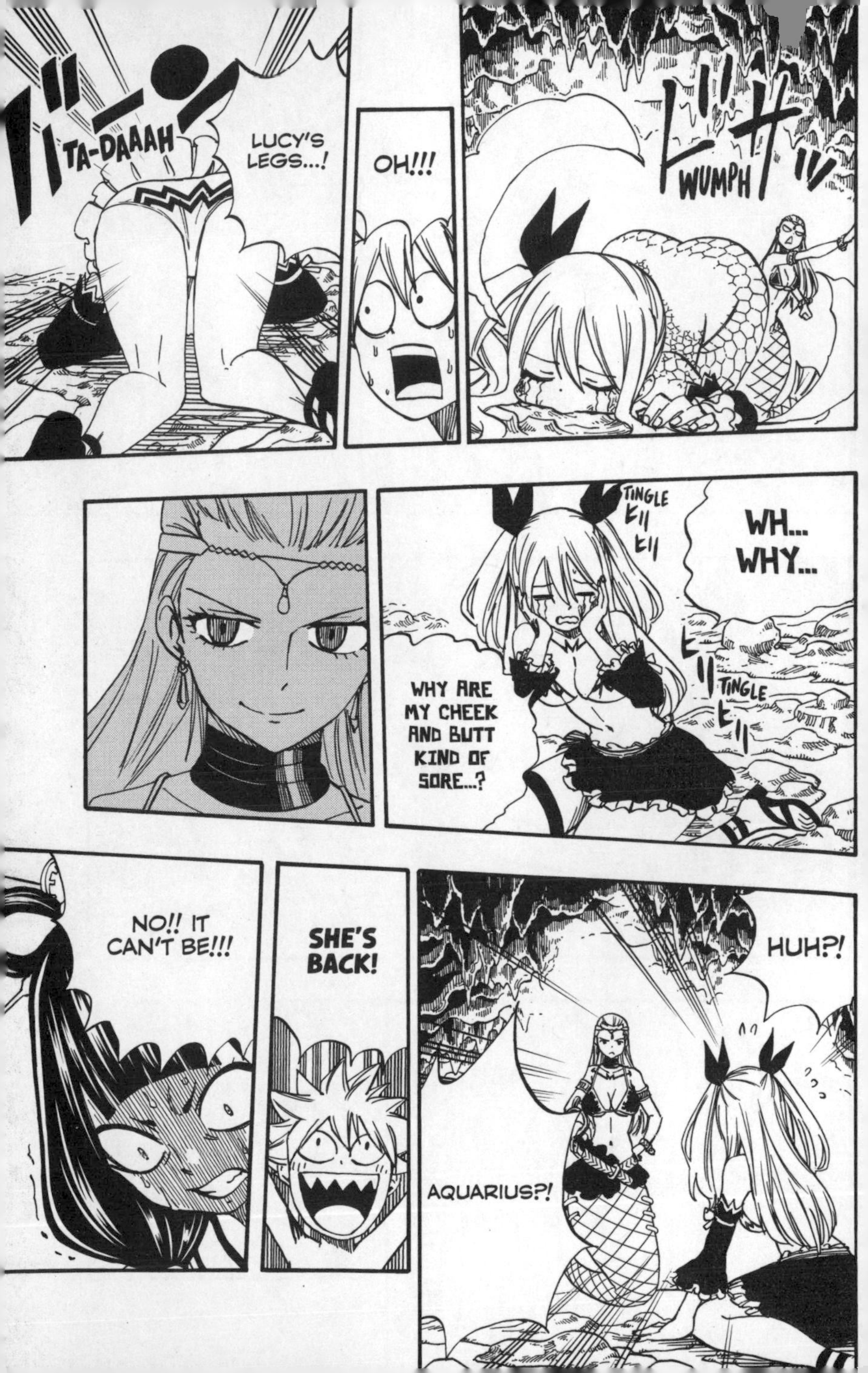

WUMPH
OH!!!
LUCY'S LEGS...!
TA-DAAAH
TINGLE
WH... WHY...
TINGLE
WHY ARE MY CHEEK AND BUTT KIND OF SORE...?
HUH?!
AQUARIUS?!
SHE'S BACK!
NO!! IT CAN'T BE!!!

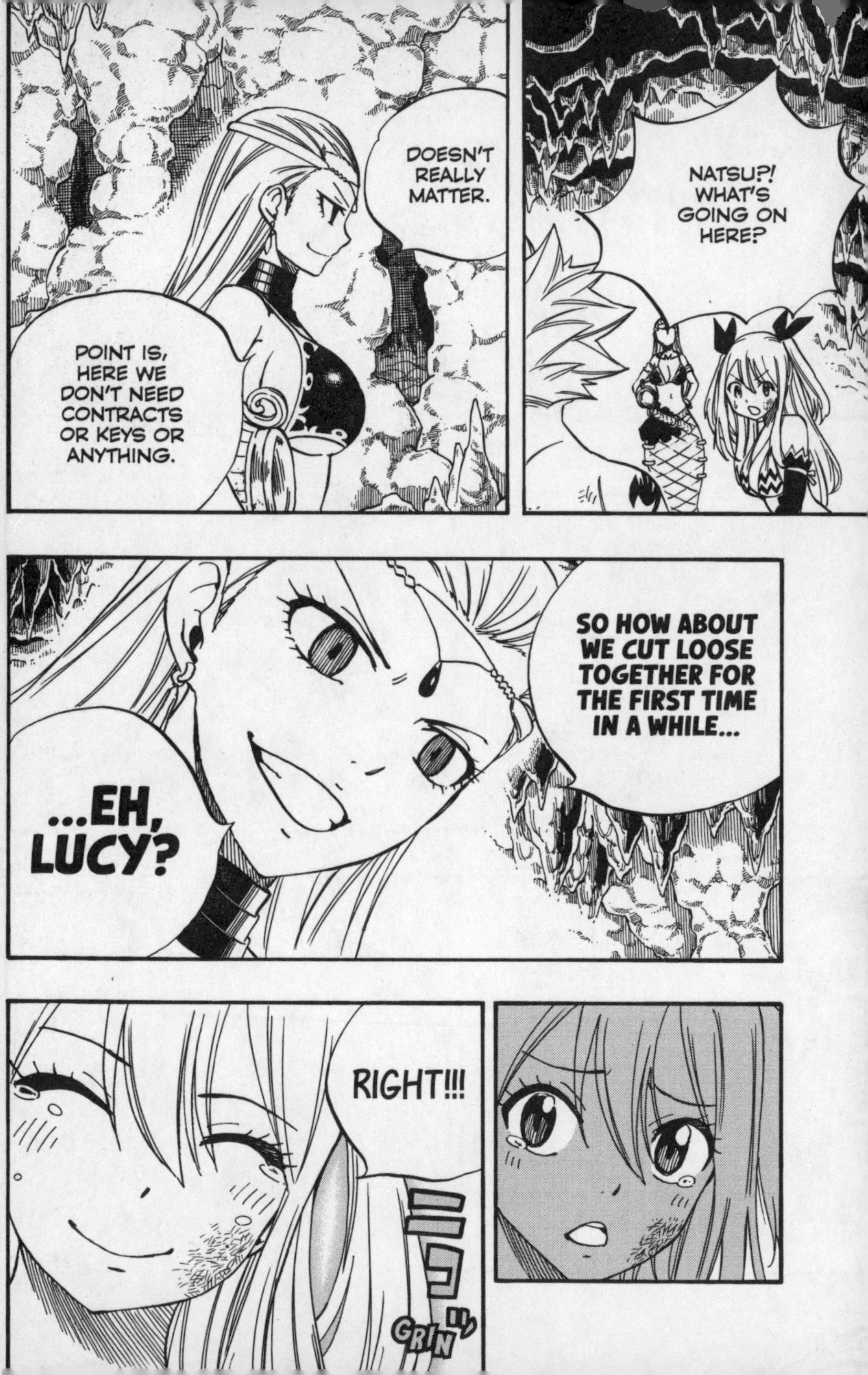
NATSU?! WHAT'S GOING ON HERE?
DOESN'T REALLY MATTER.
POINT IS, HERE WE DON'T NEED CONTRACTS OR KEYS OR ANYTHING.
SO HOW ABOUT WE CUT LOOSE TOGETHER FOR THE FIRST TIME IN A WHILE...
...EH, LUCY?
RIGHT!!!
GRIN

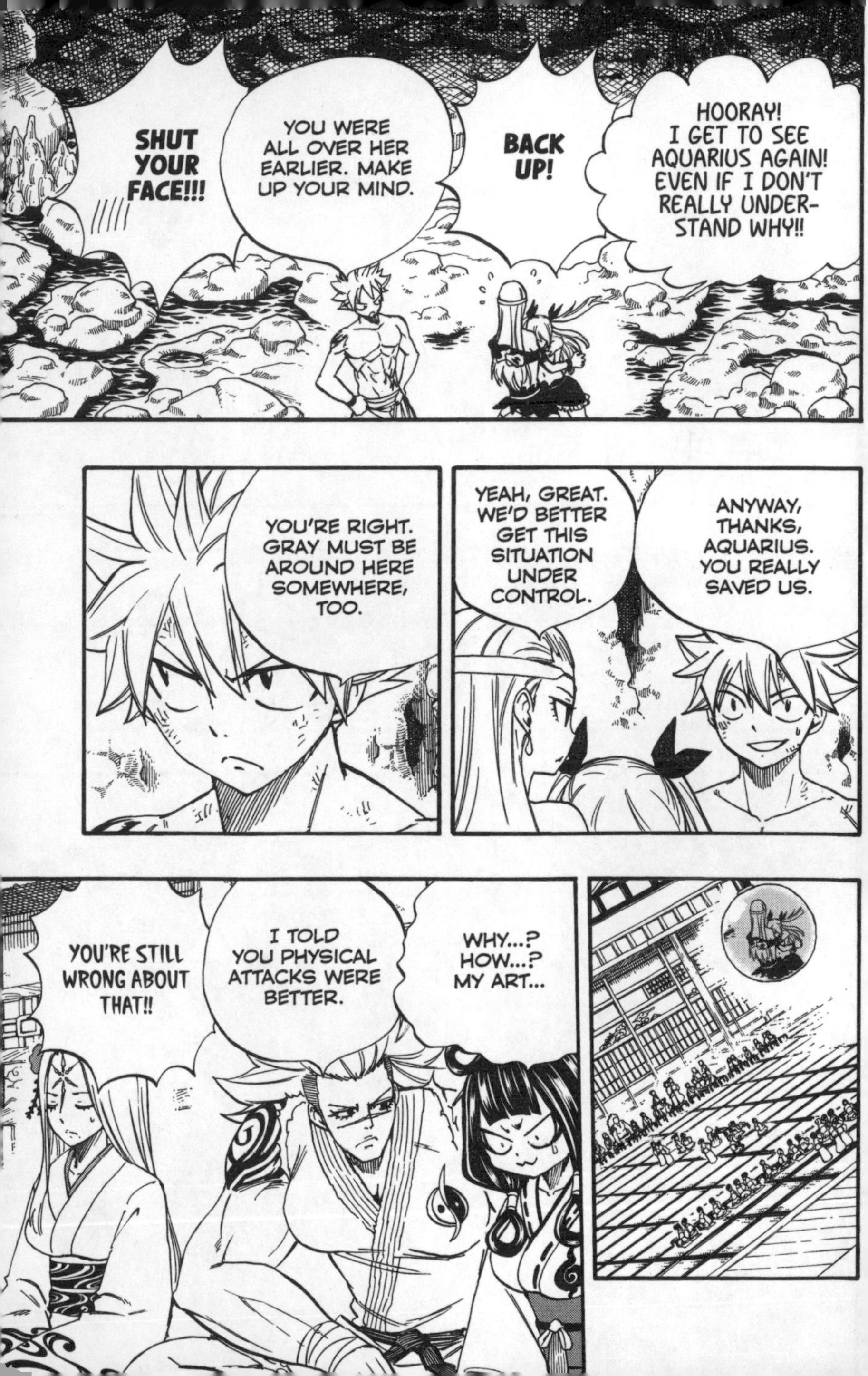
HOORAY! I GET TO SEE AQUARIUS AGAIN! EVEN IF I DON'T REALLY UNDER-STAND WHY!!
BACK UP!
YOU WERE ALL OVER HER EARLIER. MAKE UP YOUR MIND.
SHUT YOUR FACE!!!
ANYWAY, THANKS, AQUARIUS. YOU REALLY SAVED US.
YEAH, GREAT. WE'D BETTER GET THIS SITUATION UNDER CONTROL.
YOU'RE RIGHT. GRAY MUST BE AROUND HERE SOMEWHERE, TOO.
WHY...? HOW...? MY ART...
I TOLD YOU PHYSICAL ATTACKS WERE BETTER.
YOU'RE STILL WRONG ABOUT THAT!!

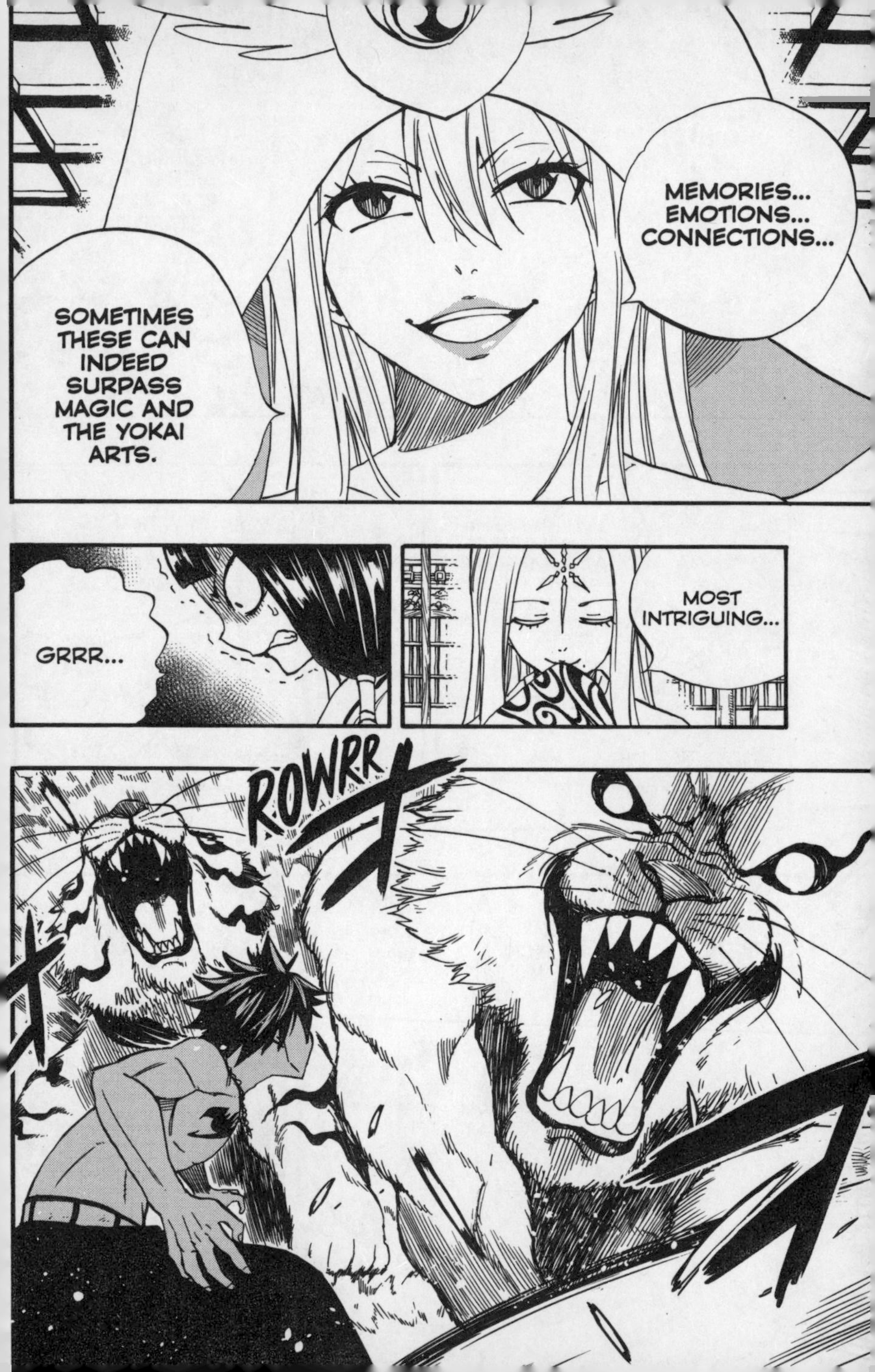
MEMORIES... EMOTIONS... CONNECTIONS...
SOMETIMES THESE CAN INDEED SURPASS MAGIC AND THE YOKAI ARTS.
MOST INTRIGUING...
GRRR...
ROWRR

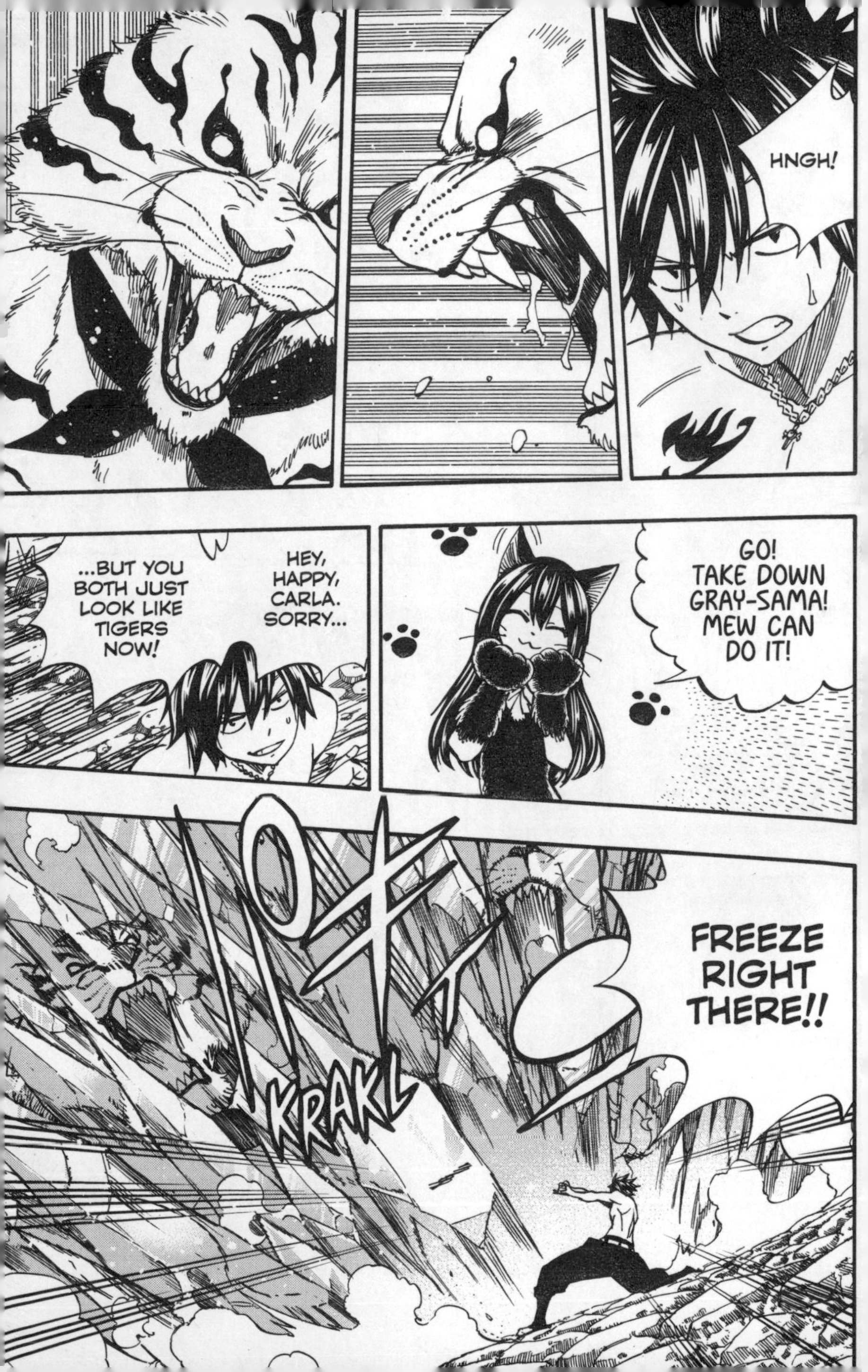
HNGH!
GO! TAKE DOWN GRAY-SAMA! MEW CAN DO IT!
HEY, HAPPY, CARLA. SORRY...
...BUT YOU BOTH JUST LOOK LIKE TIGERS NOW!
FREEZE RIGHT THERE!!
KRAK!

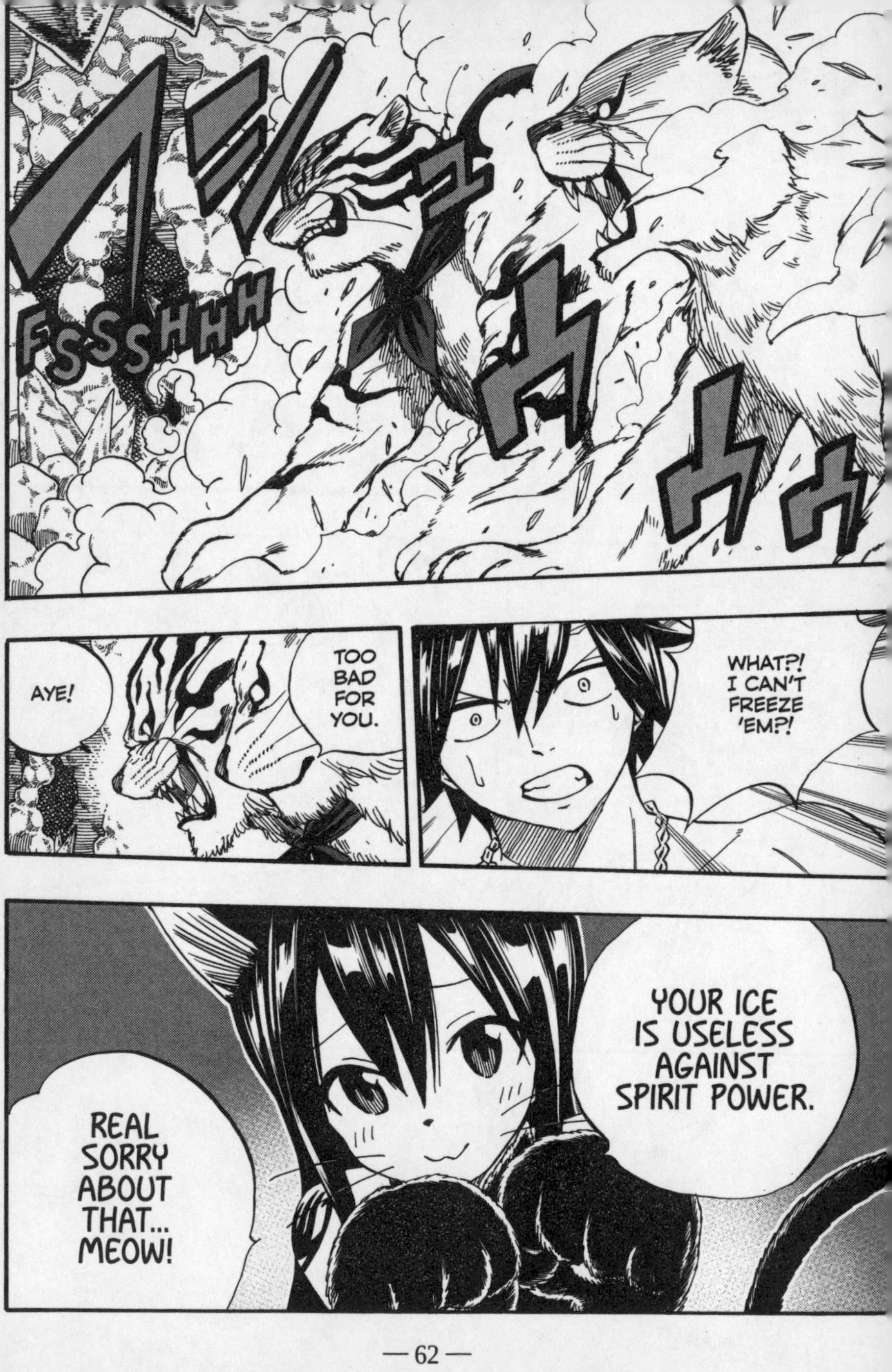
FSSHHH
WHAT?! I CAN'T FREEZE 'EM?!
TOO BAD FOR YOU.
AYE!
YOUR ICE IS USELESS AGAINST SPIRIT POWER.
REAL SORRY ABOUT THAT... MEOW!

FAIRY TAIL 100 YEARS QUEST

Chapter 76: Dance of the Twin Tigers

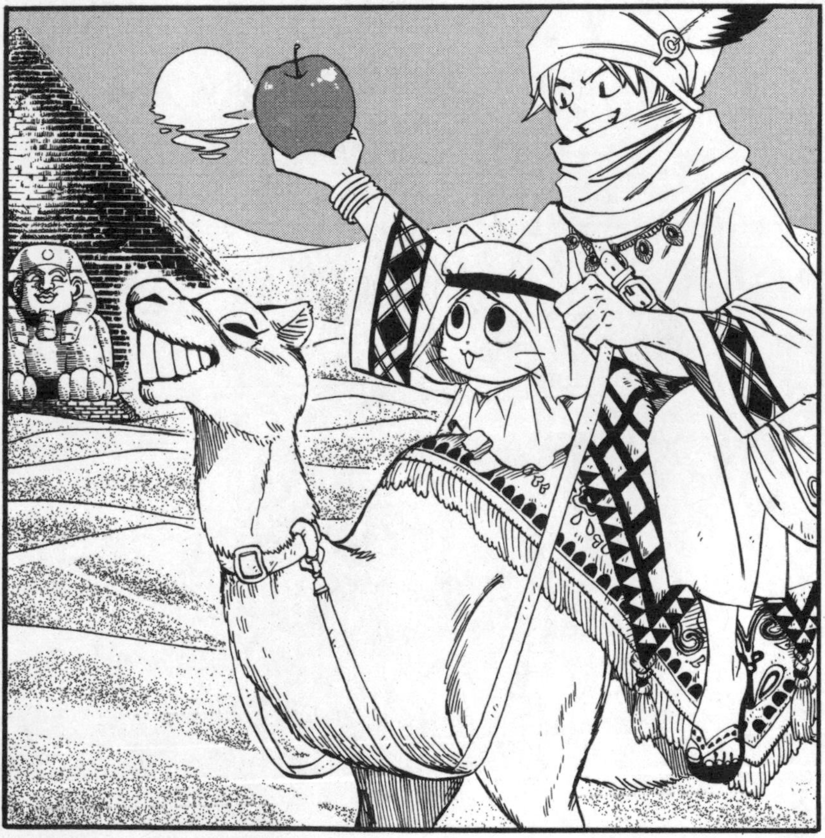

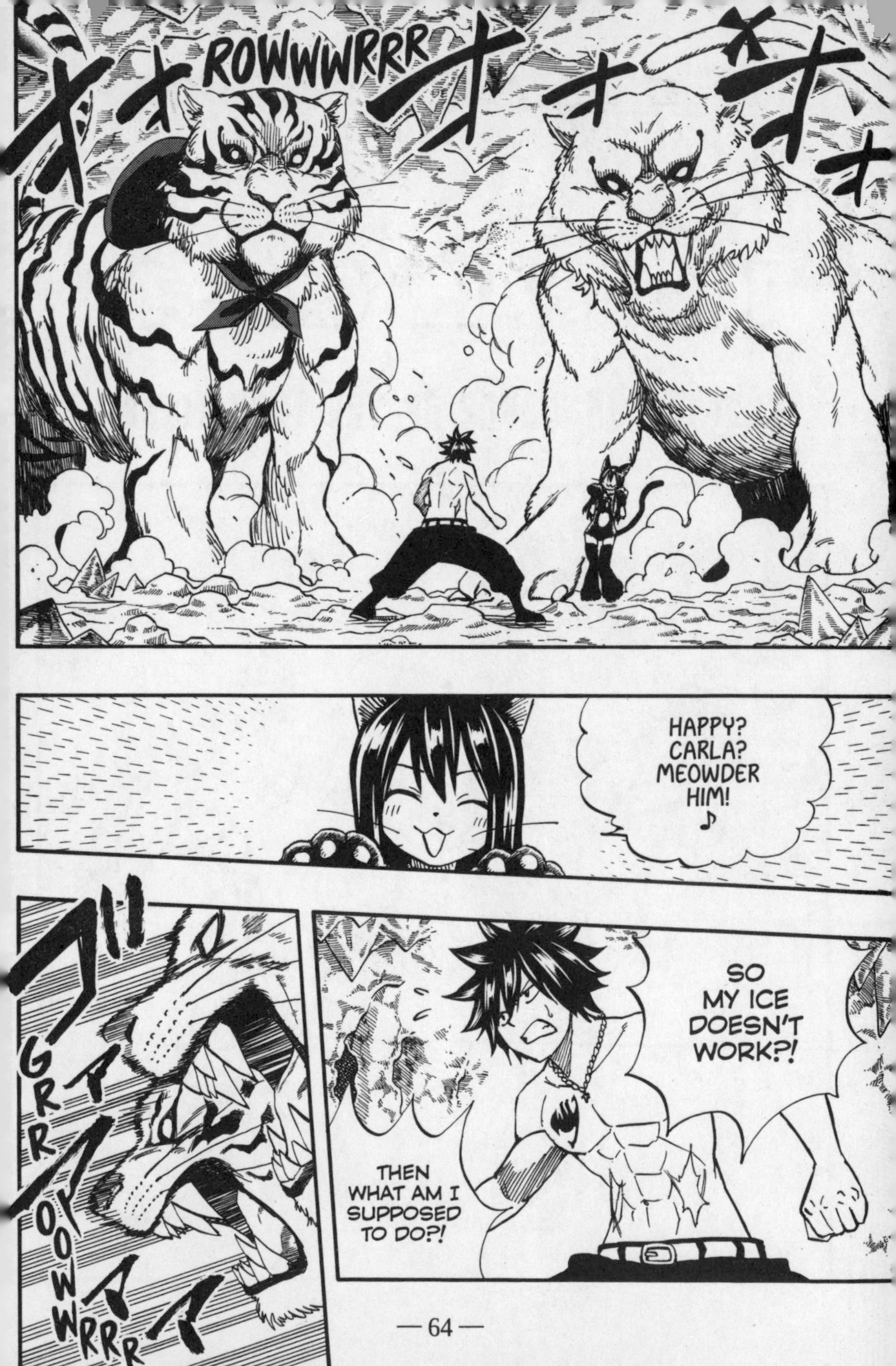
ROWWWRRR
HAPPY? CARLA? MEOWDER HIM! ♪
SO MY ICE DOESN'T WORK?!
THEN WHAT AM I SUPPOSED TO DO?!
GRROOOWWRRR

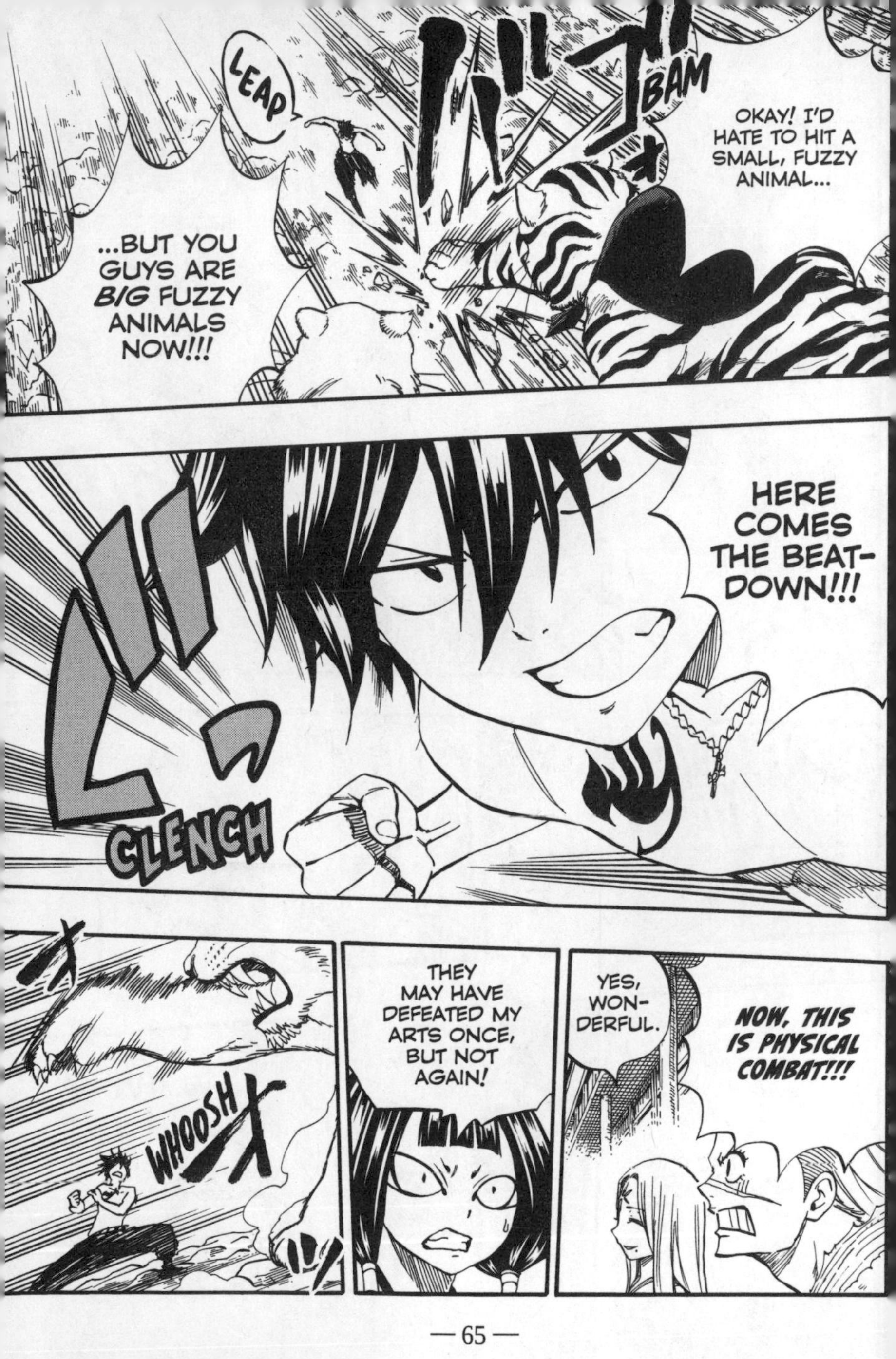
OKAY! I'D HATE TO HIT A SMALL, FUZZY ANIMAL...
BAM
LEAP
...BUT YOU GUYS ARE *BIG* FUZZY ANIMALS NOW!!!
HERE COMES THE BEAT-DOWN!!!
CLENCH
NOW, THIS IS PHYSICAL COMBAT!!!
YES, WON-DERFUL.
THEY MAY HAVE DEFEATED MY ARTS ONCE, BUT NOT AGAIN!
WHOOSH

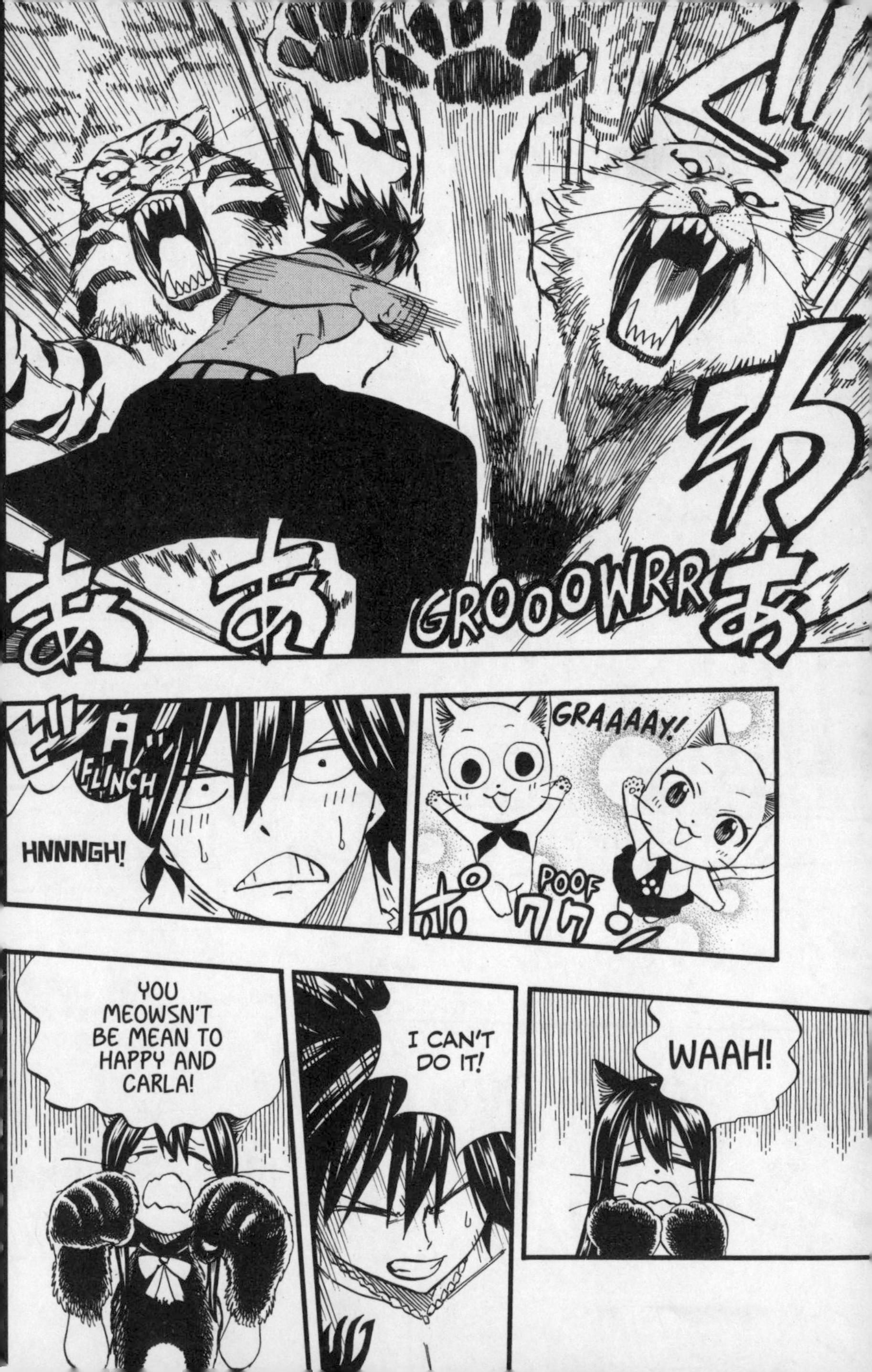
GROOOWRR
GRAAAAY!
POOF
FLINCH
HNNNGH!
WAAH!
I CAN'T DO IT!
YOU MEOWSN'T BE MEAN TO HAPPY AND CARLA!

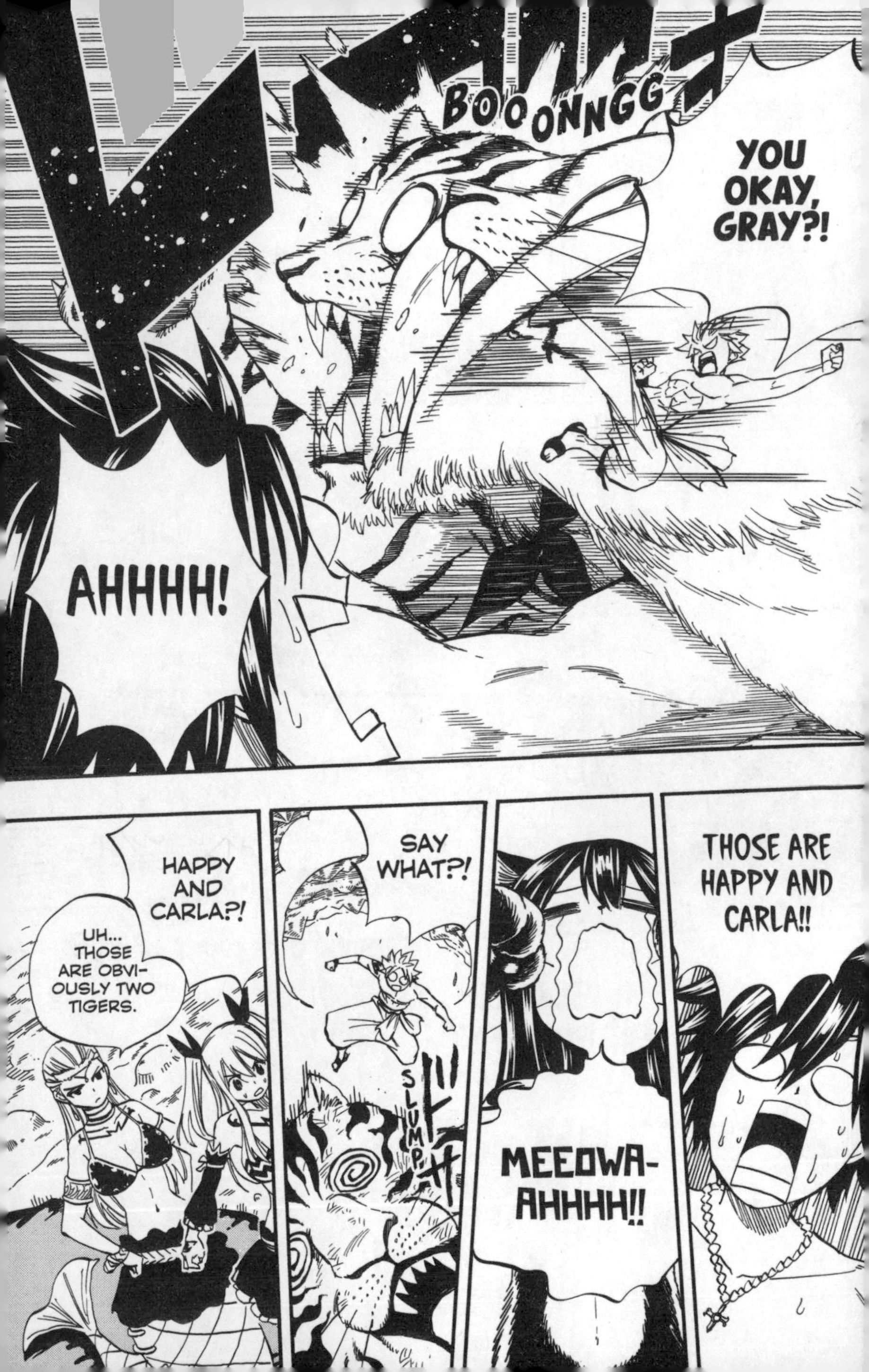
BOOONNGG
YOU OKAY, GRAY?!
AHHHH!
THOSE ARE HAPPY AND CARLA!!
MEEOWA-AHHHH!!
SAY WHAT?!
SLUMP
HAPPY AND CARLA?!
UH... THOSE ARE OBVIOUSLY TWO TIGERS.

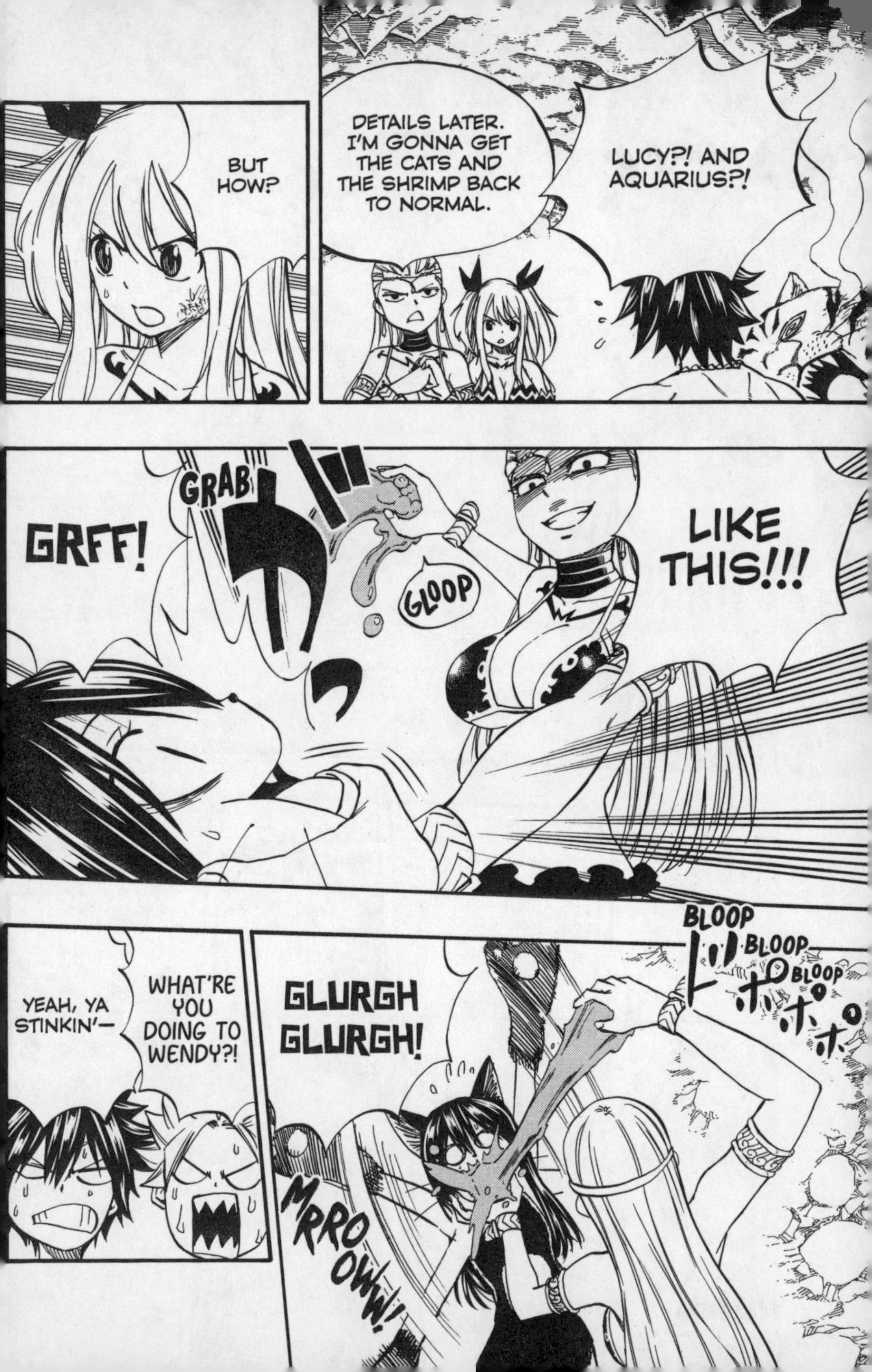
LUCY?! AND AQUARIUS?!
DETAILS LATER. I'M GONNA GET THE CATS AND THE SHRIMP BACK TO NORMAL.
BUT HOW?
LIKE THIS!!!
GLOOP
GRAB
GRFF!
BLOOP
BLOOP
BLOOP
GLURGH GLURGH!
MRROOWW!
WHAT'RE YOU DOING TO WENDY?!
YEAH, YA STINKIN'—

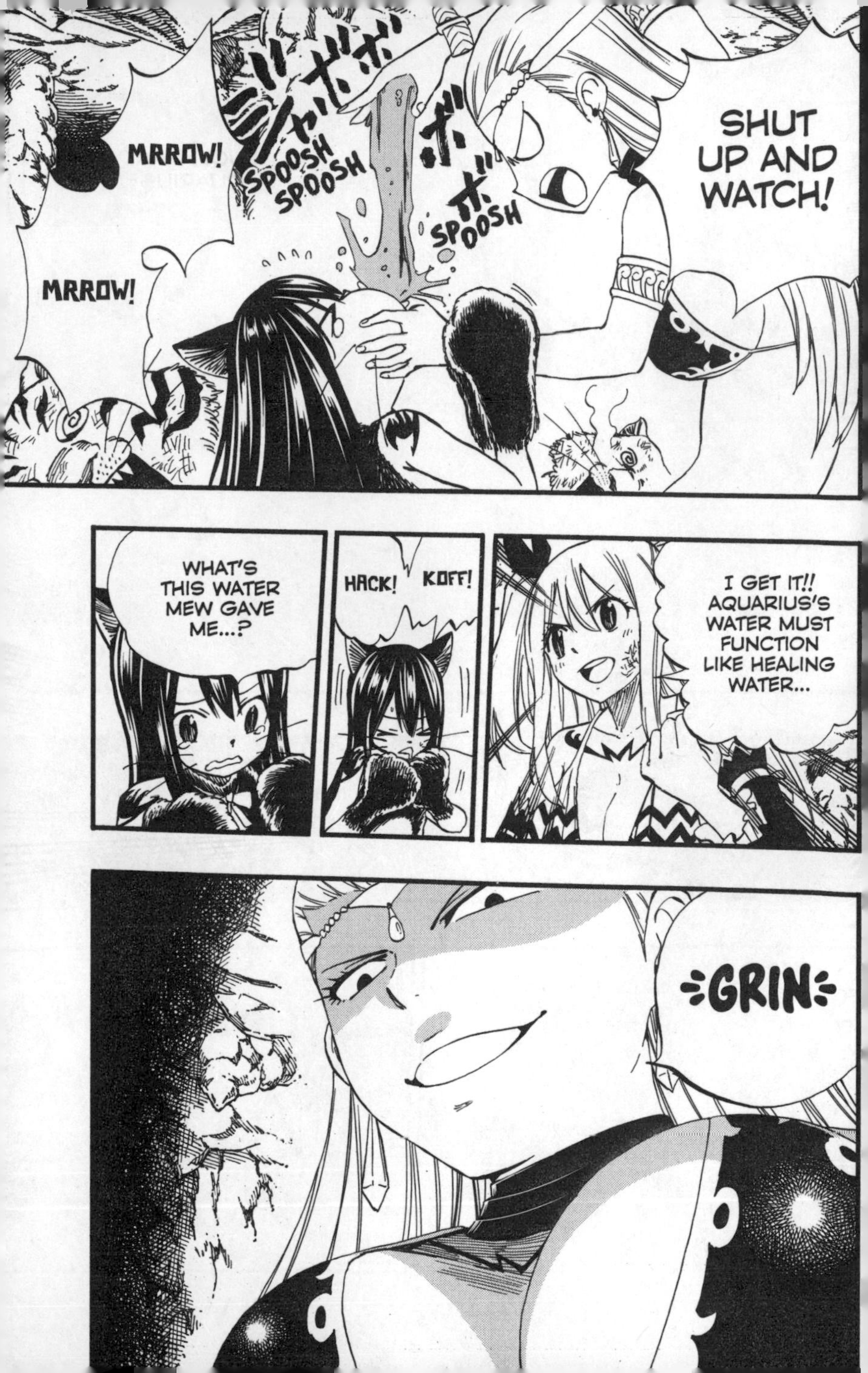
SHUT UP AND WATCH!
SPOOSH
SPOOSH SPOOSH
MRROW!
MRROW!
I GET IT!! AQUARIUS'S WATER MUST FUNCTION LIKE HEALING WATER...
KOFF!
HACK!
WHAT'S THIS WATER MEW GAVE ME...?
GRIN

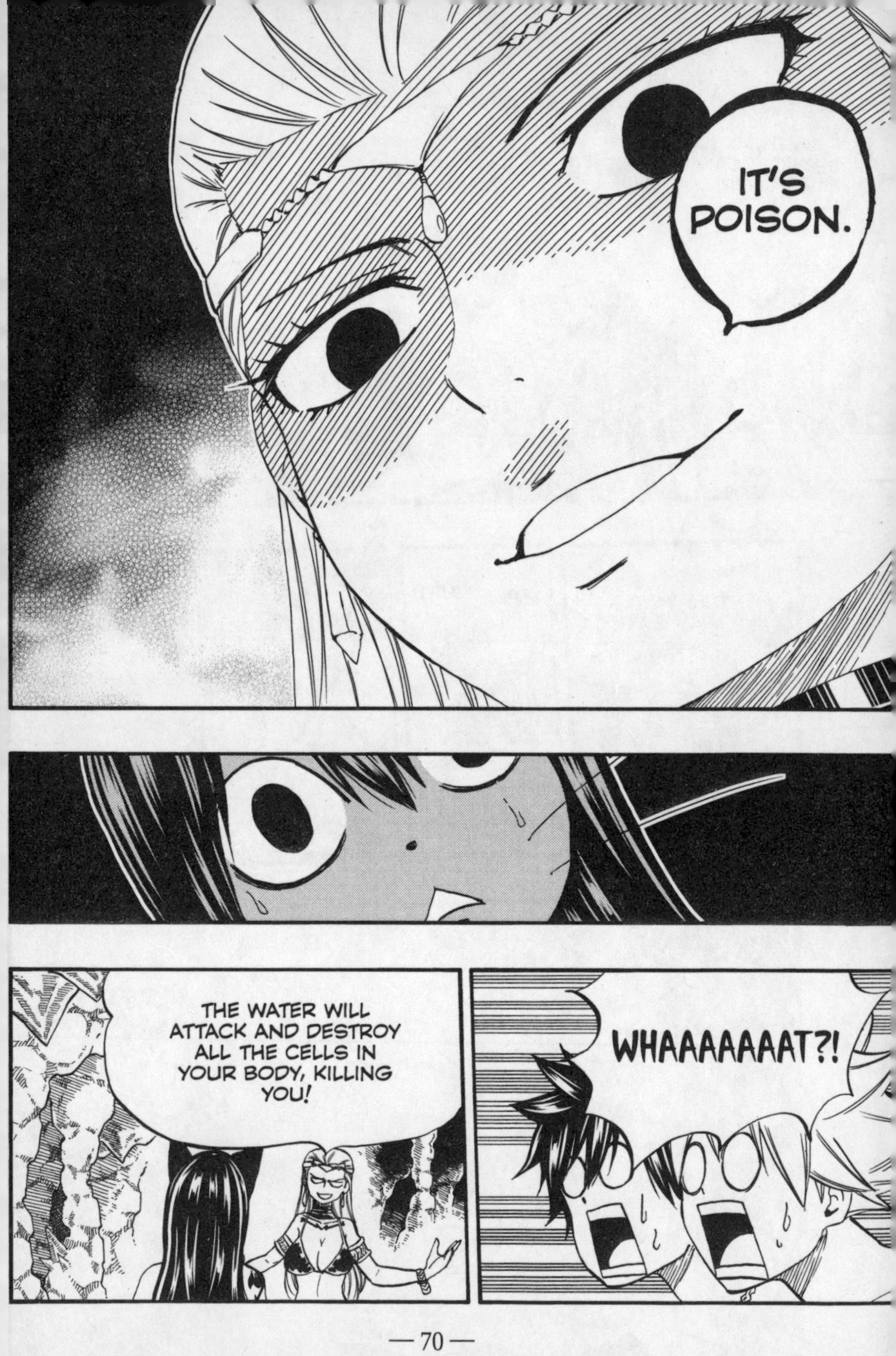
IT'S POISON.
WHAAAAAAAT?!
THE WATER WILL ATTACK AND DESTROY ALL THE CELLS IN YOUR BODY, KILLING YOU!

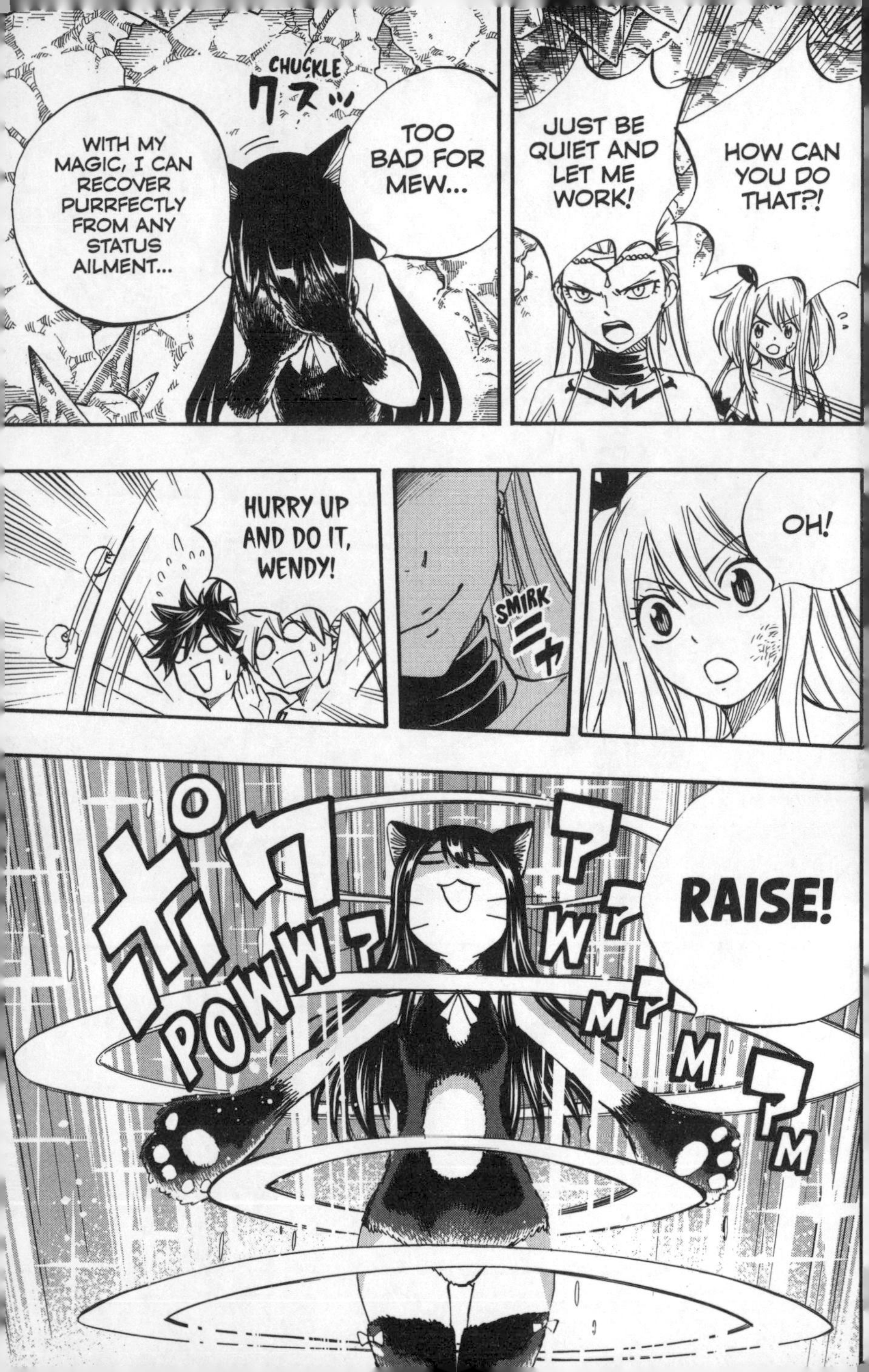
HOW CAN YOU DO THAT?!
JUST BE QUIET AND LET ME WORK!
CHUCKLE
TOO BAD FOR MEW...
WITH MY MAGIC, I CAN RECOVER PURRFECTLY FROM ANY STATUS AILMENT...
OH!
SMIRK
HURRY UP AND DO IT, WENDY!
RAISE!
POWWWMMMM

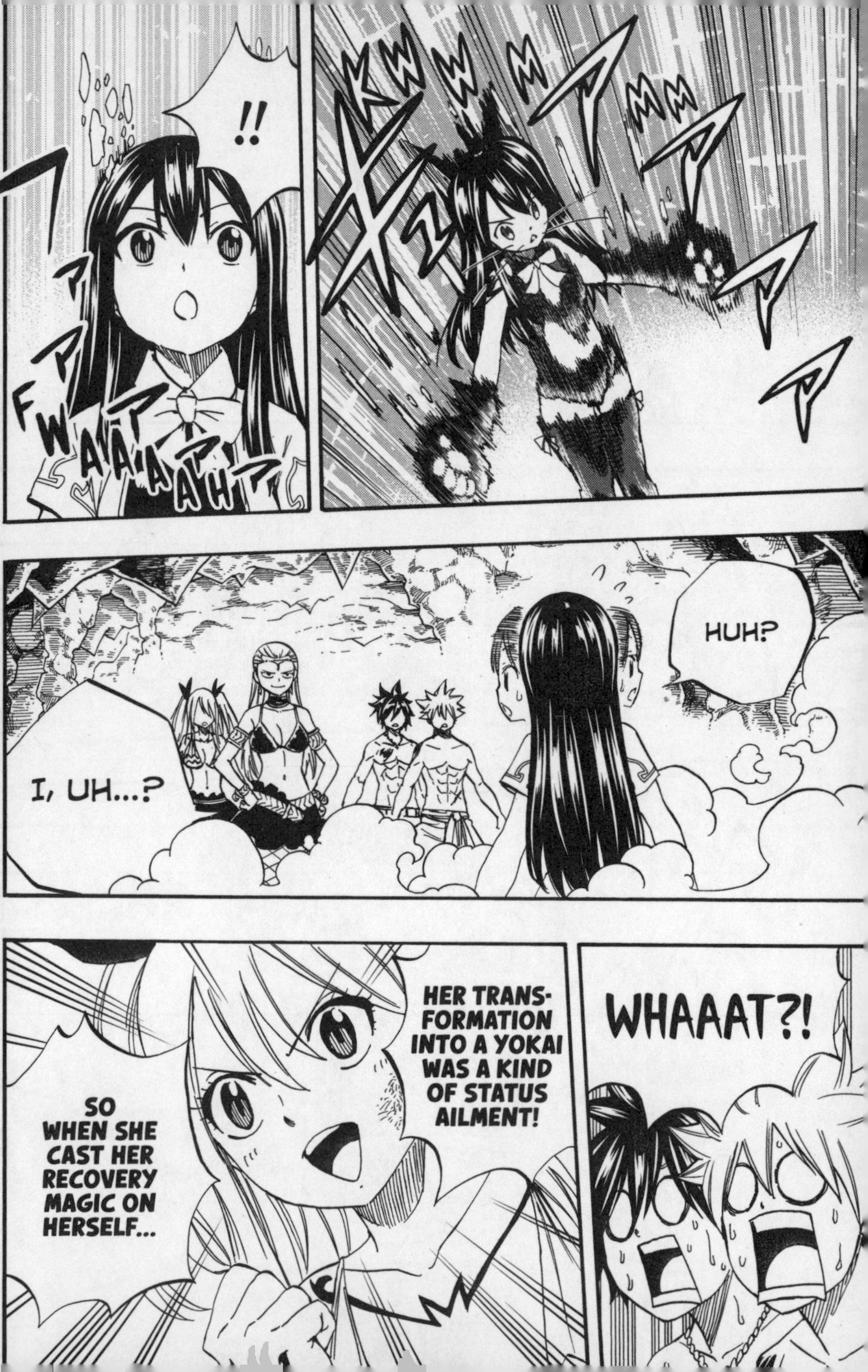

!!
FWAAAAH
HUH?
I, UH...?
WHAAAT?!
HER TRANS-FORMATION INTO A YOKAI WAS A KIND OF STATUS AILMENT!
SO WHEN SHE CAST HER RECOVERY MAGIC ON HERSELF...

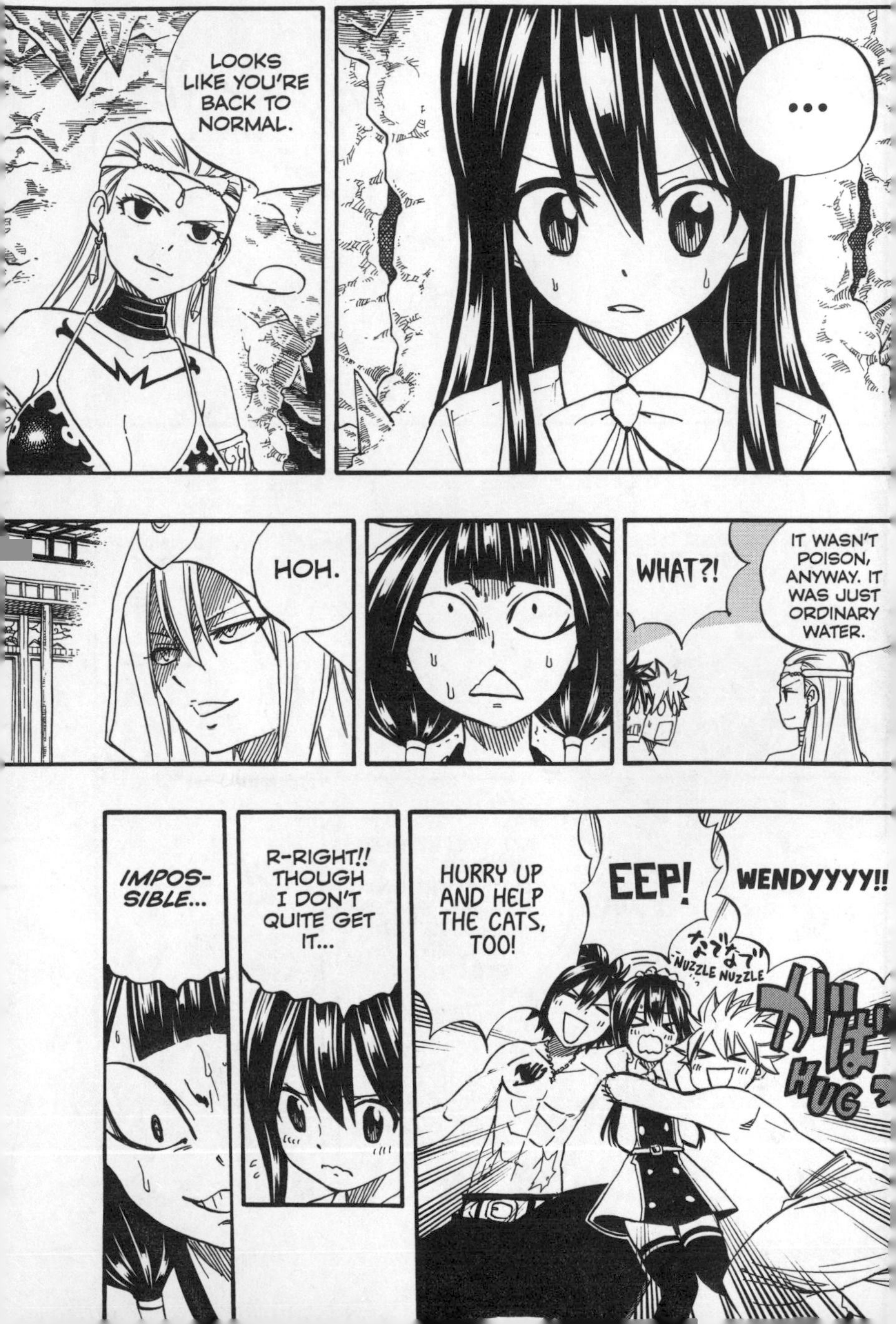
...
LOOKS LIKE YOU'RE BACK TO NORMAL.
IT WASN'T POISON, ANYWAY. IT WAS JUST ORDINARY WATER.
WHAT?!
HOH.
WENDYYYY!!
EEP!
HURRY UP AND HELP THE CATS, TOO!
かばっ HUG
なでなで NUZZLE NUZZLE
R-RIGHT!! THOUGH I DON'T QUITE GET IT...
IMPOS-SIBLE...

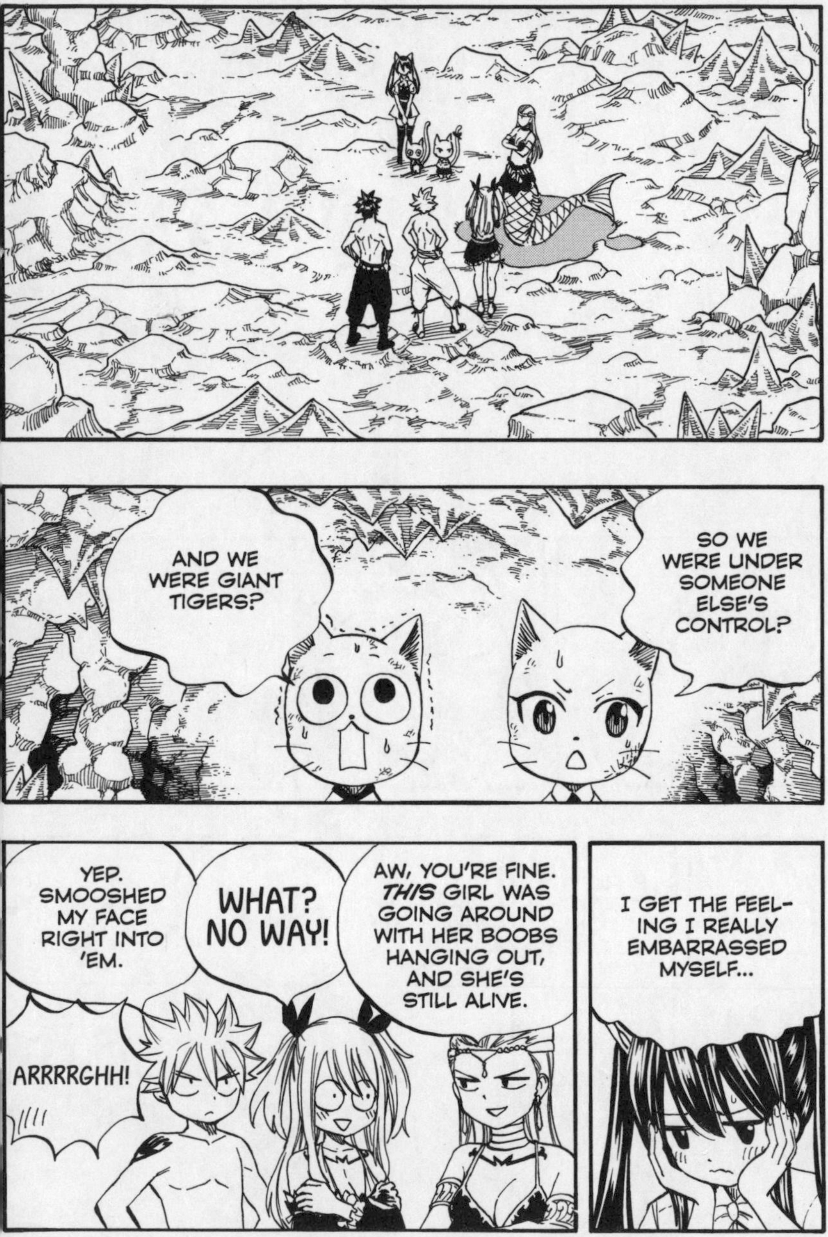
SO WE WERE UNDER SOMEONE ELSE'S CONTROL?
AND WE WERE GIANT TIGERS?
I GET THE FEEL-ING I REALLY EMBARRASSED MYSELF...
AW, YOU'RE FINE. *THIS* GIRL WAS GOING AROUND WITH HER BOOBS HANGING OUT, AND SHE'S STILL ALIVE.
WHAT? NO WAY!
YEP. SMOOSHED MY FACE RIGHT INTO 'EM.
ARRRRGHH!

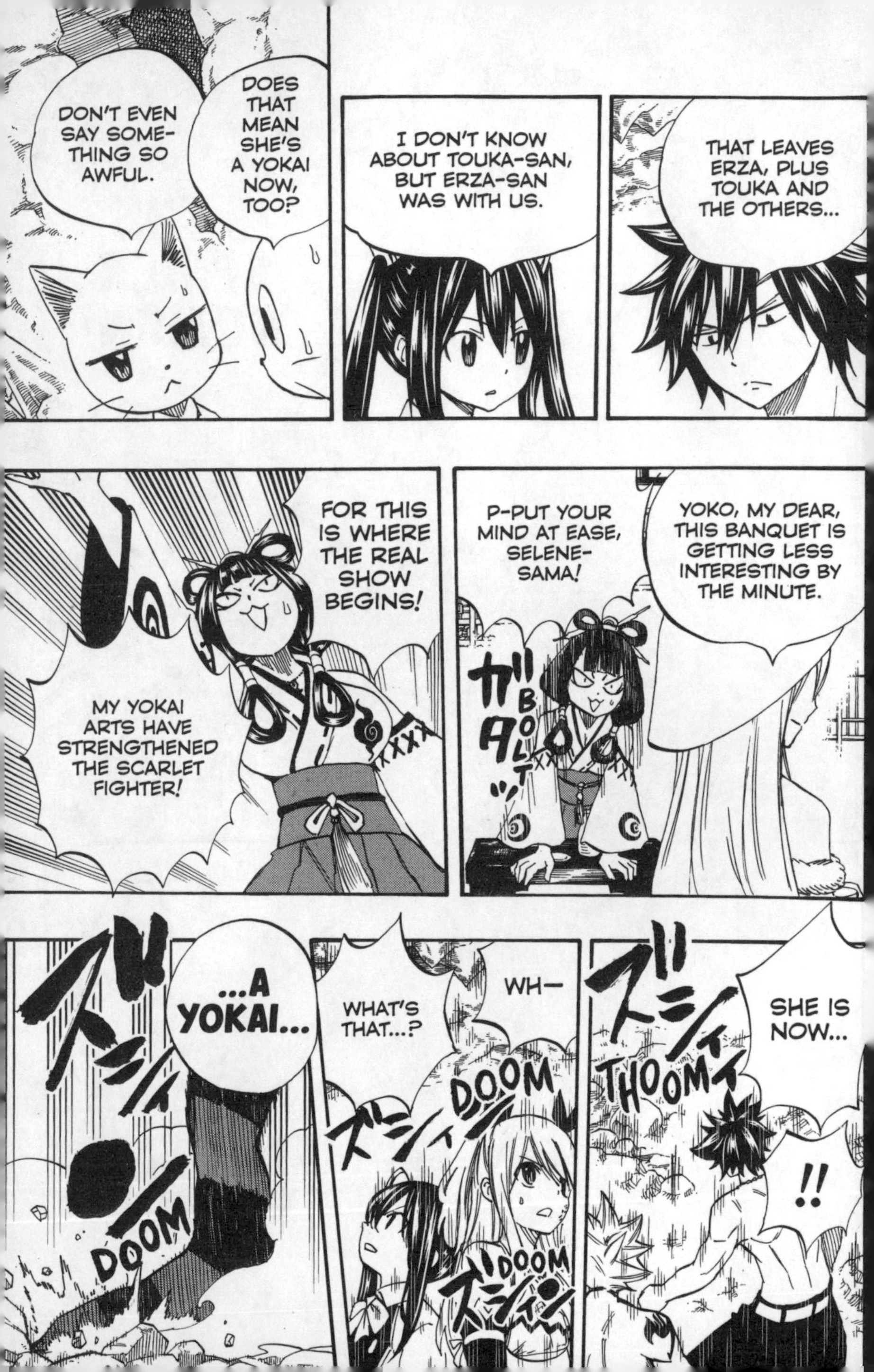
THAT LEAVES ERZA, PLUS TOUKA AND THE OTHERS...
I DON'T KNOW ABOUT TOUKA-SAN, BUT ERZA-SAN WAS WITH US.
DOES THAT MEAN SHE'S A YOKAI NOW, TOO?
DON'T EVEN SAY SOMETHING SO AWFUL.
YOKO, MY DEAR, THIS BANQUET IS GETTING LESS INTERESTING BY THE MINUTE.
P-PUT YOUR MIND AT EASE, SELENE-SAMA!
BOLT
FOR THIS IS WHERE THE REAL SHOW BEGINS!
MY YOKAI ARTS HAVE STRENGTHENED THE SCARLET FIGHTER!
SHE IS NOW...
THOOM
!!
WH—
WHAT'S THAT...?
DOOM
DOOM
...A YOKAI...
DOOM

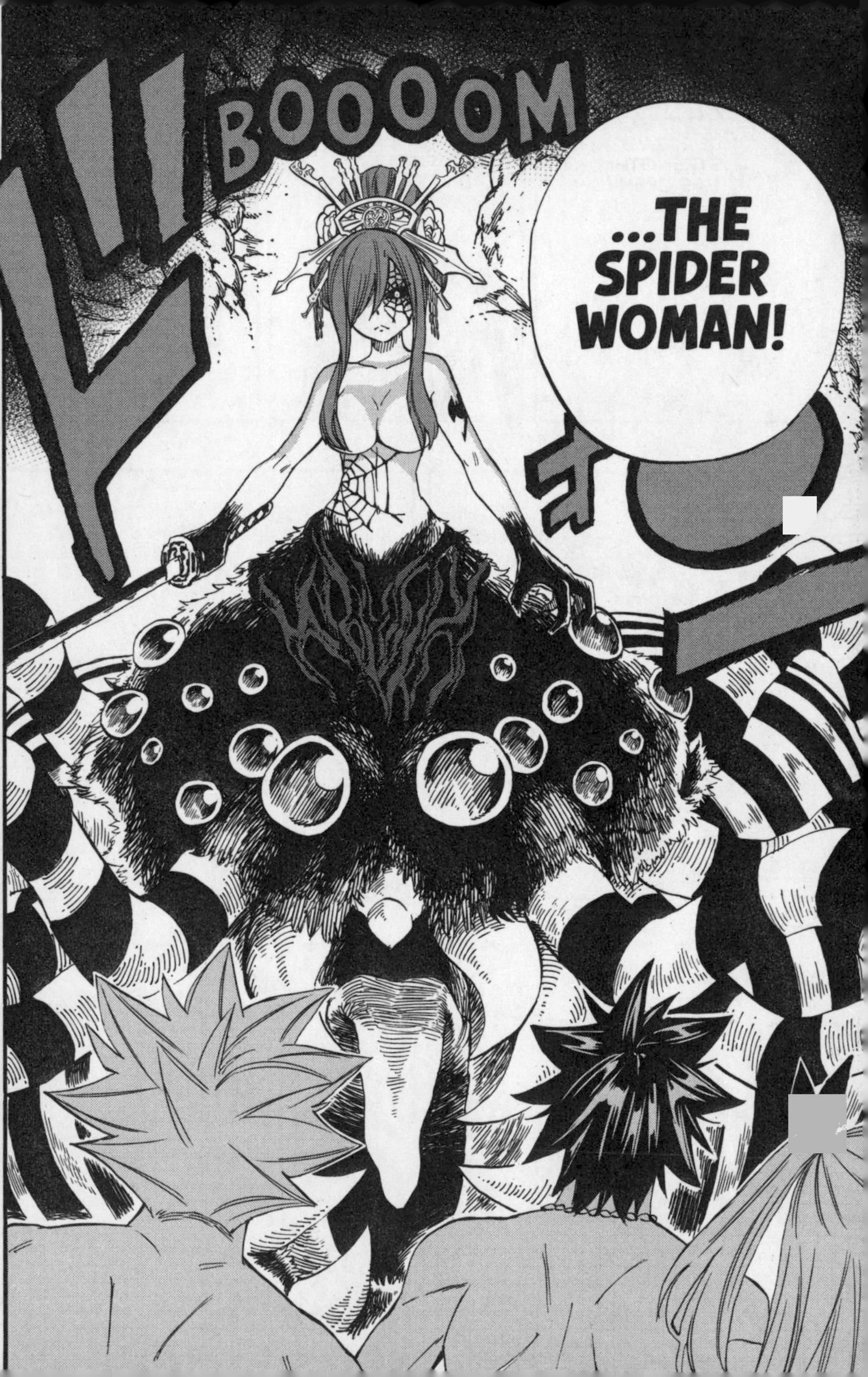
...THE SPIDER WOMAN!
BOOOOM

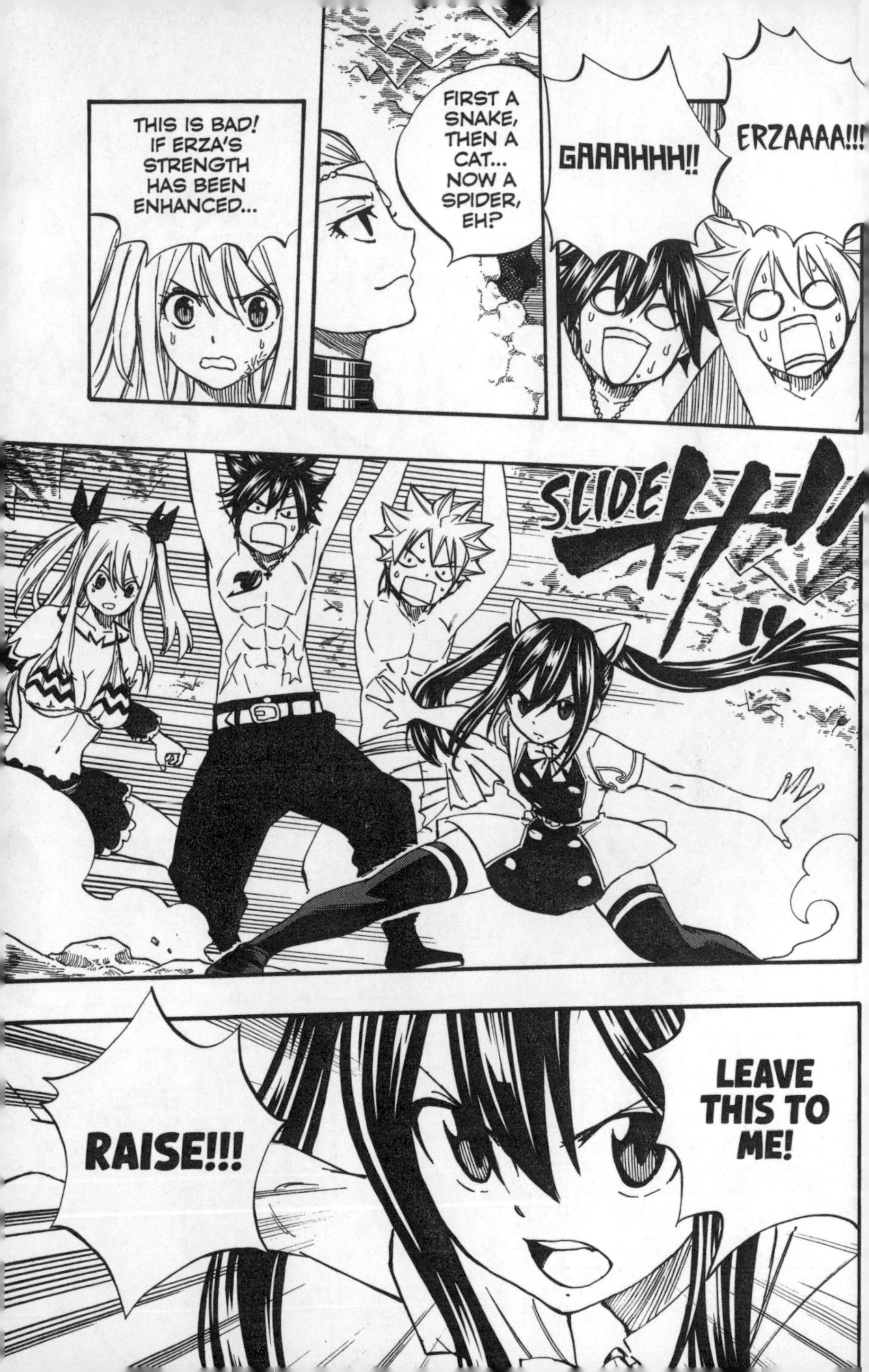
ERZAAAA!!!
GAAAHHH!!
FIRST A SNAKE, THEN A CAT... NOW A SPIDER, EH?
THIS IS BAD! IF ERZA'S STRENGTH HAS BEEN ENHANCED...
SLIDE
LEAVE THIS TO ME!
RAISE!!!

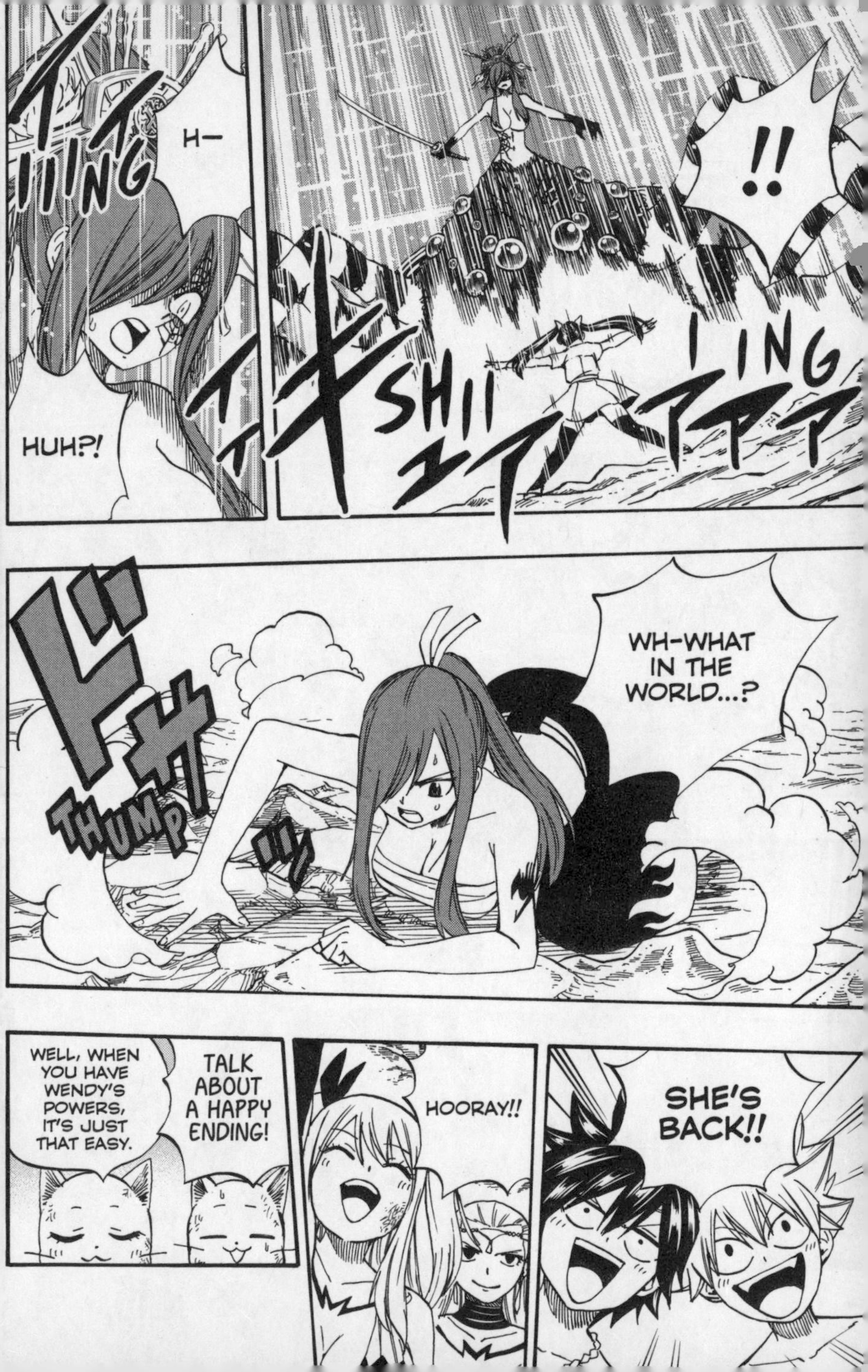
!!
SHII
ING
IIING
H—
HUH?!
WH-WHAT IN THE WORLD...?
THUMP!
SHE'S BACK!!
HOORAY!!
TALK ABOUT A HAPPY ENDING!
WELL, WHEN YOU HAVE WENDY'S POWERS, IT'S JUST THAT EASY.

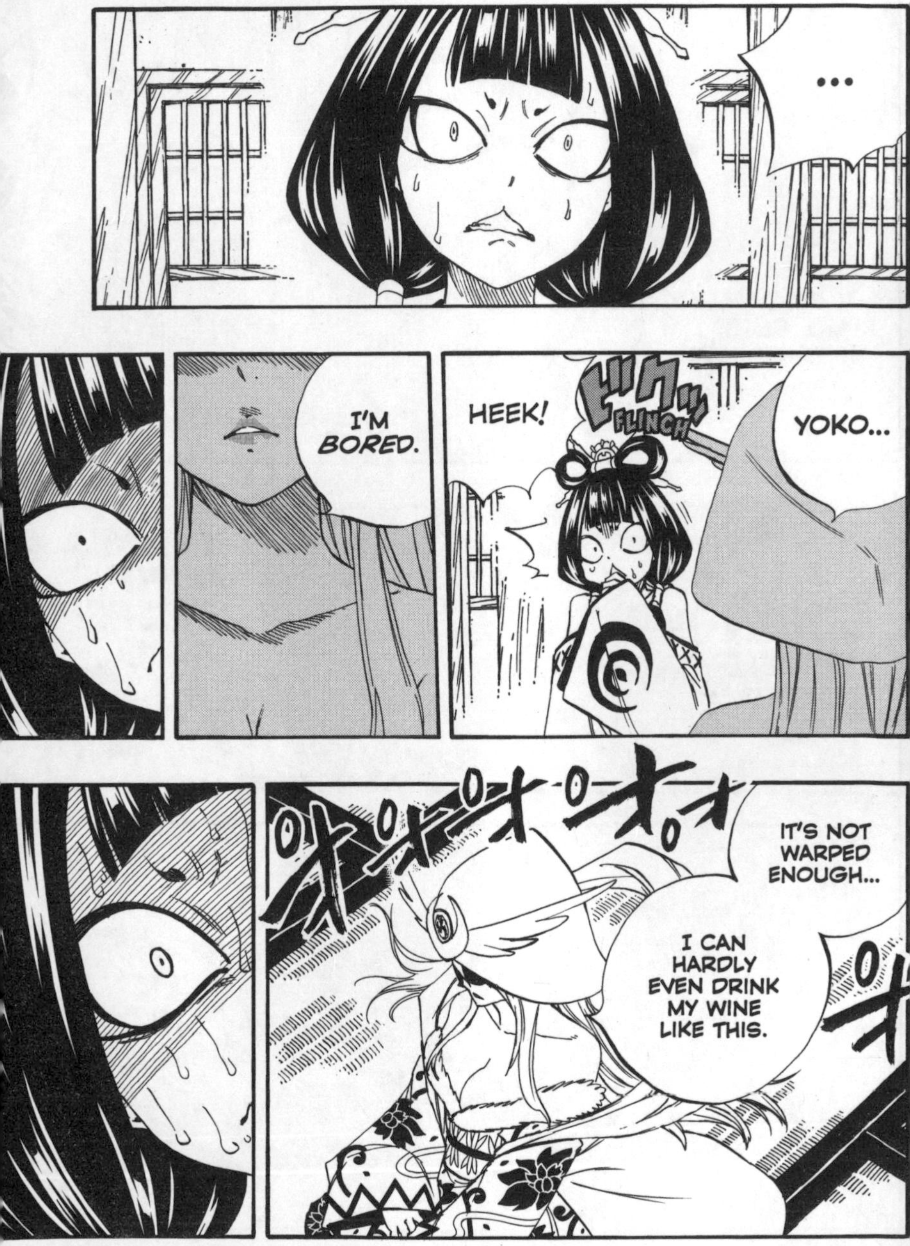
...
YOKO...
HEEK!
FLINCH
I'M BORED.
IT'S NOT WARPED ENOUGH...
I CAN HARDLY EVEN DRINK MY WINE LIKE THIS.

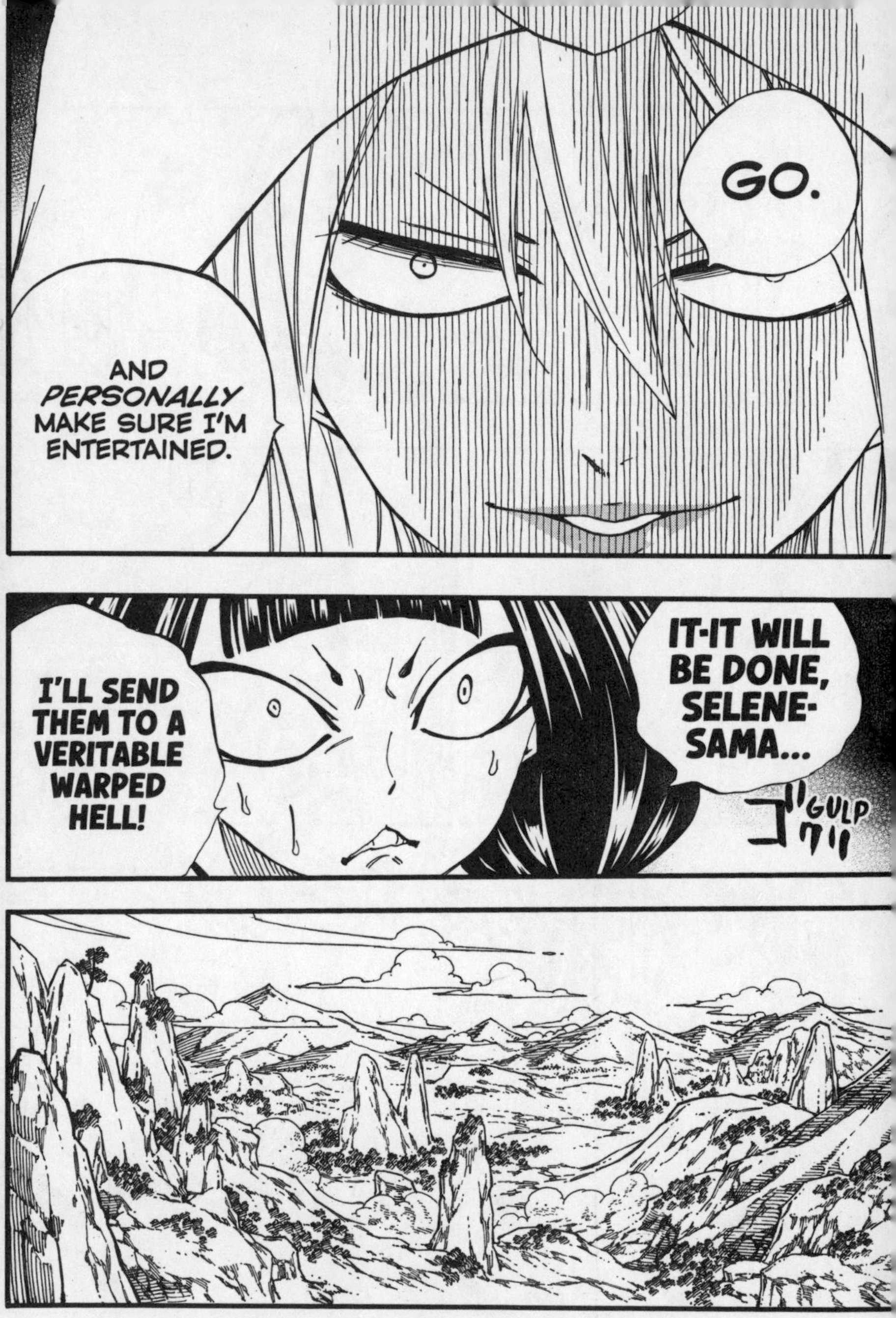
GO.
AND PERSONALLY MAKE SURE I'M ENTERTAINED.
IT-IT WILL BE DONE, SELENE-SAMA...
GULP
I'LL SEND THEM TO A VERITABLE WARPED HELL!

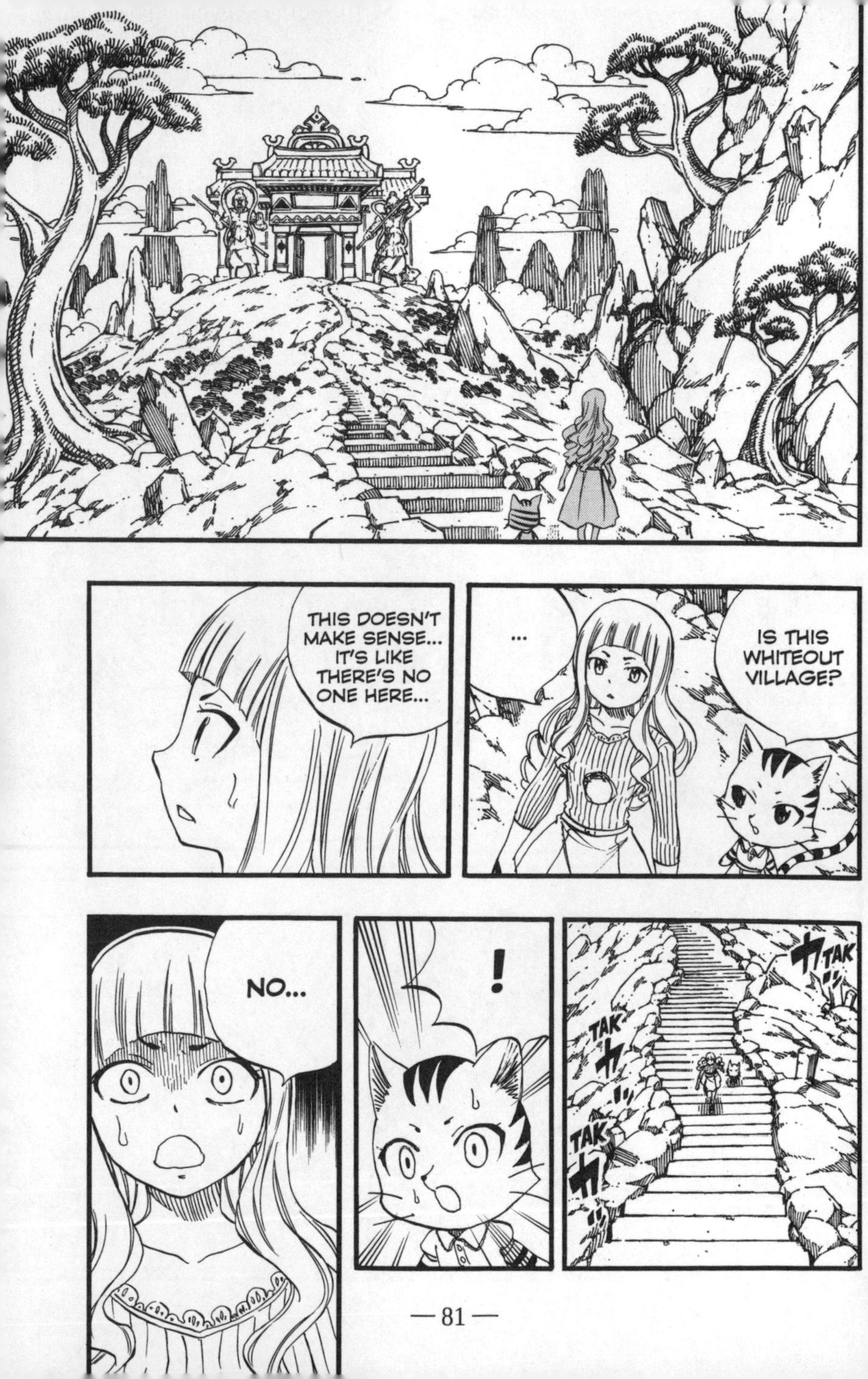
IS THIS WHITEOUT VILLAGE?
...
THIS DOESN'T MAKE SENSE... IT'S LIKE THERE'S NO ONE HERE...
TAK
TAK
TAK
!
NO...

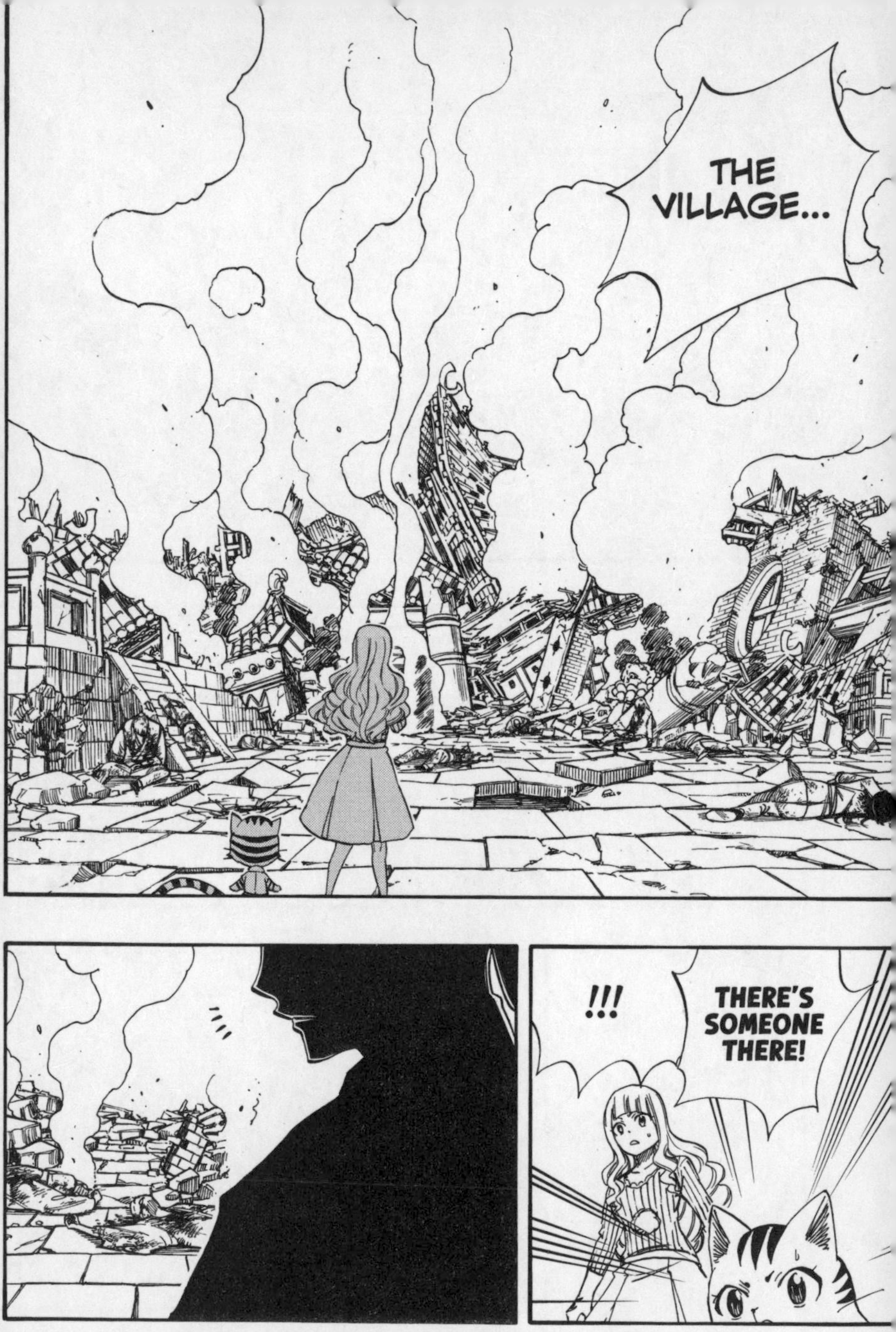
THE VILLAGE...
THERE'S SOMEONE THERE!
!!!

FAIRY TAIL
100 YEARS QUEST

Chapter 77: Whiteout Village

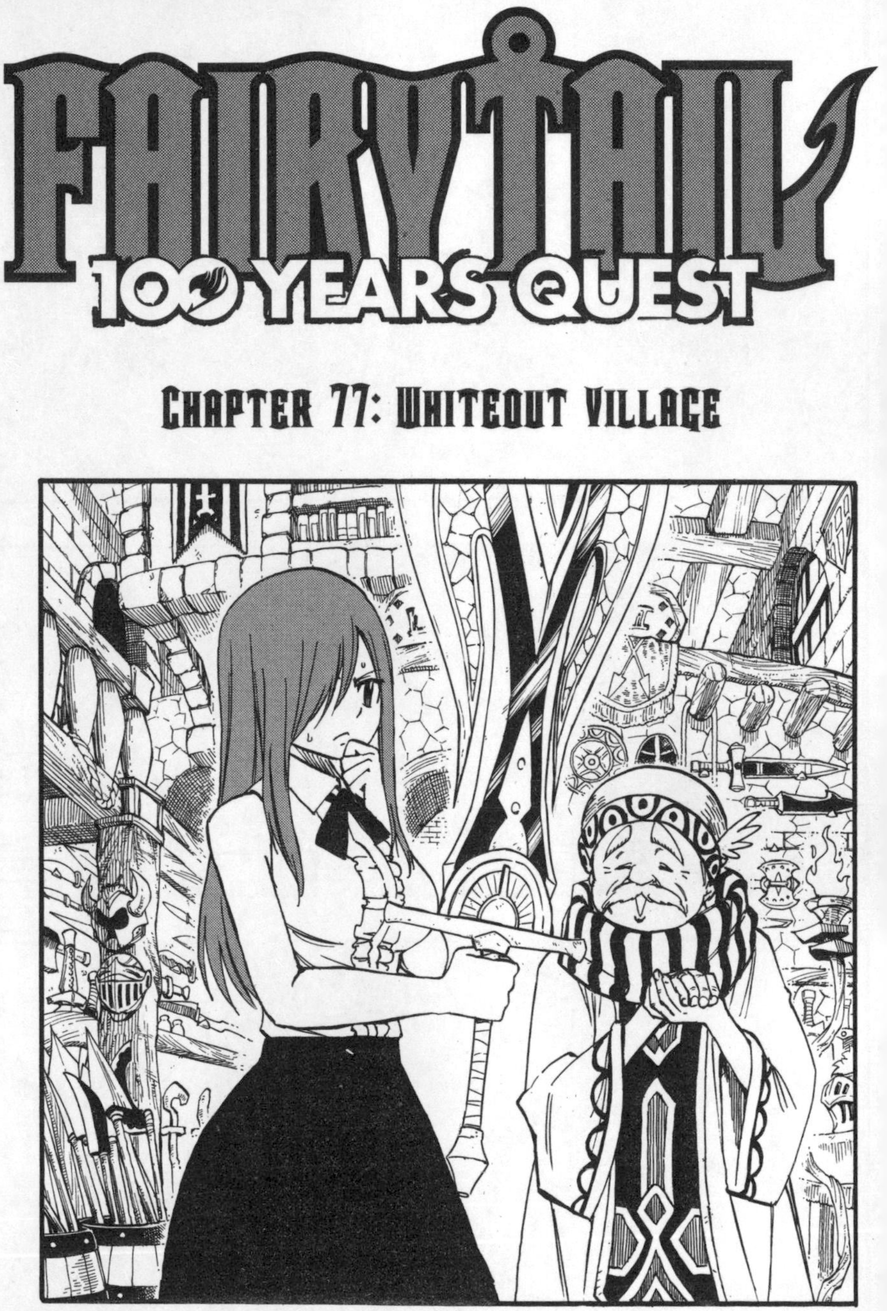

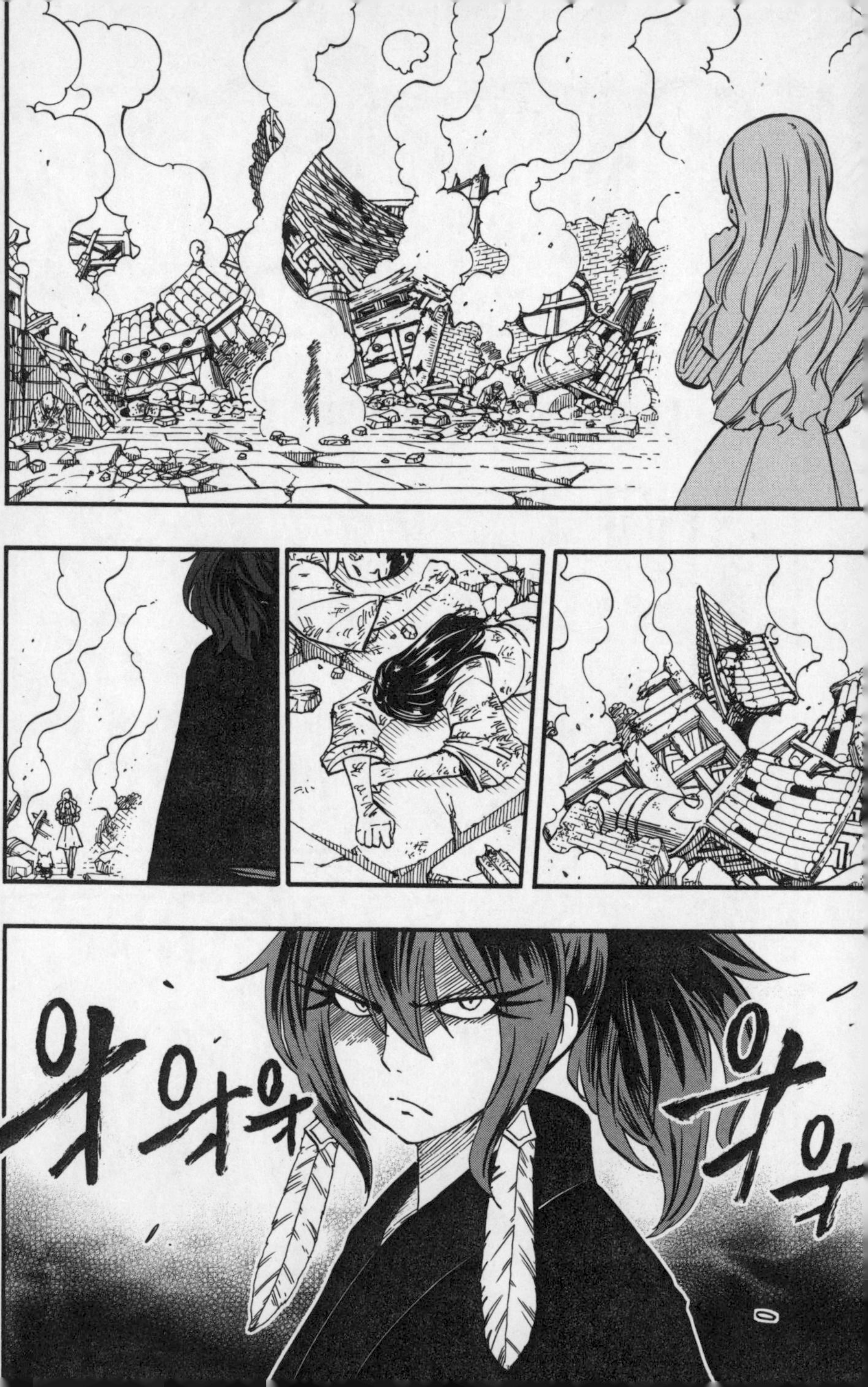
워어
어어워

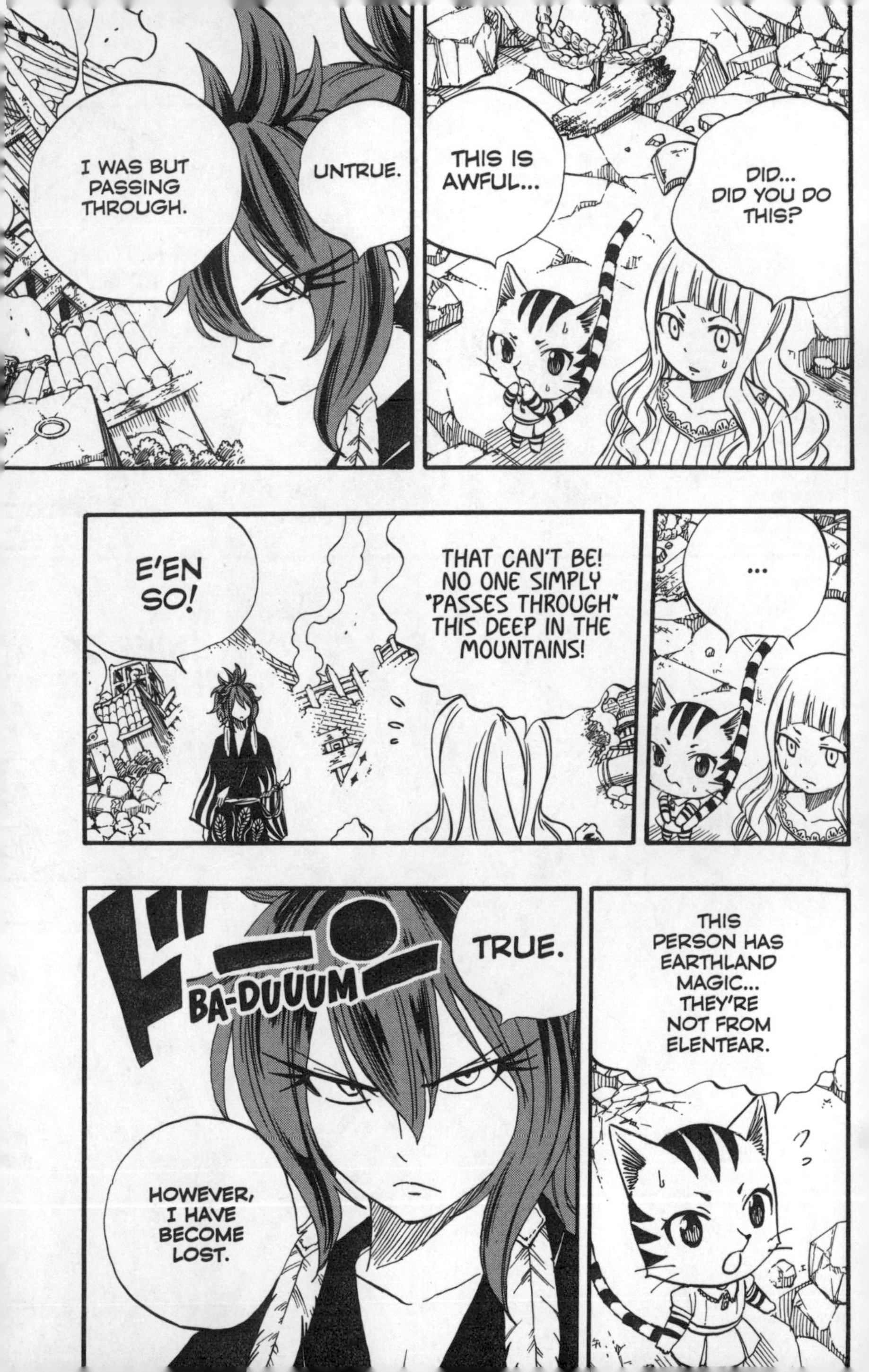
DID... DID YOU DO THIS?
THIS IS AWFUL...
UNTRUE.
I WAS BUT PASSING THROUGH.
...
THAT CAN'T BE! NO ONE SIMPLY "PASSES THROUGH" THIS DEEP IN THE MOUNTAINS!
E'EN SO!
THIS PERSON HAS EARTHLAND MAGIC... THEY'RE NOT FROM ELENTEAR.
TRUE.
BA-DUUUM
HOWEVER, I HAVE BECOME LOST.

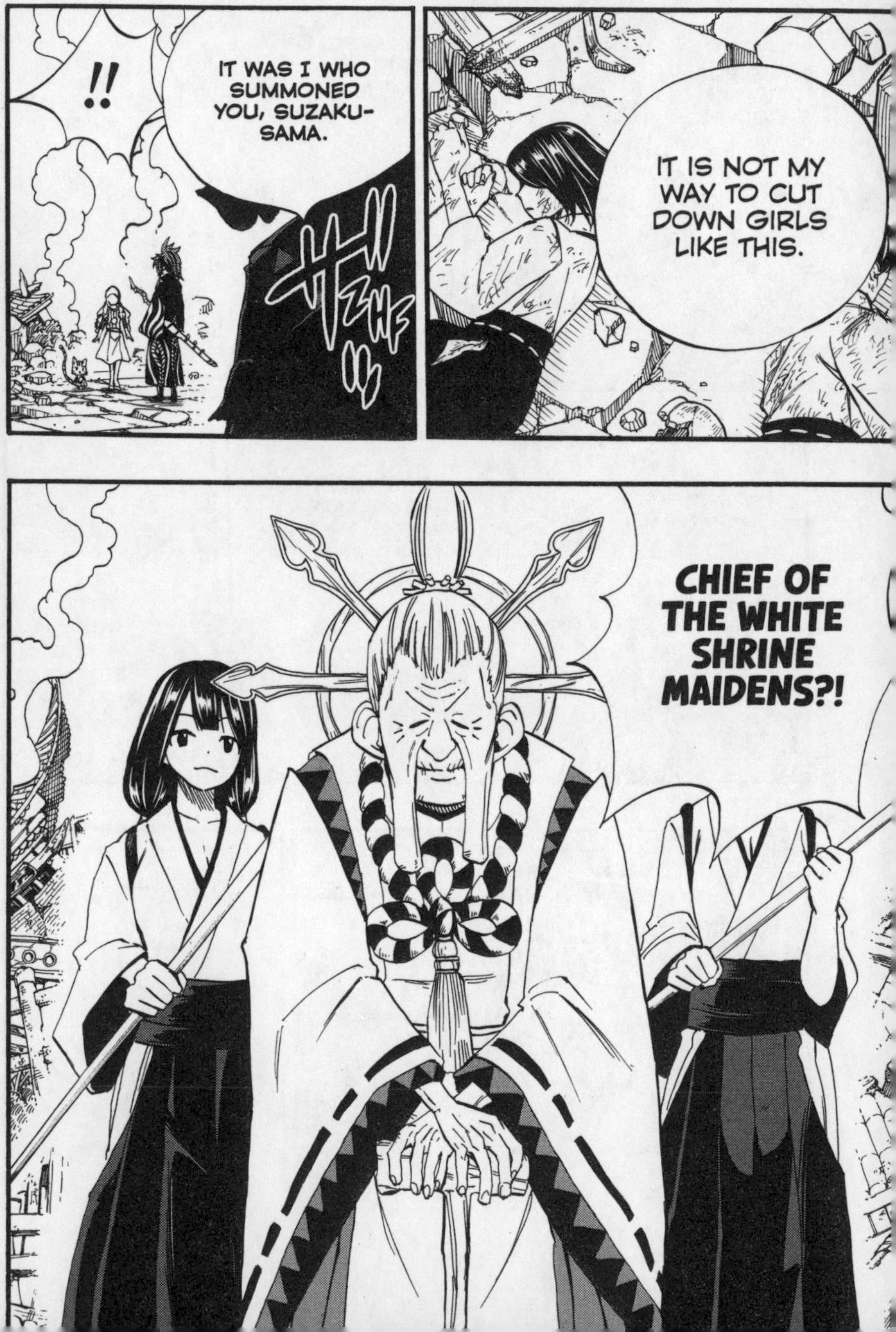
IT IS NOT MY WAY TO CUT DOWN GIRLS LIKE THIS.
!!
IT WAS I WHO SUMMONED YOU, SUZAKU-SAMA.
CHIEF OF THE WHITE SHRINE MAIDENS?!

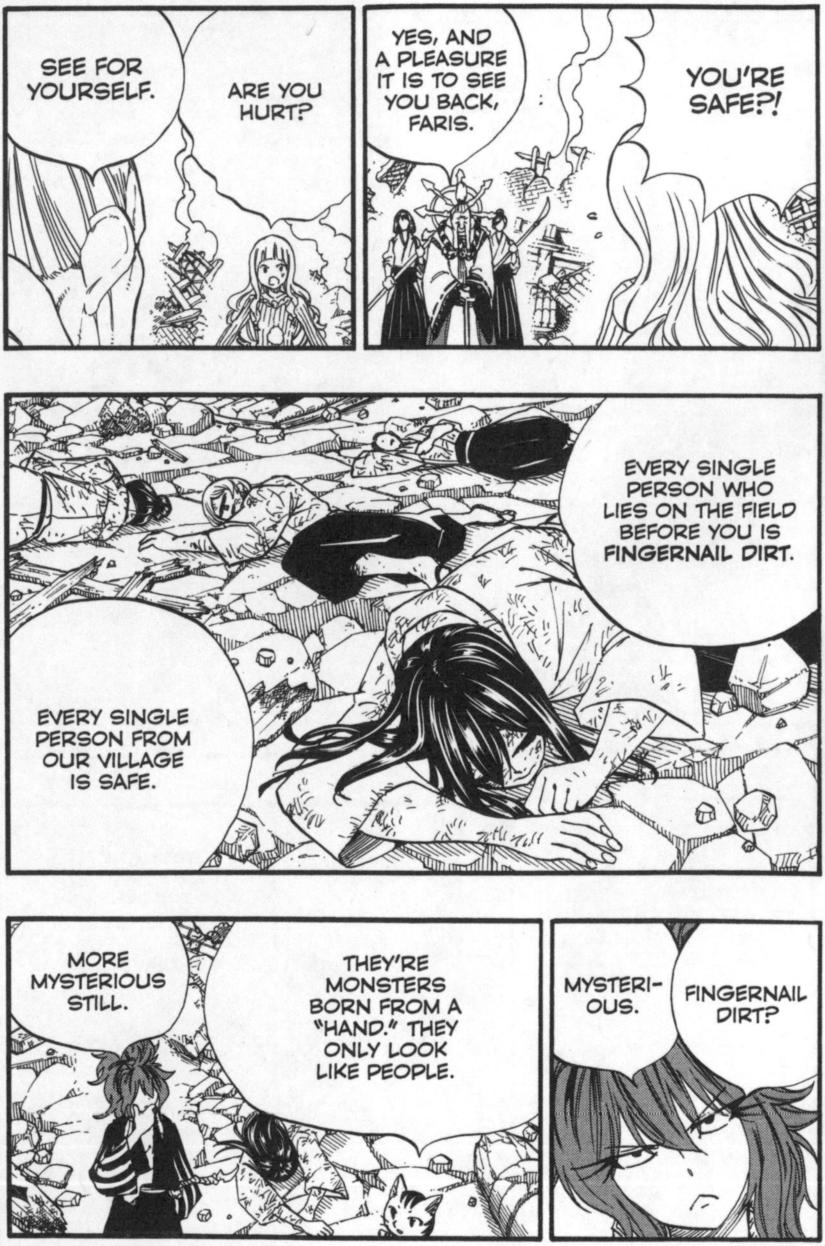
YOU'RE SAFE?!
YES, AND A PLEASURE IT IS TO SEE YOU BACK, FARIS.
ARE YOU HURT?
SEE FOR YOURSELF.
EVERY SINGLE PERSON WHO LIES ON THE FIELD BEFORE YOU IS FINGERNAIL DIRT.
EVERY SINGLE PERSON FROM OUR VILLAGE IS SAFE.
FINGERNAIL DIRT?
MYSTERI-OUS.
THEY'RE MONSTERS BORN FROM A "HAND." THEY ONLY LOOK LIKE PEOPLE.
MORE MYSTERIOUS STILL.

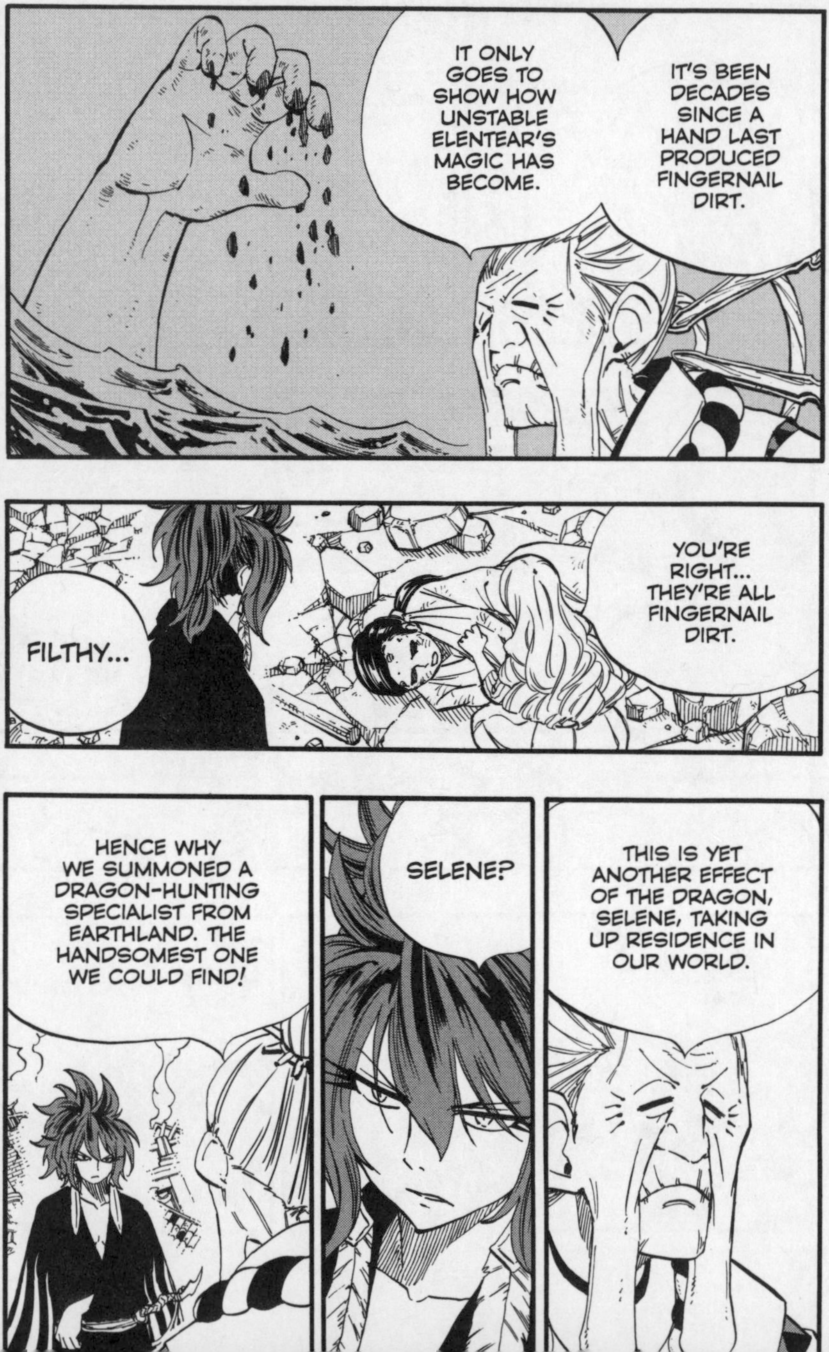
IT'S BEEN DECADES SINCE A HAND LAST PRODUCED FINGERNAIL DIRT.
IT ONLY GOES TO SHOW HOW UNSTABLE ELENTEAR'S MAGIC HAS BECOME.
YOU'RE RIGHT... THEY'RE ALL FINGERNAIL DIRT.
FILTHY...
THIS IS YET ANOTHER EFFECT OF THE DRAGON, SELENE, TAKING UP RESIDENCE IN OUR WORLD.
SELENE?
HENCE WHY WE SUMMONED A DRAGON-HUNTING SPECIALIST FROM EARTHLAND. THE HANDSOMEST ONE WE COULD FIND!

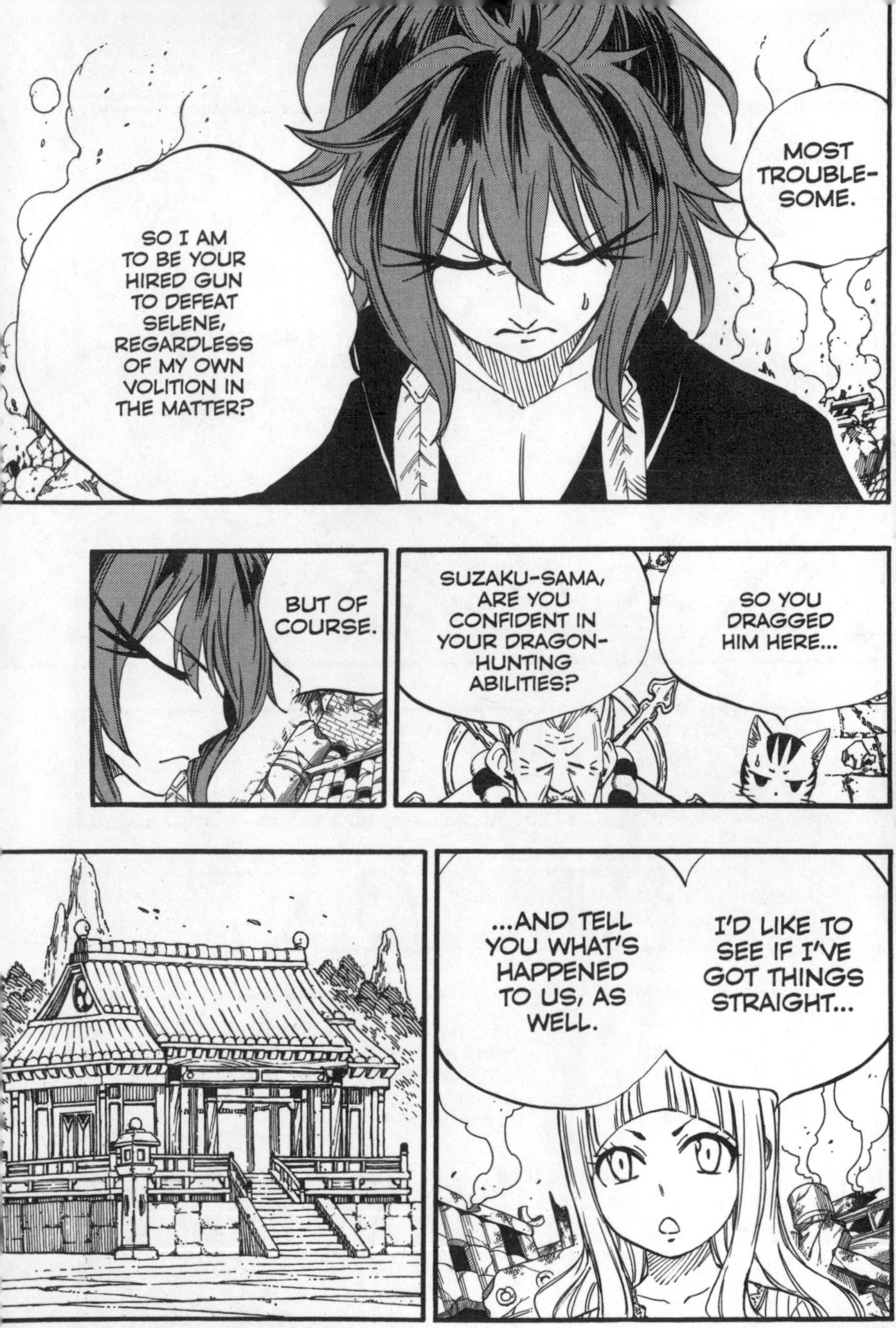
MOST TROUBLE-SOME.
SO I AM TO BE YOUR HIRED GUN TO DEFEAT SELENE, REGARDLESS OF MY OWN VOLITION IN THE MATTER?
SO YOU DRAGGED HIM HERE...
SUZAKU-SAMA, ARE YOU CONFIDENT IN YOUR DRAGON-HUNTING ABILITIES?
BUT OF COURSE.
I'D LIKE TO SEE IF I'VE GOT THINGS STRAIGHT...
...AND TELL YOU WHAT'S HAPPENED TO US, AS WELL.

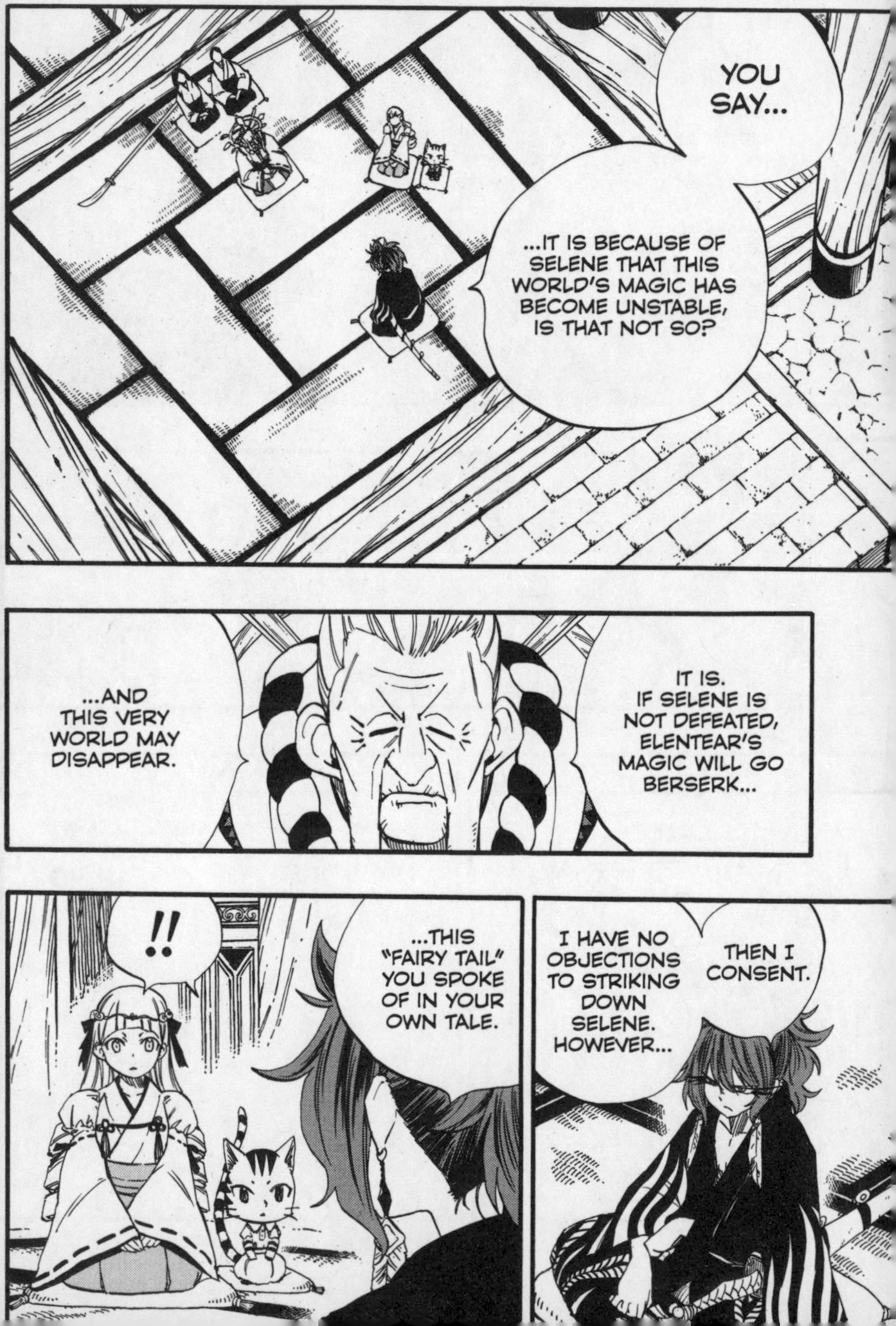
YOU SAY...
...IT IS BECAUSE OF SELENE THAT THIS WORLD'S MAGIC HAS BECOME UNSTABLE, IS THAT NOT SO?
IT IS. IF SELENE IS NOT DEFEATED, ELENTEAR'S MAGIC WILL GO BERSERK...
...AND THIS VERY WORLD MAY DISAPPEAR.
THEN I CONSENT.
I HAVE NO OBJECTIONS TO STRIKING DOWN SELENE. HOWEVER...
...THIS "FAIRY TAIL" YOU SPOKE OF IN YOUR OWN TALE.
!!

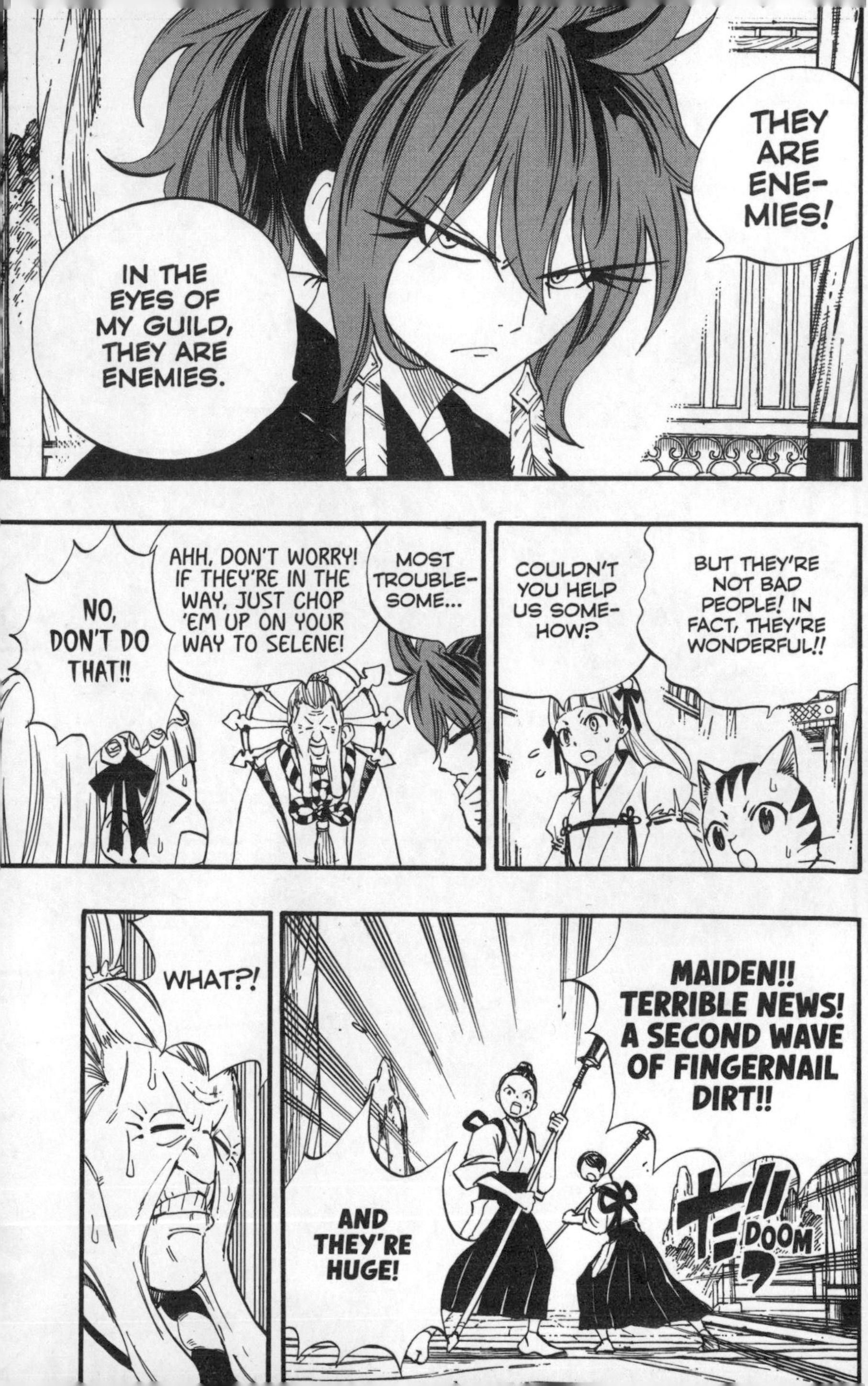
THEY ARE ENE-MIES!
IN THE EYES OF MY GUILD, THEY ARE ENEMIES.
BUT THEY'RE NOT BAD PEOPLE! IN FACT, THEY'RE WONDERFUL!!
COULDN'T YOU HELP US SOME-HOW?
MOST TROUBLE-SOME...
AHH, DON'T WORRY! IF THEY'RE IN THE WAY, JUST CHOP 'EM UP ON YOUR WAY TO SELENE!
NO, DON'T DO THAT!!
MAIDEN!! TERRIBLE NEWS! A SECOND WAVE OF FINGERNAIL DIRT!!
DOOM
AND THEY'RE HUGE!
WHAT?!

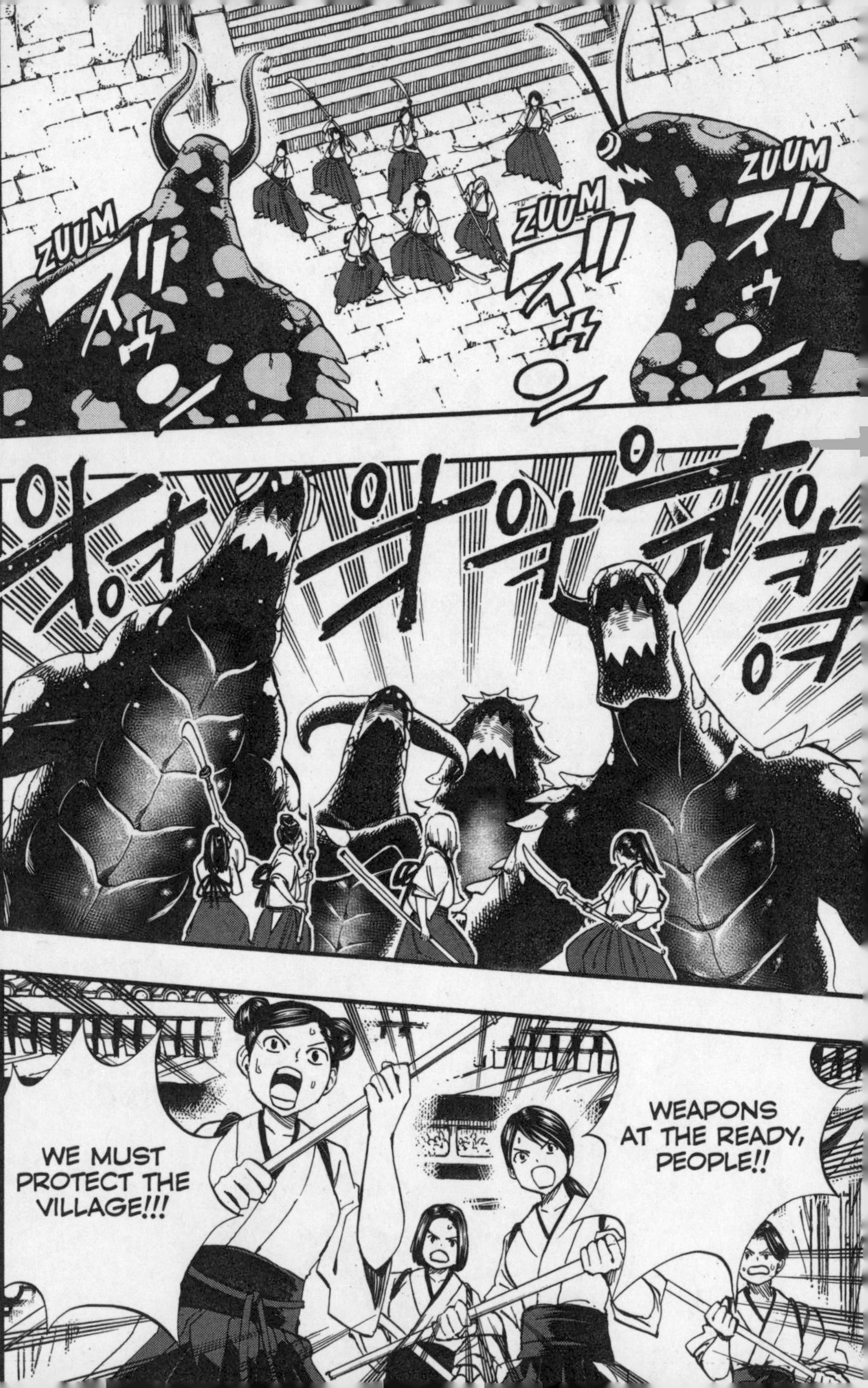
ZUUM
ZUUM
ZUUM
WEAPONS AT THE READY, PEOPLE!!
WE MUST PROTECT THE VILLAGE!!!

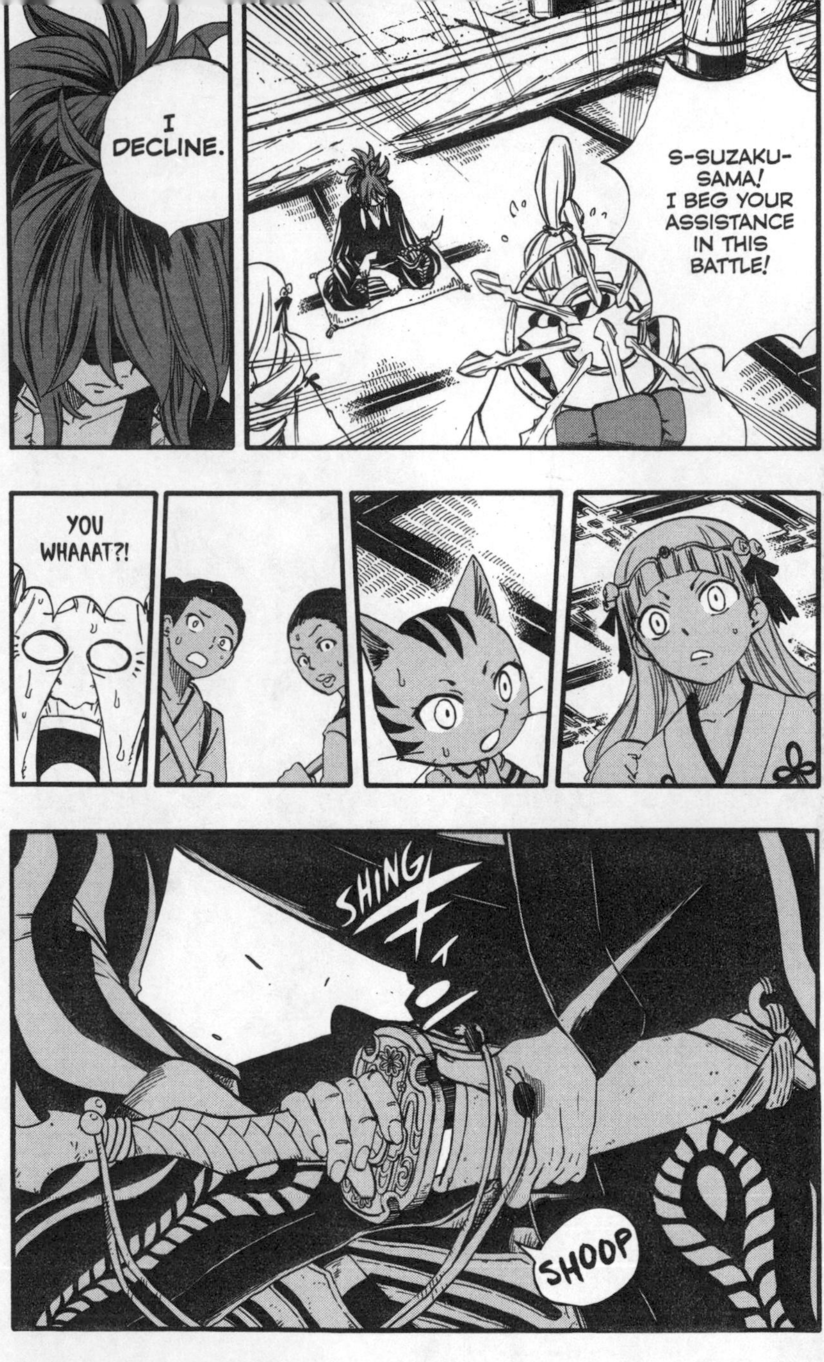
S-SUZAKU-SAMA! I BEG YOUR ASSISTANCE IN THIS BATTLE!
I DECLINE.
YOU WHAAAT?!
SHING
SHOOP

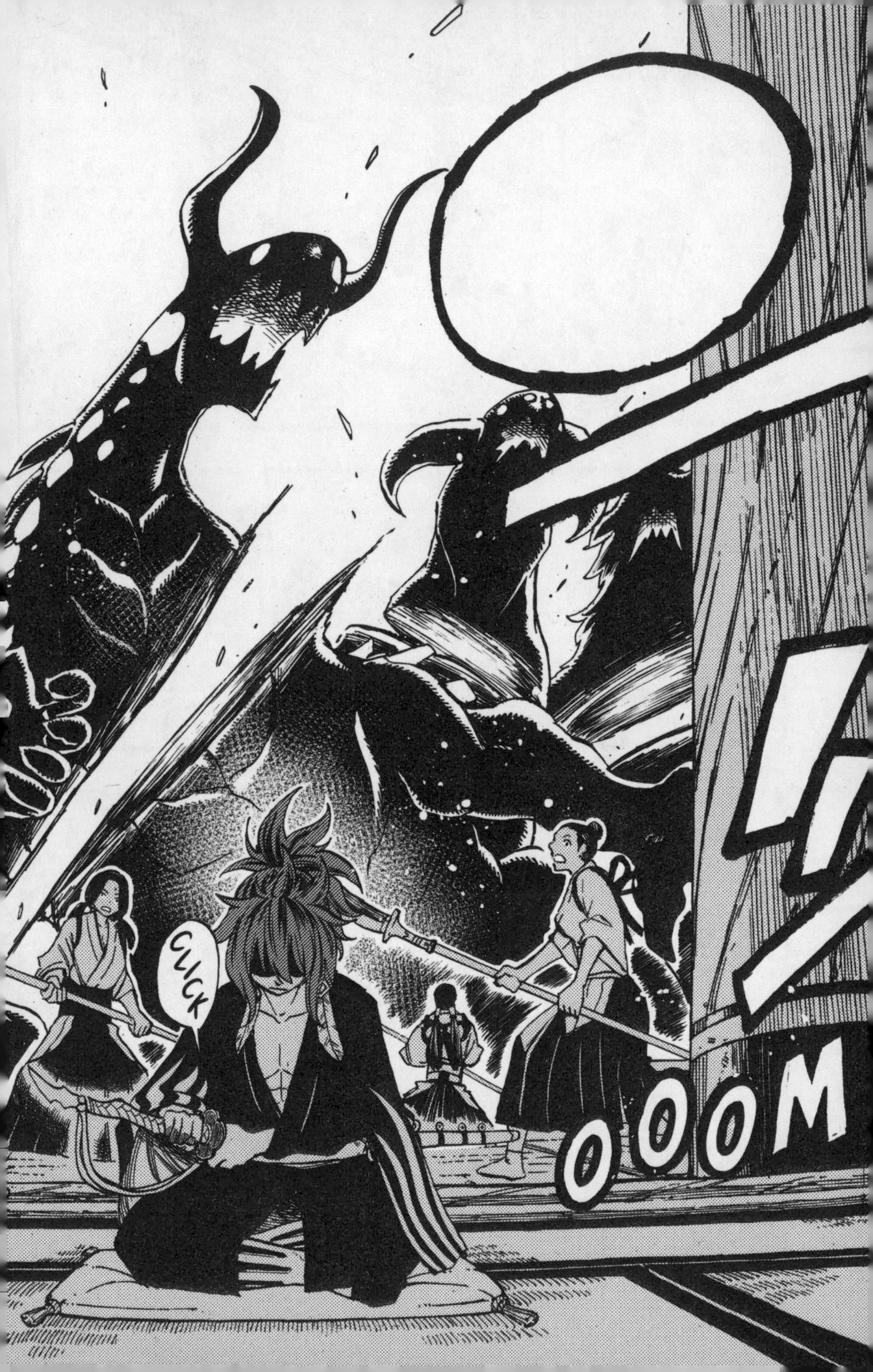
OOOM
CLICK

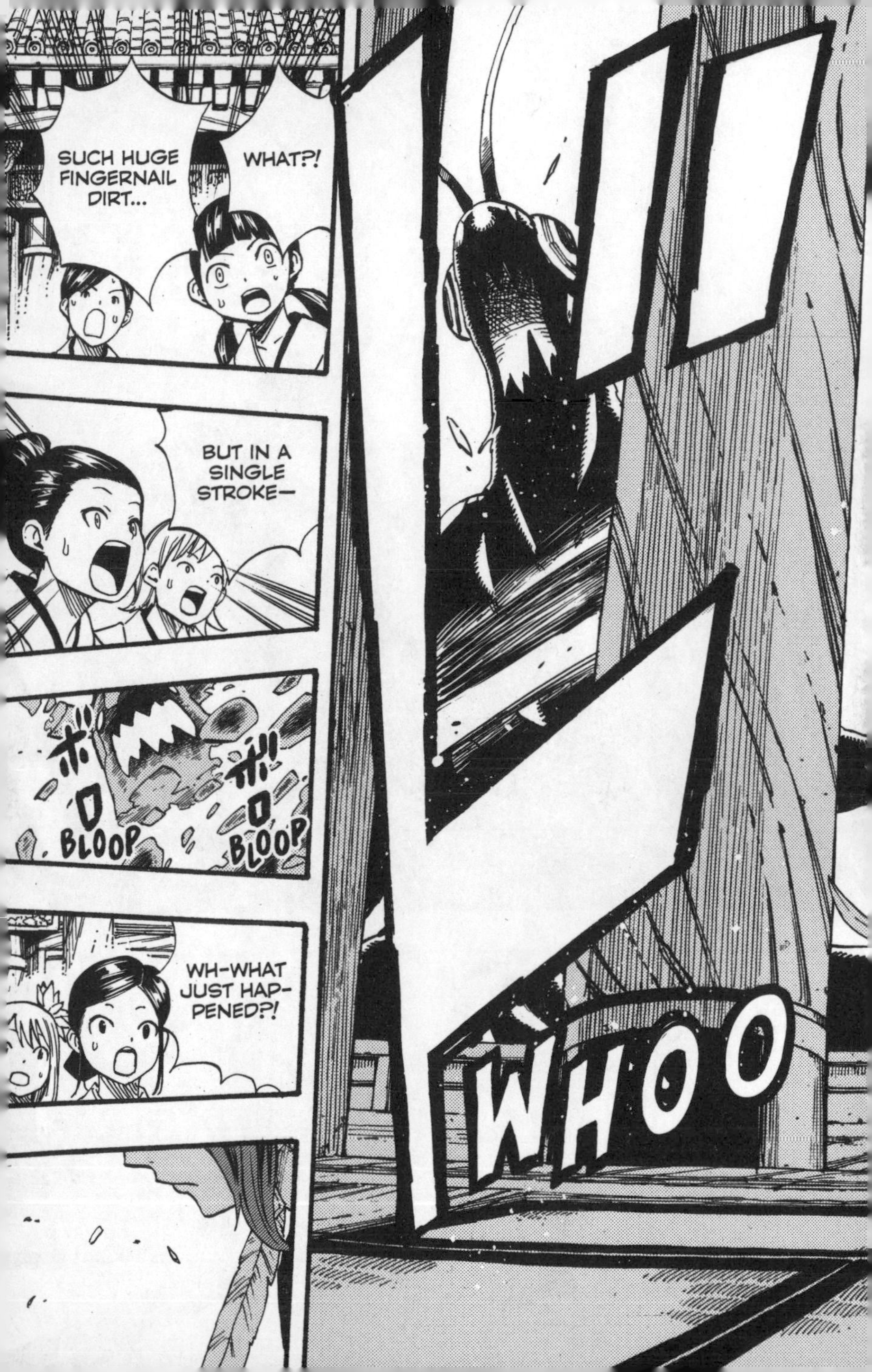
WHOOO
WHAT?!
SUCH HUGE FINGERNAIL DIRT...
BUT IN A SINGLE STROKE—
BLOOP
BLOOP
WH-WHAT JUST HAPPENED?!

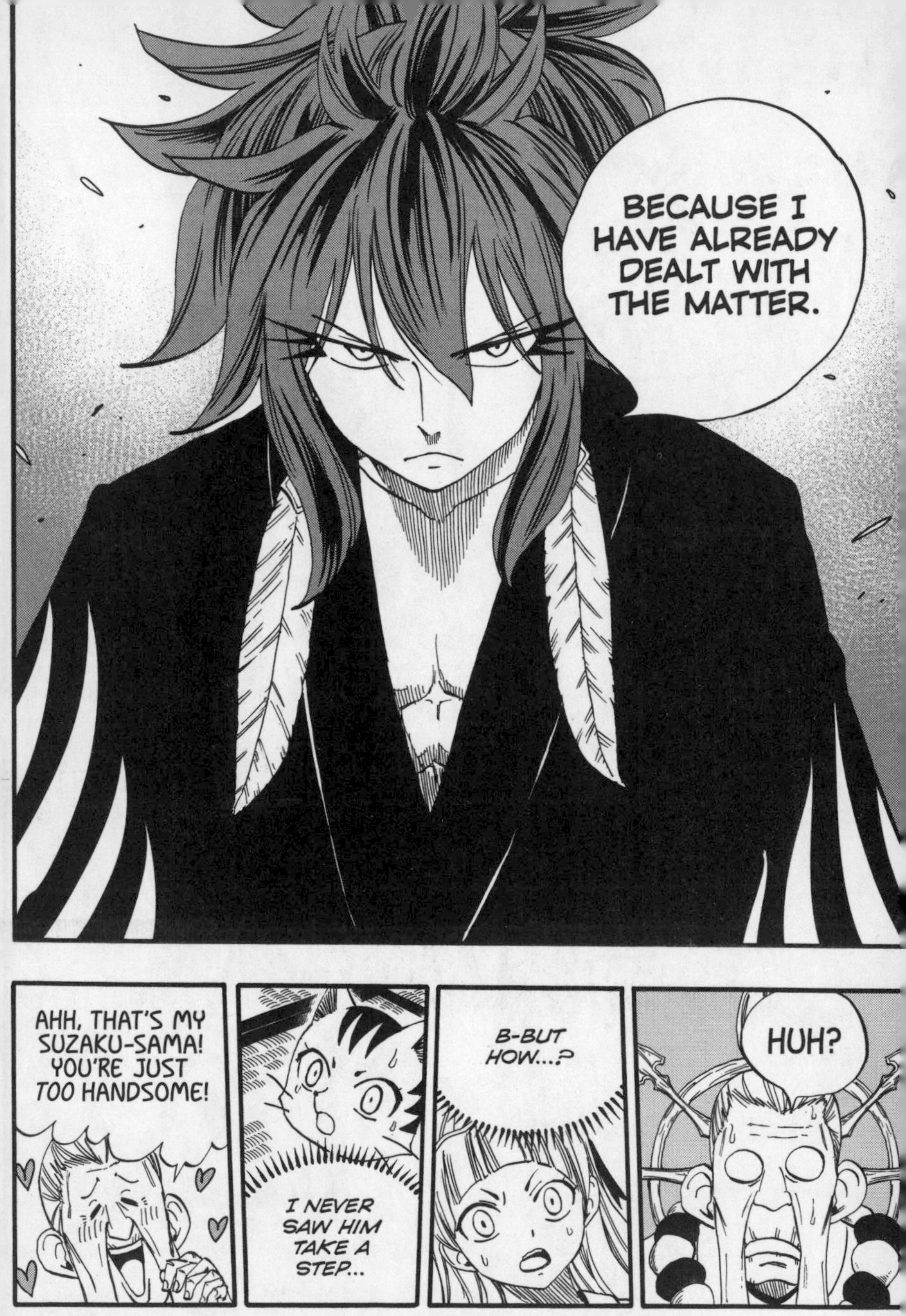
BECAUSE I HAVE ALREADY DEALT WITH THE MATTER.
HUH?
B-BUT HOW...?
I NEVER SAW HIM TAKE A STEP...
AHH, THAT'S MY SUZAKU-SAMA! YOU'RE JUST *TOO* HANDSOME!

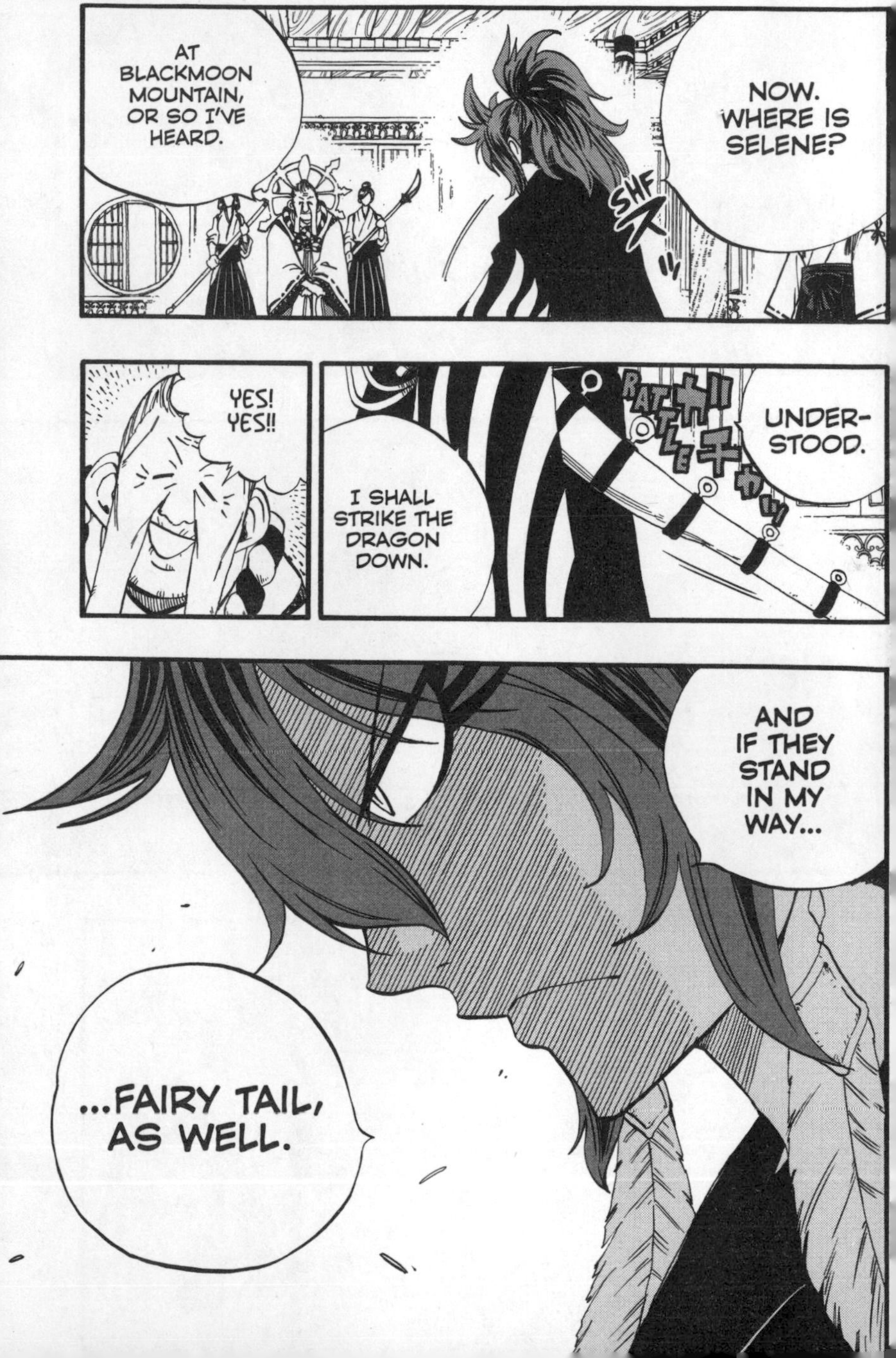
NOW. WHERE IS SELENE?
SHF
AT BLACKMOON MOUNTAIN, OR SO I'VE HEARD.
UNDER-STOOD.
RATTLE
I SHALL STRIKE THE DRAGON DOWN.
YES! YES!!
AND IF THEY STAND IN MY WAY...
...FAIRY TAIL, AS WELL.

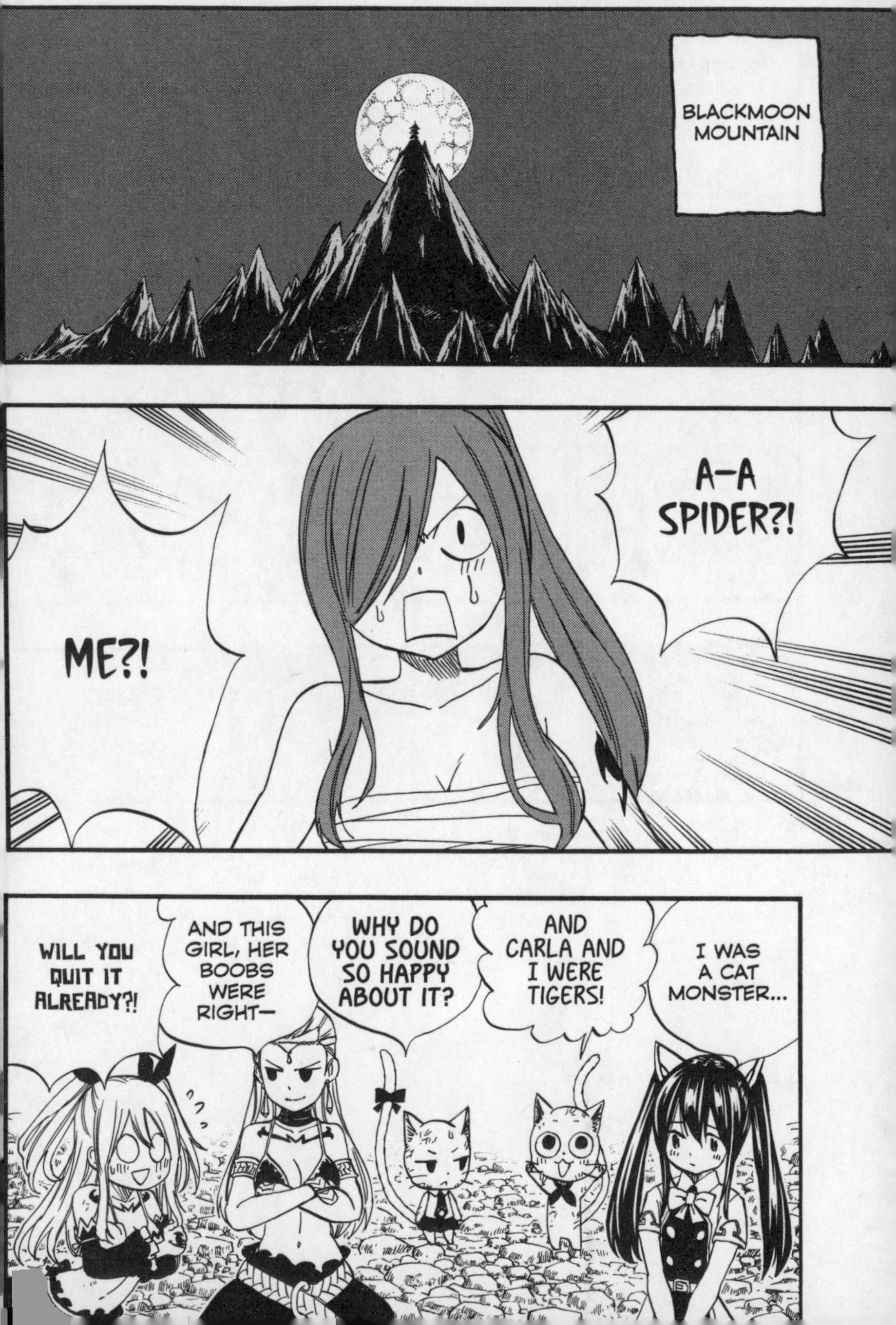
BLACKMOON MOUNTAIN
A-A SPIDER?!
ME?!
I WAS A CAT MONSTER...
AND CARLA AND I WERE TIGERS!
WHY DO YOU SOUND SO HAPPY ABOUT IT?
AND THIS GIRL, HER BOOBS WERE RIGHT—
WILL YOU QUIT IT ALREADY?!

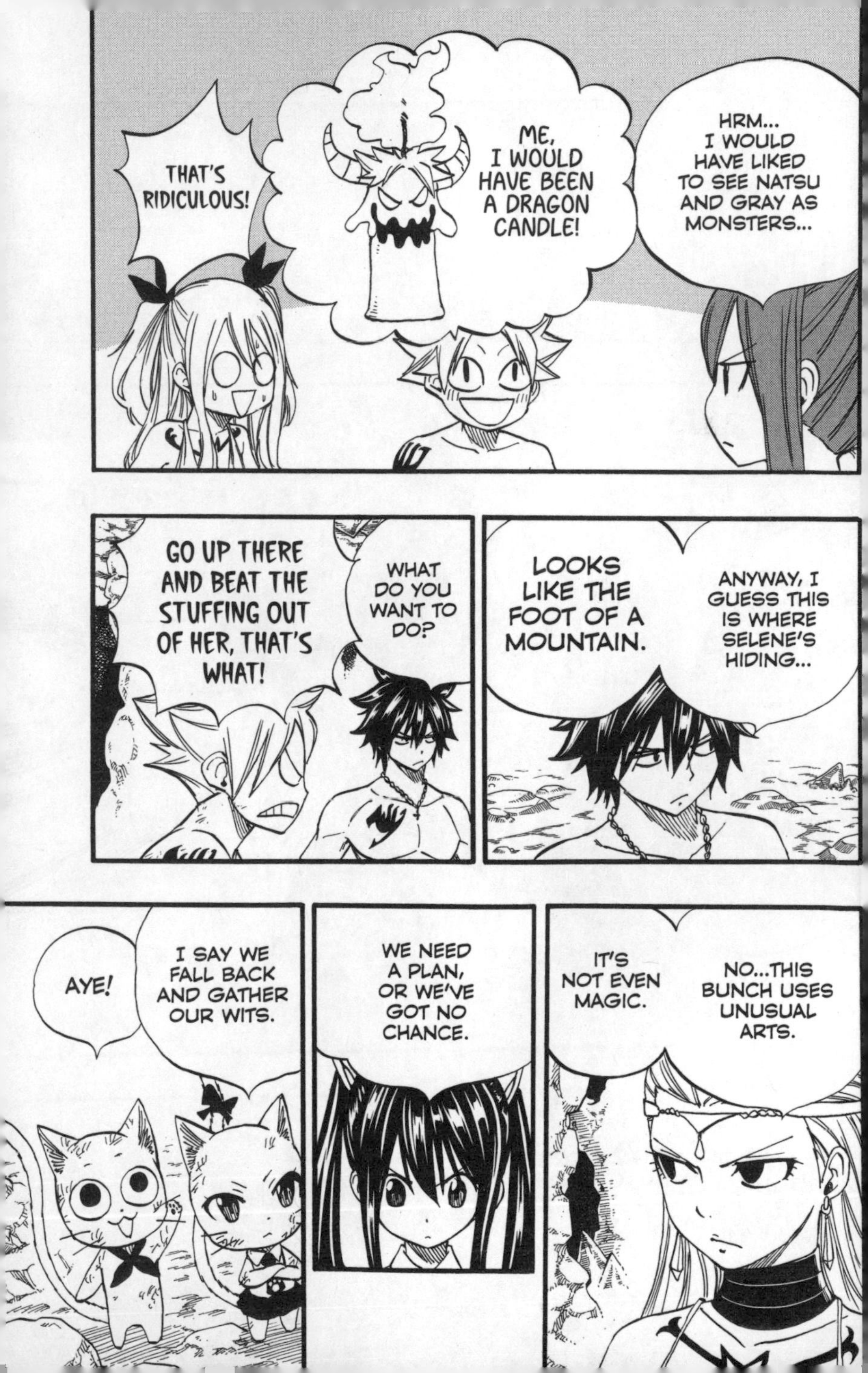
HRM... I WOULD HAVE LIKED TO SEE NATSU AND GRAY AS MONSTERS...
ME, I WOULD HAVE BEEN A DRAGON CANDLE!
THAT'S RIDICULOUS!
ANYWAY, I GUESS THIS IS WHERE SELENE'S HIDING...
LOOKS LIKE THE FOOT OF A MOUNTAIN.
WHAT DO YOU WANT TO DO?
GO UP THERE AND BEAT THE STUFFING OUT OF HER, THAT'S WHAT!
NO...THIS BUNCH USES UNUSUAL ARTS.
IT'S NOT EVEN MAGIC.
WE NEED A PLAN, OR WE'VE GOT NO CHANCE.
I SAY WE FALL BACK AND GATHER OUR WITS.
AYE!

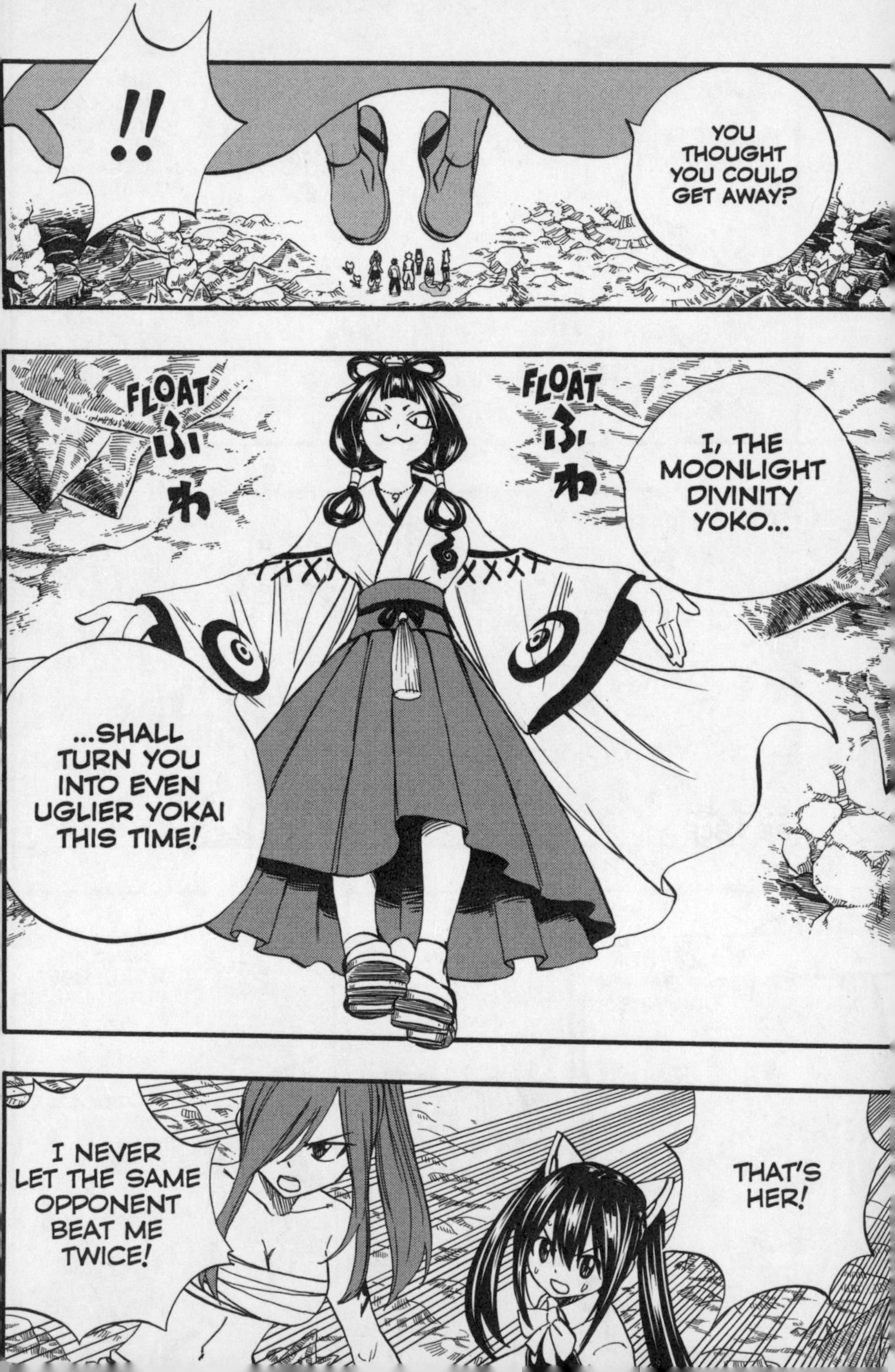
YOU THOUGHT YOU COULD GET AWAY?
!!
FLOAT ふわ
FLOAT ふわ
I, THE MOONLIGHT DIVINITY YOKO...
...SHALL TURN YOU INTO EVEN UGLIER YOKAI THIS TIME!
THAT'S HER!
I NEVER LET THE SAME OPPONENT BEAT ME TWICE!

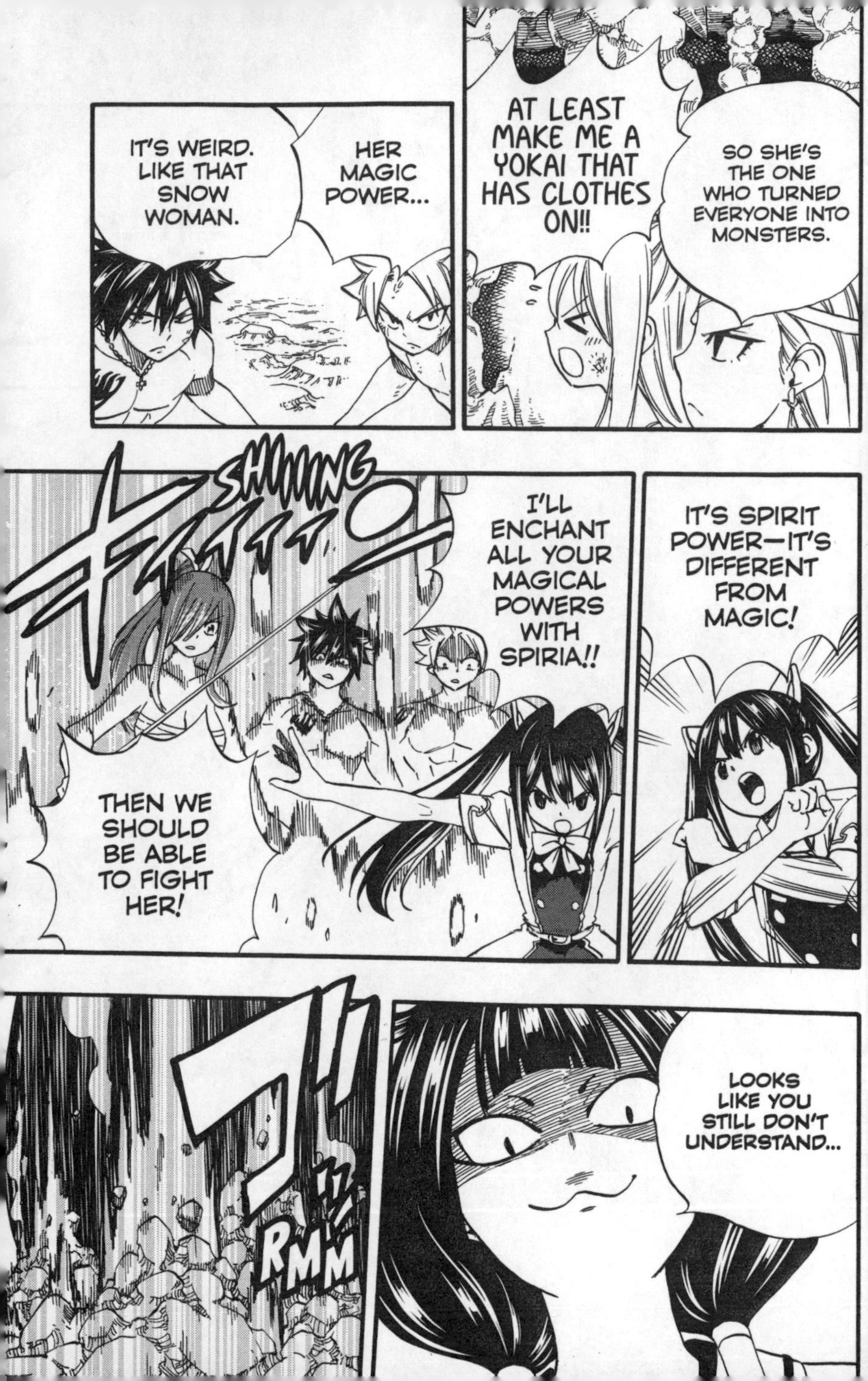
SO SHE'S THE ONE WHO TURNED EVERYONE INTO MONSTERS.
AT LEAST MAKE ME A YOKAI THAT HAS CLOTHES ON!!
HER MAGIC POWER...
IT'S WEIRD. LIKE THAT SNOW WOMAN.
IT'S SPIRIT POWER—IT'S DIFFERENT FROM MAGIC!
I'LL ENCHANT ALL YOUR MAGICAL POWERS WITH SPIRIA!!
SHIIIING
THEN WE SHOULD BE ABLE TO FIGHT HER!
LOOKS LIKE YOU STILL DON'T UNDERSTAND...
RMM

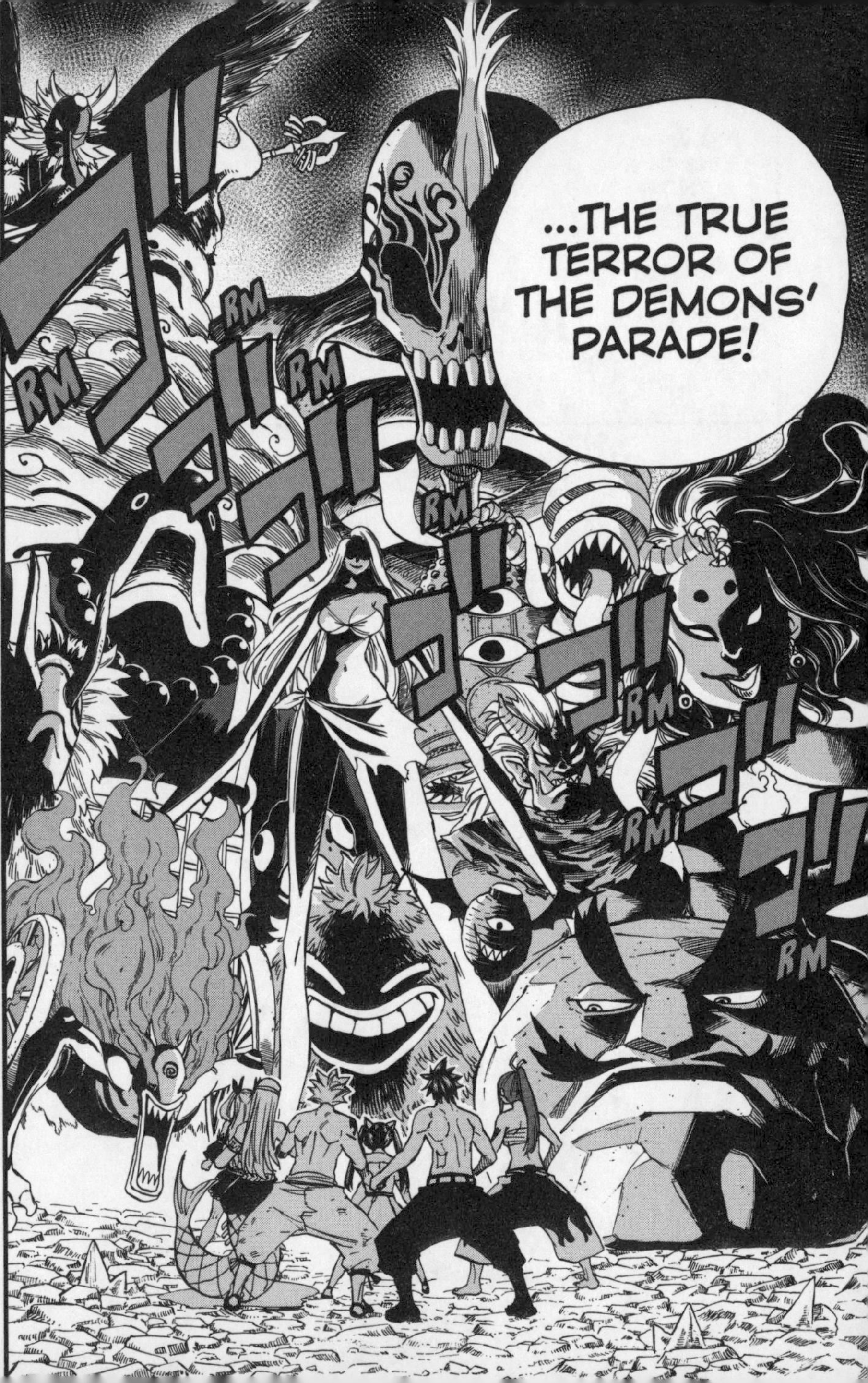
...THE TRUE TERROR OF THE DEMONS' PARADE!
RM
RM
RM
RM
RM
RM
RM

FAIRY TAIL 100 YEARS QUEST

Chapter 78: The Demons' Parade

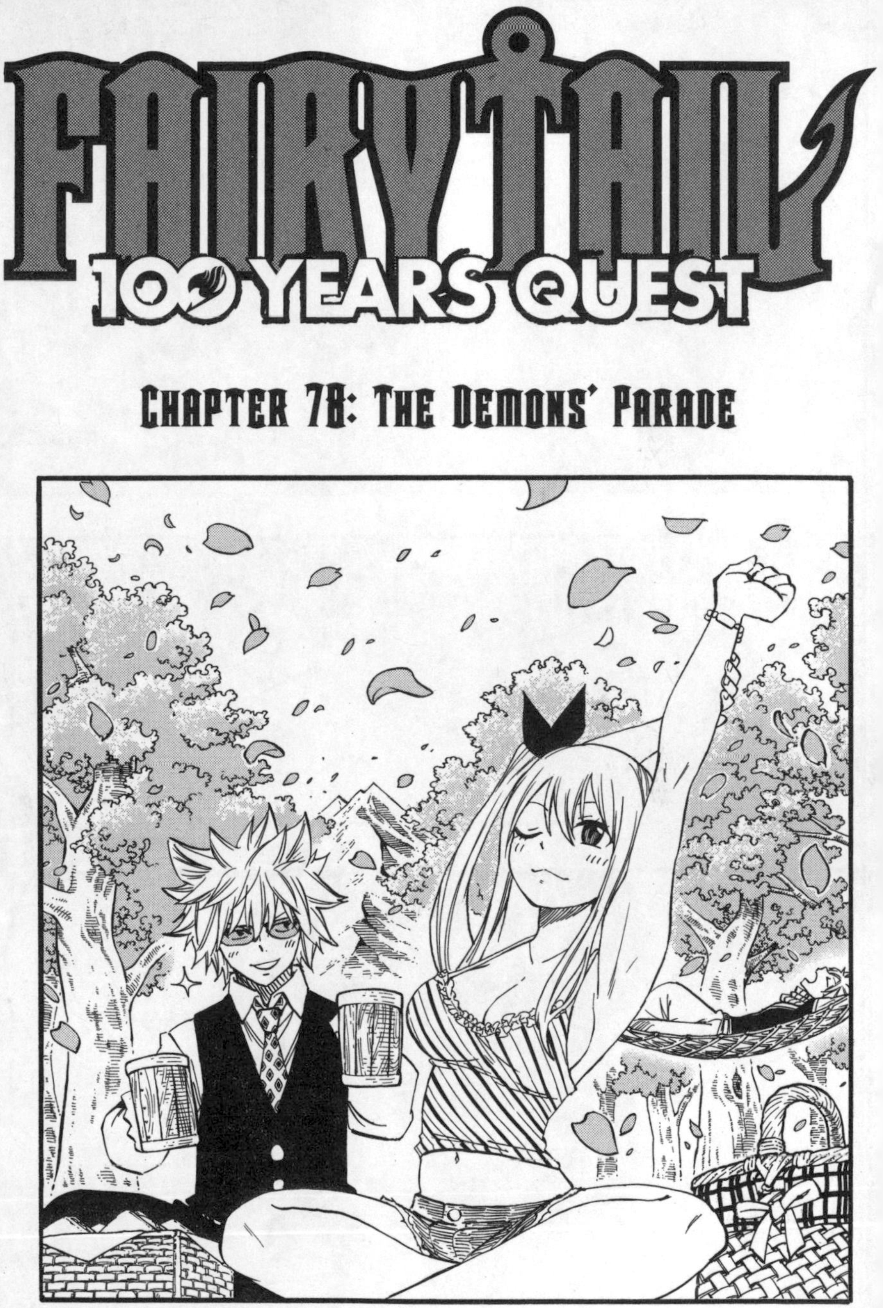

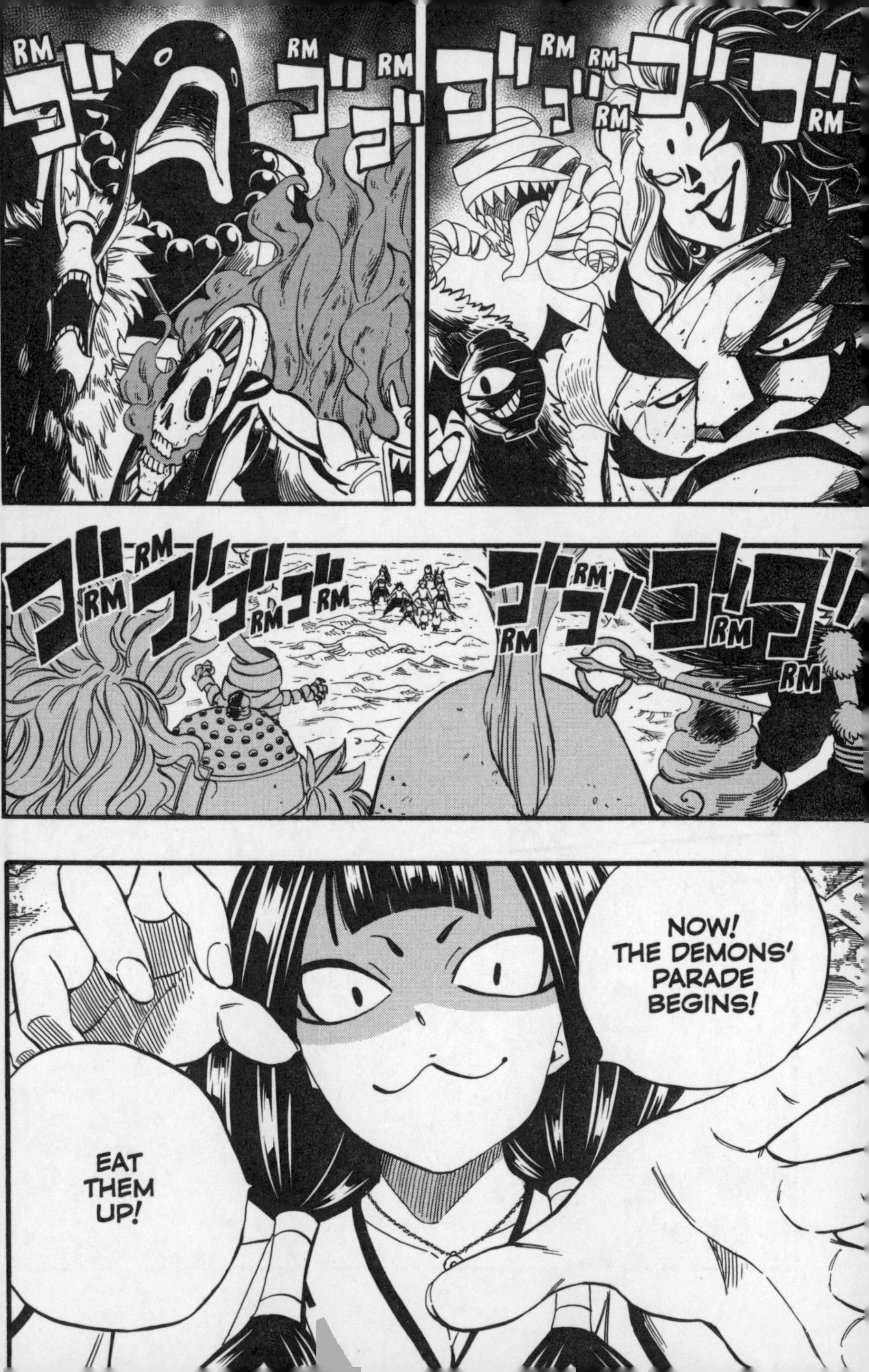
RM RM RM RM RM
ゴゴゴゴ
RM RM RM
ゴゴゴ
RM RM RM RM RM RM RM RM RM
ゴゴゴゴゴゴゴゴゴ
NOW! THE DEMONS' PARADE BEGINS!
EAT THEM UP!

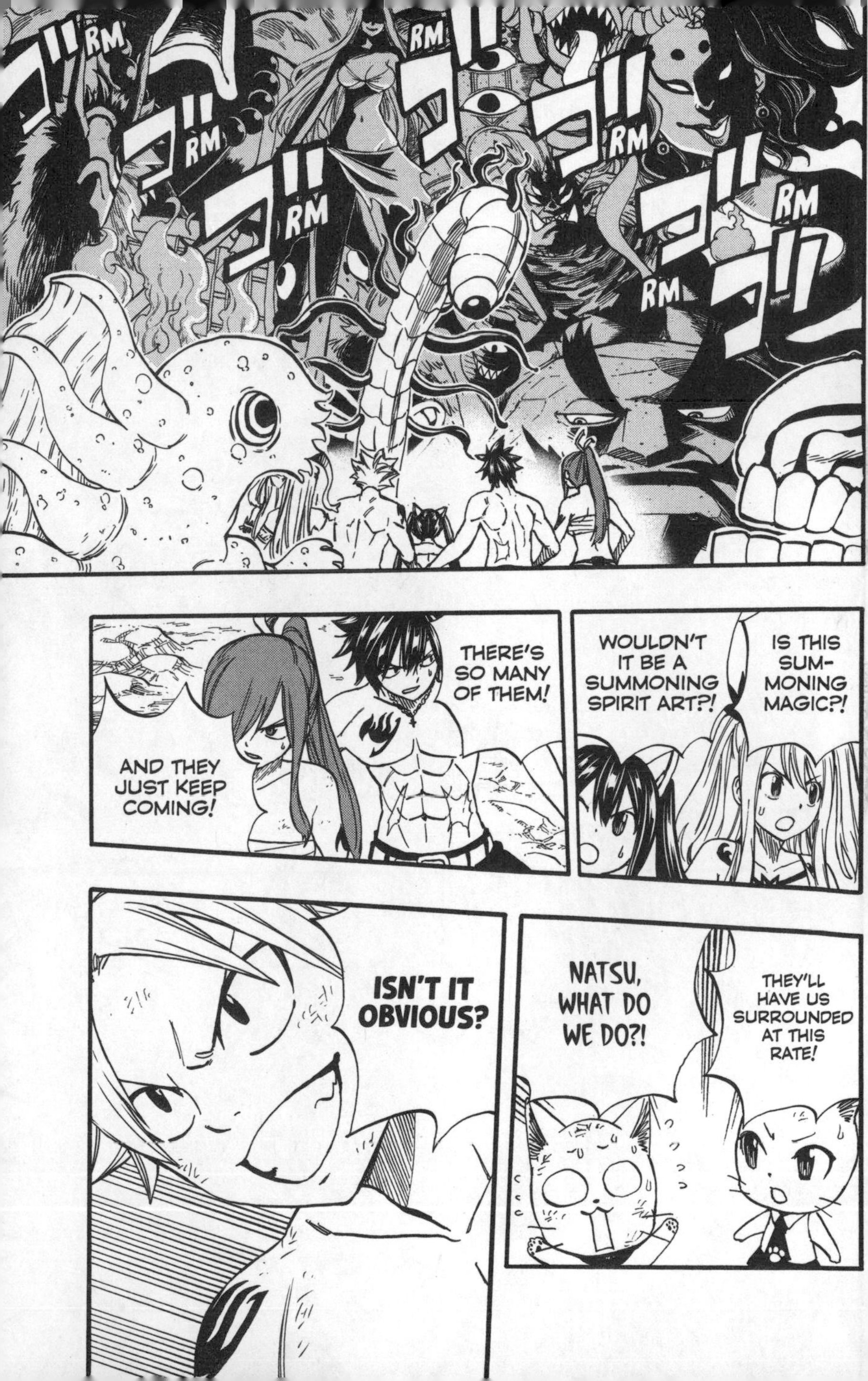
RM
RM
RM
RM
RM
RM
RM
RM
IS THIS SUM-MONING MAGIC?!
WOULDN'T IT BE A SUMMONING SPIRIT ART?!
THERE'S SO MANY OF THEM!
AND THEY JUST KEEP COMING!
THEY'LL HAVE US SURROUNDED AT THIS RATE!
NATSU, WHAT DO WE DO?!
ISN'T IT OBVIOUS?

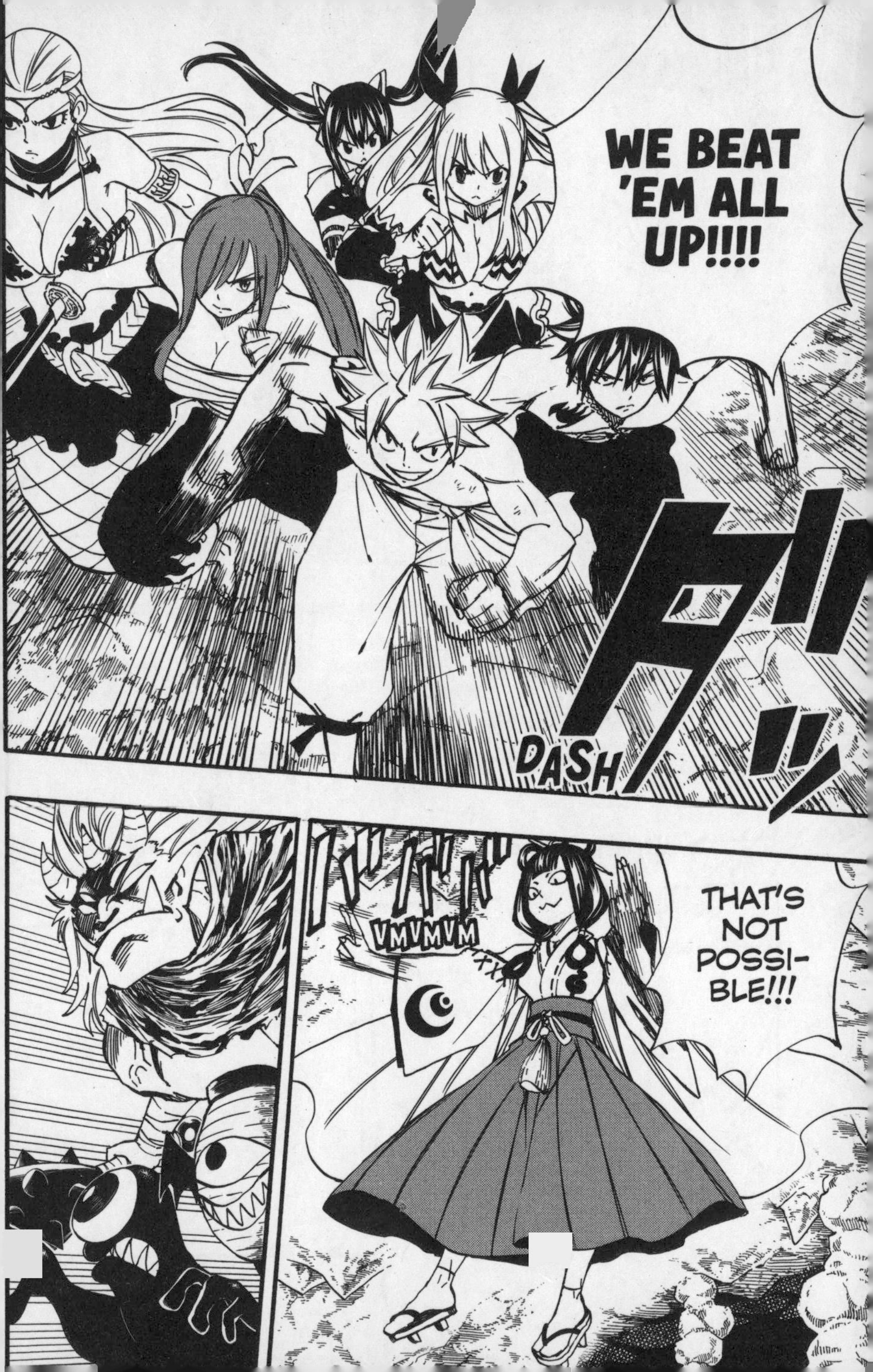
WE BEAT 'EM ALL UP!!!!
DASH
THAT'S NOT POSSI-BLE!!!
VMVMVM

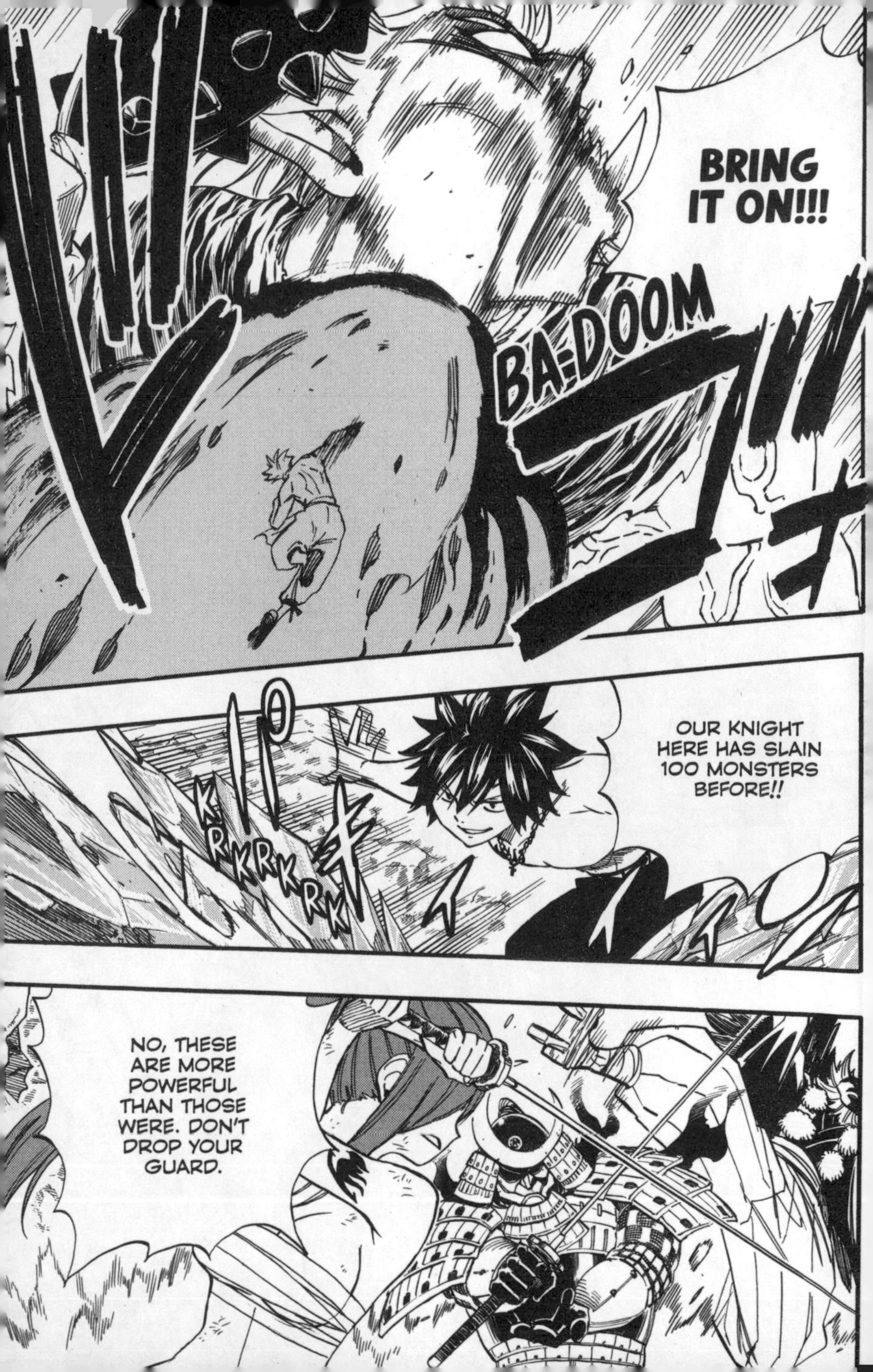
BRING IT ON!!!
BA-DOOM
OUR KNIGHT HERE HAS SLAIN 100 MONSTERS BEFORE!!
KRKRKRKRK
NO, THESE ARE MORE POWERFUL THAN THOSE WERE. DON'T DROP YOUR GUARD.

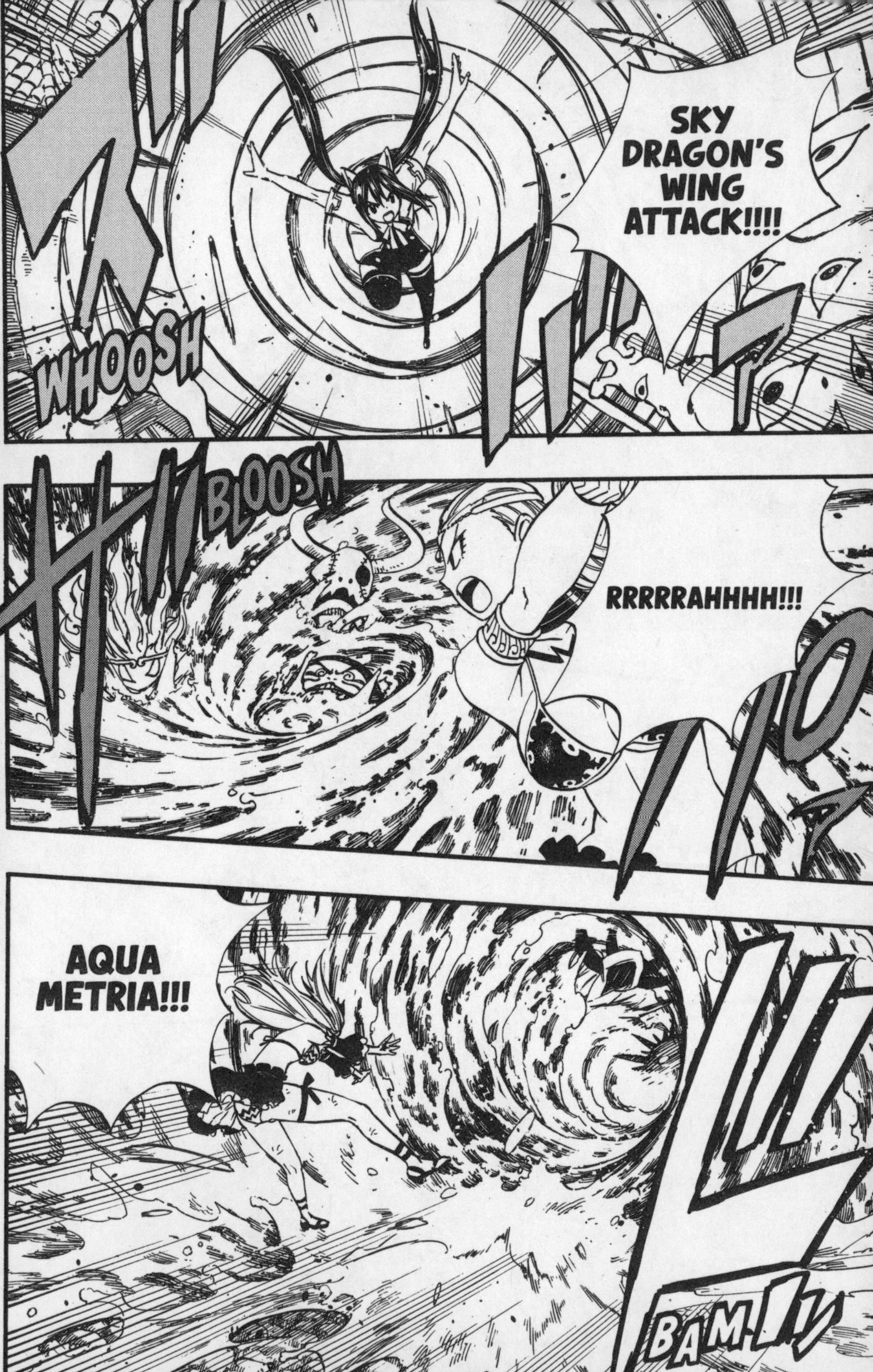
SKY DRAGON'S WING ATTACK!!!!
WHOOSH
RRRRRAHHHH!!!
BLOOSH
AQUA METRIA!!!
BAM

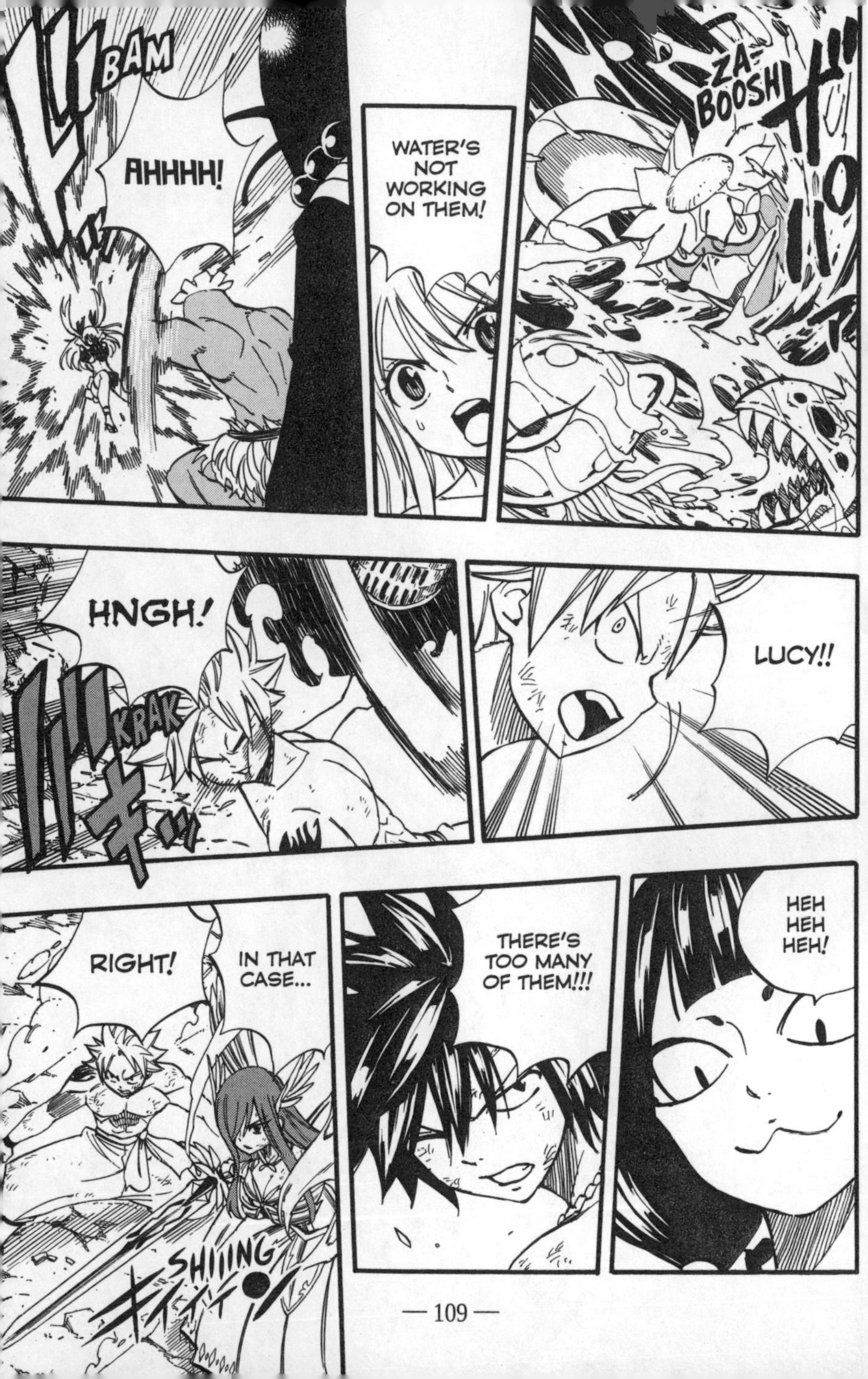
ZA-BOOSH
WATER'S NOT WORKING ON THEM!
BAM
AHHHH!
LUCY!!
HNGH!
KRAK
HEH HEH HEH!
THERE'S TOO MANY OF THEM!!!
IN THAT CASE...
RIGHT!
SHIIING

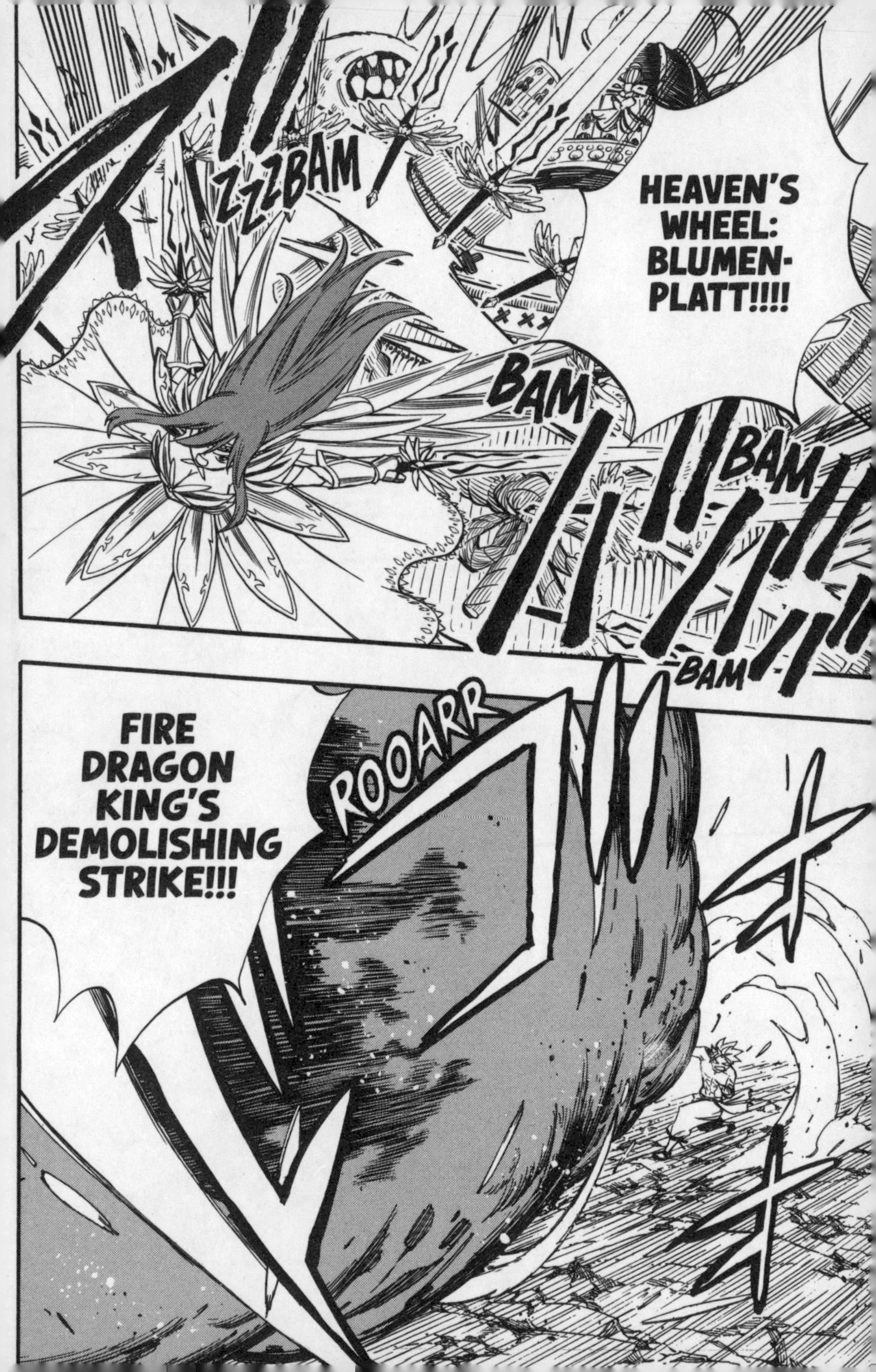
HEAVEN'S WHEEL: BLUMEN-PLATT!!!!
ZZZBAM
BAM
BAM
BAM
ROOARR
FIRE DRAGON KING'S DEMOLISHING STRIKE!!!

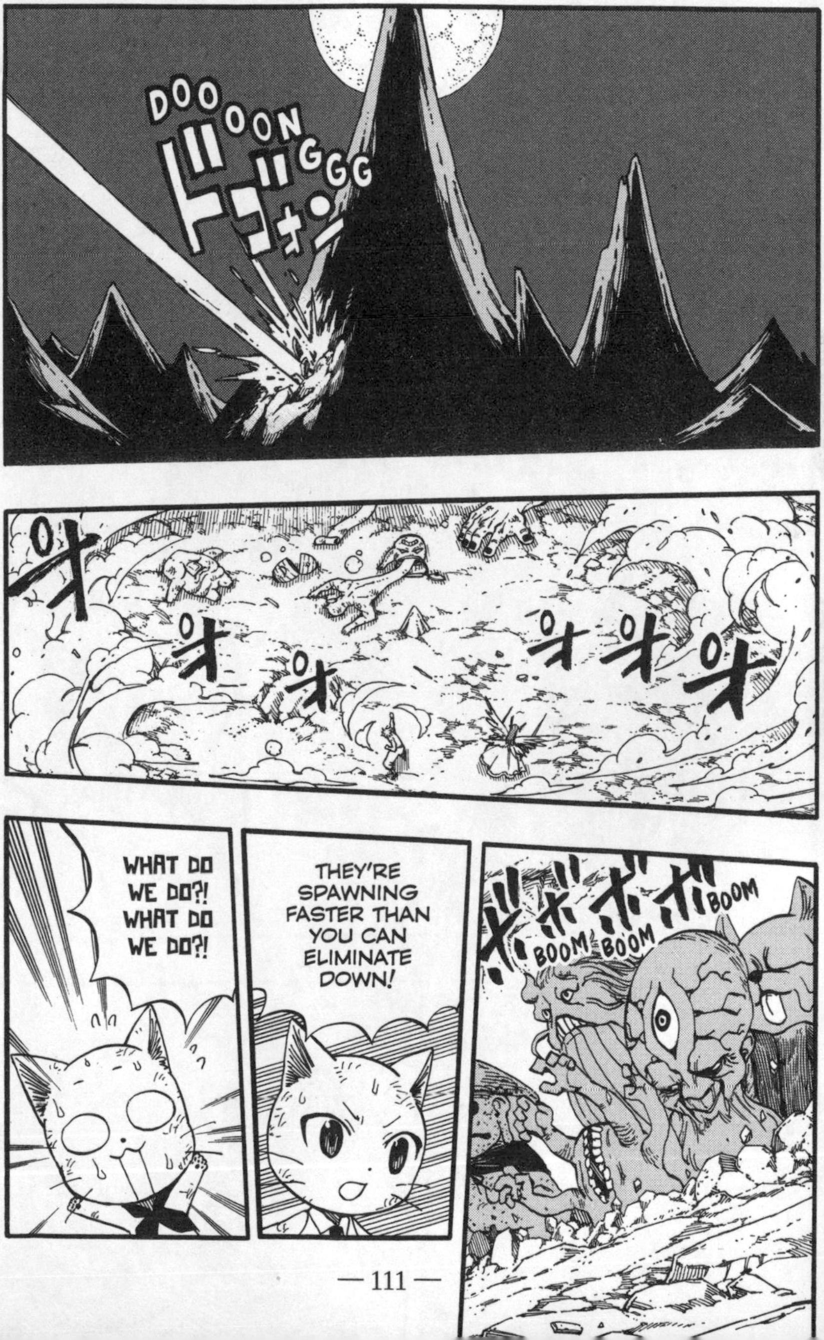
DOOOONGGG
ドゴォン
BOOM BOOM BOOM
THEY'RE SPAWNING FASTER THAN YOU CAN ELIMINATE DOWN!
WHAT DO WE DO?! WHAT DO WE DO?!

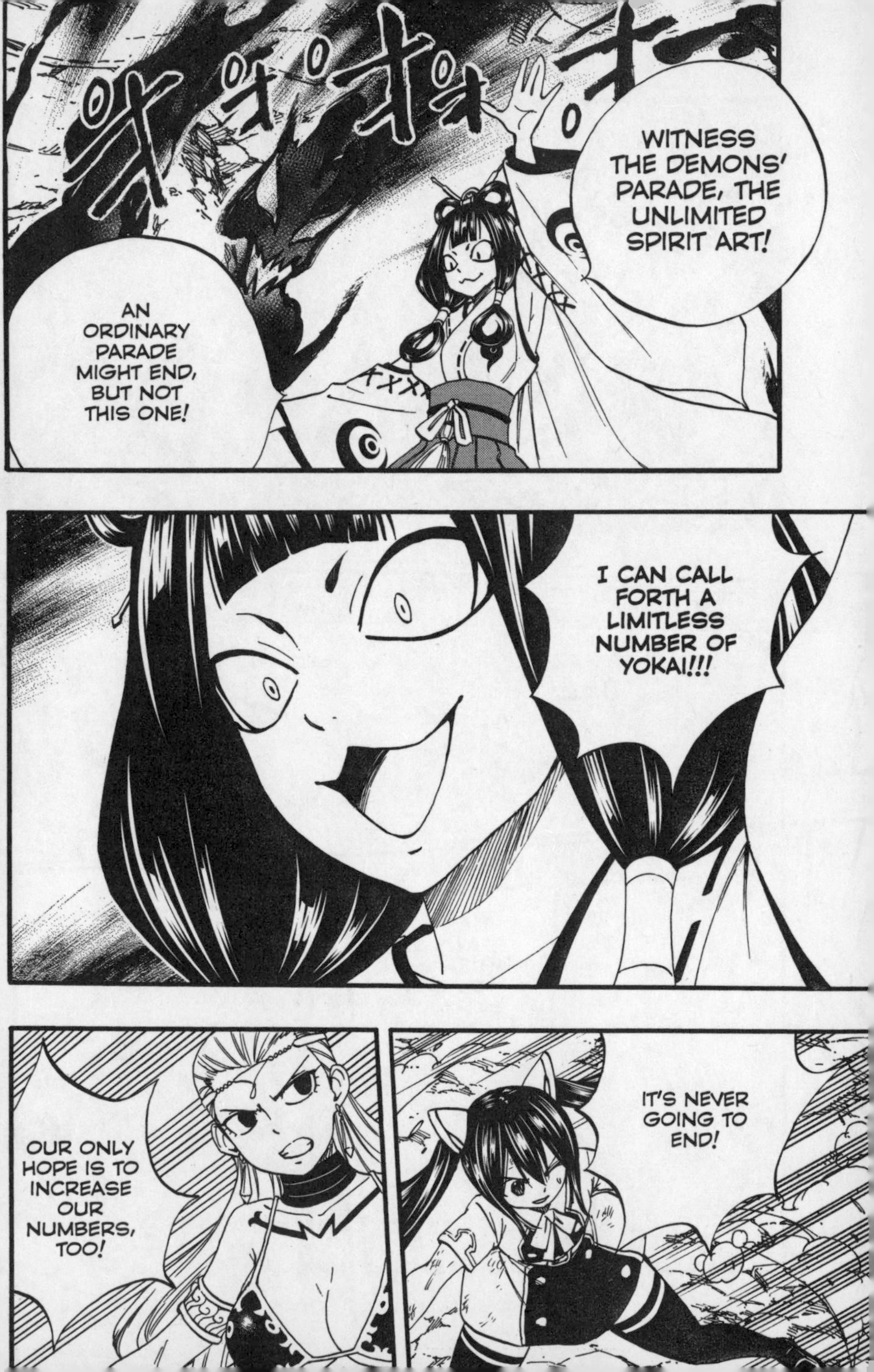

WITNESS THE DEMONS' PARADE, THE UNLIMITED SPIRIT ART!
AN ORDINARY PARADE MIGHT END, BUT NOT THIS ONE!
I CAN CALL FORTH A LIMITLESS NUMBER OF YOKAI!!!
IT'S NEVER GOING TO END!
OUR ONLY HOPE IS TO INCREASE OUR NUMBERS, TOO!

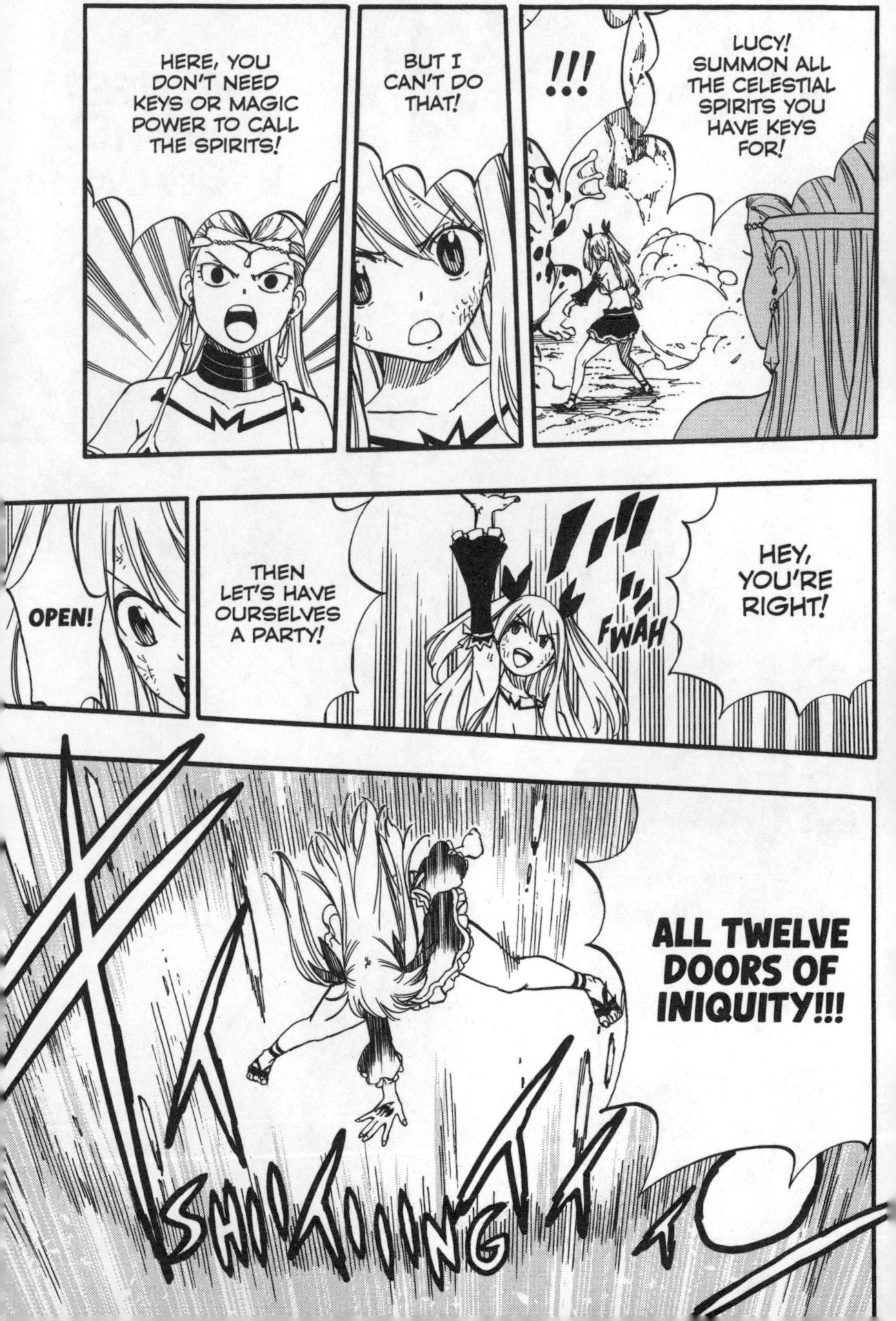
LUCY! SUMMON ALL THE CELESTIAL SPIRITS YOU HAVE KEYS FOR!
!!!
BUT I CAN'T DO THAT!
HERE, YOU DON'T NEED KEYS OR MAGIC POWER TO CALL THE SPIRITS!
HEY, YOU'RE RIGHT!
FWAH
THEN LET'S HAVE OURSELVES A PARTY!
OPEN!
ALL TWELVE DOORS OF INIQUITY!!!

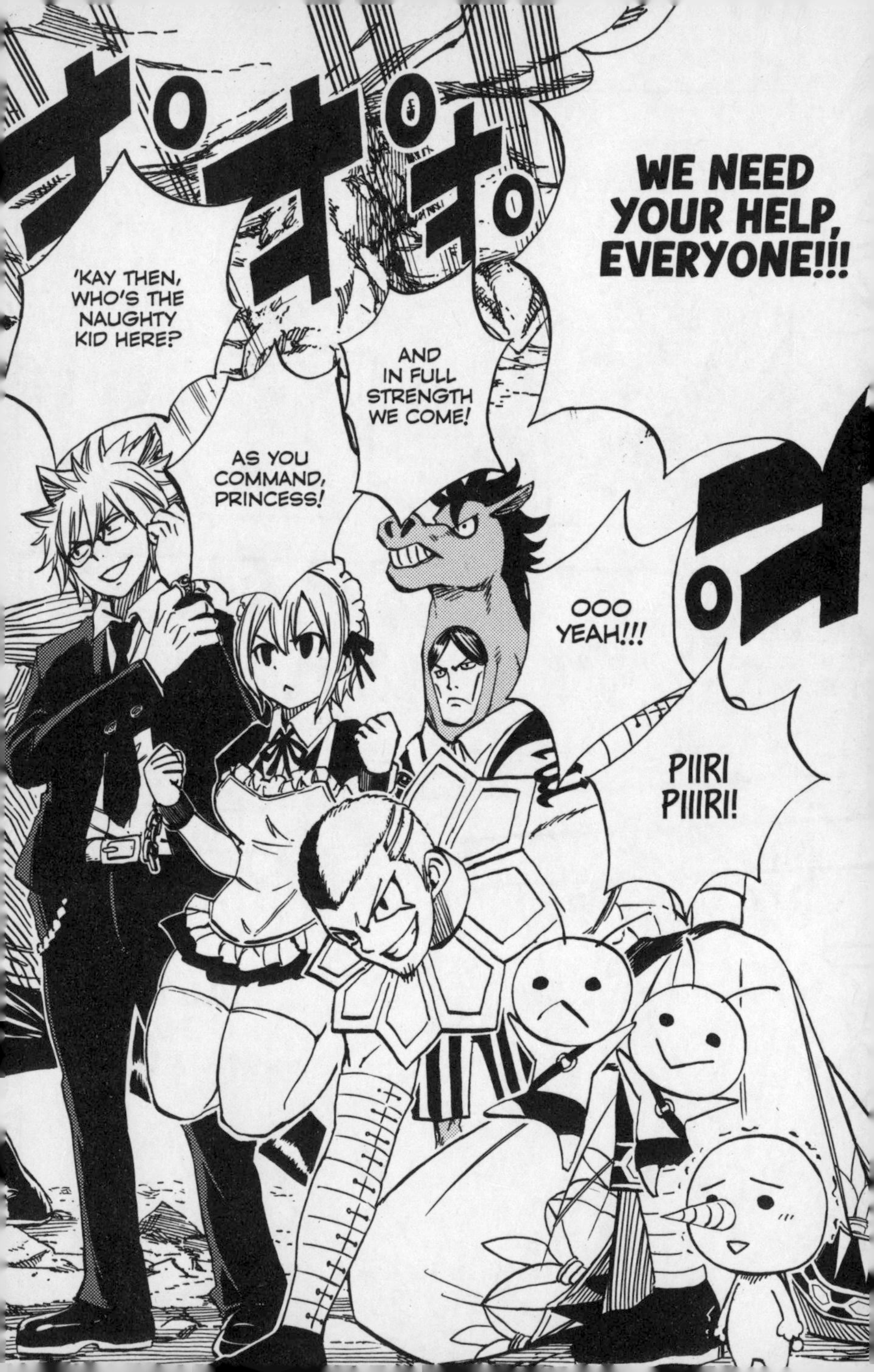
WE NEED YOUR HELP, EVERYONE!!!
'KAY THEN, WHO'S THE NAUGHTY KID HERE?
AND IN FULL STRENGTH WE COME!
AS YOU COMMAND, PRINCESS!
OOO YEAH!!!
PIIRI PIIIRI!

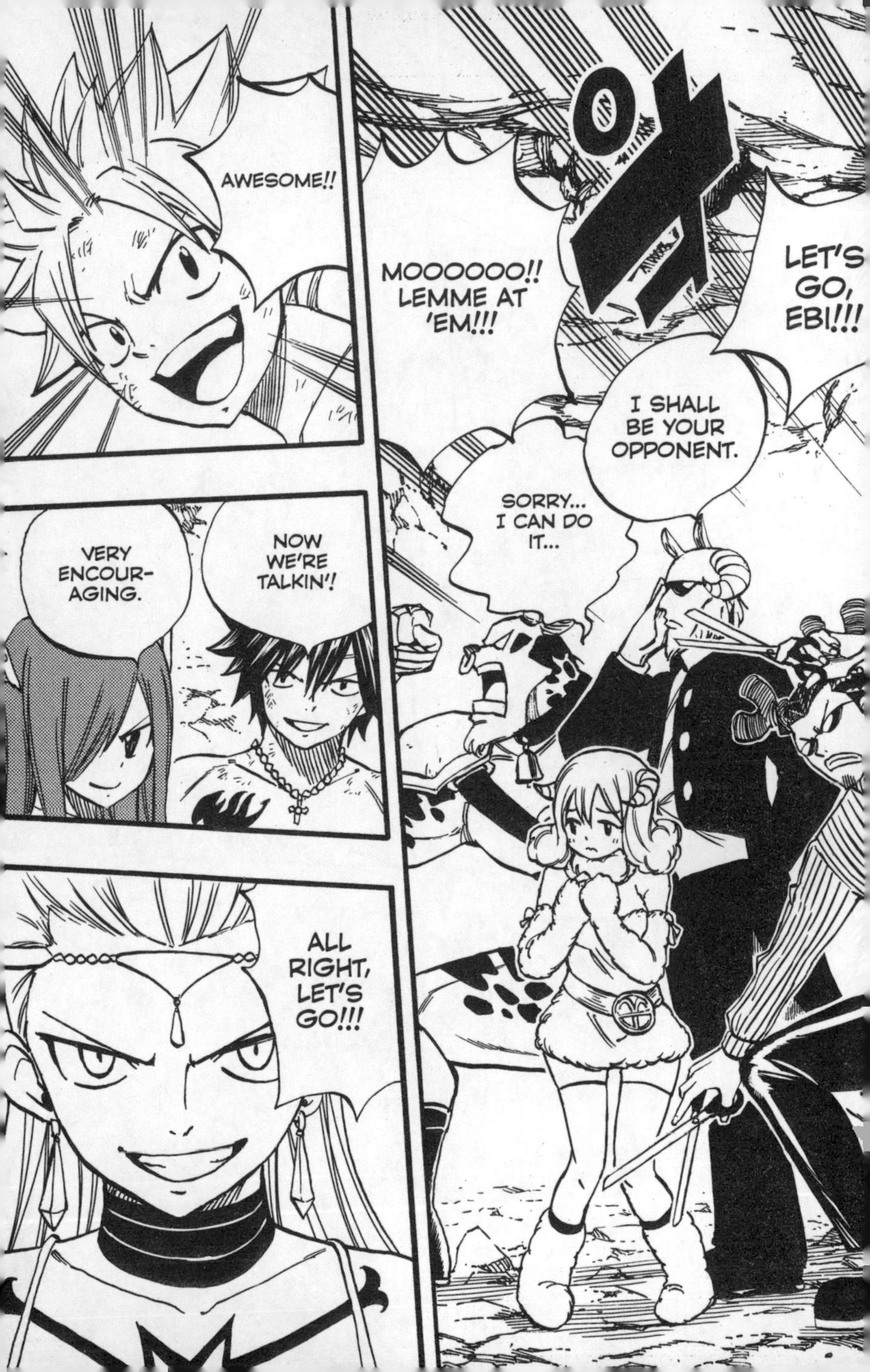
LET'S GO, EBI!!!
MOOOOOO!! LEMME AT 'EM!!!
I SHALL BE YOUR OPPONENT.
SORRY... I CAN DO IT...
AWESOME!!
NOW WE'RE TALKIN'!
VERY ENCOUR-AGING.
ALL RIGHT, LET'S GO!!!

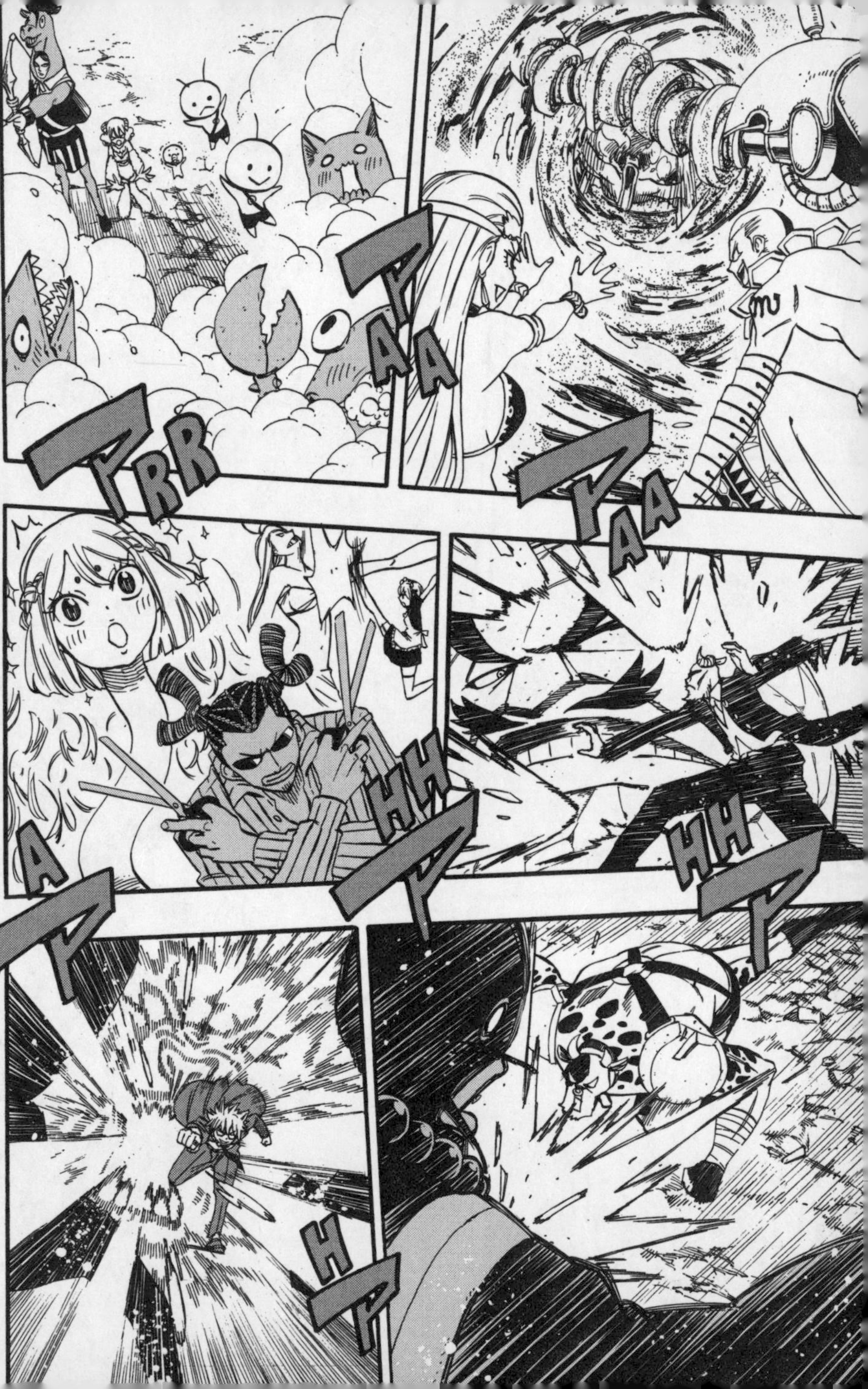

PYAA
PAA
PRR
PHH
PHH
PA
PH

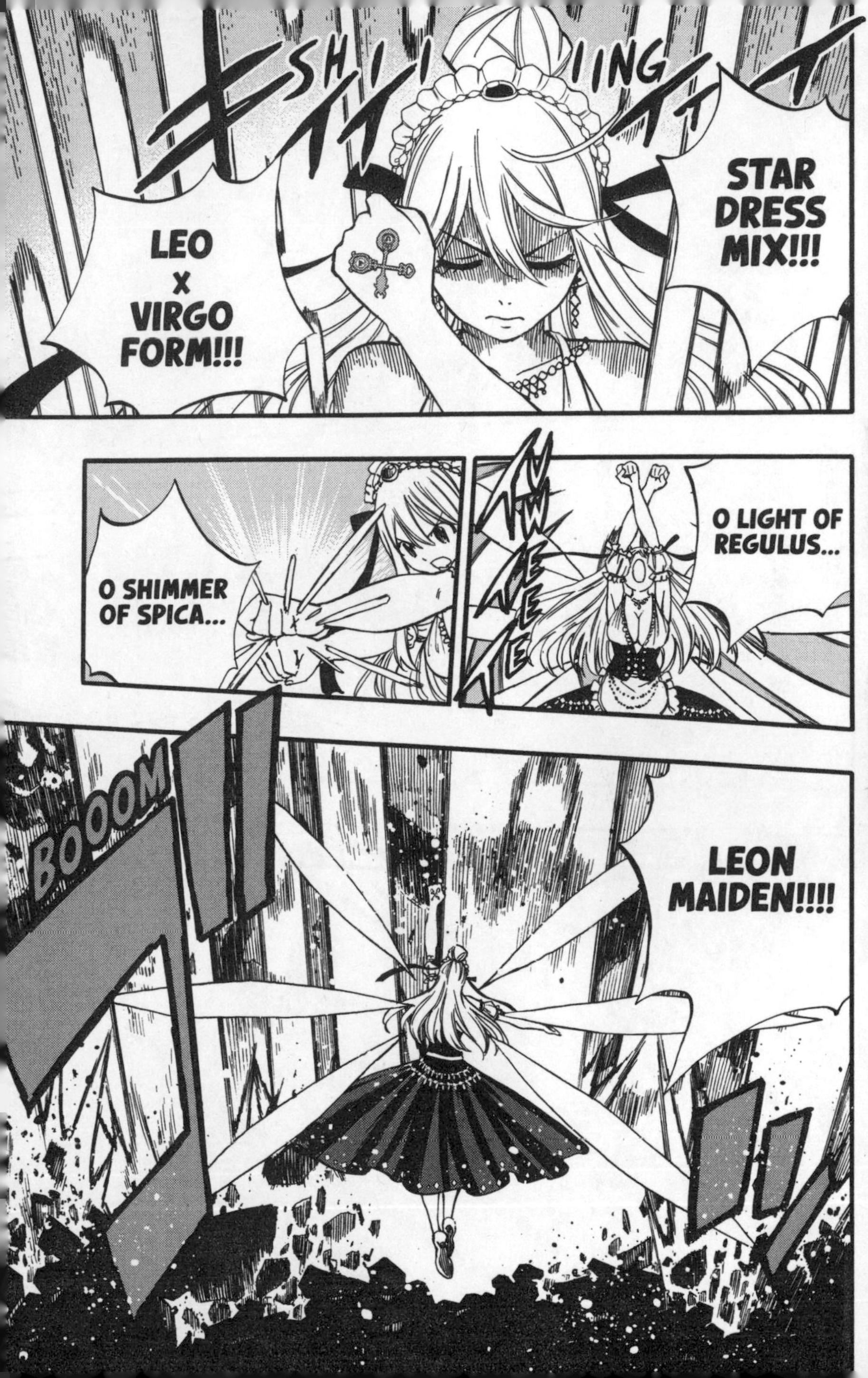
SHIIIING
STAR DRESS MIX!!!
LEO x VIRGO FORM!!!
O LIGHT OF REGULUS...
O SHIMMER OF SPICA...
LEON MAIDEN!!!!
BOOOM

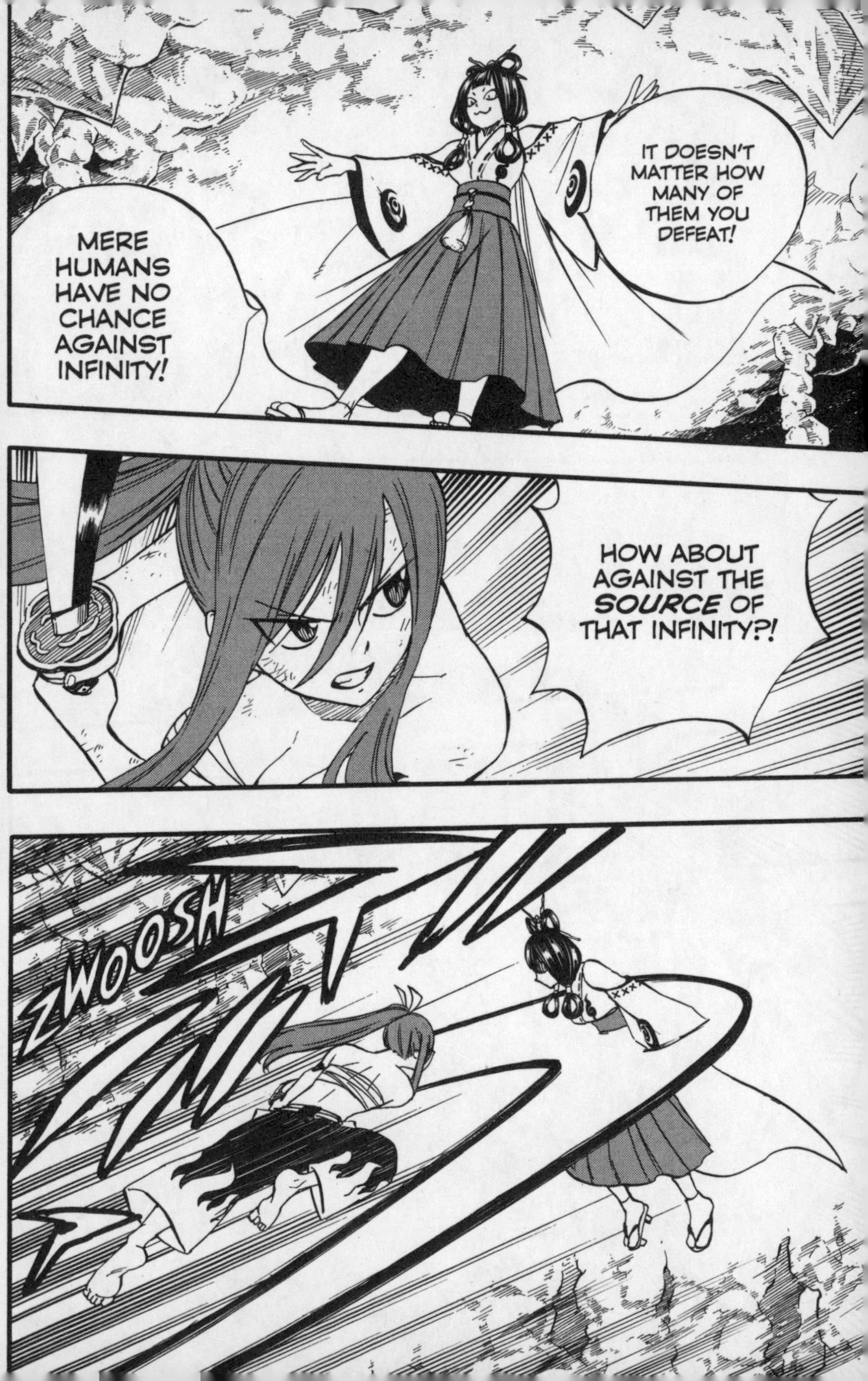
IT DOESN'T MATTER HOW MANY OF THEM YOU DEFEAT!
MERE HUMANS HAVE NO CHANCE AGAINST INFINITY!
HOW ABOUT AGAINST THE *SOURCE* OF THAT INFINITY?!
ZWOOSH

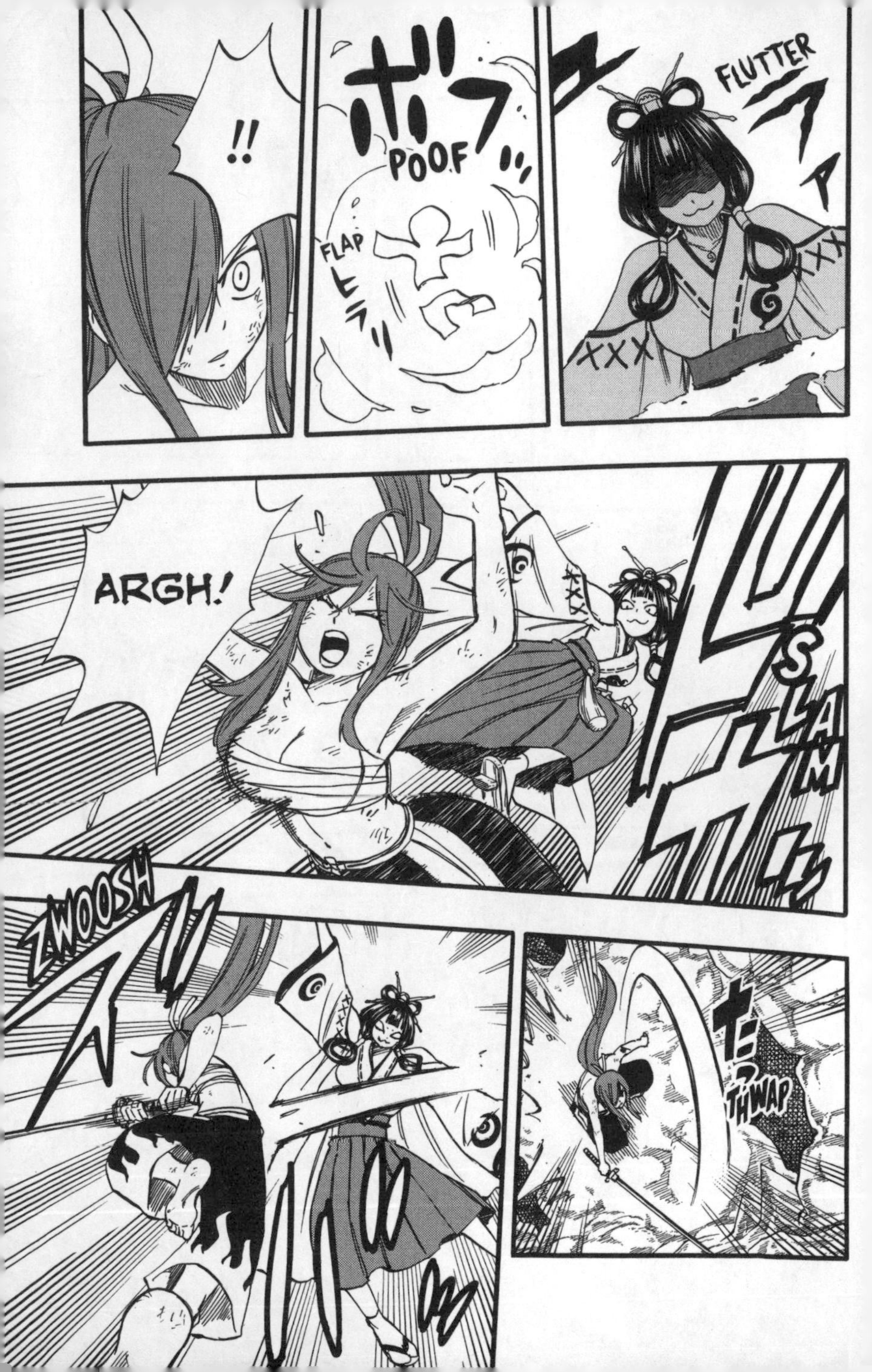
FLUTTER
POOF
FLAP
!!
SLAM
ARGH!
THWAP
ZWOOSH

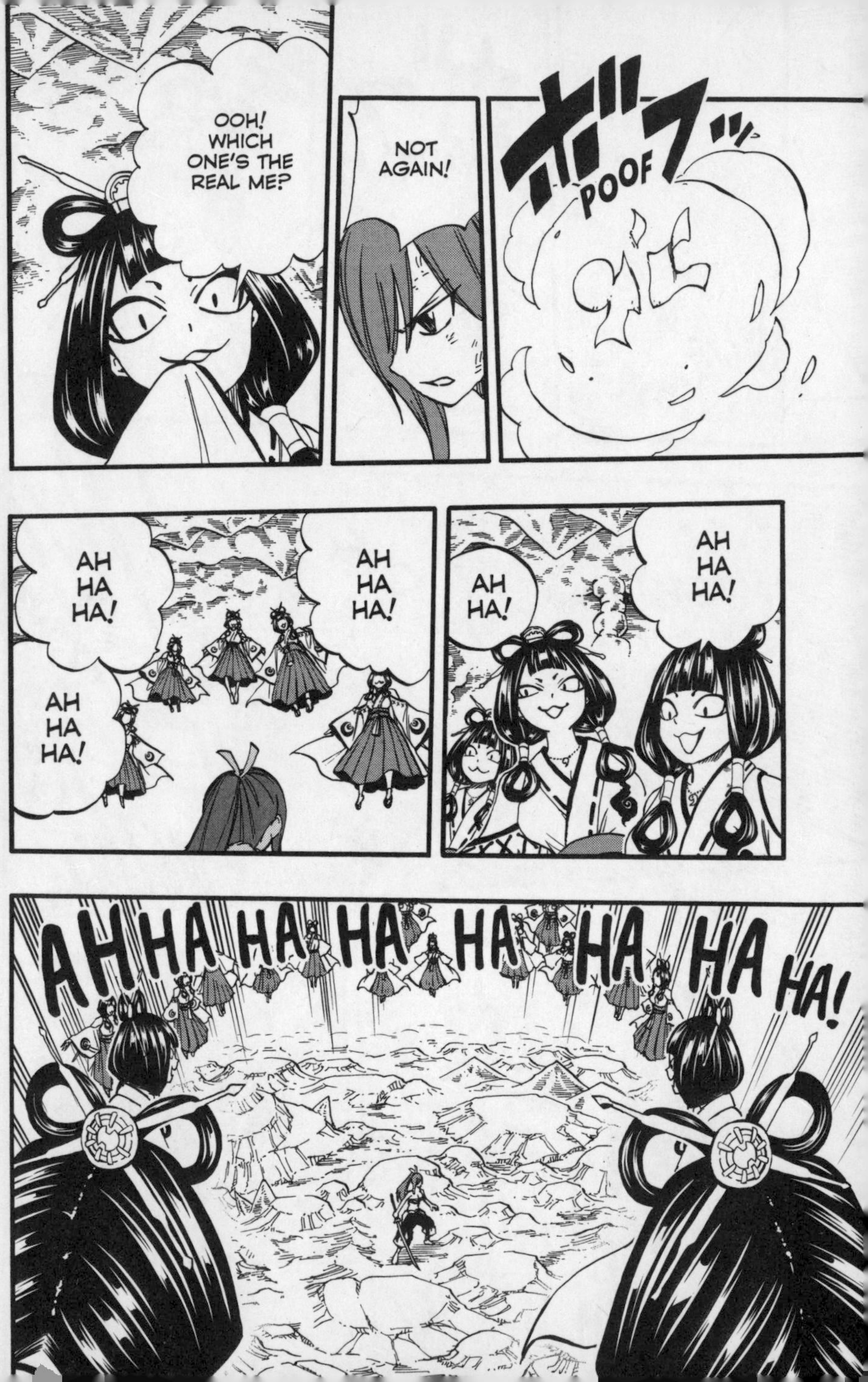
POOF
NOT AGAIN!
OOH! WHICH ONE'S THE REAL ME?
AH HA HA!
AH HA!
AH HA HA!
AH HA HA!
AH HA HA!
AH HA HA HA HA HA HA HA HA!

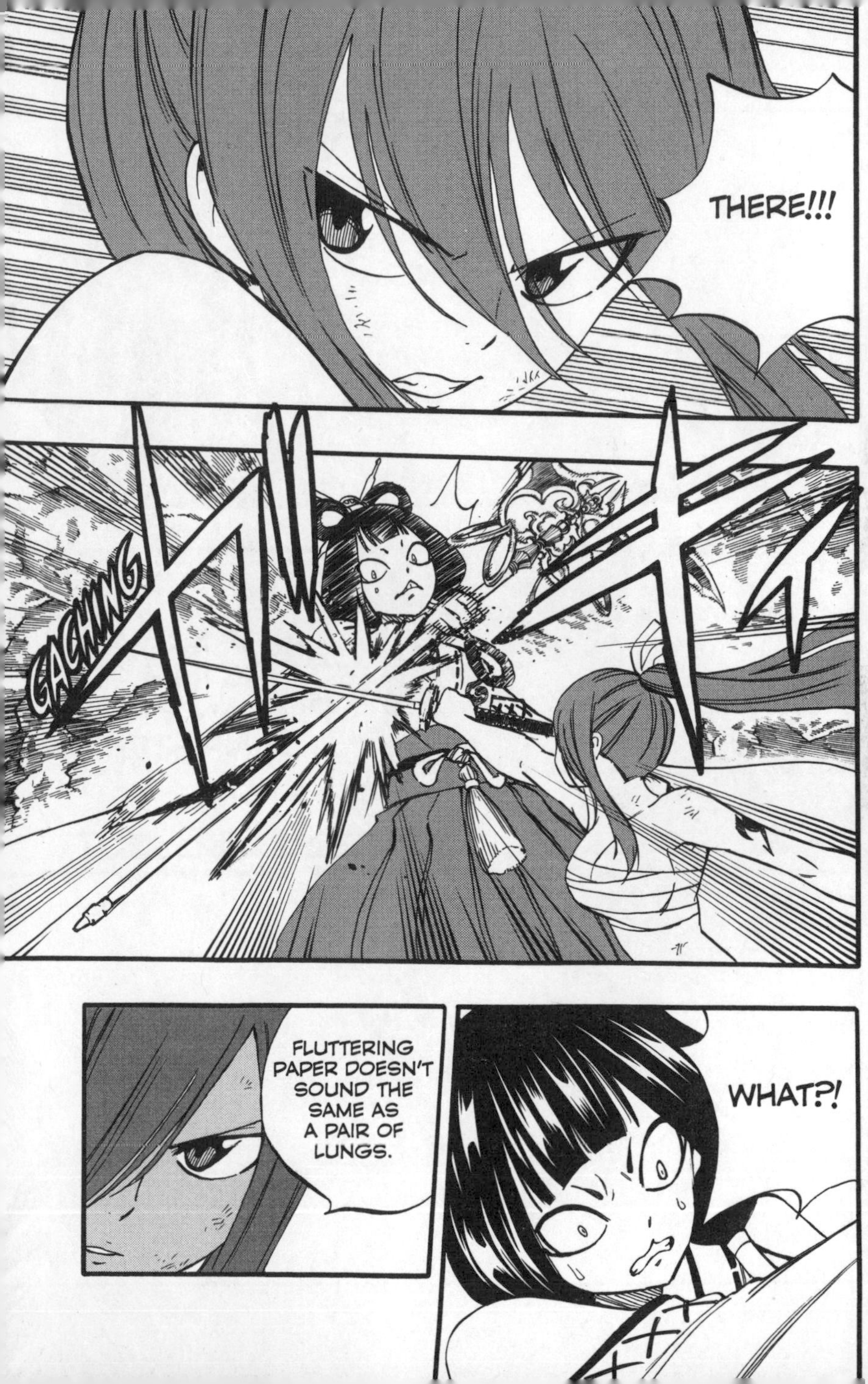
THERE!!!
GACHING
WHAT?!
FLUTTERING PAPER DOESN'T SOUND THE SAME AS A PAIR OF LUNGS.

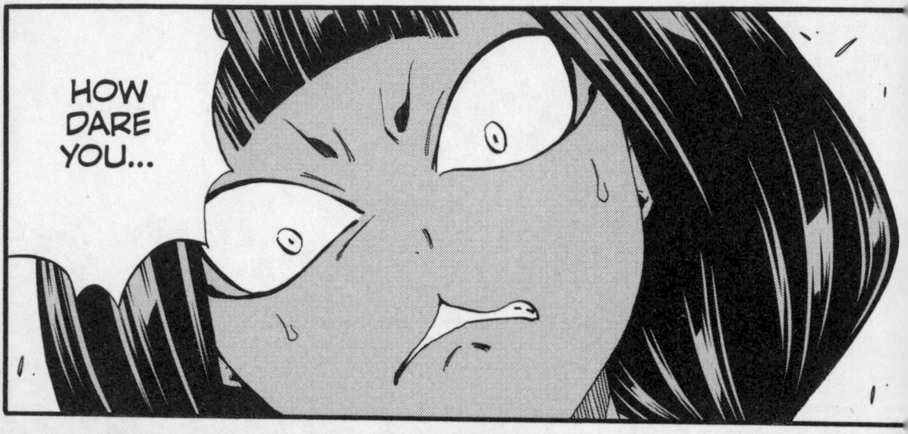
HOW DARE YOU...
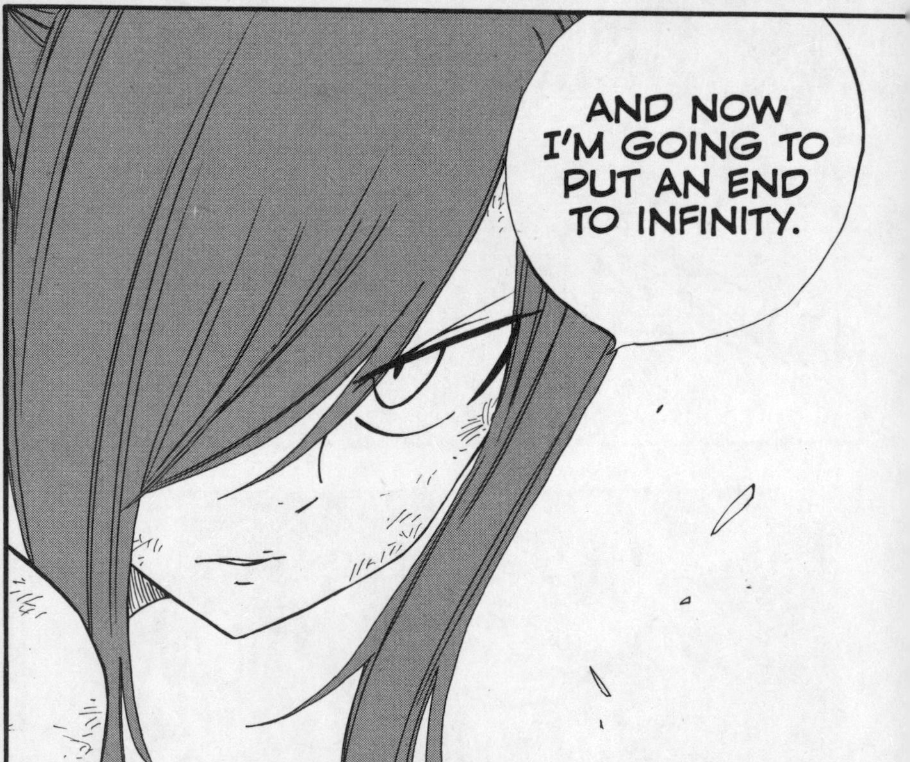
AND NOW I'M GOING TO PUT AN END TO INFINITY.

FAIRY TAIL 100 YEARS QUEST

Chapter 79: The Inhuman Path: Ohmagatoki

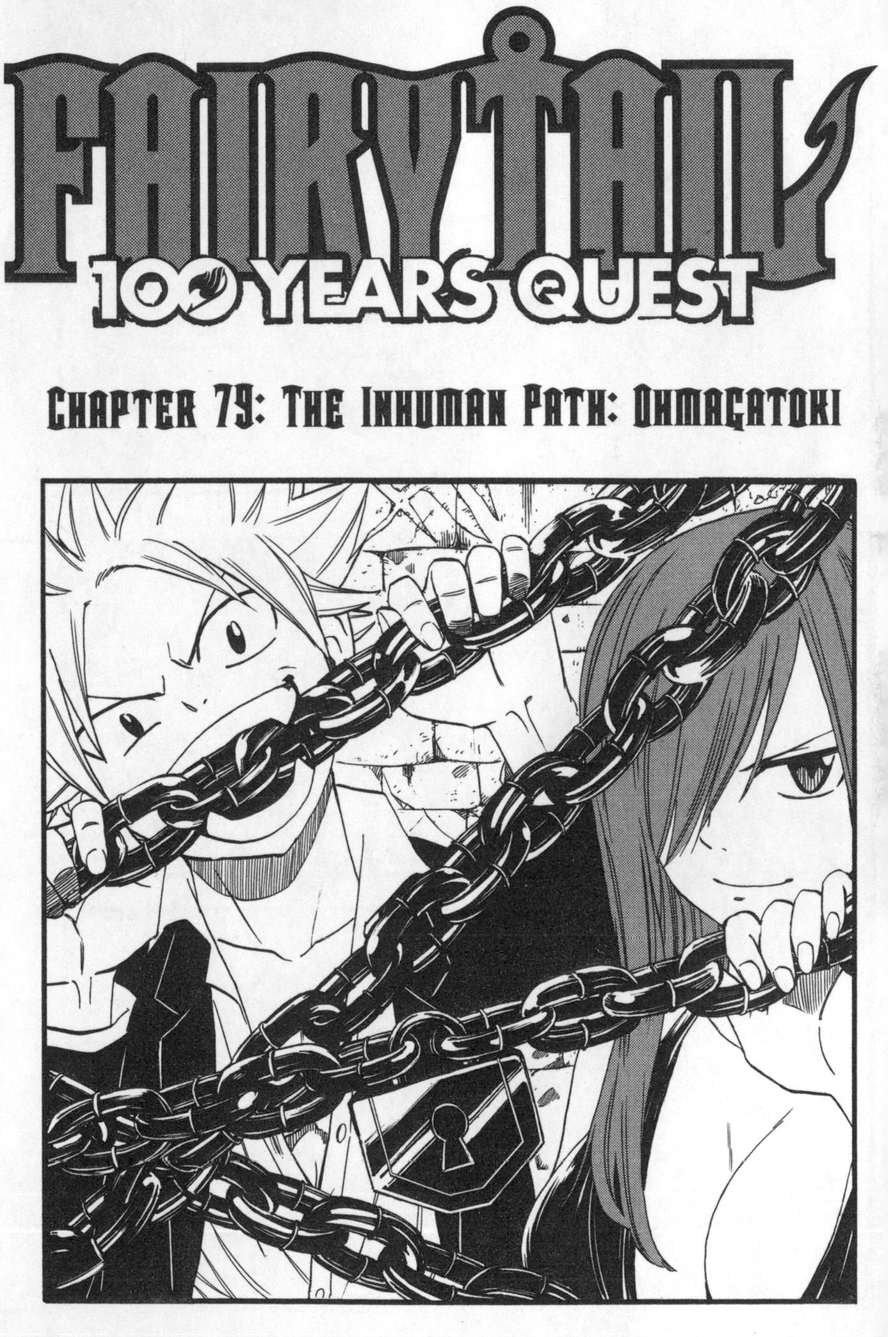

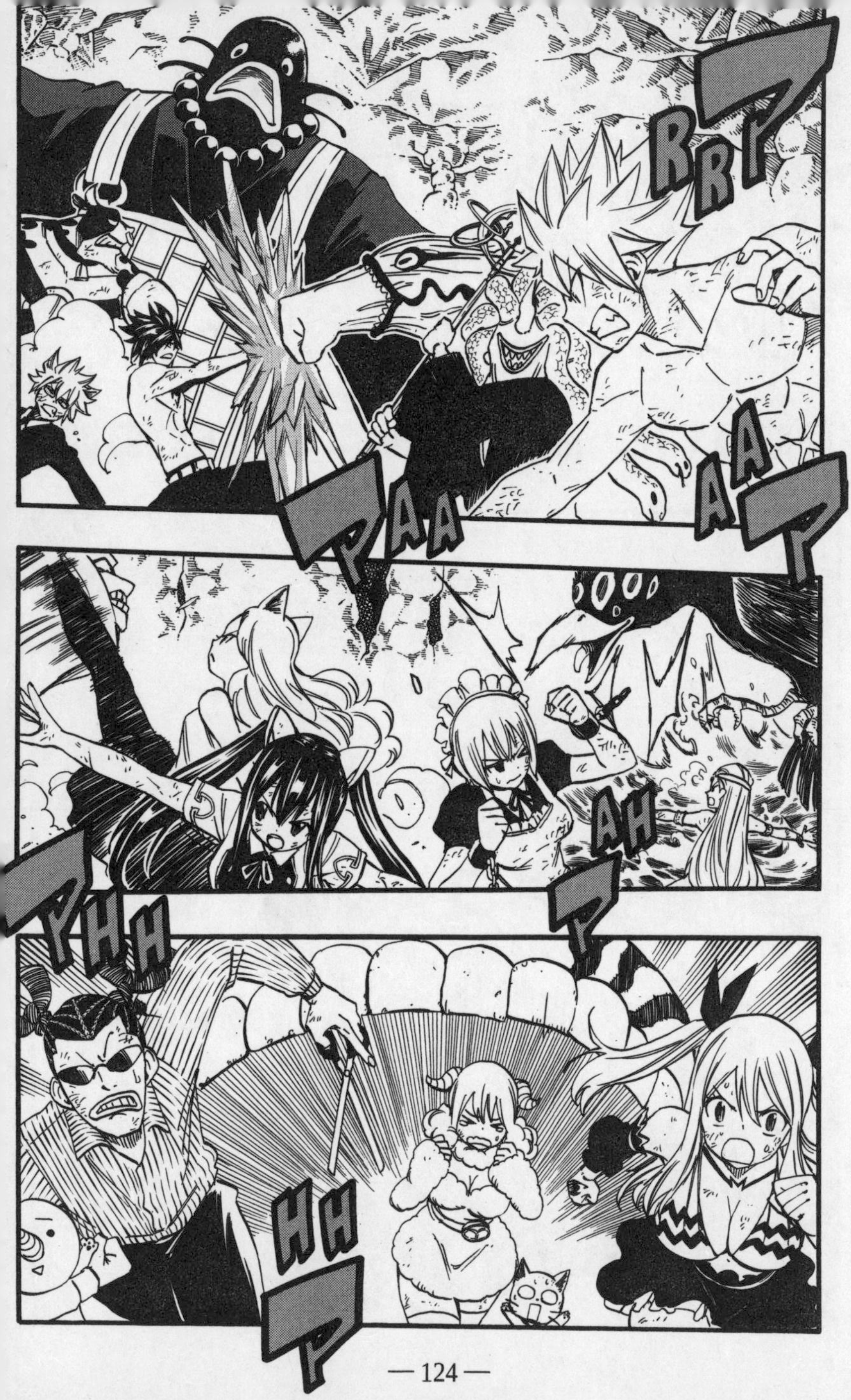
RRR
AA
PAA
AH
PHH
HH
P

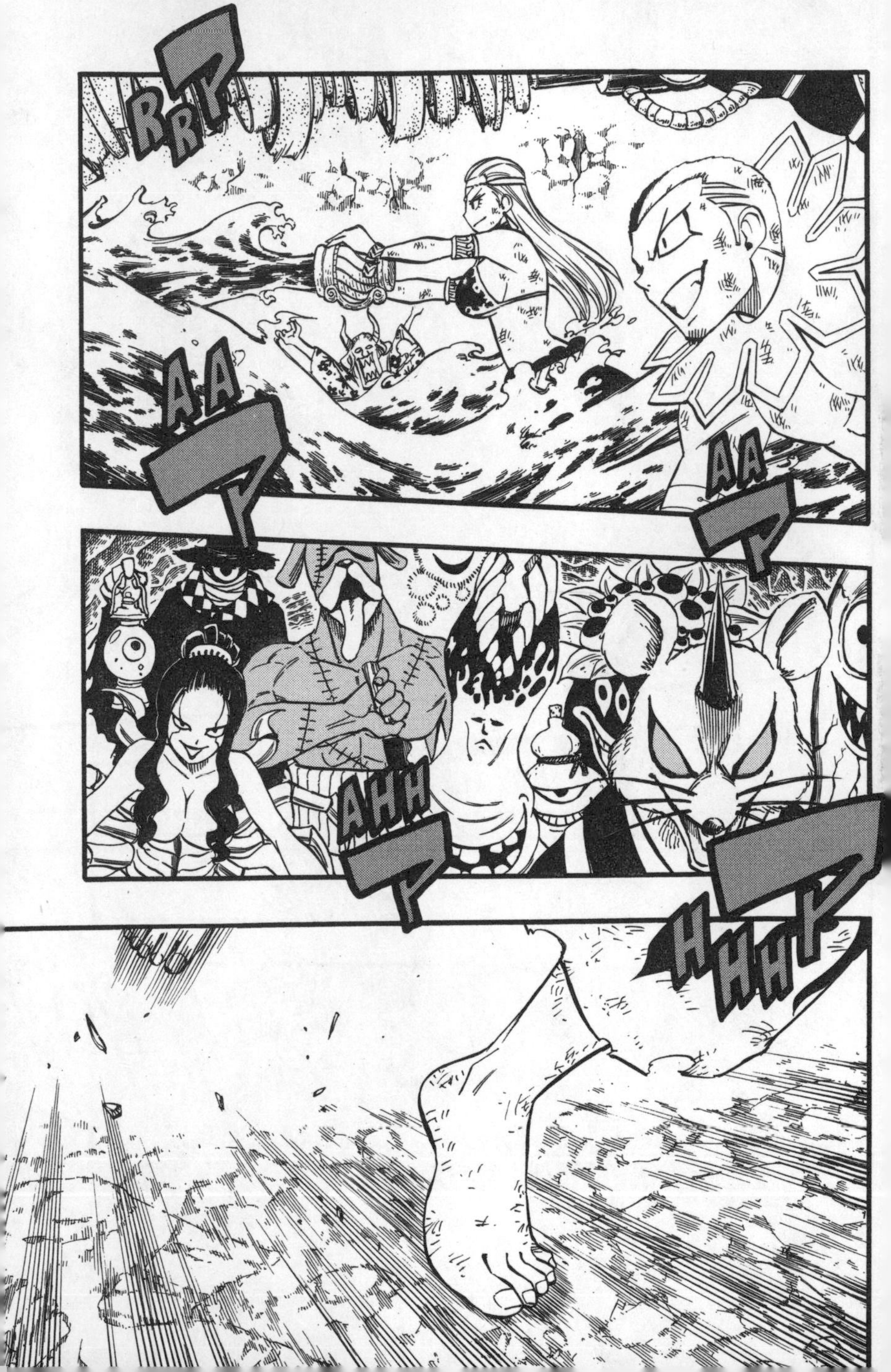
RR
AA
AA
AHH
HHH

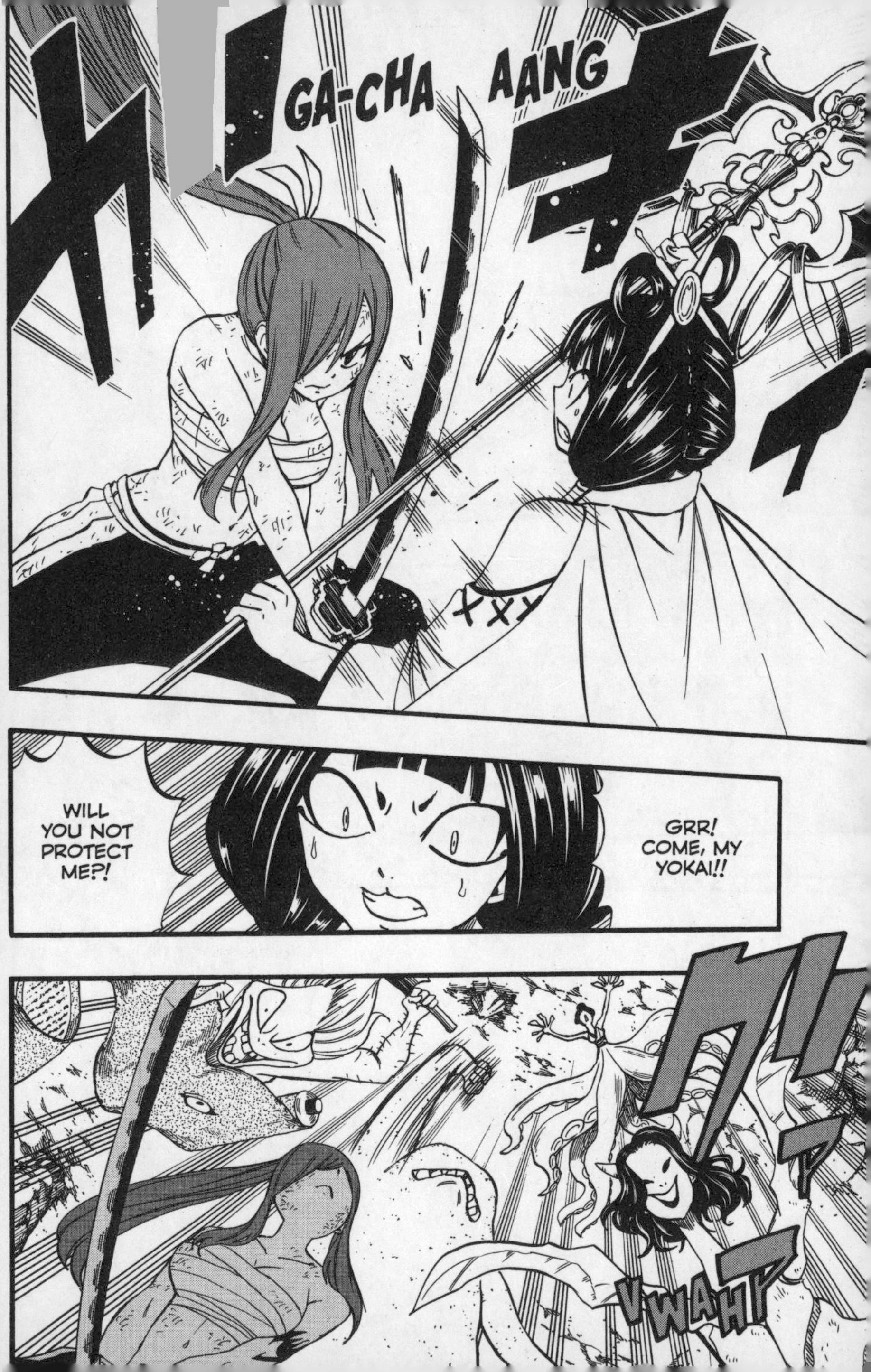
GA-CHA
AANG
GRR! COME, MY YOKAI!!
WILL YOU NOT PROTECT ME?!
VWAHT

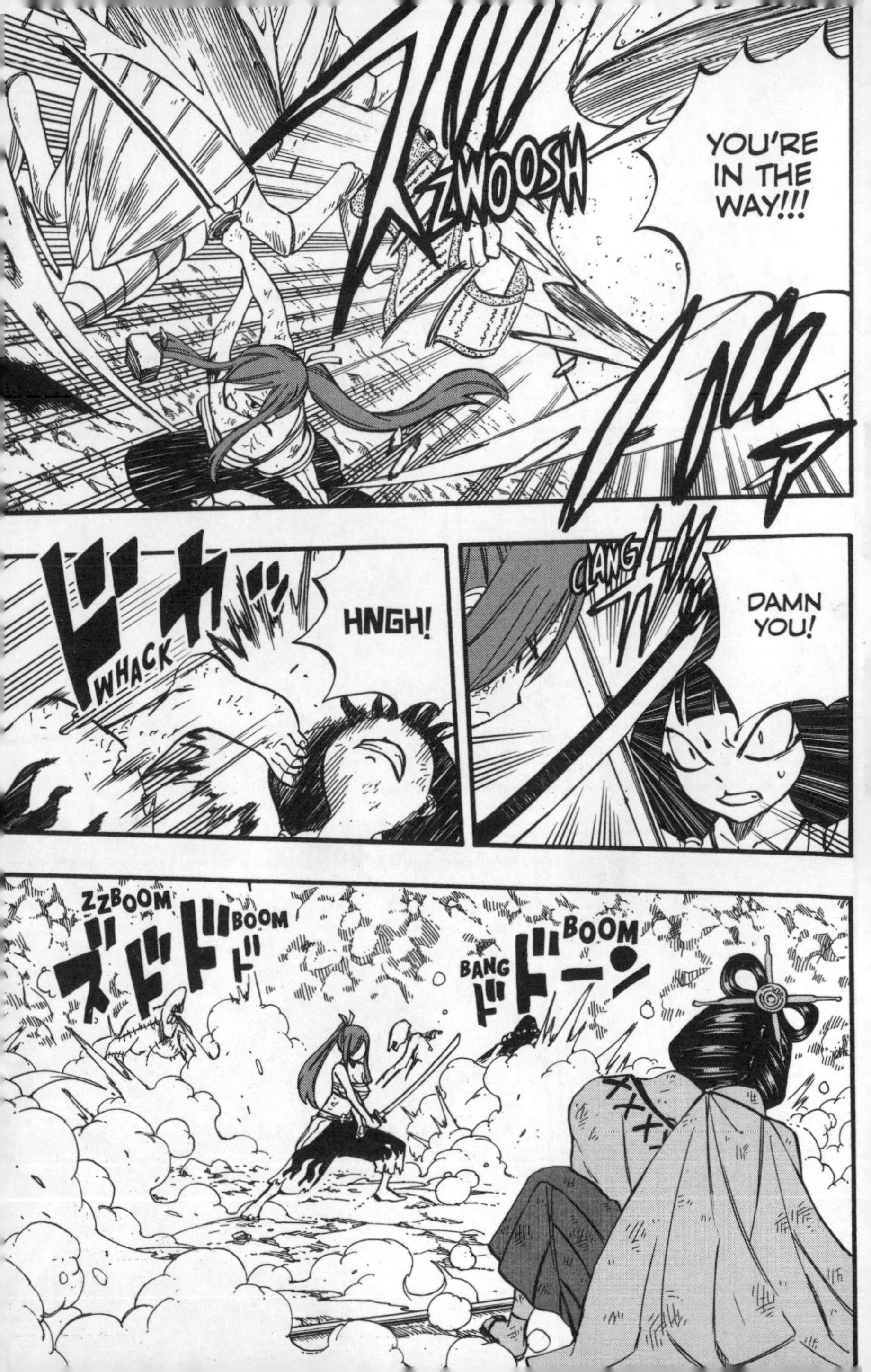
YOU'RE IN THE WAY!!!
ZWOOSH
DAMN YOU!
CLANG
HNGH!
WHACK
BOOM
BANG
ZZBOOM
BOOM

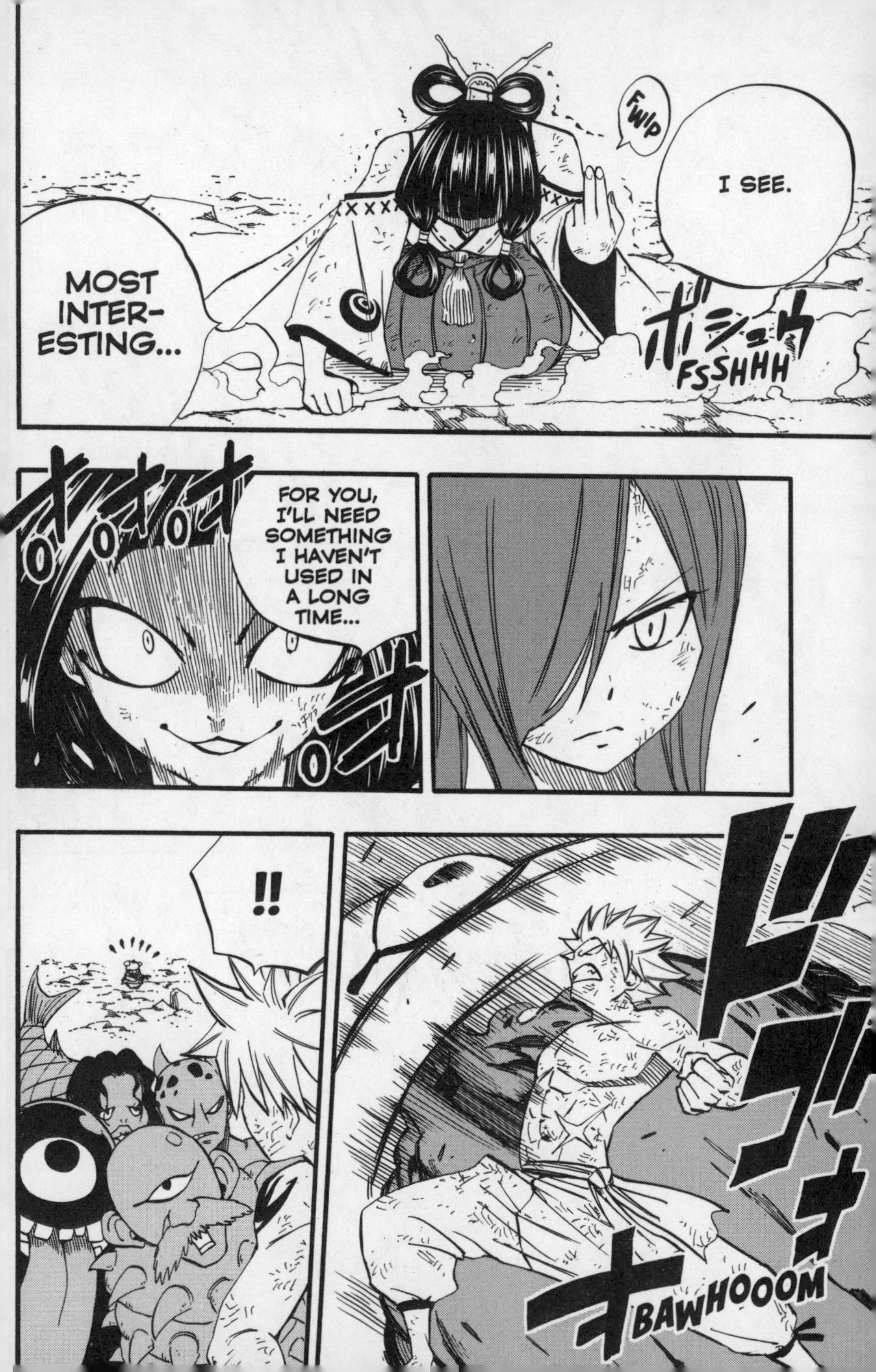
I SEE.
FWIP
FSSHHH
MOST INTER-ESTING...
FOR YOU, I'LL NEED SOMETHING I HAVEN'T USED IN A LONG TIME...
BAWHOOOM
!!

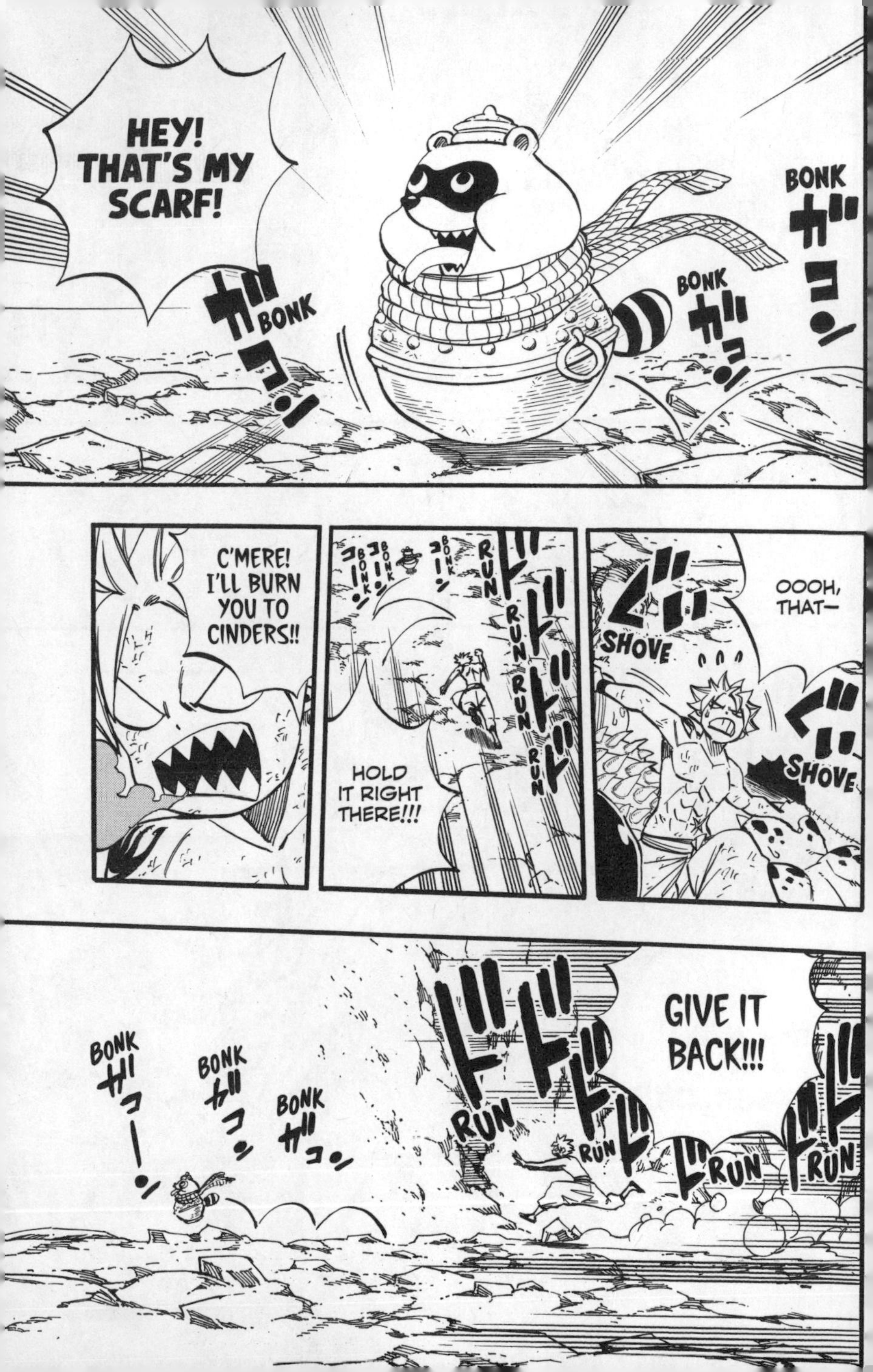
BONK
BONK
HEY! THAT'S MY SCARF!
BONK
OOOH, THAT—
SHOVE
SHOVE
RUN
RUN
RUN
RUN
BONK
BONK
BONK
HOLD IT RIGHT THERE!!!
C'MERE! I'LL BURN YOU TO CINDERS!!
GIVE IT BACK!!!
RUN
RUN
RUN
RUN
BONK
BONK
BONK

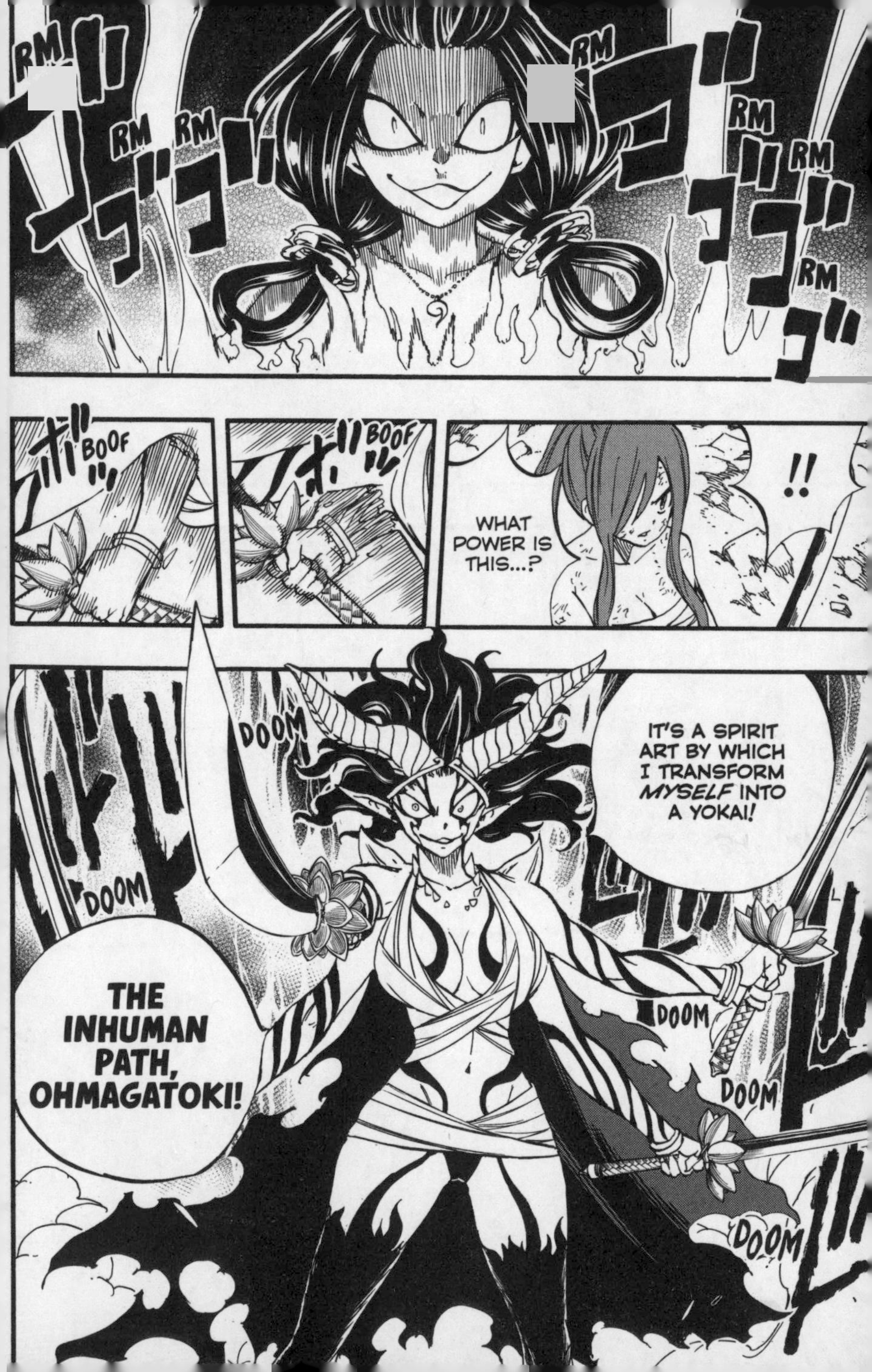

RM
RM
RM
RM
RM
RM
RM
!!
WHAT POWER IS THIS...?
BOOF
BOOF
IT'S A SPIRIT ART BY WHICH I TRANSFORM *MYSELF* INTO A YOKAI!
DOOM
DOOM
DOOM
DOOM
DOOM
DOOM
THE INHUMAN PATH, OHMAGATOKI!

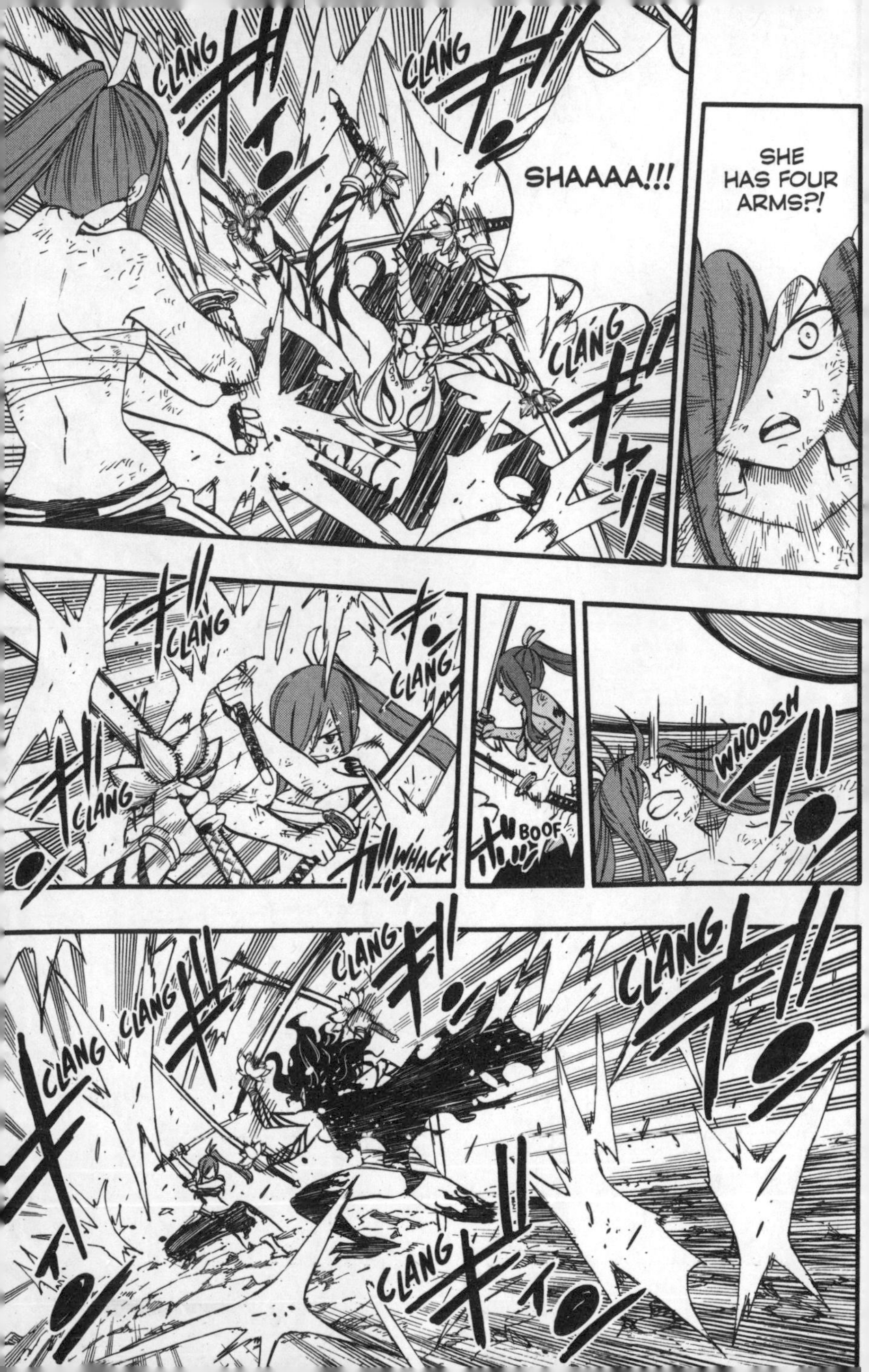

SHE HAS FOUR ARMS?!
CLANG
CLANG
SHAAAA!!!
CLANG
WHOOSH
BOOF
CLANG
CLANG
CLANG
WHACK
CLANG
CLANG
CLANG
CLANG
CLANG
CLANG

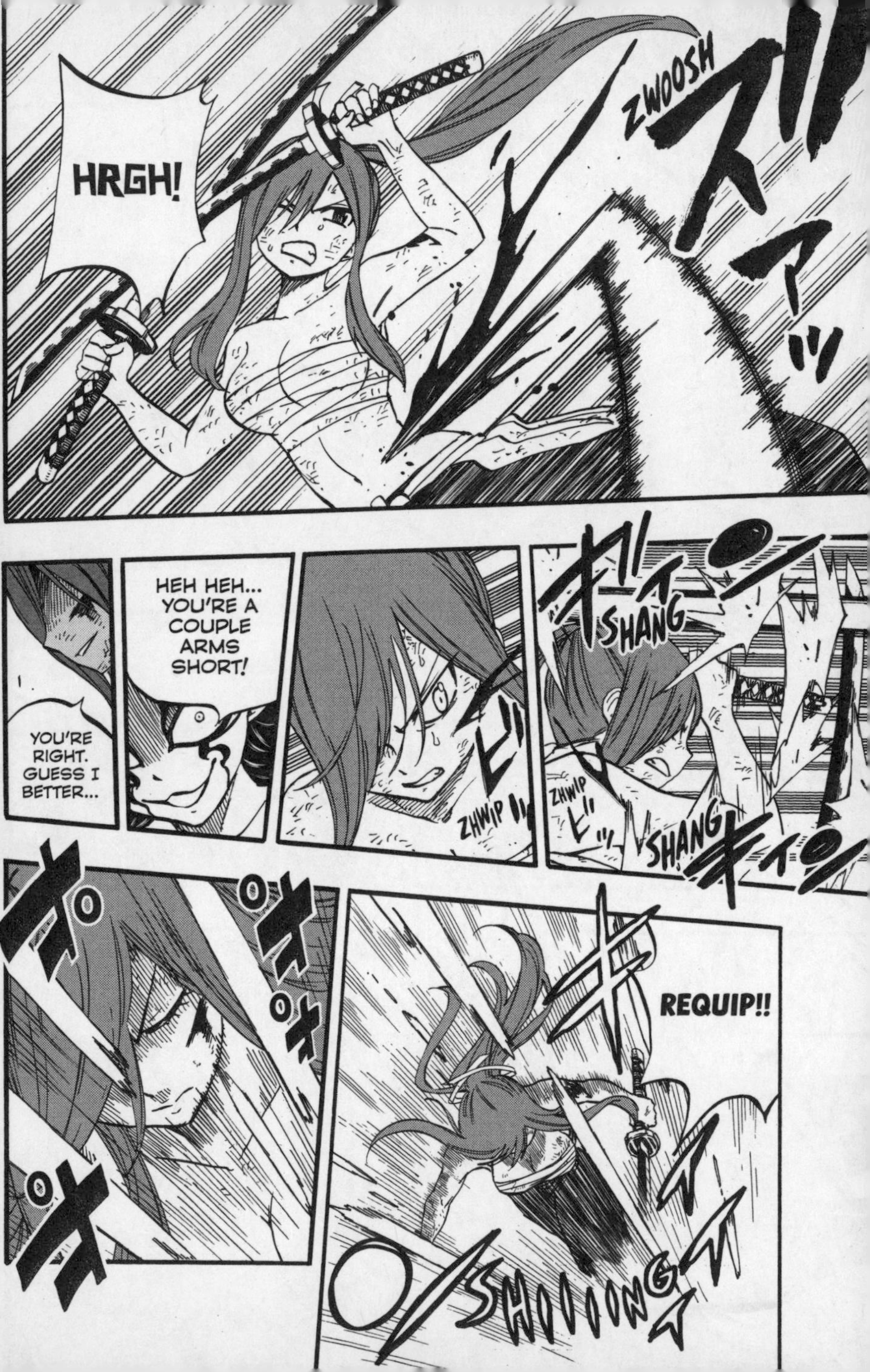
HRGH!
ZWOOSH
SHANG
ZHWIP
SHANG
ZHWIP
HEH HEH... YOU'RE A COUPLE ARMS SHORT!
YOU'RE RIGHT. GUESS I BETTER...
REQUIP!!
SHIIIING

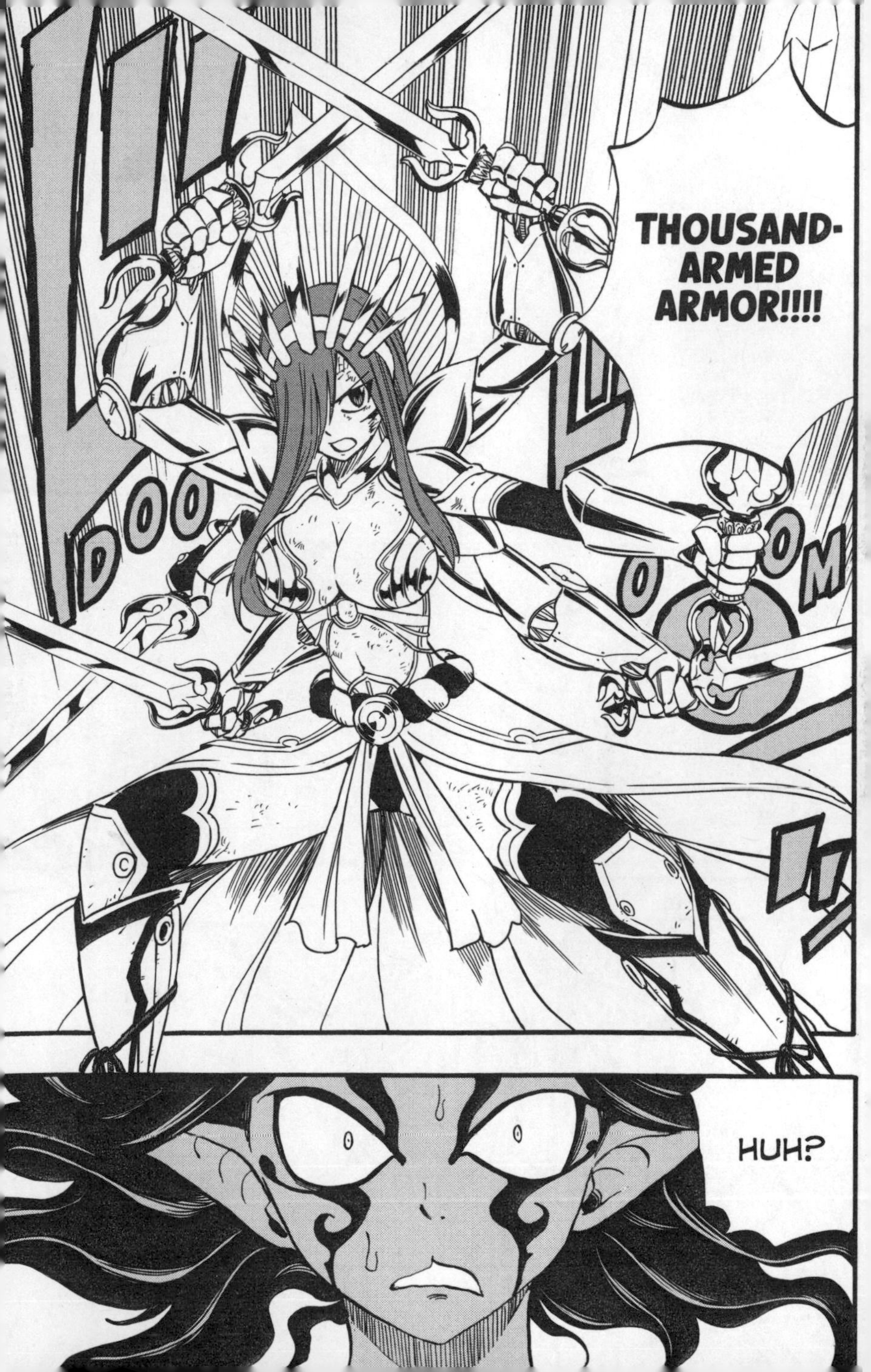
THOUSAND-ARMED ARMOR!!!!
DOOOOM
HUH?

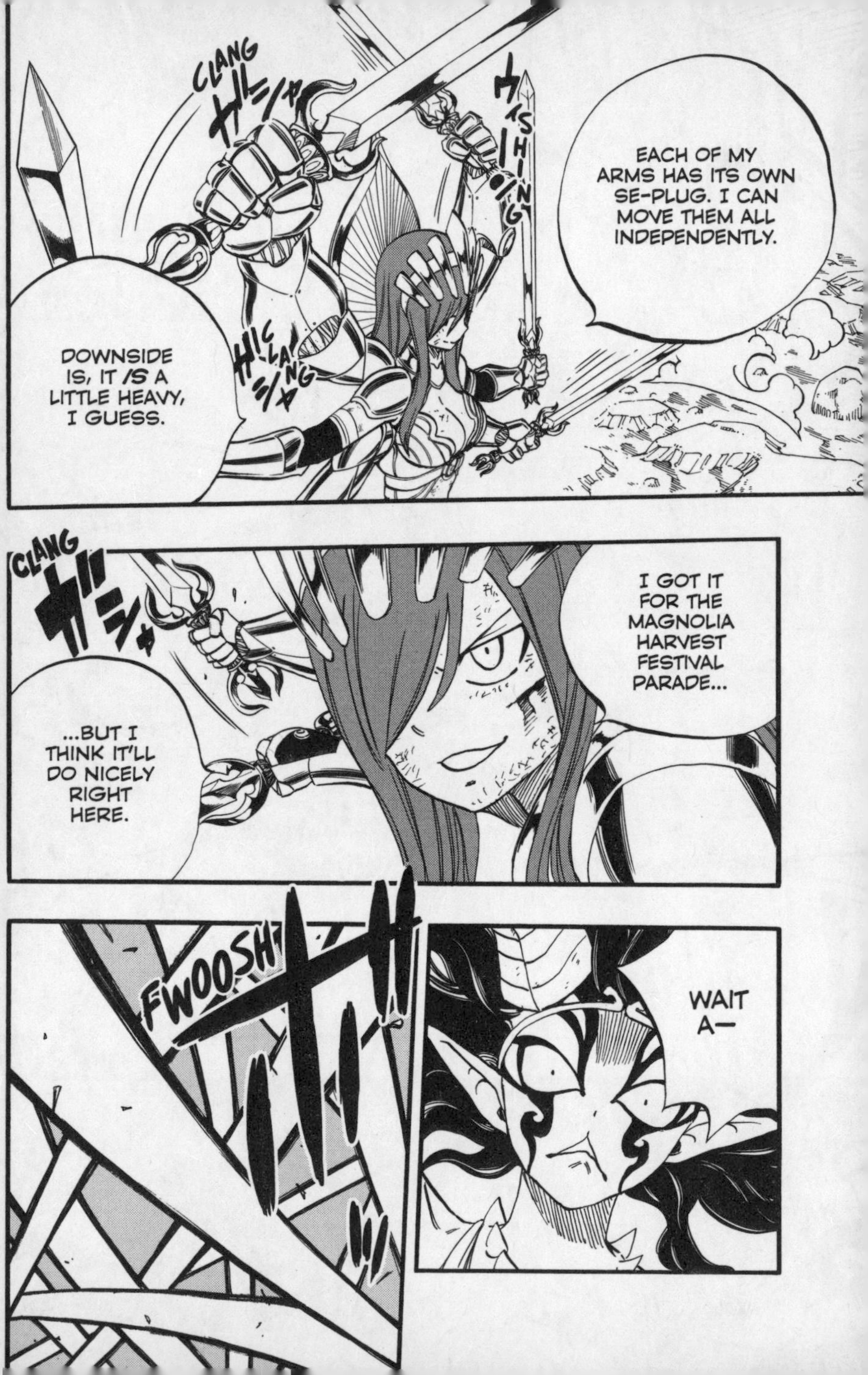
EACH OF MY ARMS HAS ITS OWN SE-PLUG. I CAN MOVE THEM ALL INDEPENDENTLY.
SHING
CLANG
CLANG
DOWNSIDE IS, IT IS A LITTLE HEAVY, I GUESS.
I GOT IT FOR THE MAGNOLIA HARVEST FESTIVAL PARADE...
CLANG
...BUT I THINK IT'LL DO NICELY RIGHT HERE.
WAIT A—
FWOOSH

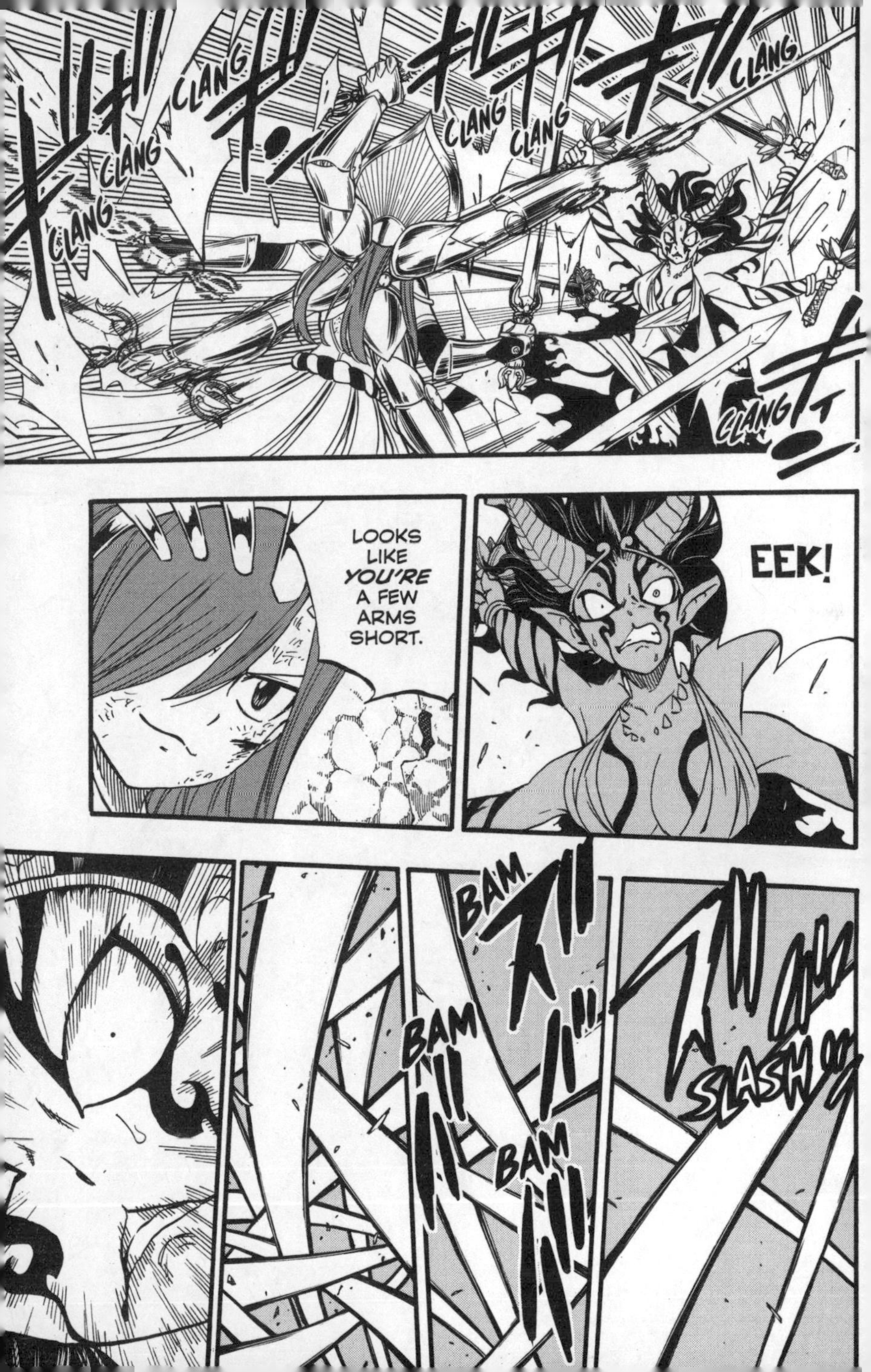
CLANG
CLANG
CLANG
CLANG
CLANG
CLANG
CLANG
EEK!
LOOKS LIKE *YOU'RE* A FEW ARMS SHORT.
SLASH
BAM
BAM
BAM

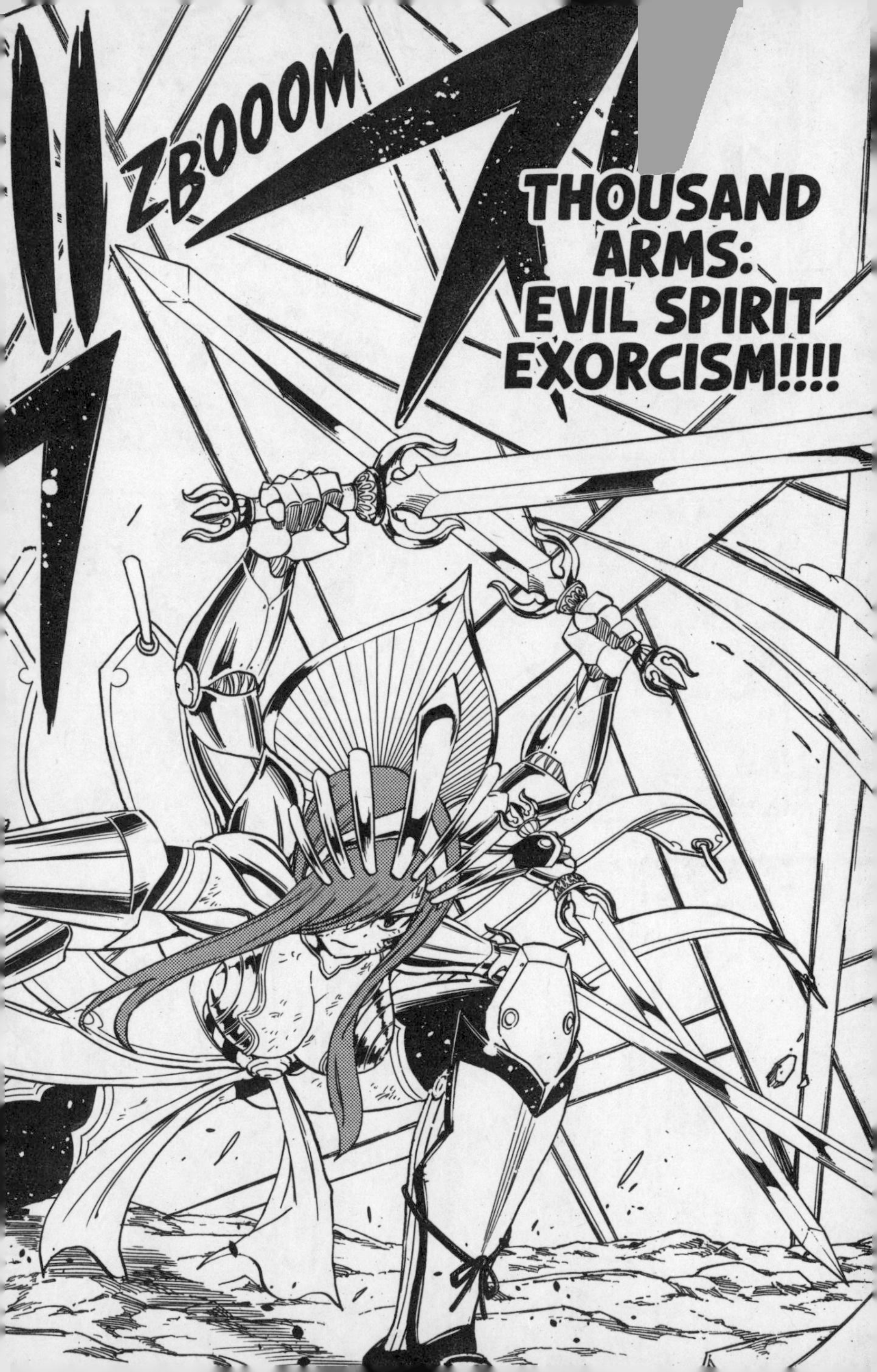
ZBOOOM
THOUSAND ARMS: EVIL SPIRIT EXORCISM!!!!

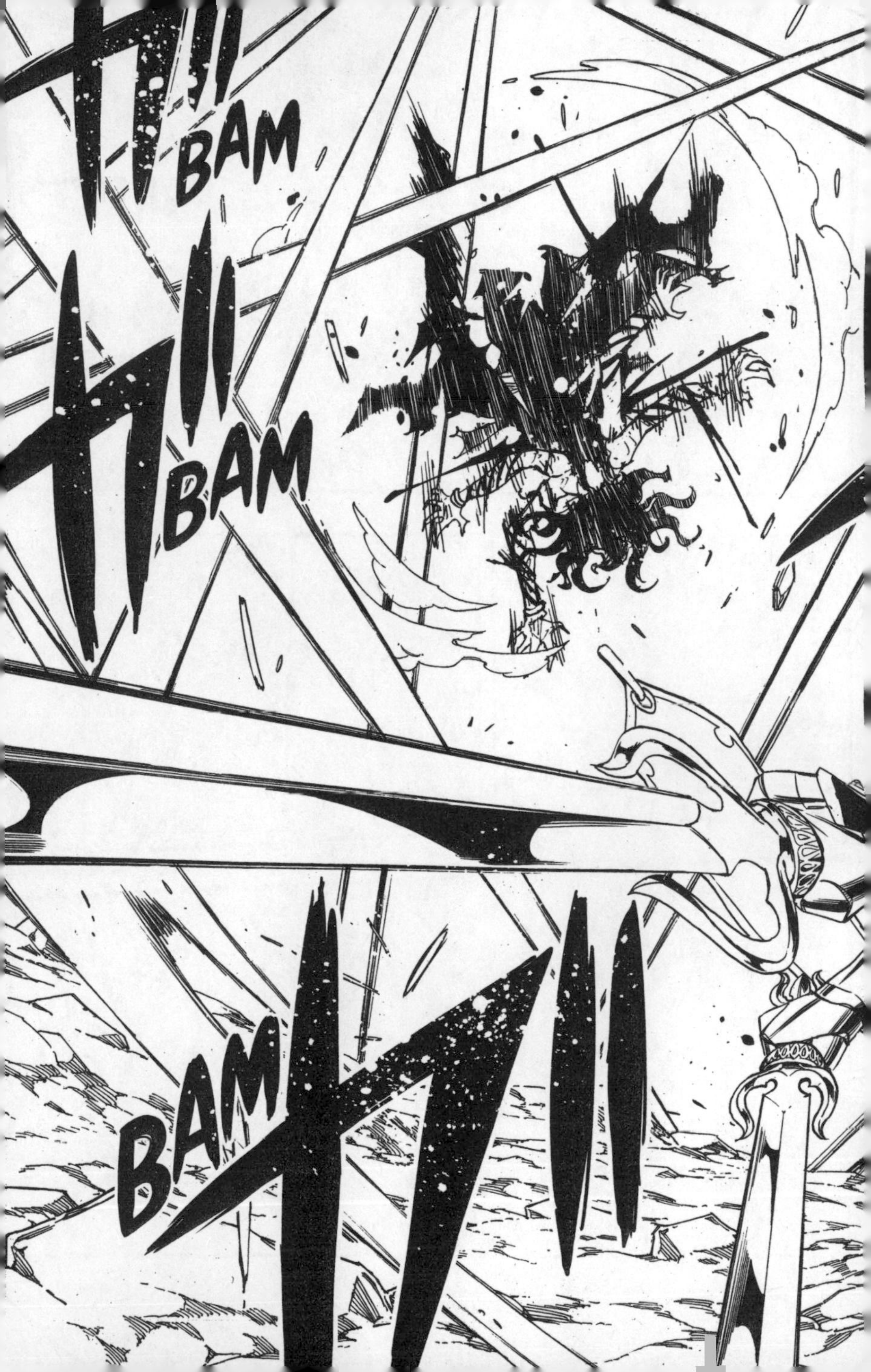
BAM
BAM
BAM

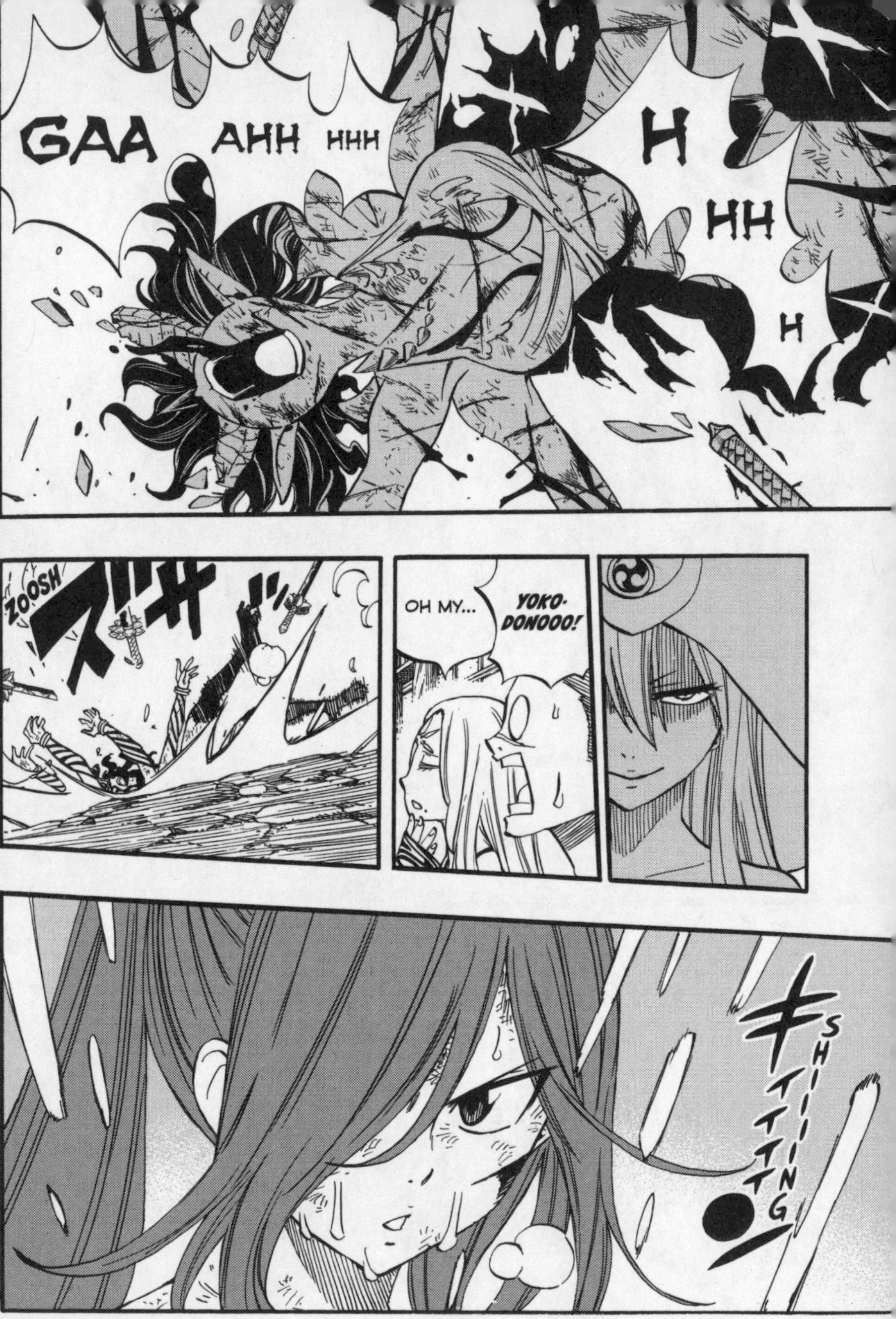
GAA AHH HHH H HH H
YOKO-DONOOO!
OH MY...
ZOOSH
SHIIIING

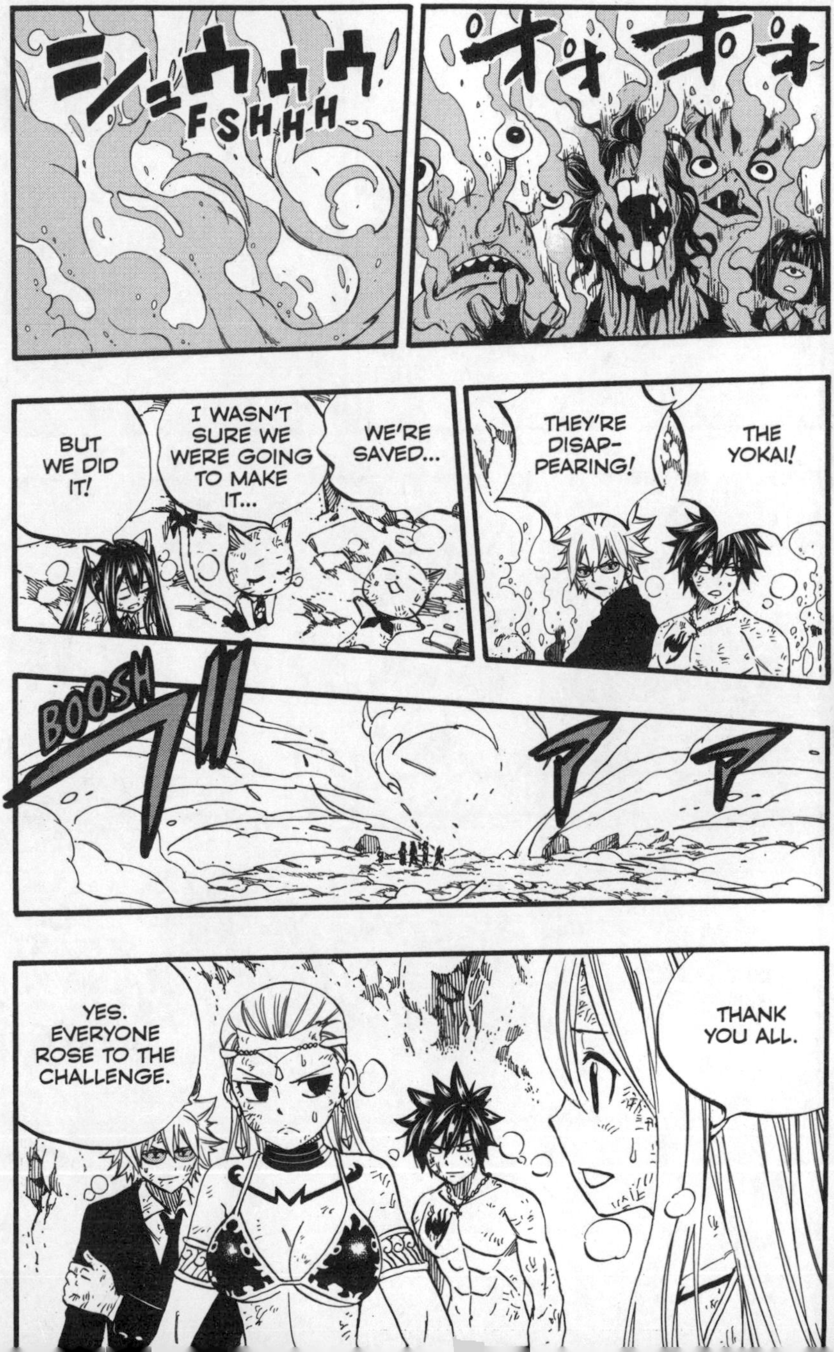
FSHHH
THE YOKAI!
THEY'RE DISAPPEARING!
WE'RE SAVED...
I WASN'T SURE WE WERE GOING TO MAKE IT...
BUT WE DID IT!
BOOSH
THANK YOU ALL.
YES. EVERYONE ROSE TO THE CHALLENGE.

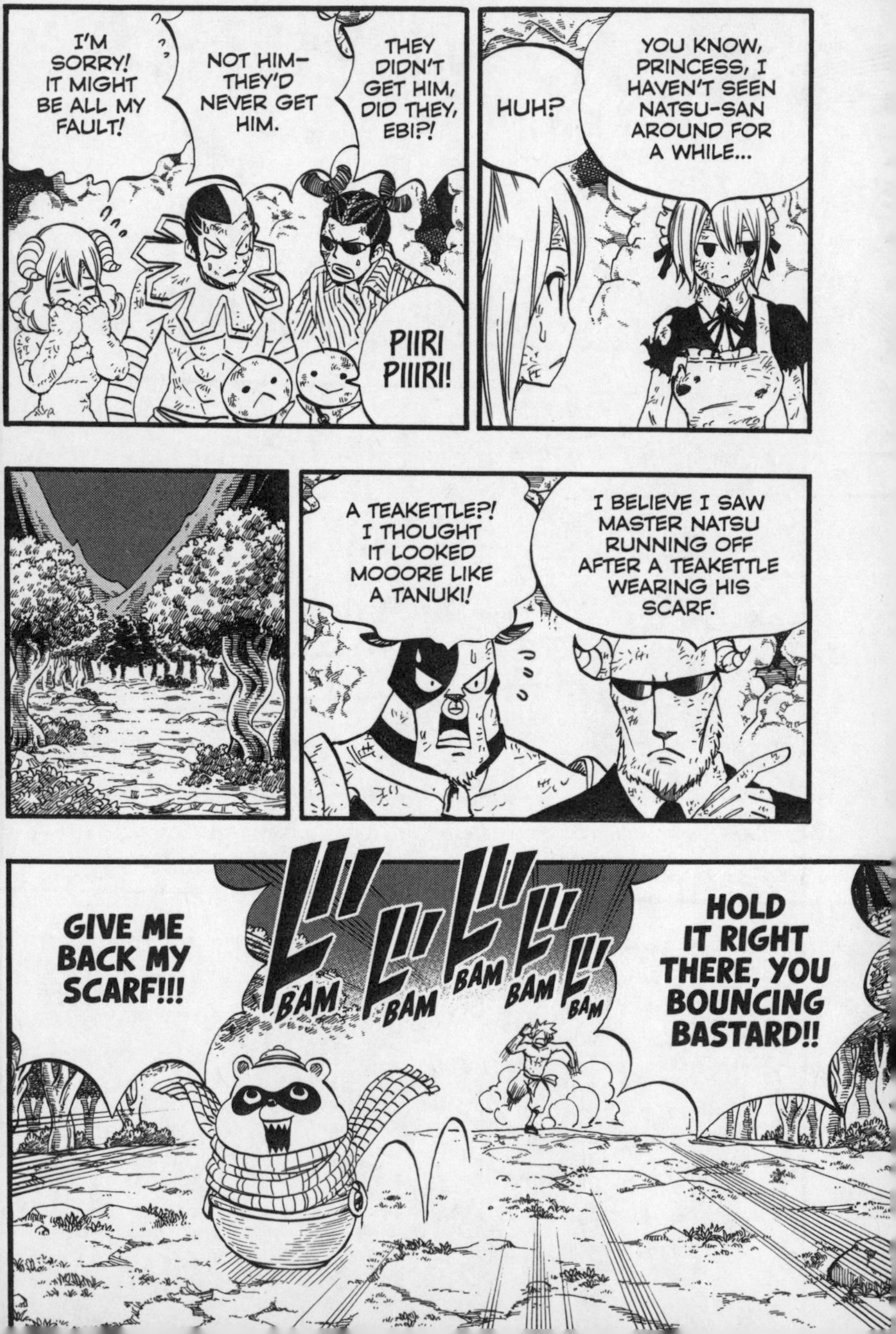
YOU KNOW, PRINCESS, I HAVEN'T SEEN NATSU-SAN AROUND FOR A WHILE...
HUH?
THEY DIDN'T GET HIM, DID THEY, EBI?!
NOT HIM— THEY'D NEVER GET HIM.
I'M SORRY! IT MIGHT BE ALL MY FAULT!
PIIRI PIIIRI!
I BELIEVE I SAW MASTER NATSU RUNNING OFF AFTER A TEAKETTLE WEARING HIS SCARF.
A TEAKETTLE?! I THOUGHT IT LOOKED MOOORE LIKE A TANUKI!
HOLD IT RIGHT THERE, YOU BOUNCING BASTARD!!
BAM BAM BAM BAM BAM
GIVE ME BACK MY SCARF!!!

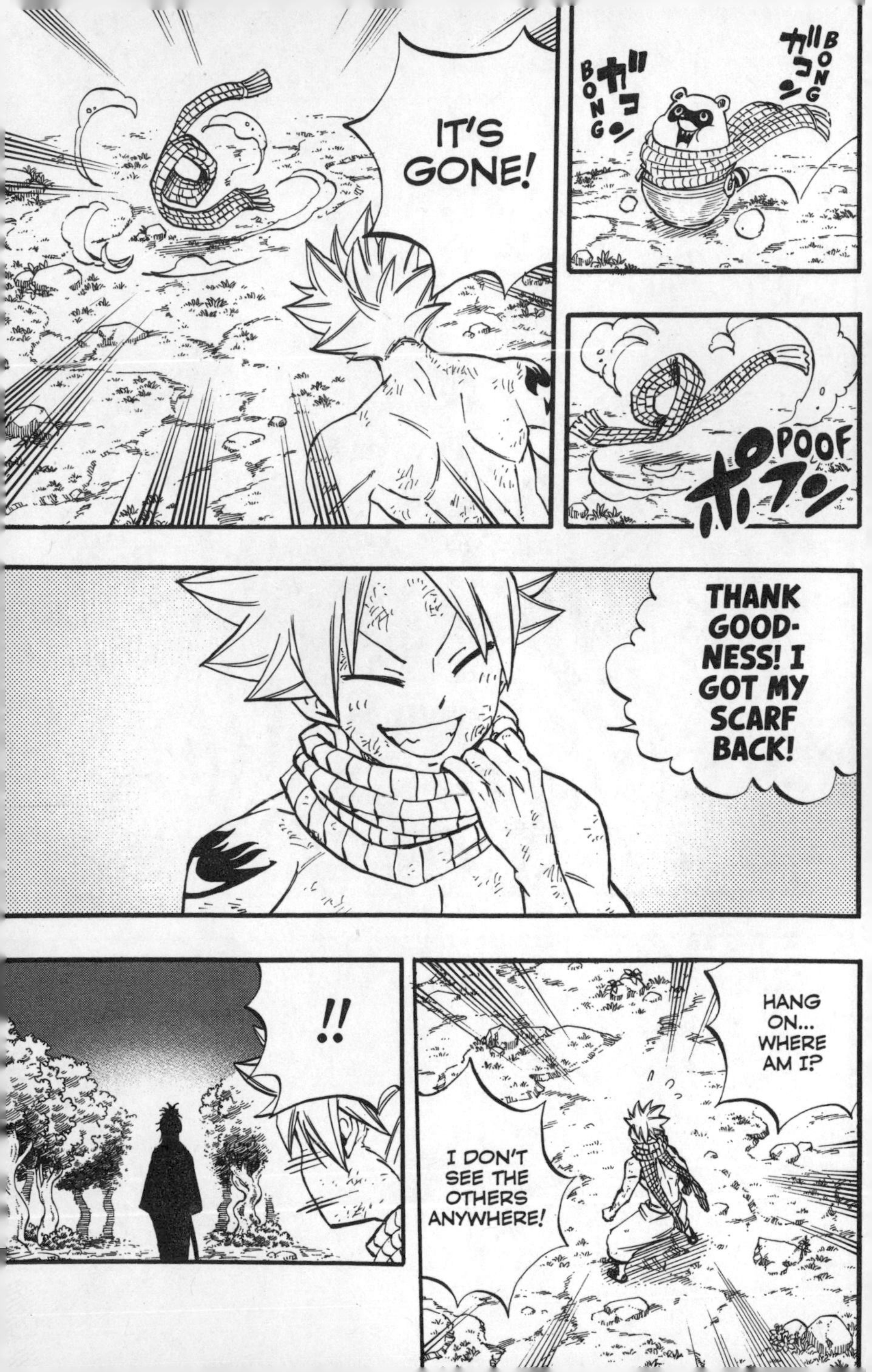

BONG
ガコン
BONG
ガコン
POOF
ポフン
IT'S GONE!
THANK GOOD-NESS! I GOT MY SCARF BACK!
HANG ON... WHERE AM I?
I DON'T SEE THE OTHERS ANYWHERE!
!!

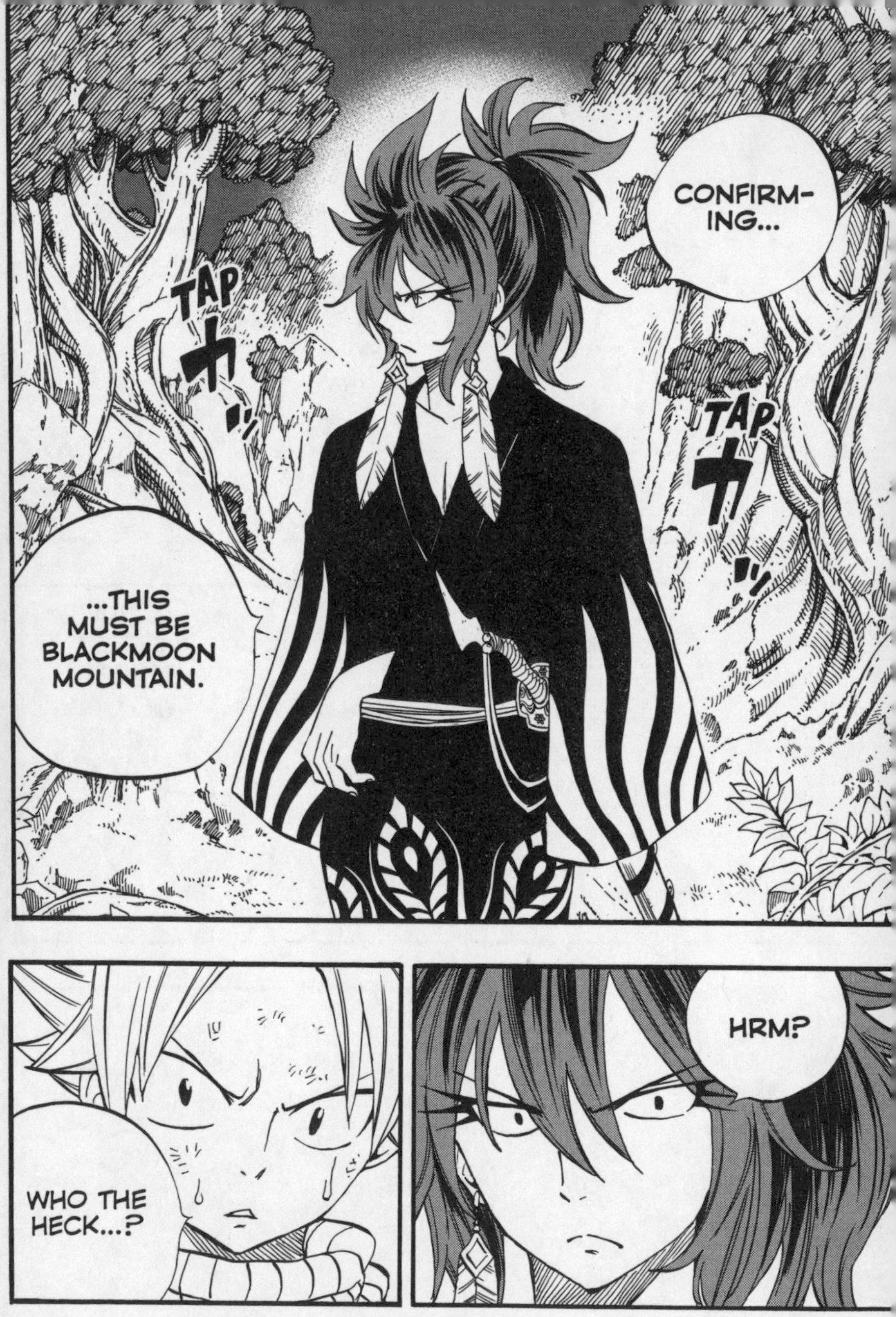
CONFIRMING-
ING...
TAP
TAP
...THIS MUST BE BLACKMOON MOUNTAIN.
HRM?
WHO THE HECK...?

FAIRY TAIL 100 YEARS QUEST

Chapter 80: Suzaku

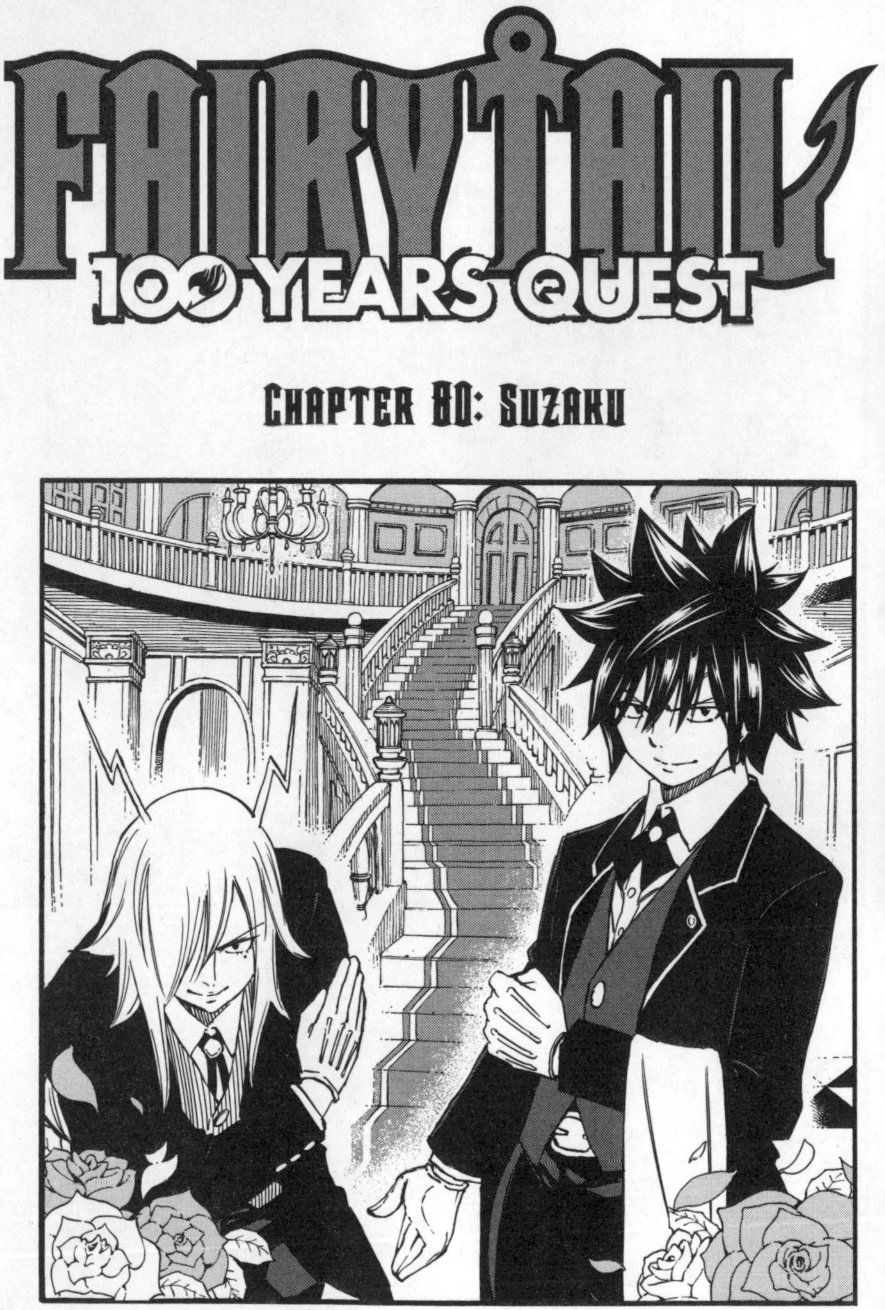

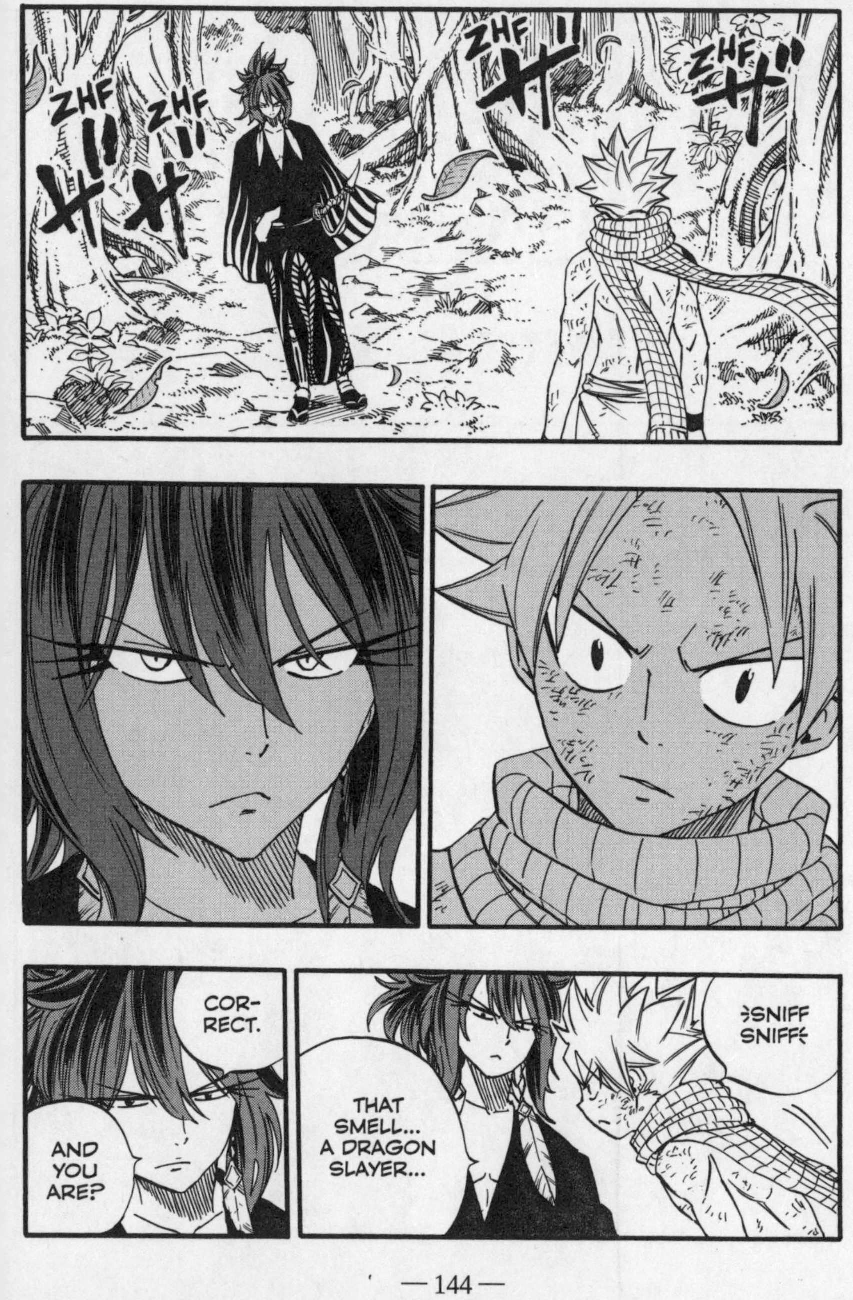
ZHF
ZHF
ZHF
ZHF
⁝SNIFF SNIFF⁝
THAT SMELL... A DRAGON SLAYER...
COR-RECT.
AND YOU ARE?

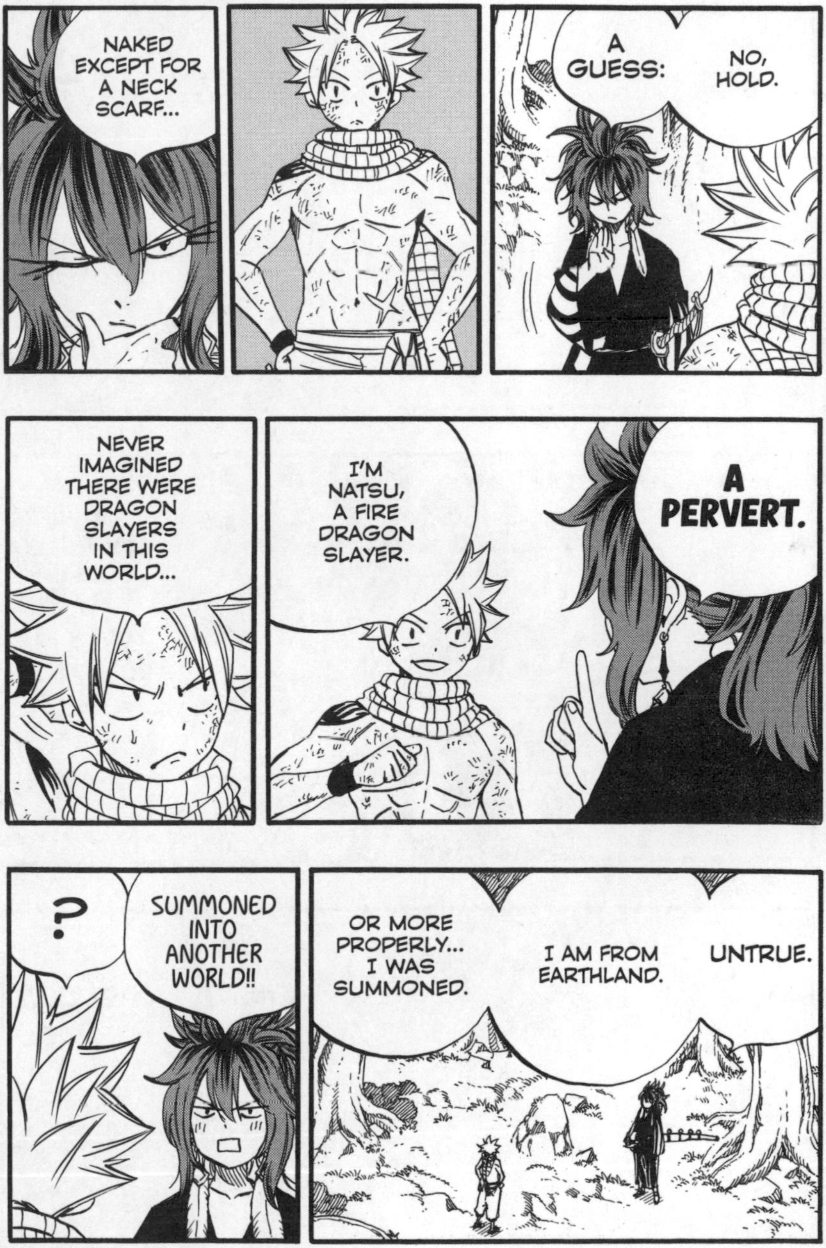
NO, HOLD.
A GUESS:
NAKED EXCEPT FOR A NECK SCARF...
A PERVERT.
I'M NATSU, A FIRE DRAGON SLAYER.
NEVER IMAGINED THERE WERE DRAGON SLAYERS IN THIS WORLD...
UNTRUE.
I AM FROM EARTHLAND.
OR MORE PROPERLY... I WAS SUMMONED.
SUMMONED INTO ANOTHER WORLD!!
?

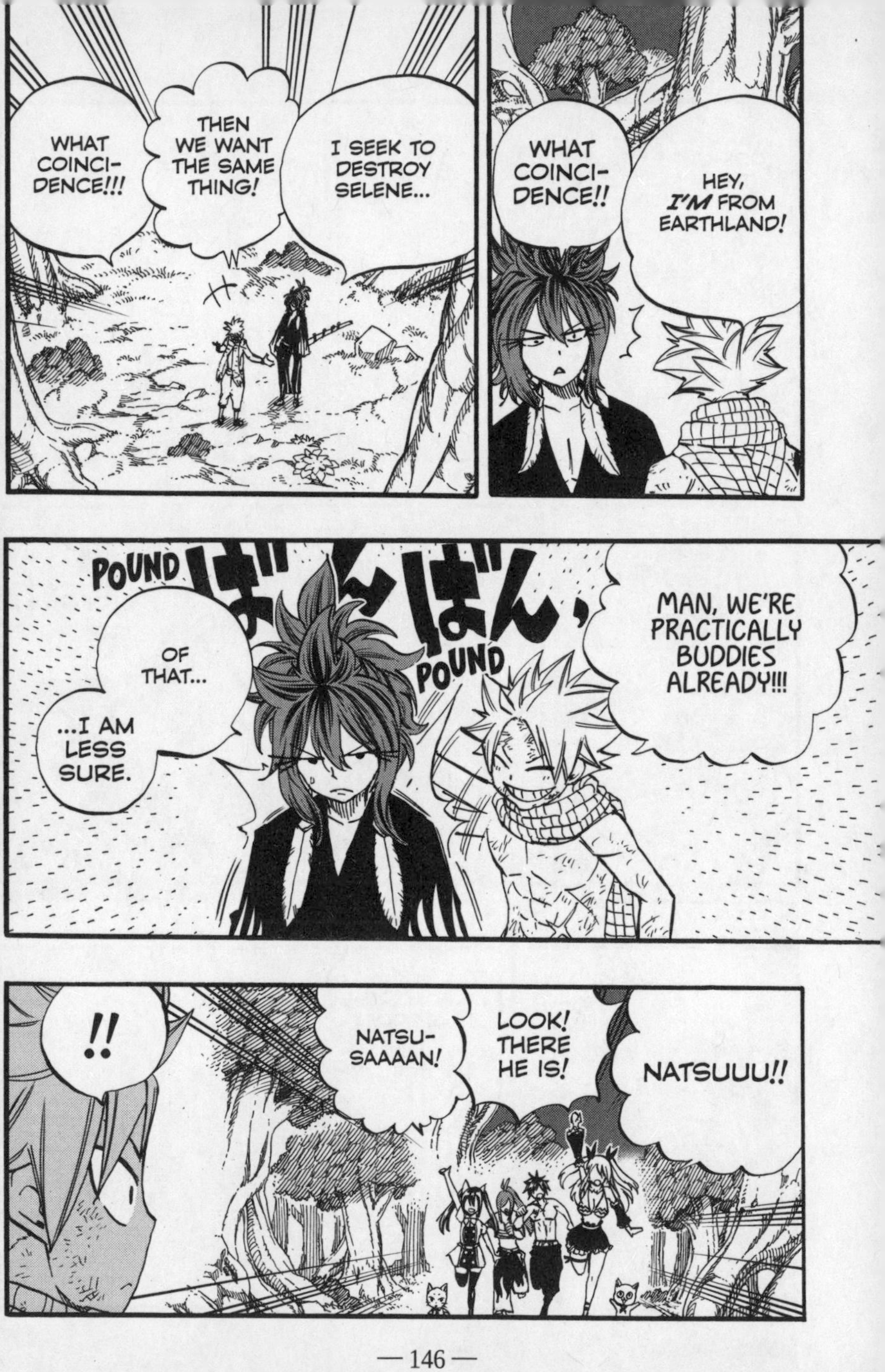
HEY, *I'M* FROM EARTHLAND!
WHAT COINCI-DENCE!!
I SEEK TO DESTROY SELENE...
THEN WE WANT THE SAME THING!
WHAT COINCI-DENCE!!!
MAN, WE'RE PRACTICALLY BUDDIES ALREADY!!!
POUND
POUND
ばんばん,
OF THAT...
...I AM LESS SURE.
NATSUUU!!
LOOK! THERE HE IS!
NATSU-SAAAAN!
!!

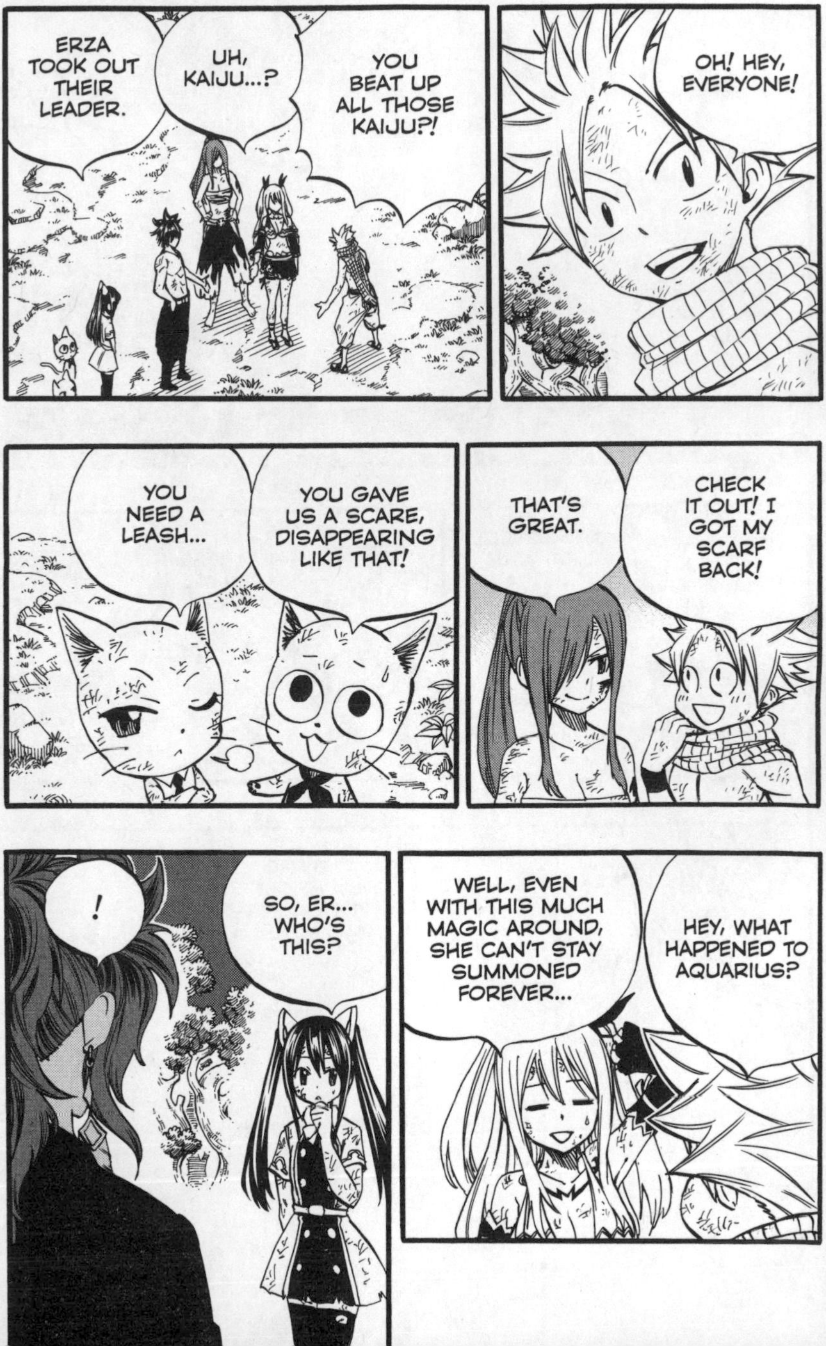
OH! HEY, EVERYONE!
YOU BEAT UP ALL THOSE KAIJU?!
UH, KAIJU...?
ERZA TOOK OUT THEIR LEADER.
CHECK IT OUT! I GOT MY SCARF BACK!
THAT'S GREAT.
YOU GAVE US A SCARE, DISAPPEARING LIKE THAT!
YOU NEED A LEASH...
HEY, WHAT HAPPENED TO AQUARIUS?
WELL, EVEN WITH THIS MUCH MAGIC AROUND, SHE CAN'T STAY SUMMONED FOREVER...
SO, ER... WHO'S THIS?
!

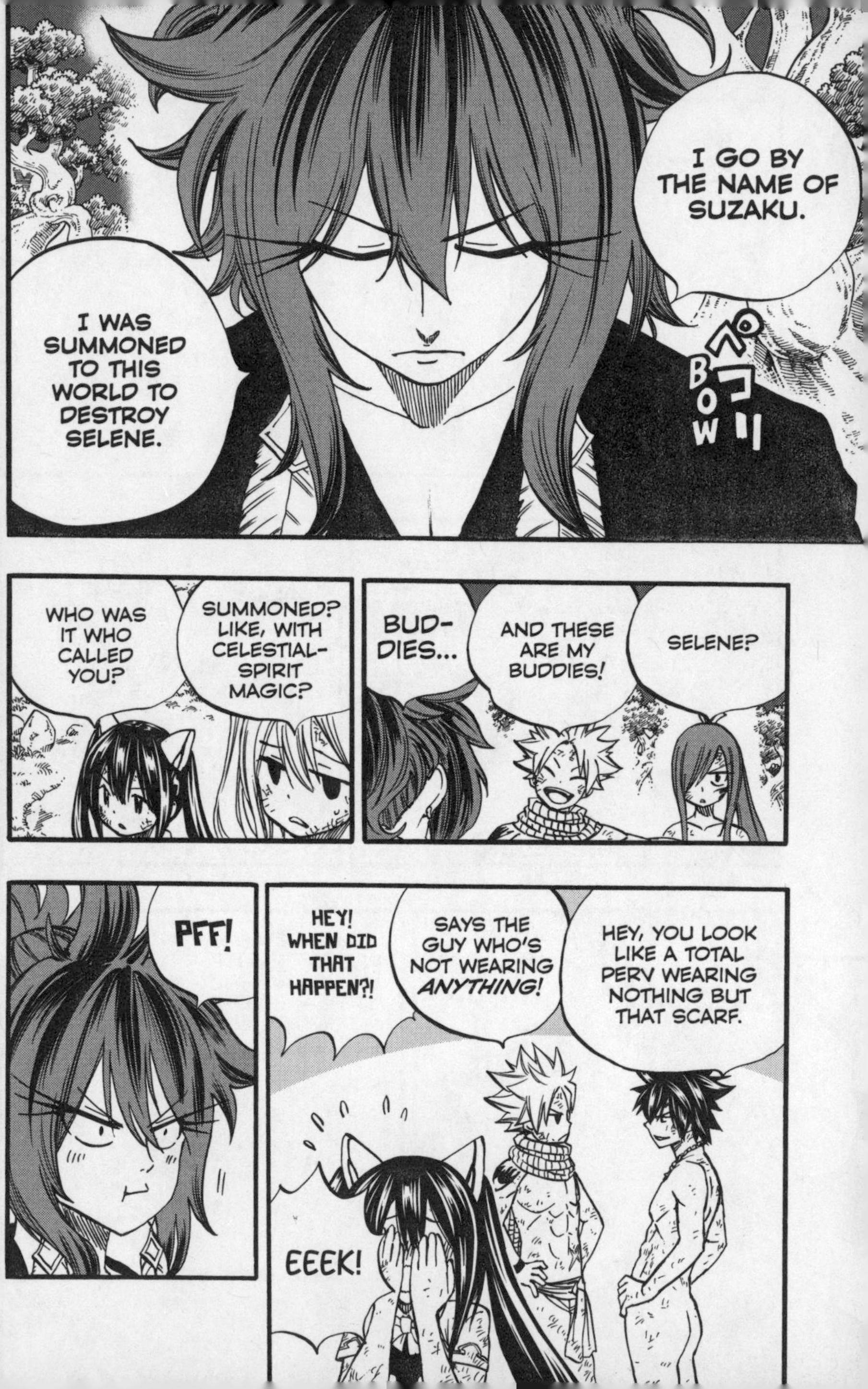

I GO BY THE NAME OF SUZAKU.
BOW
I WAS SUMMONED TO THIS WORLD TO DESTROY SELENE.
SELENE?
AND THESE ARE MY BUDDIES!
BUD-DIES...
SUMMONED? LIKE, WITH CELESTIAL-SPIRIT MAGIC?
WHO WAS IT WHO CALLED YOU?
HEY, YOU LOOK LIKE A TOTAL PERV WEARING NOTHING BUT THAT SCARF.
SAYS THE GUY WHO'S NOT WEARING *ANYTHING*!
HEY! WHEN DID THAT HAPPEN?!
EEEK!
PFF!

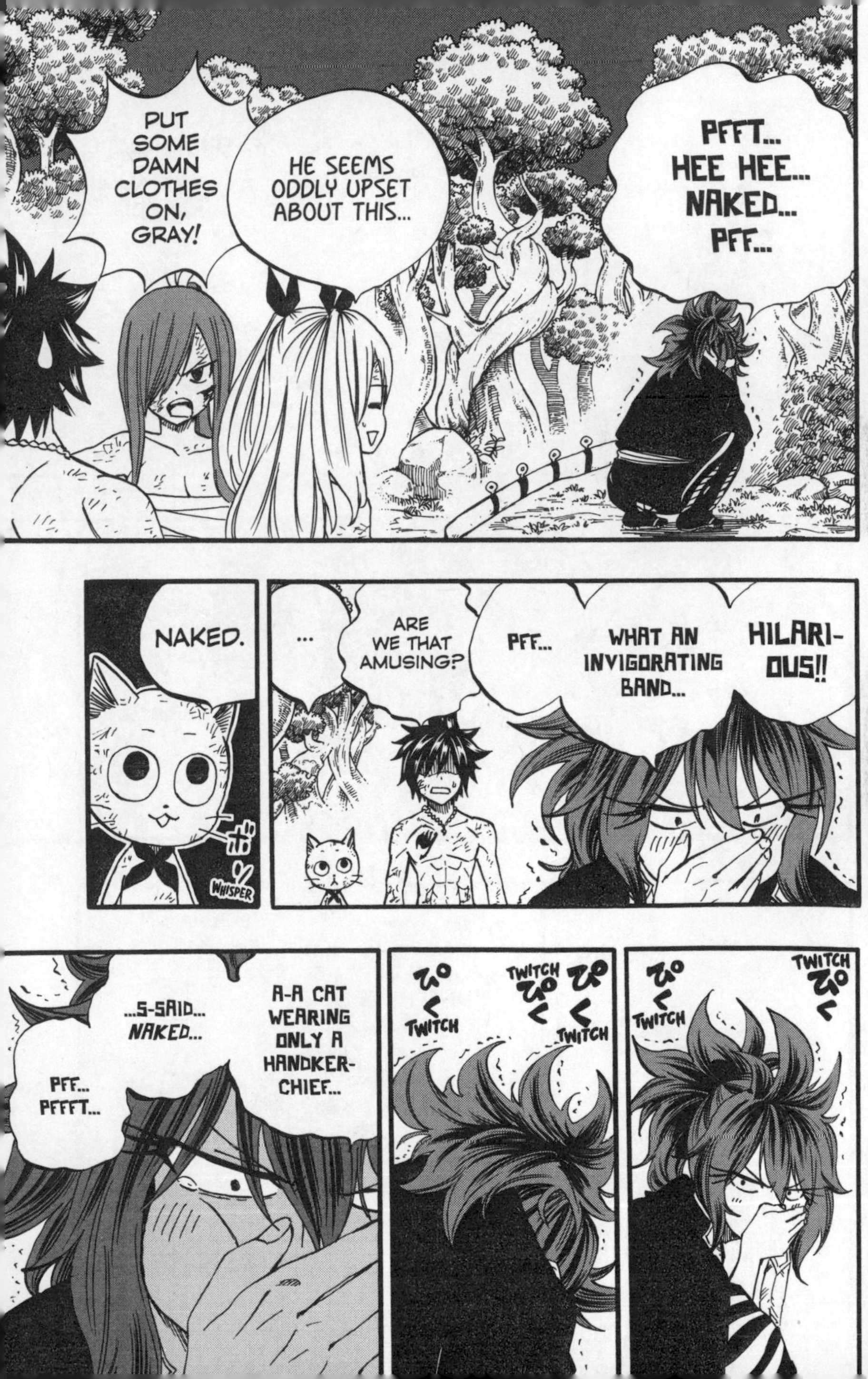
PFFT... HEE HEE... NAKED... PFF...
HE SEEMS ODDLY UPSET ABOUT THIS...
PUT SOME DAMN CLOTHES ON, GRAY!
HILARI-OUS!!
WHAT AN INVIGORATING BAND...
PFF...
ARE WE THAT AMUSING?
...
NAKED.
WHISPER
TWITCH
TWITCH
TWITCH
TWITCH
A-A CAT WEARING ONLY A HANDKER-CHIEF...
...S-SAID... NAKED...
PFF... PFFFT...

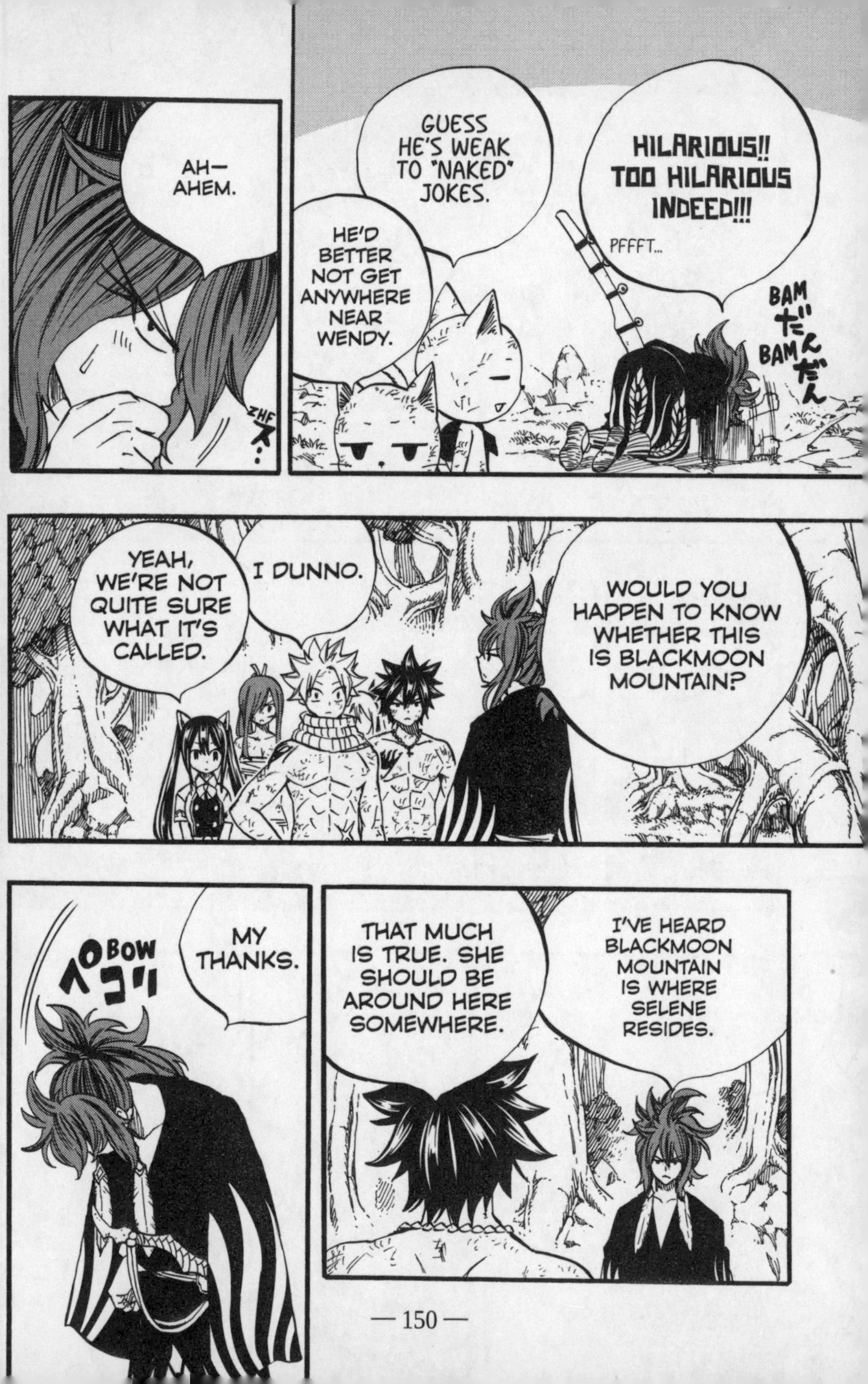
HILARIOUS!! TOO HILARIOUS INDEED!!!
PFFFT...
BAM だん BAM だん
GUESS HE'S WEAK TO "NAKED" JOKES.
HE'D BETTER NOT GET ANYWHERE NEAR WENDY.
AH— AHEM.
ZHF ズ…
WOULD YOU HAPPEN TO KNOW WHETHER THIS IS BLACKMOON MOUNTAIN?
I DUNNO.
YEAH, WE'RE NOT QUITE SURE WHAT IT'S CALLED.
I'VE HEARD BLACKMOON MOUNTAIN IS WHERE SELENE RESIDES.
THAT MUCH IS TRUE. SHE SHOULD BE AROUND HERE SOMEWHERE.
MY THANKS.
BOW ペコリ

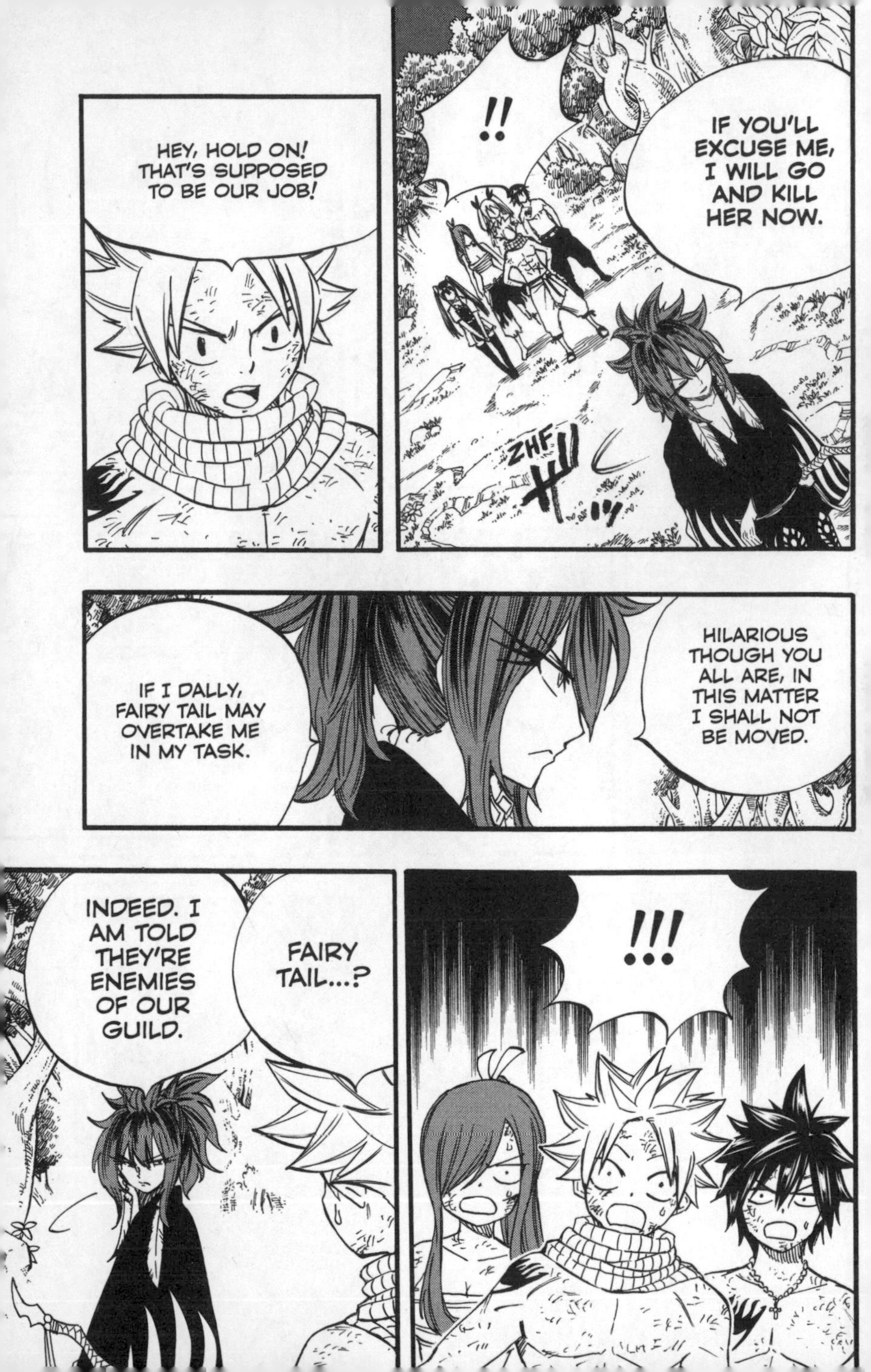
IF YOU'LL EXCUSE ME, I WILL GO AND KILL HER NOW.
!!
ZHF
HEY, HOLD ON! THAT'S SUPPOSED TO BE OUR JOB!
HILARIOUS THOUGH YOU ALL ARE, IN THIS MATTER I SHALL NOT BE MOVED.
IF I DALLY, FAIRY TAIL MAY OVERTAKE ME IN MY TASK.
!!!
FAIRY TAIL...?
INDEED. I AM TOLD THEY'RE ENEMIES OF OUR GUILD.

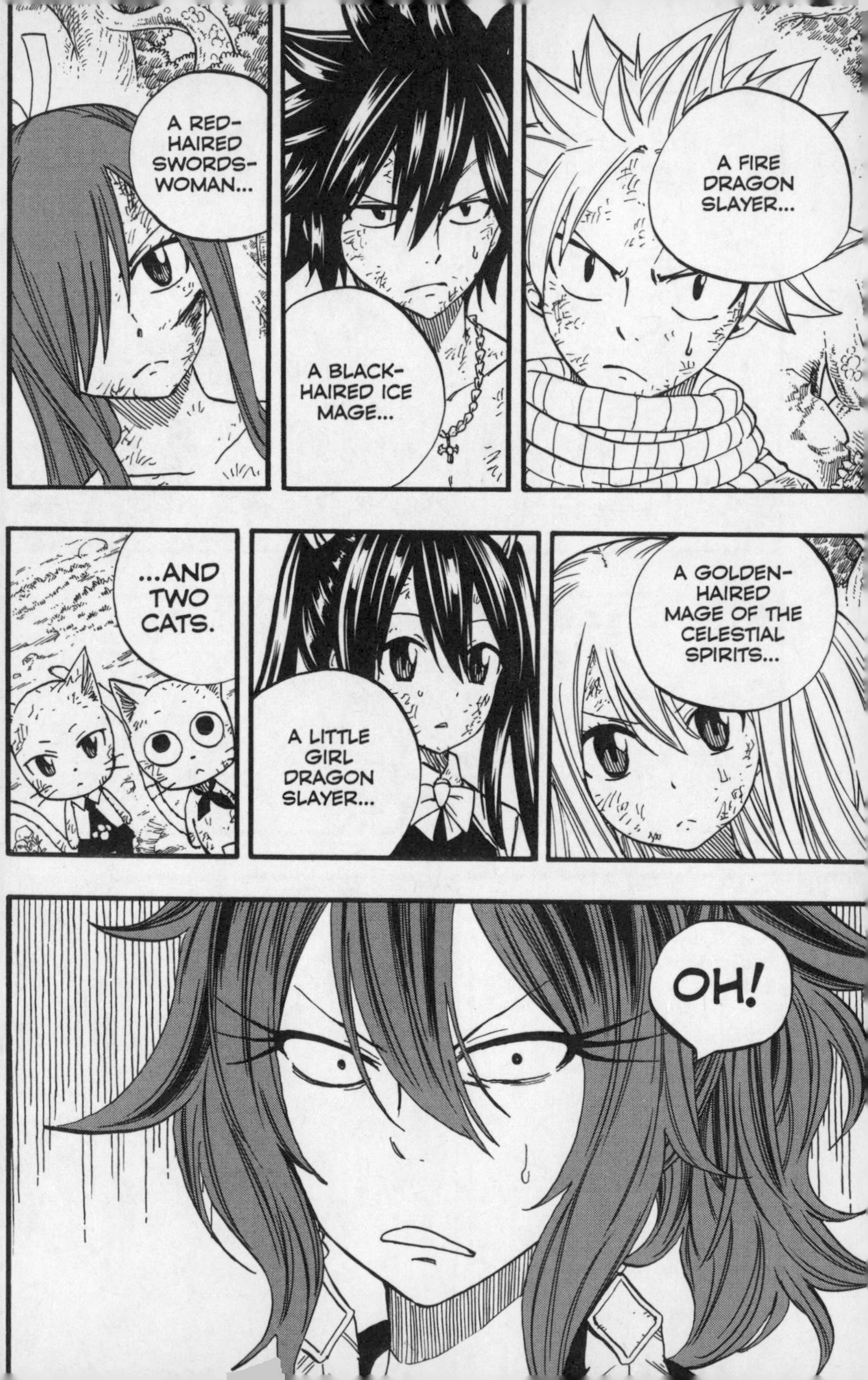
A FIRE DRAGON SLAYER...
A BLACK-HAIRED ICE MAGE...
A RED-HAIRED SWORDSWOMAN...
A GOLDEN-HAIRED MAGE OF THE CELESTIAL SPIRITS...
A LITTLE GIRL DRAGON SLAYER...
...AND TWO CATS.
OH!

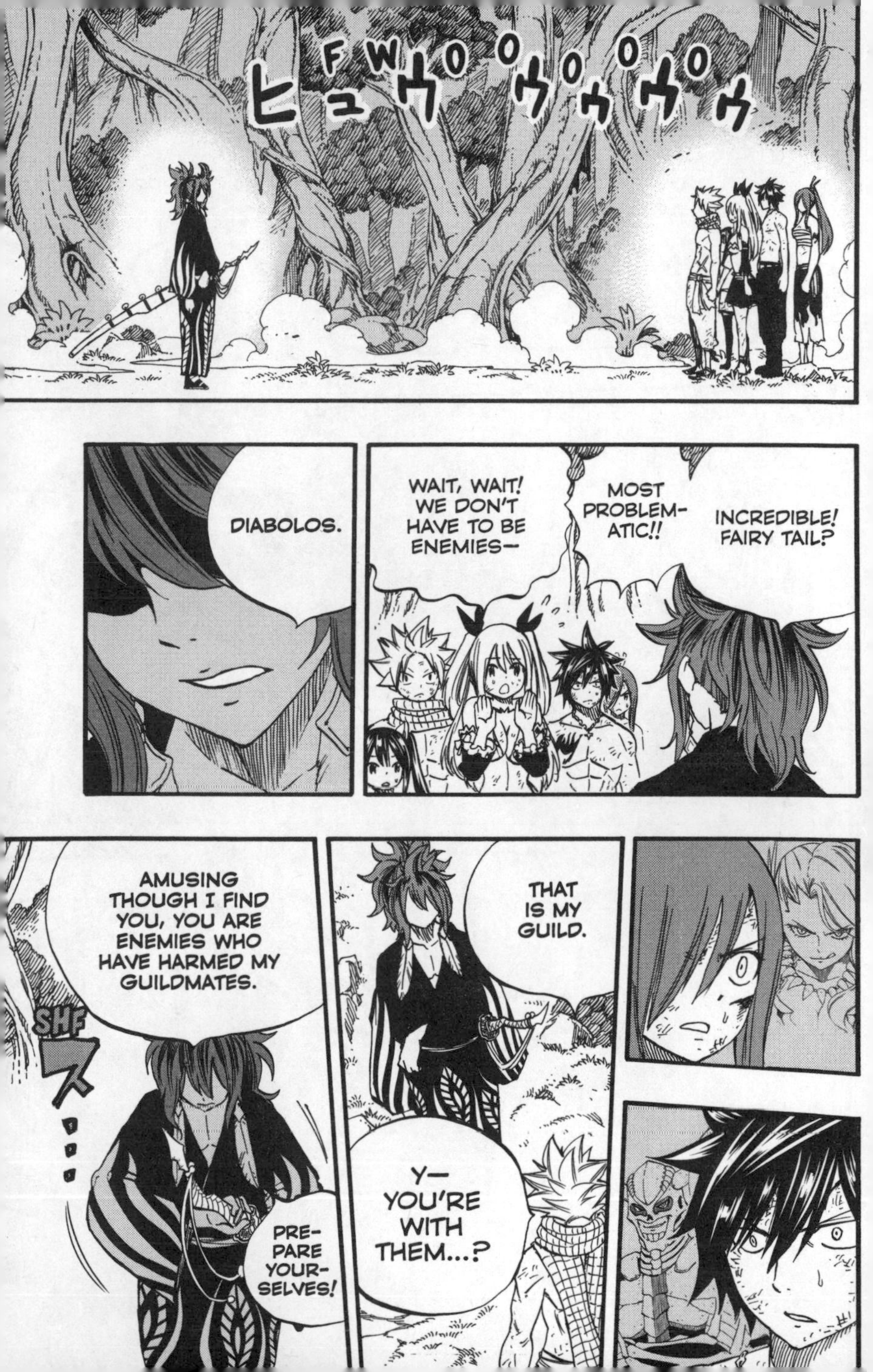
FWOOOOO
ヒュウウウウウ
INCREDIBLE! FAIRY TAIL?
MOST PROBLEM-ATIC!!
WAIT, WAIT! WE DON'T HAVE TO BE ENEMIES—
DIABOLOS.
THAT IS MY GUILD.
Y— YOU'RE WITH THEM...?
AMUSING THOUGH I FIND YOU, YOU ARE ENEMIES WHO HAVE HARMED MY GUILDMATES.
SHF
ス…
PRE-PARE YOUR-SELVES!

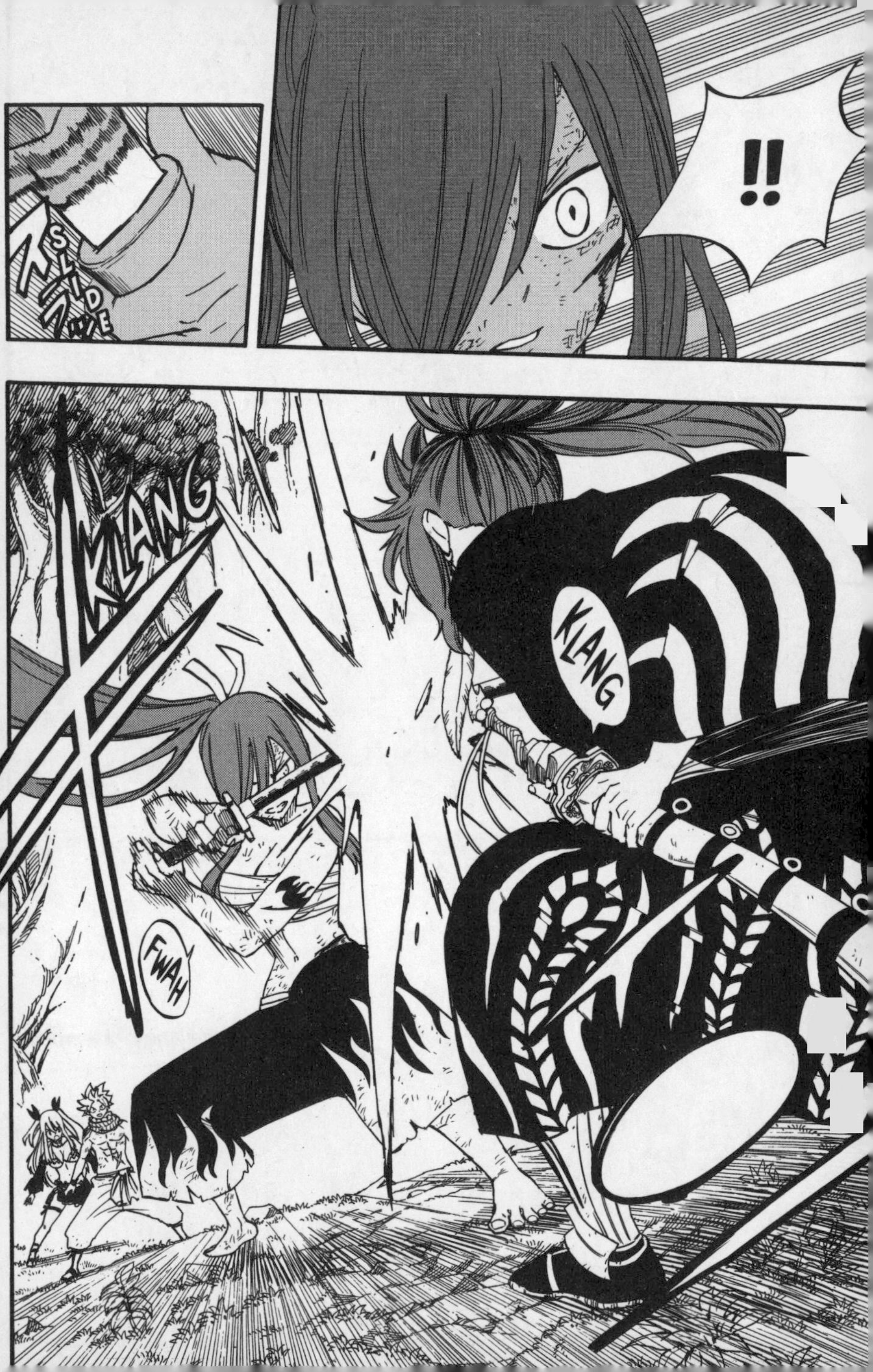
!!
SLIDE
KLANG
KLANG
FWAH

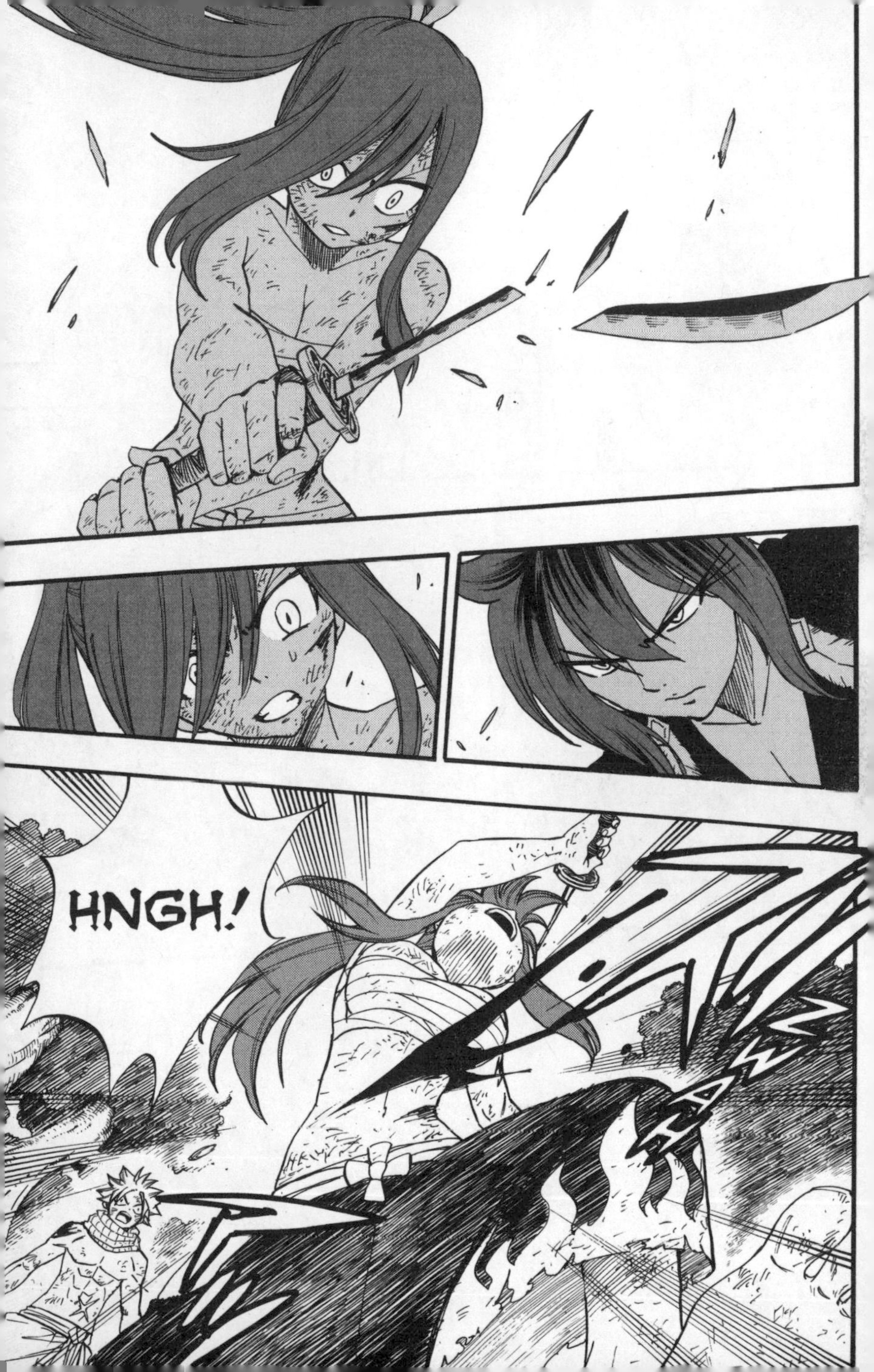
HNGH!

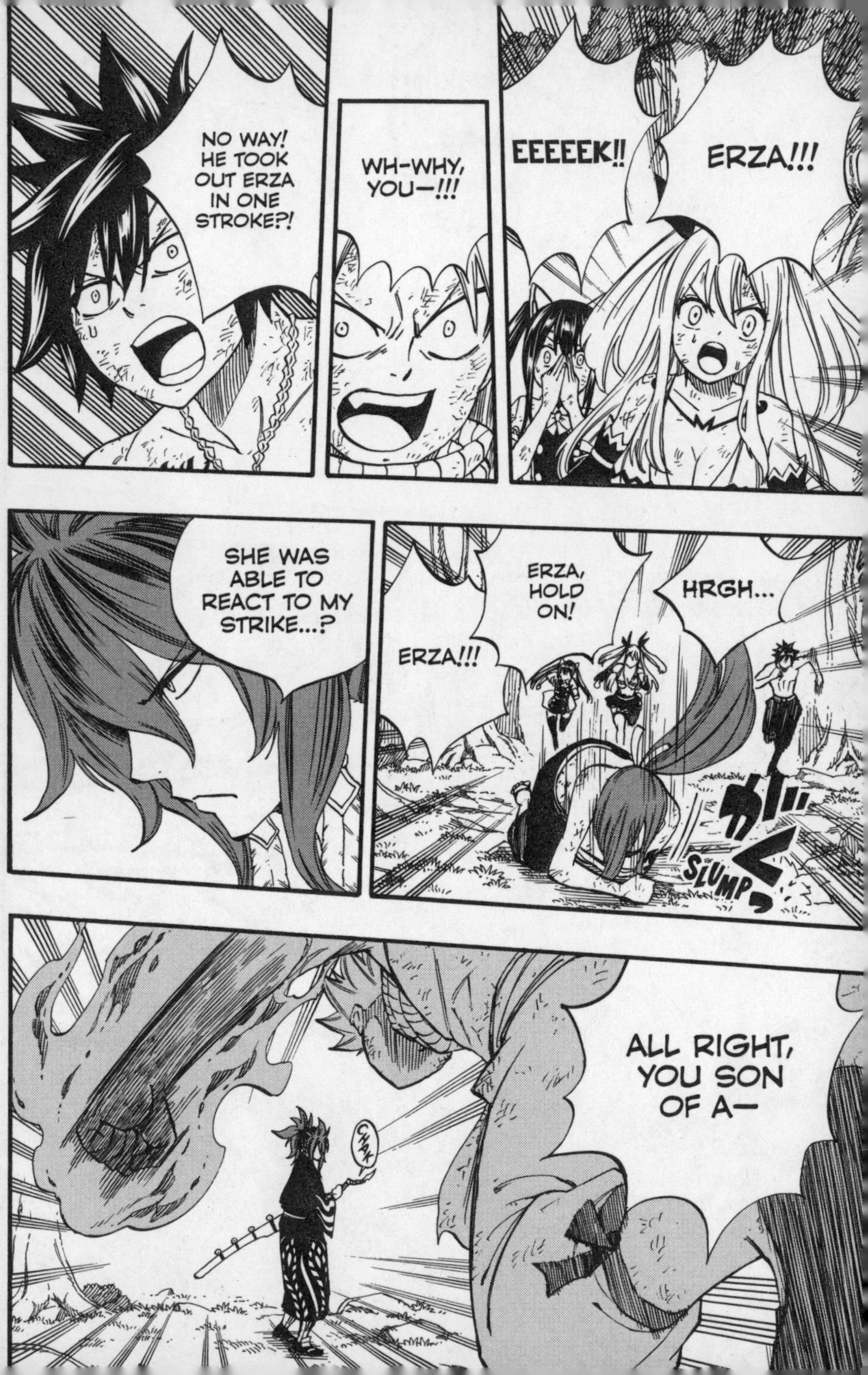
ERZA!!!
EEEEEK!!
WH-WHY, YOU—!!!
NO WAY! HE TOOK OUT ERZA IN ONE STROKE?!
HRGH...
ERZA, HOLD ON!
ERZA!!!
SLUMP
SHE WAS ABLE TO REACT TO MY STRIKE...?
ALL RIGHT, YOU SON OF A—
CHAK

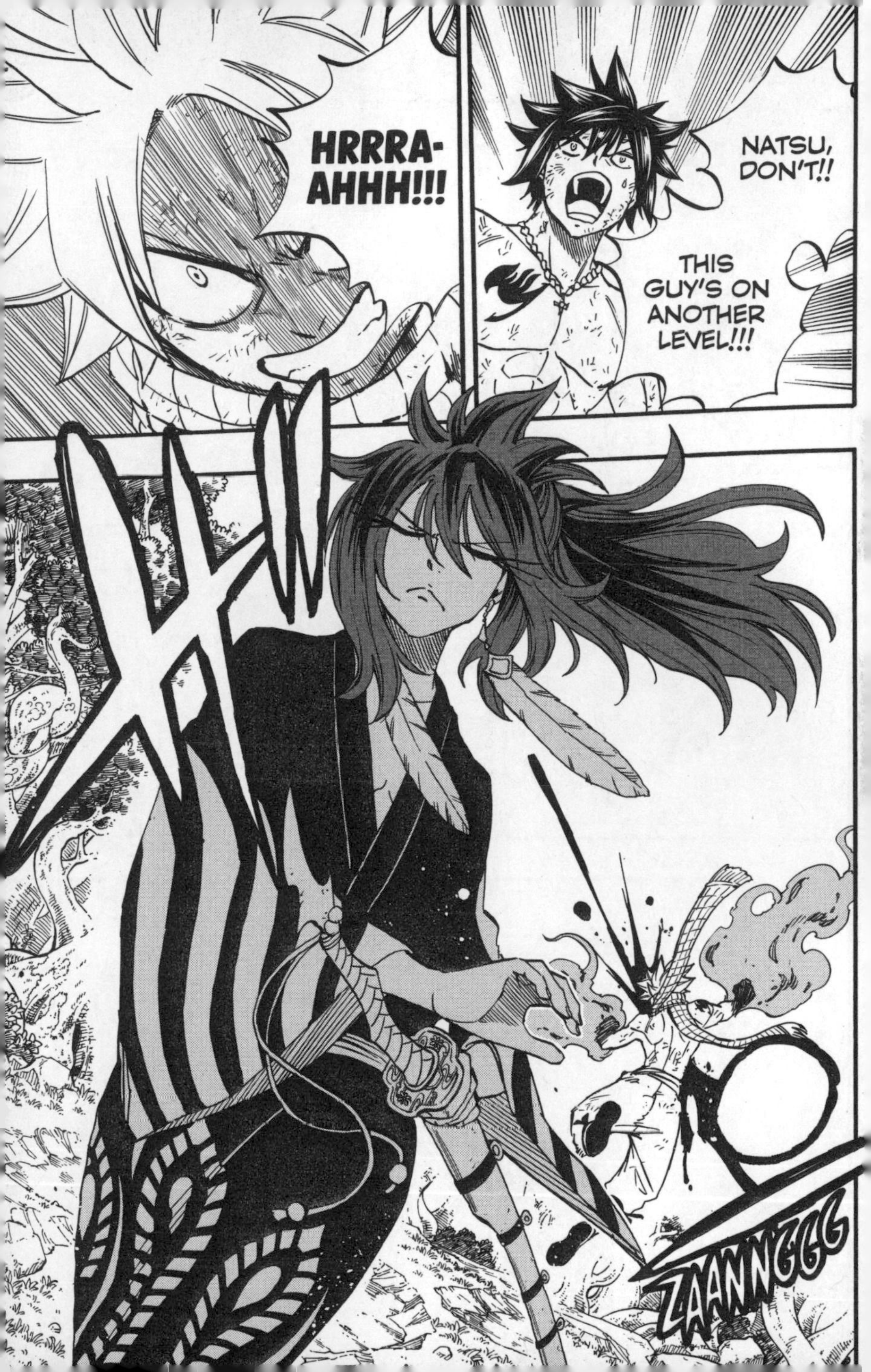
NATSU, DON'T!!
THIS GUY'S ON ANOTHER LEVEL!!!
HRRRA-AHHH!!!
ZAANNGGG

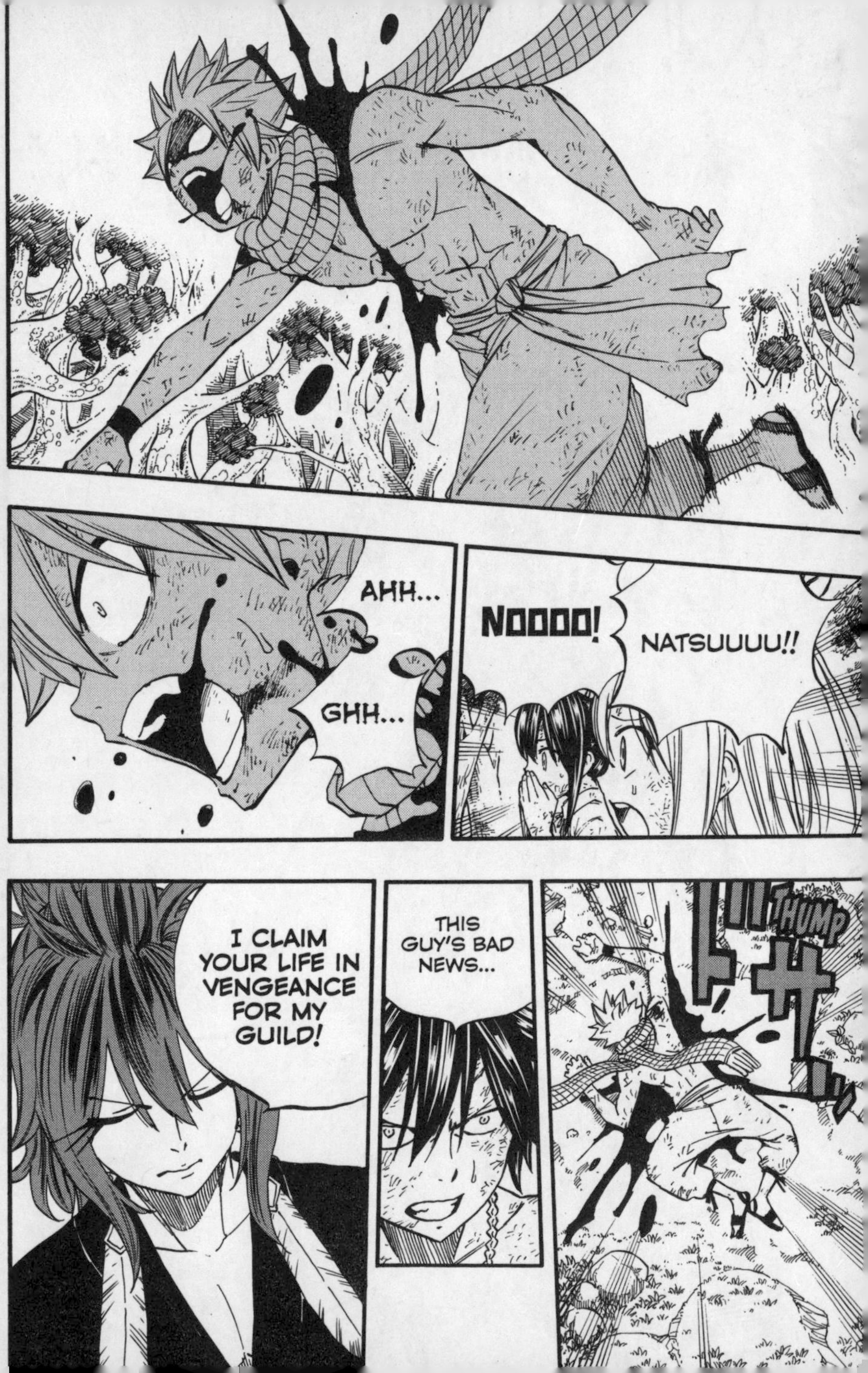
NATSUUUU!!
NOOOO!
AHH...
GHH...
THUMP
THIS GUY'S BAD NEWS...
I CLAIM YOUR LIFE IN VENGEANCE FOR MY GUILD!

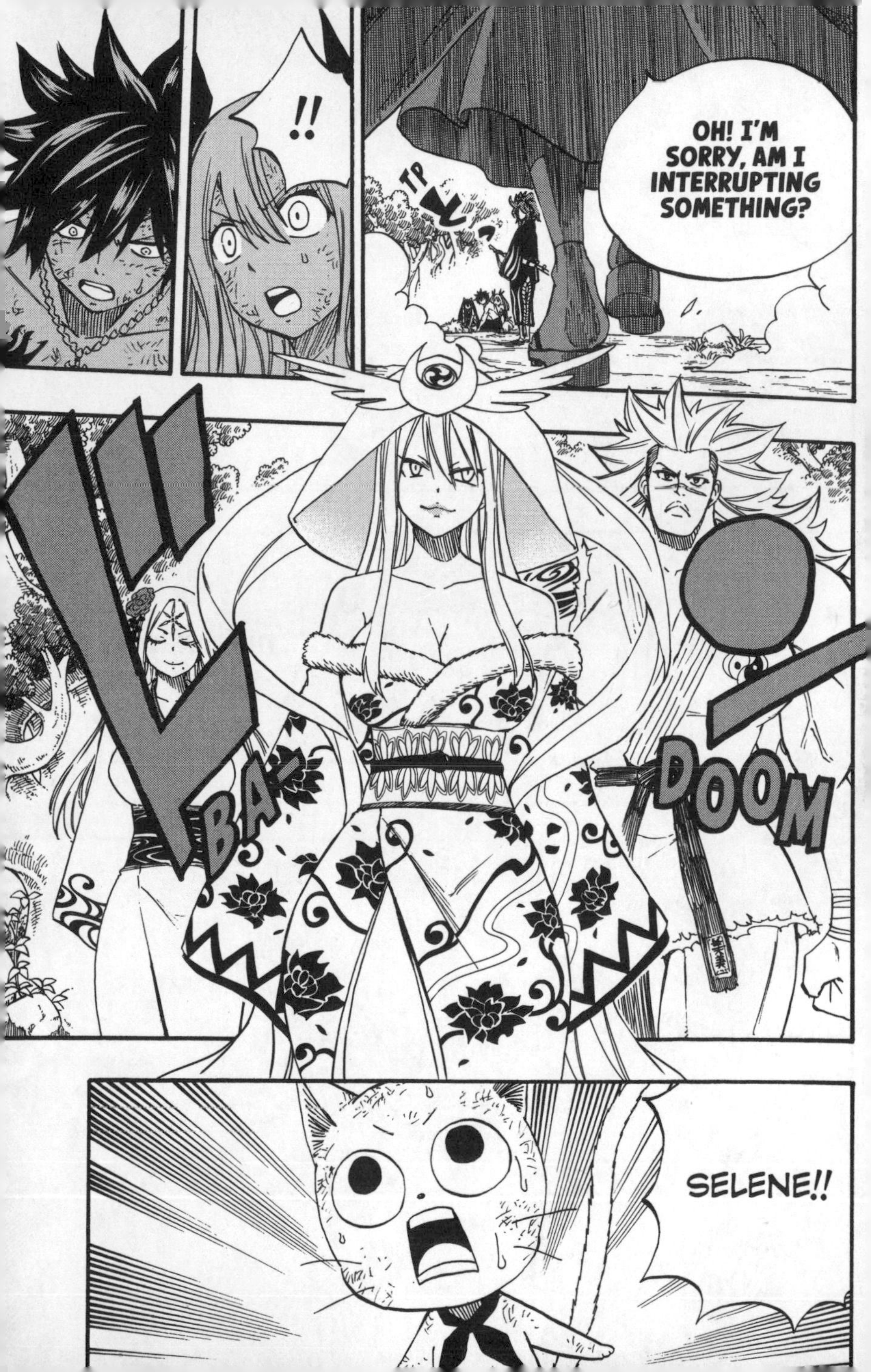
OH! I'M SORRY, AM I INTERRUPTING SOMETHING?
TP
!!
DOOM
BA-
SELENE!!

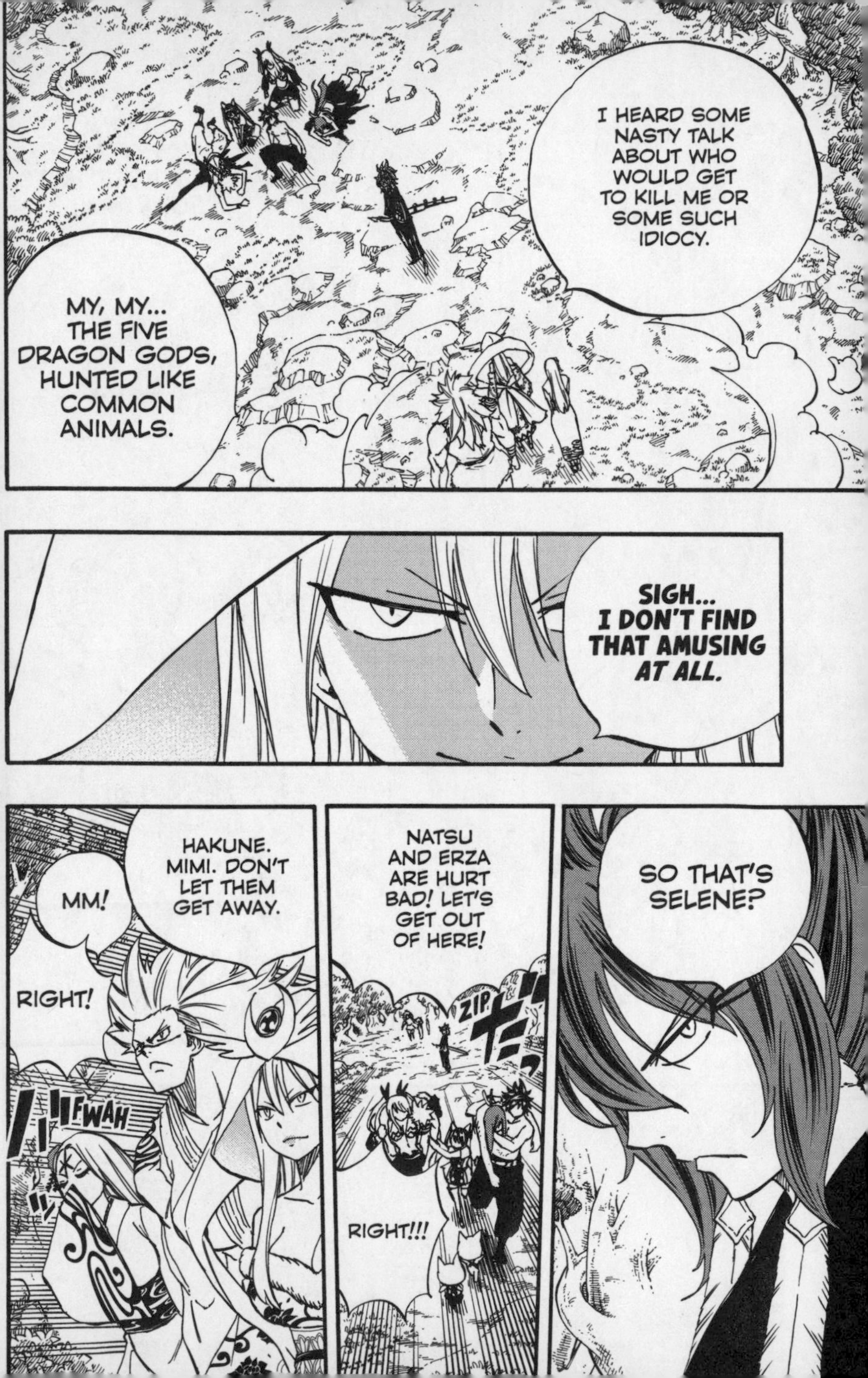
I HEARD SOME NASTY TALK ABOUT WHO WOULD GET TO KILL ME OR SOME SUCH IDIOCY.
MY, MY... THE FIVE DRAGON GODS, HUNTED LIKE COMMON ANIMALS.
SIGH... I DON'T FIND THAT AMUSING *AT ALL.*
SO THAT'S SELENE?
NATSU AND ERZA ARE HURT BAD! LET'S GET OUT OF HERE!
ZIP
RIGHT!!!
HAKUNE. MIMI. DON'T LET THEM GET AWAY.
MM!
RIGHT!
FWAH

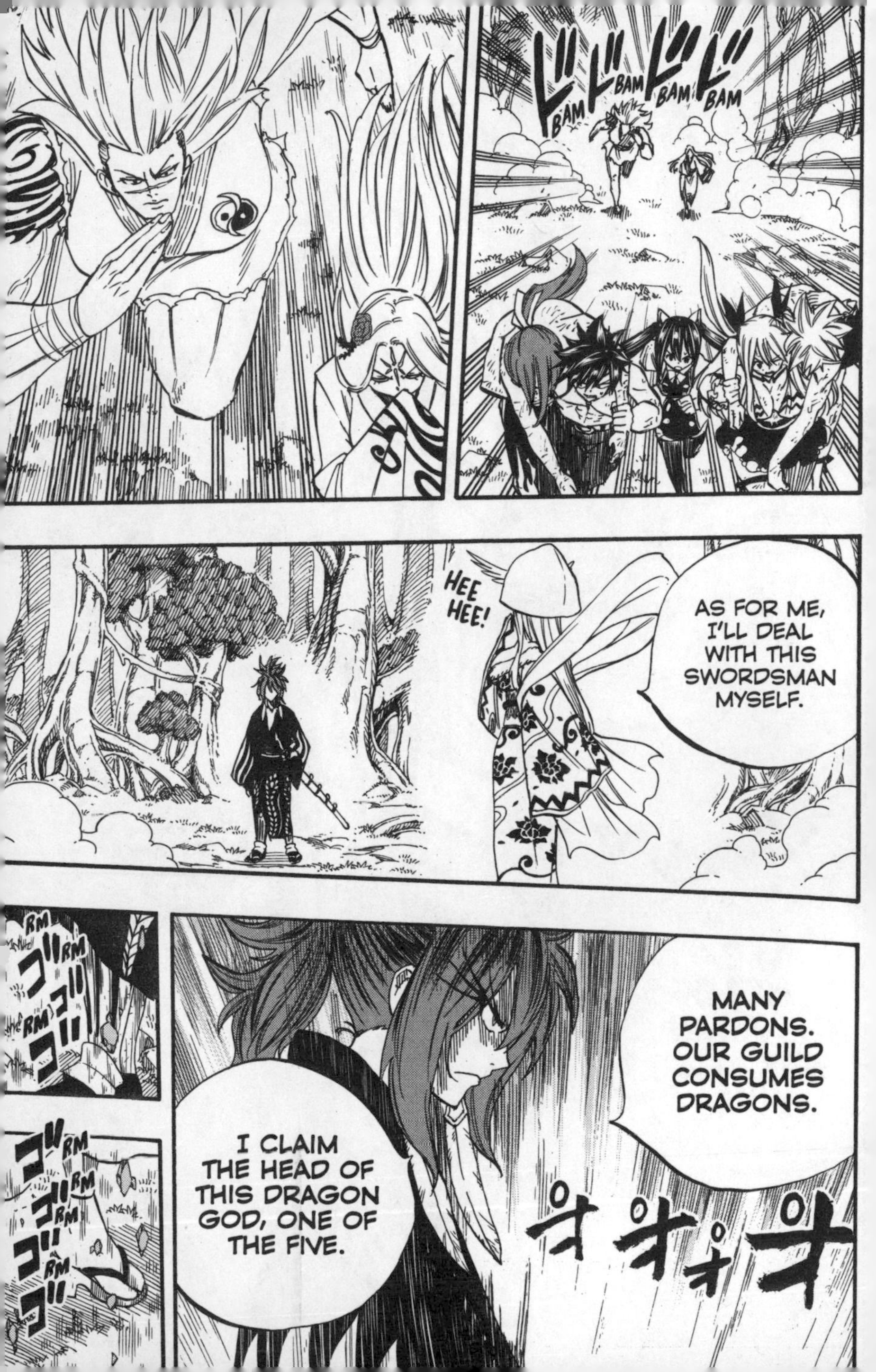
BAM BAM BAM BAM
AS FOR ME, I'LL DEAL WITH THIS SWORDSMAN MYSELF.
HEE HEE!
MANY PARDONS. OUR GUILD CONSUMES DRAGONS.
I CLAIM THE HEAD OF THIS DRAGON GOD, ONE OF THE FIVE.
RM RM RM
RM RM RM RM

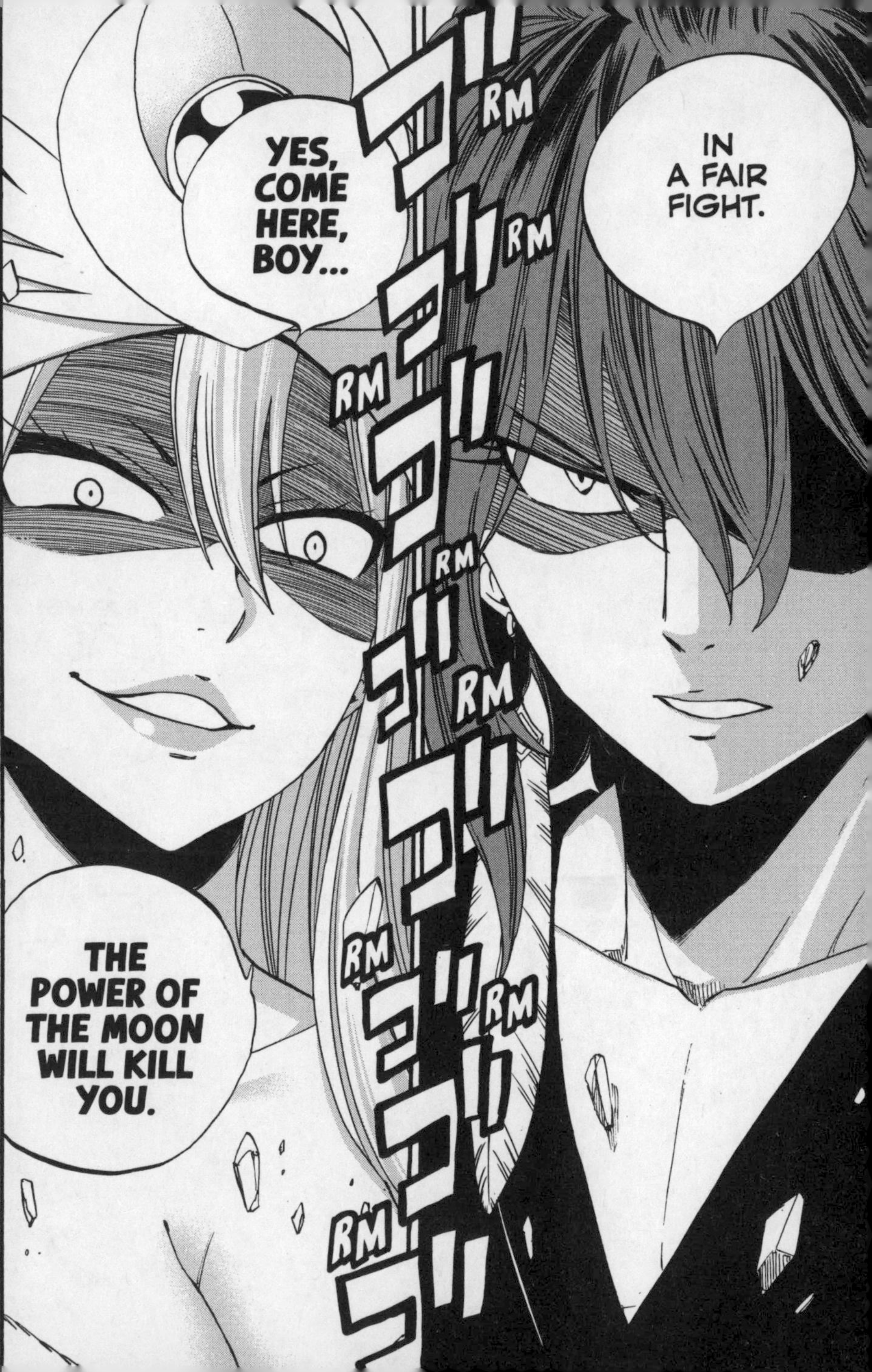
IN A FAIR FIGHT.
YES, COME HERE, BOY...
RM
RM
RM
RM
RM
RM
RM
RM
THE POWER OF THE MOON WILL KILL YOU.

FAIRY TAIL 100 YEARS QUEST

Chapter 81: Sword Saint

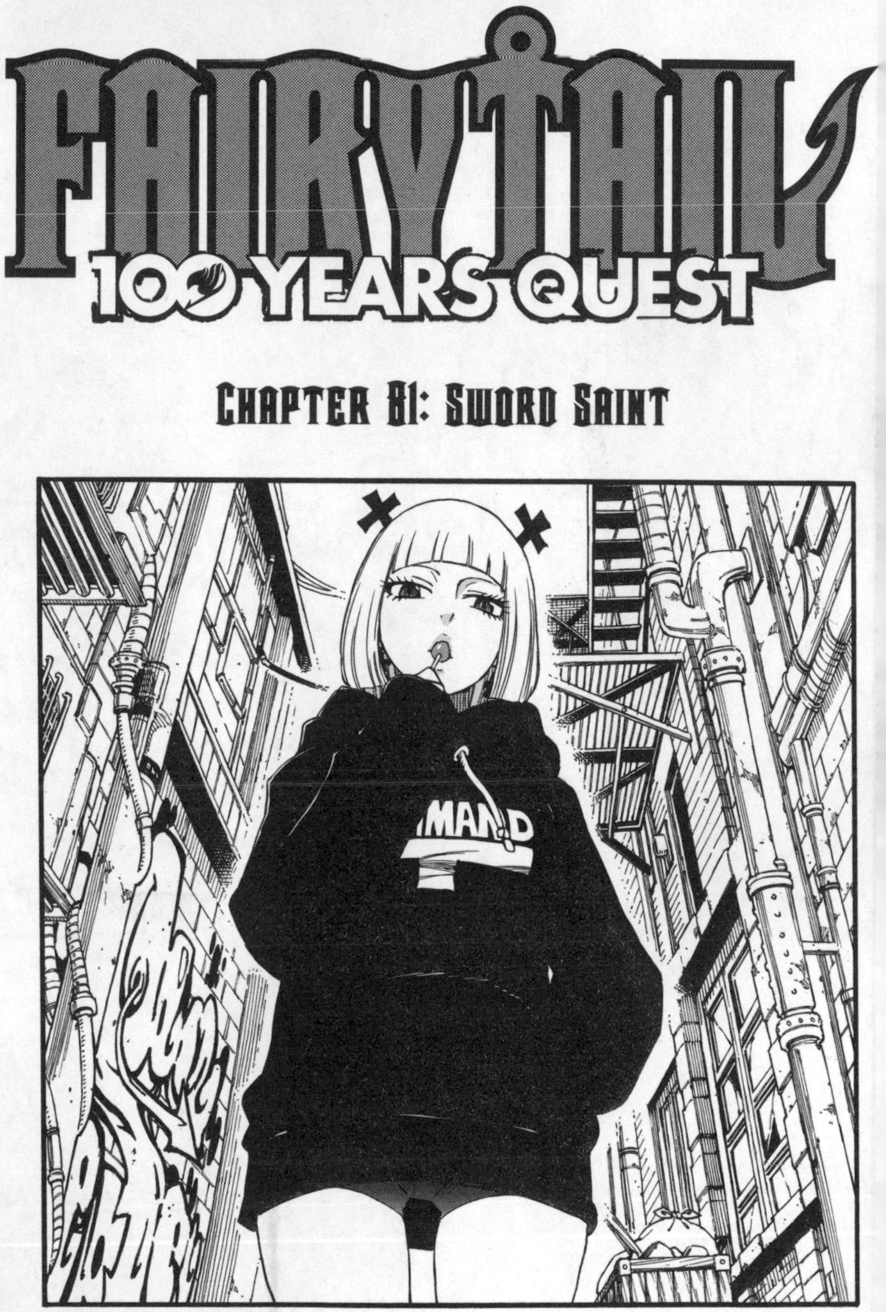

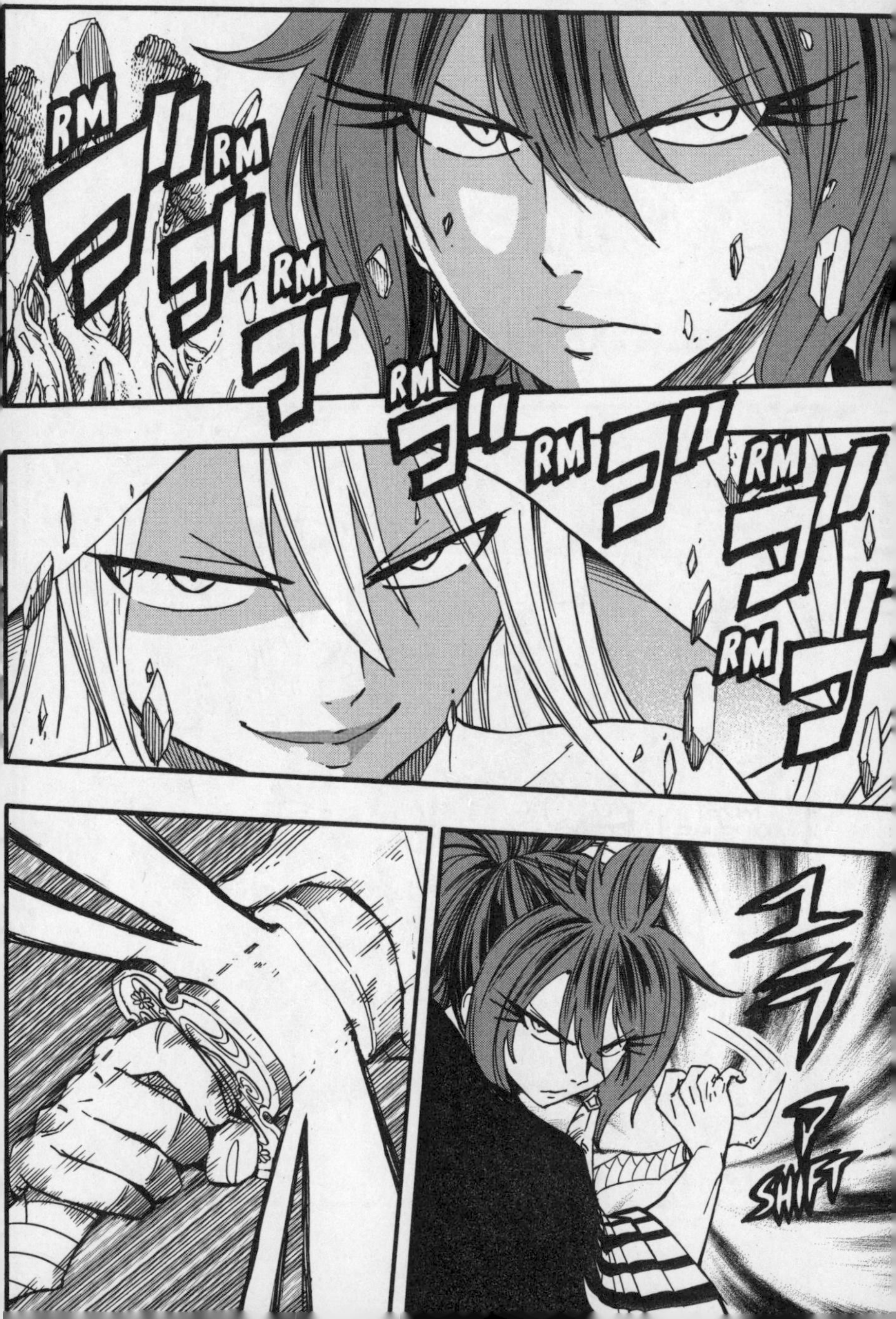
RM
RM
RM
RM
RM
RM
RM
SHIFT

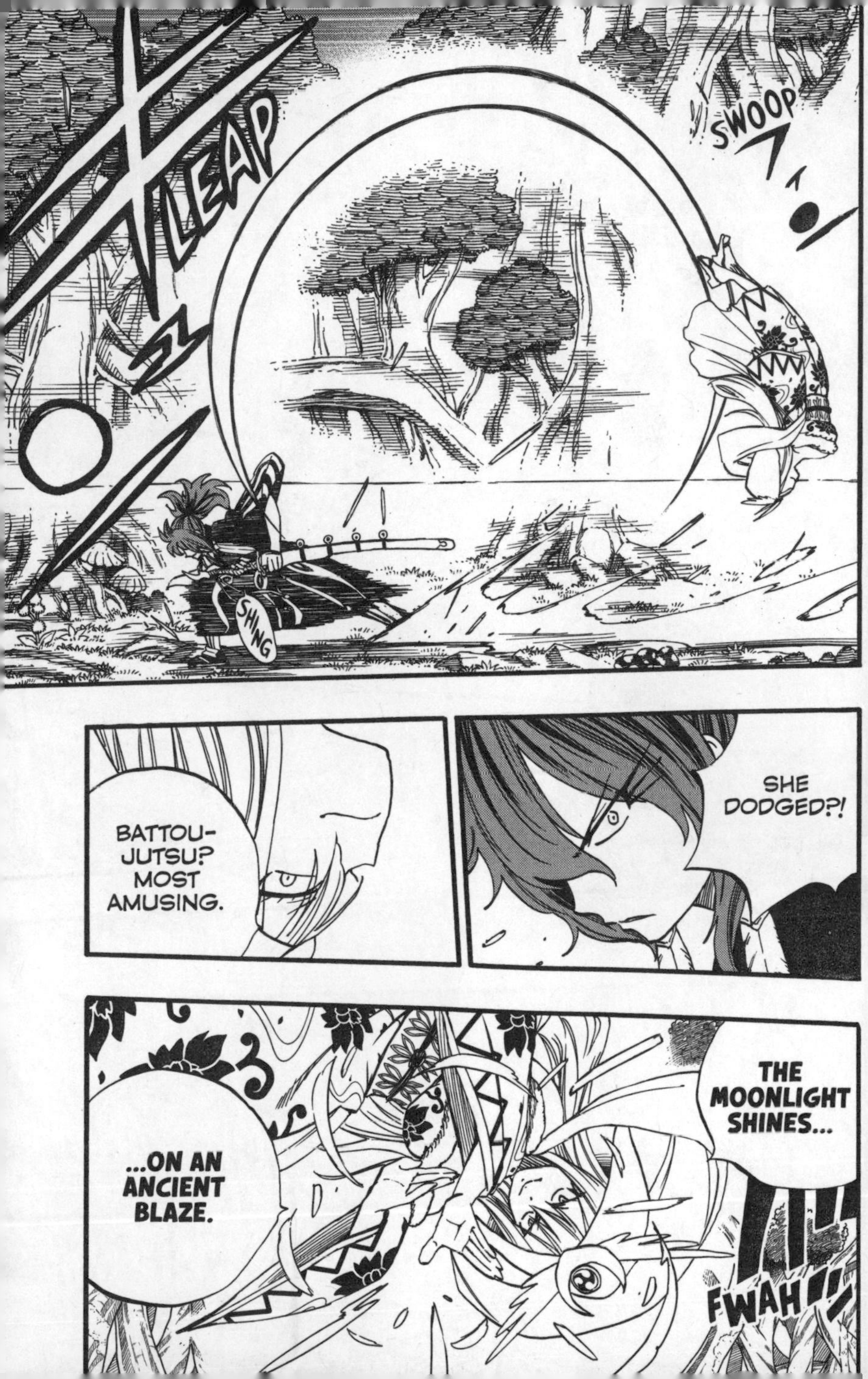
SWOOP
LEAP
SHING
SHE DODGED?!
BATTOU-JUTSU? MOST AMUSING.
THE MOONLIGHT SHINES...
...ON AN ANCIENT BLAZE.
FWAH!!

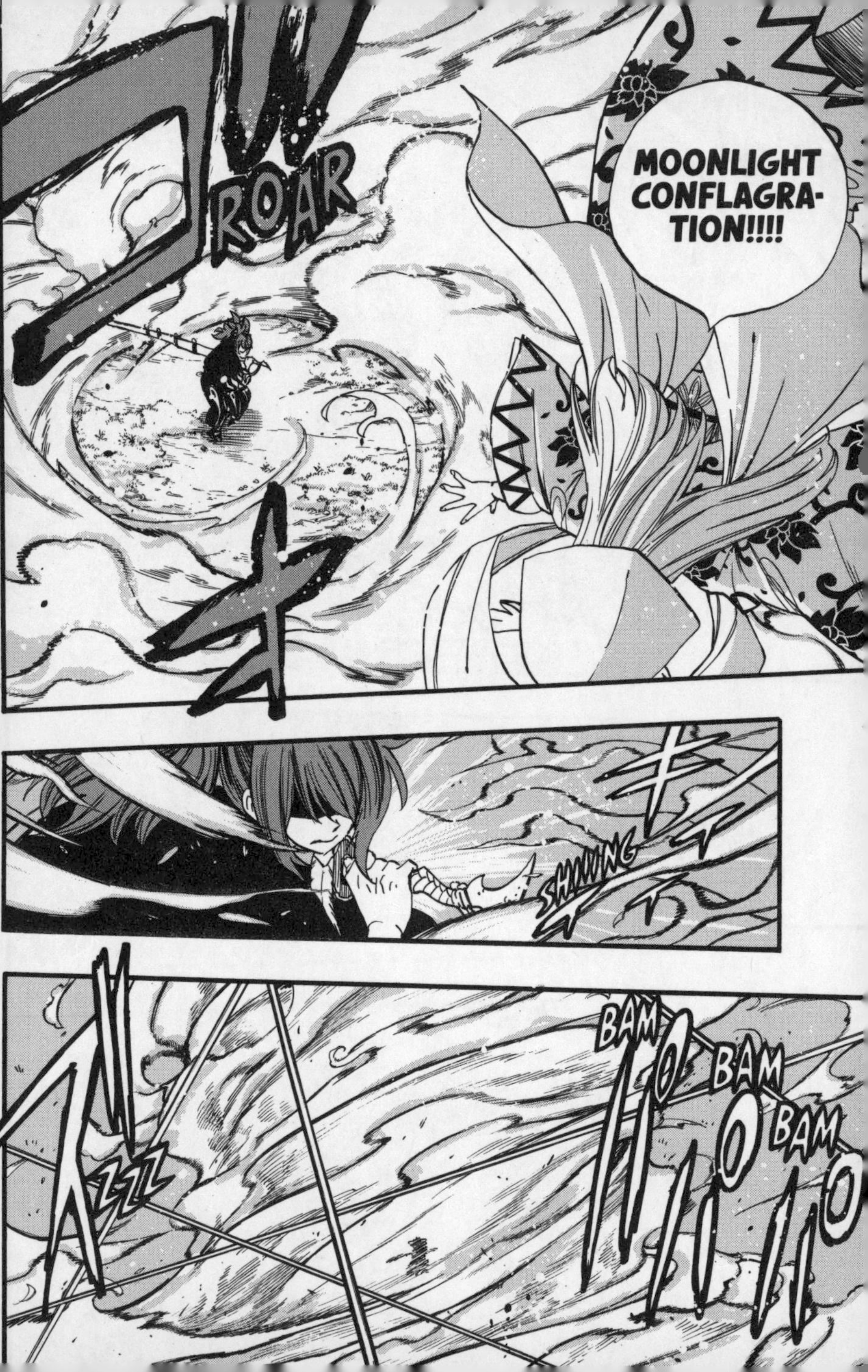
MOONLIGHT CONFLAGRA-TION!!!!
ROAR
SHIIING
BAM
BAM
BAM

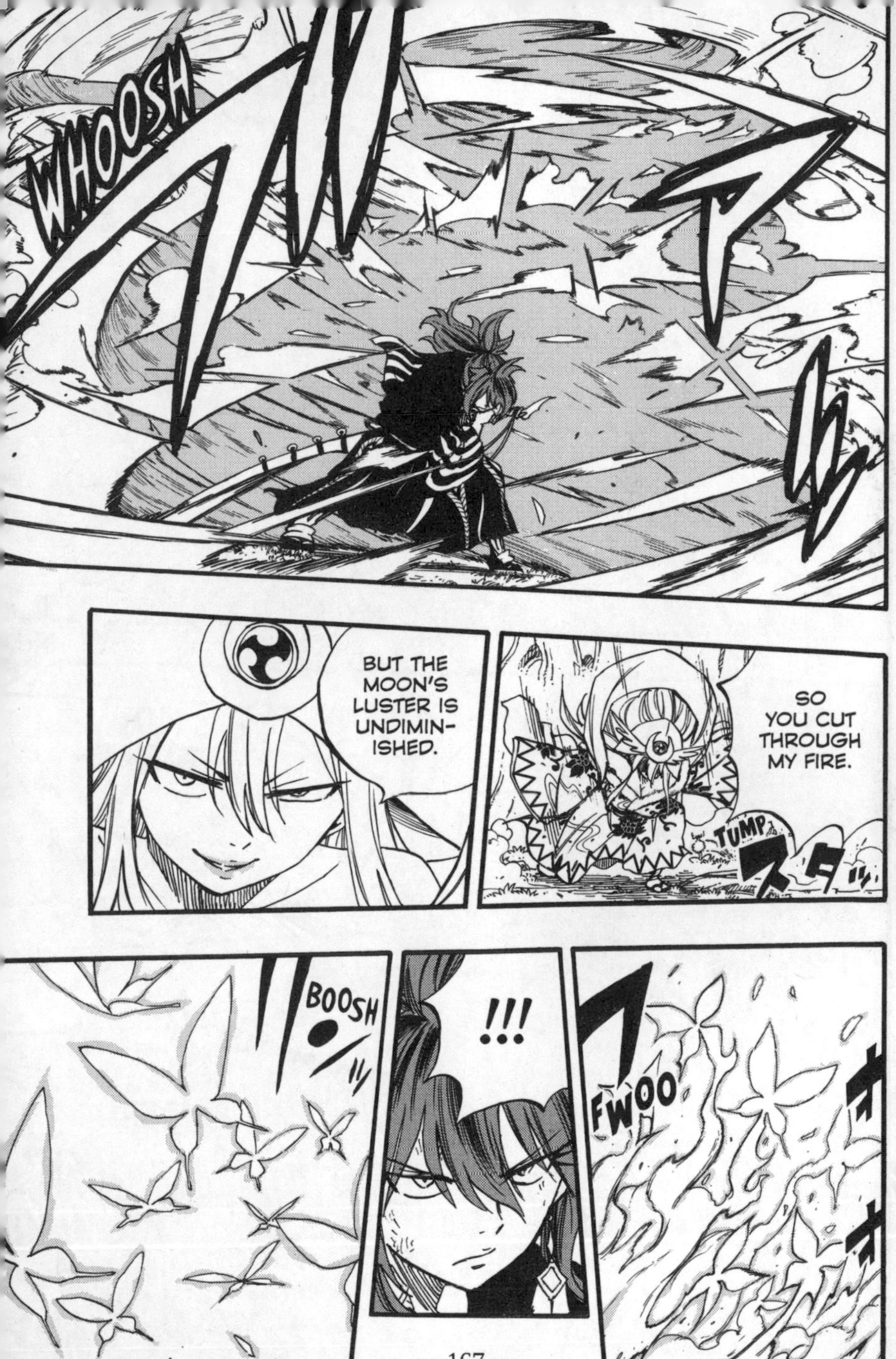
WHOOSH
SO YOU CUT THROUGH MY FIRE.
TUMP
BUT THE MOON'S LUSTER IS UNDIMINISHED.
FWOO
!!!
BOOSH

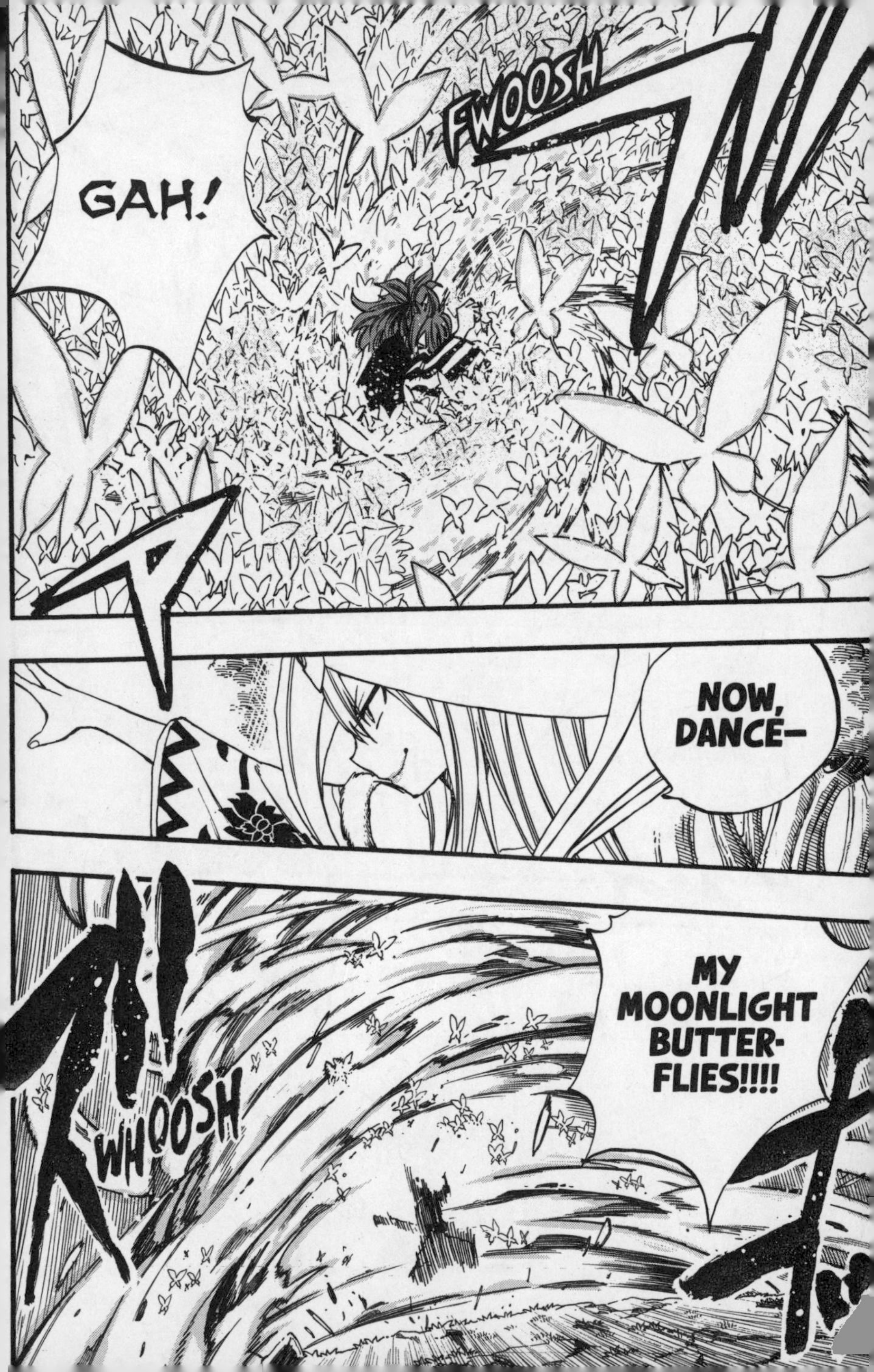
FWOOSH
GAH!
NOW, DANCE—
MY MOONLIGHT BUTTER-FLIES!!!!
WHOOSH

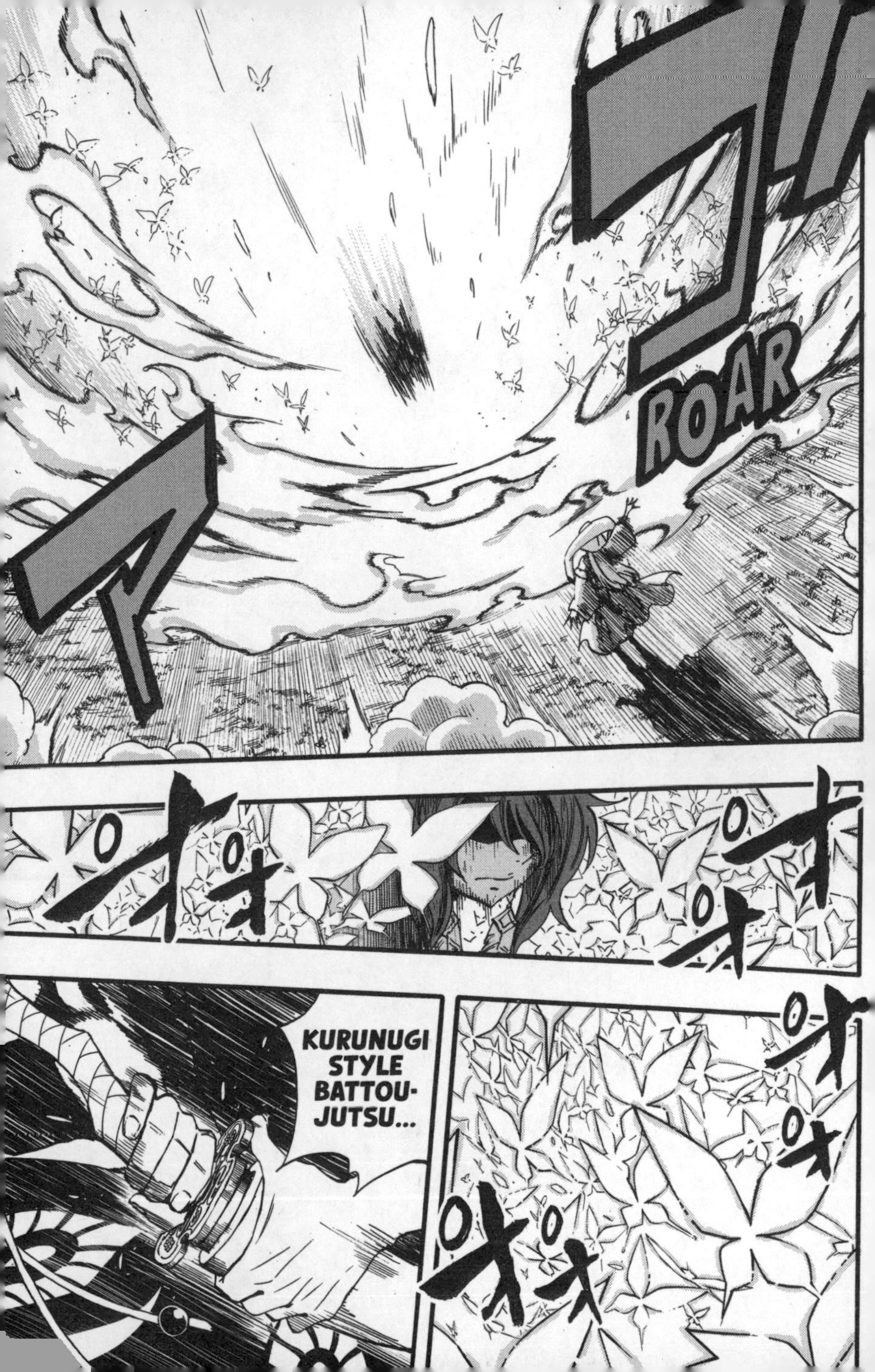
ROAR
KURUNUGI STYLE BATTOU-JUTSU...

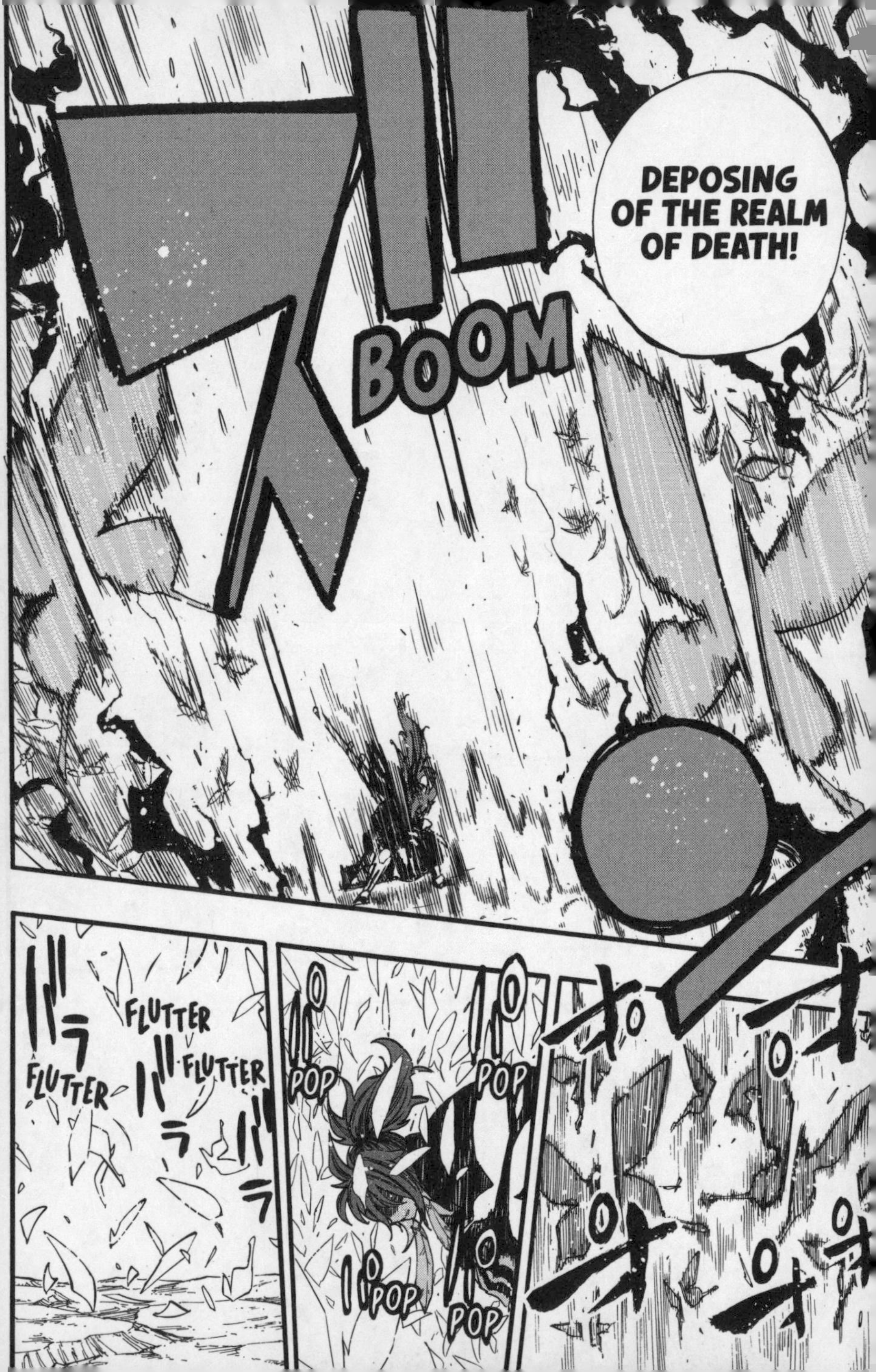
DEPOSING OF THE REALM OF DEATH!
BOOM
POP
POP
POP
POP
FLUTTER
FLUTTER
FLUTTER

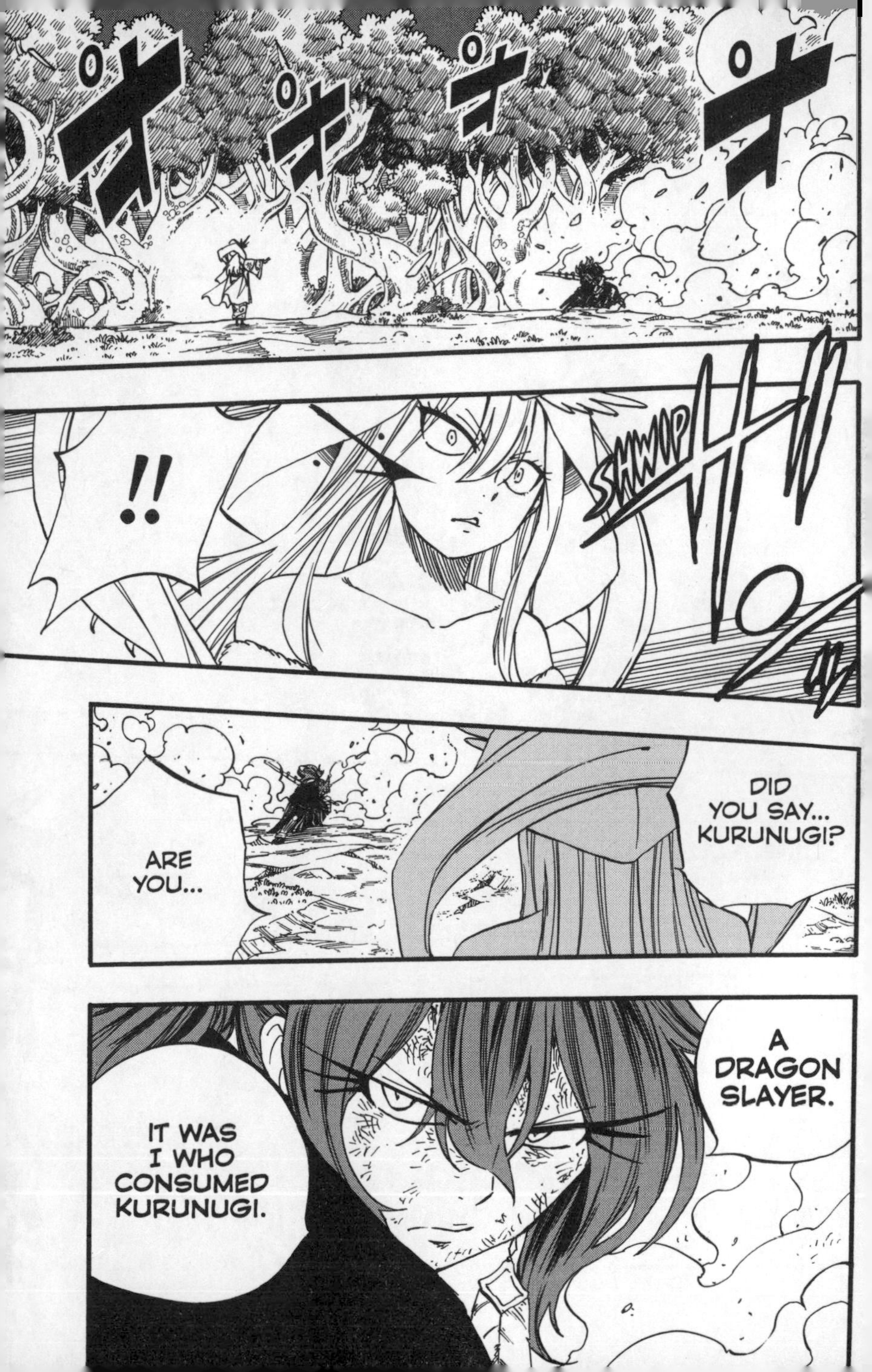
SHWIP
!!
DID YOU SAY... KURUNUGI?
ARE YOU...
A DRAGON SLAYER.
IT WAS I WHO CONSUMED KURUNUGI.

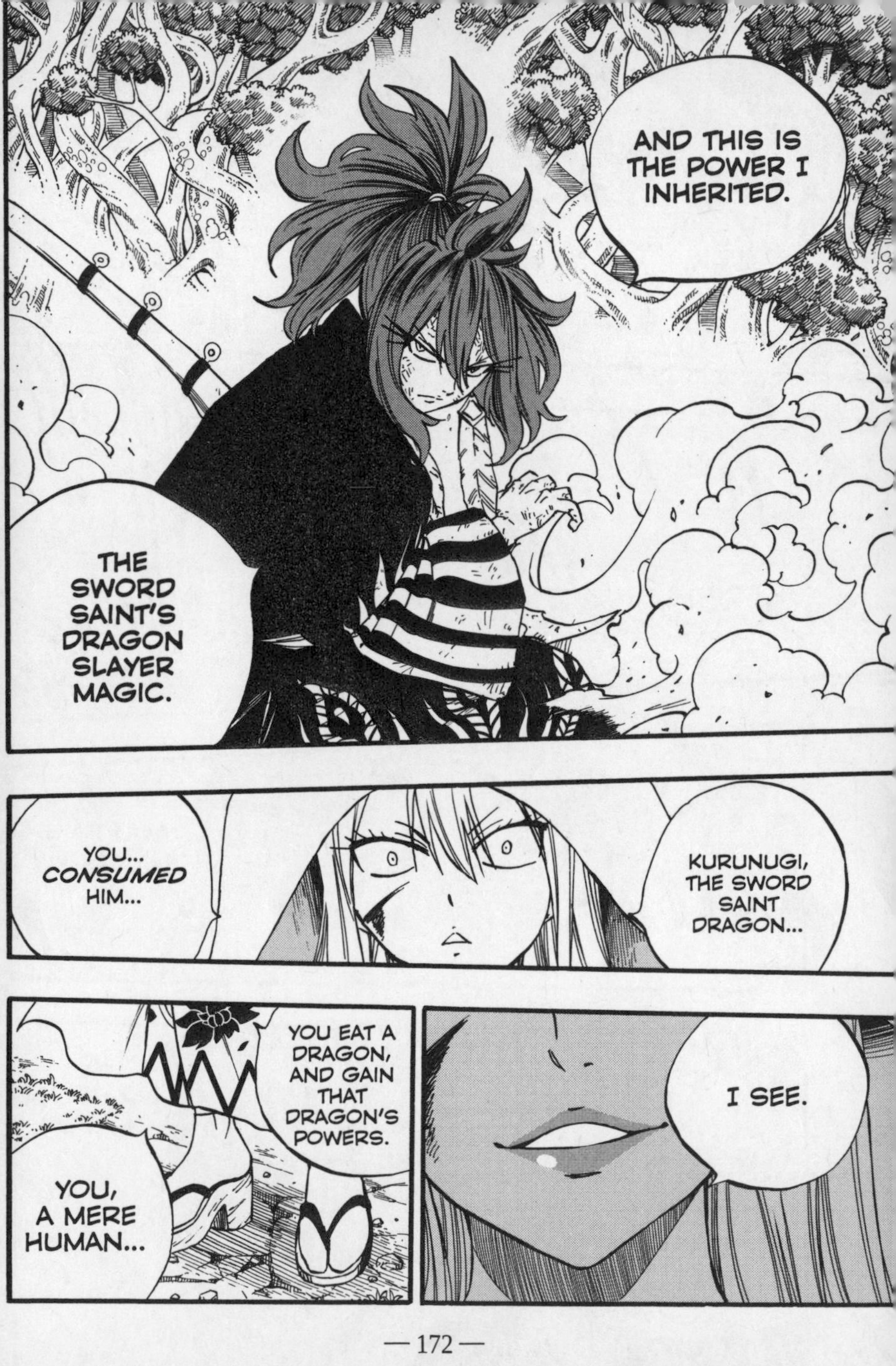
AND THIS IS THE POWER I INHERITED.
THE SWORD SAINT'S DRAGON SLAYER MAGIC.
KURUNUGI, THE SWORD SAINT DRAGON...
YOU... *CONSUMED* HIM...
I SEE.
YOU EAT A DRAGON, AND GAIN THAT DRAGON'S POWERS.
YOU, A MERE HUMAN...

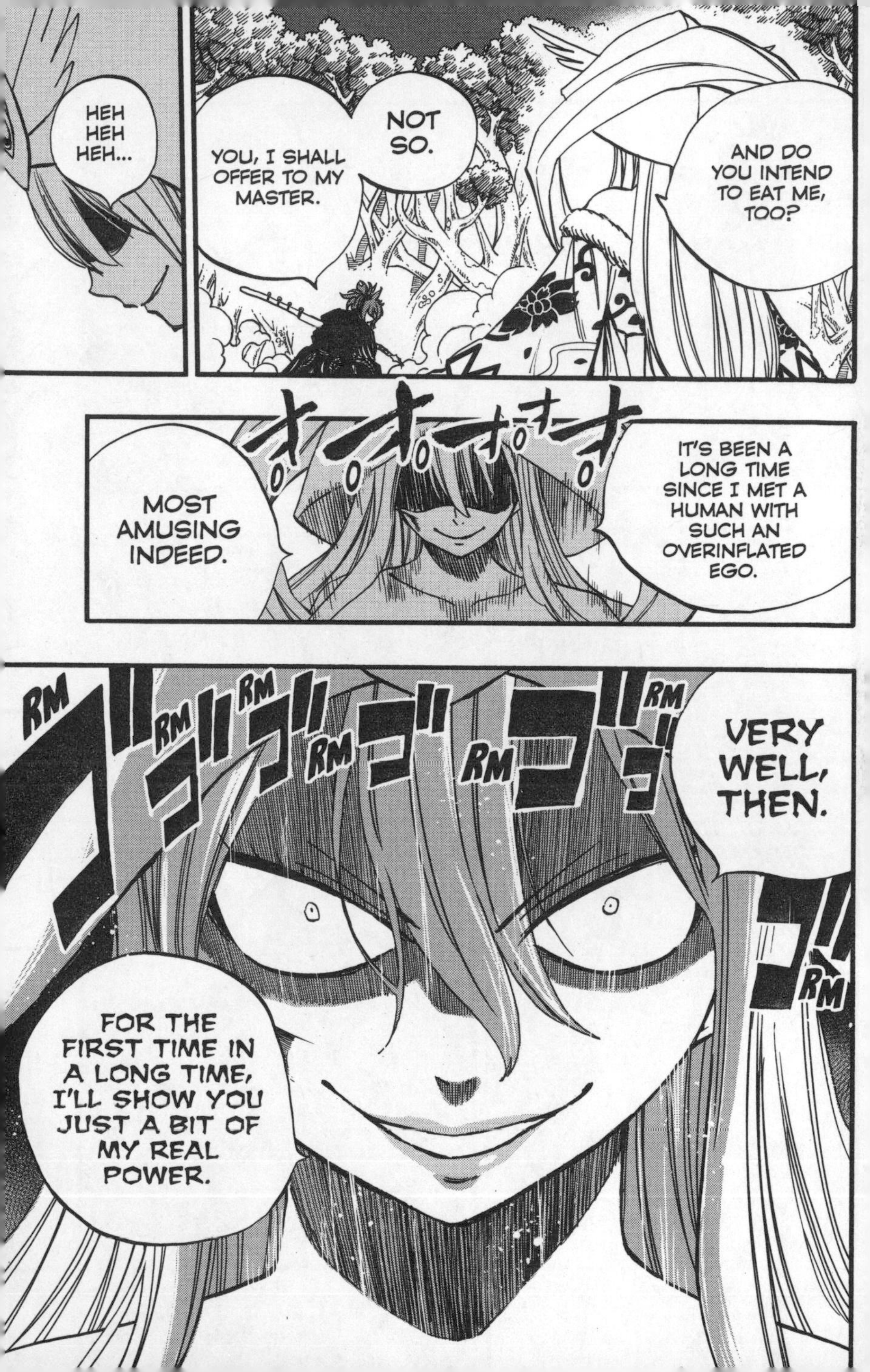
AND DO YOU INTEND TO EAT ME, TOO?
NOT SO.
YOU, I SHALL OFFER TO MY MASTER.
HEH HEH HEH...
IT'S BEEN A LONG TIME SINCE I MET A HUMAN WITH SUCH AN OVERINFLATED EGO.
MOST AMUSING INDEED.
RM
RM
RM
RM
RM
RM
RM
VERY WELL, THEN.
RM
FOR THE FIRST TIME IN A LONG TIME, I'LL SHOW YOU JUST A BIT OF MY REAL POWER.

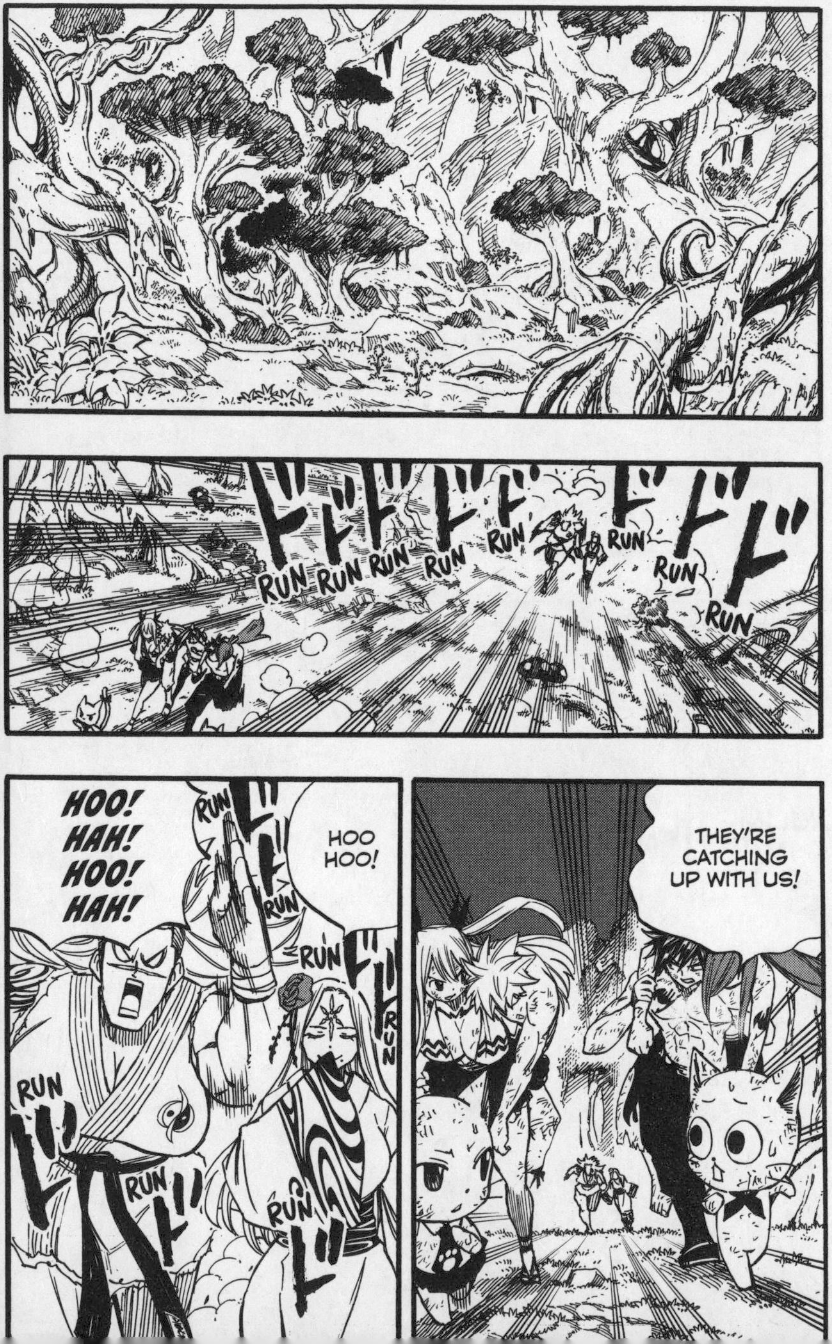
RUN
RUN
RUN
RUN
RUN
RUN
RUN
RUN
THEY'RE CATCHING UP WITH US!
HOO HOO!
RUN
RUN
RUN
HOO! HAH! HOO! HAH!
RUN
RUN
RUN
RUN

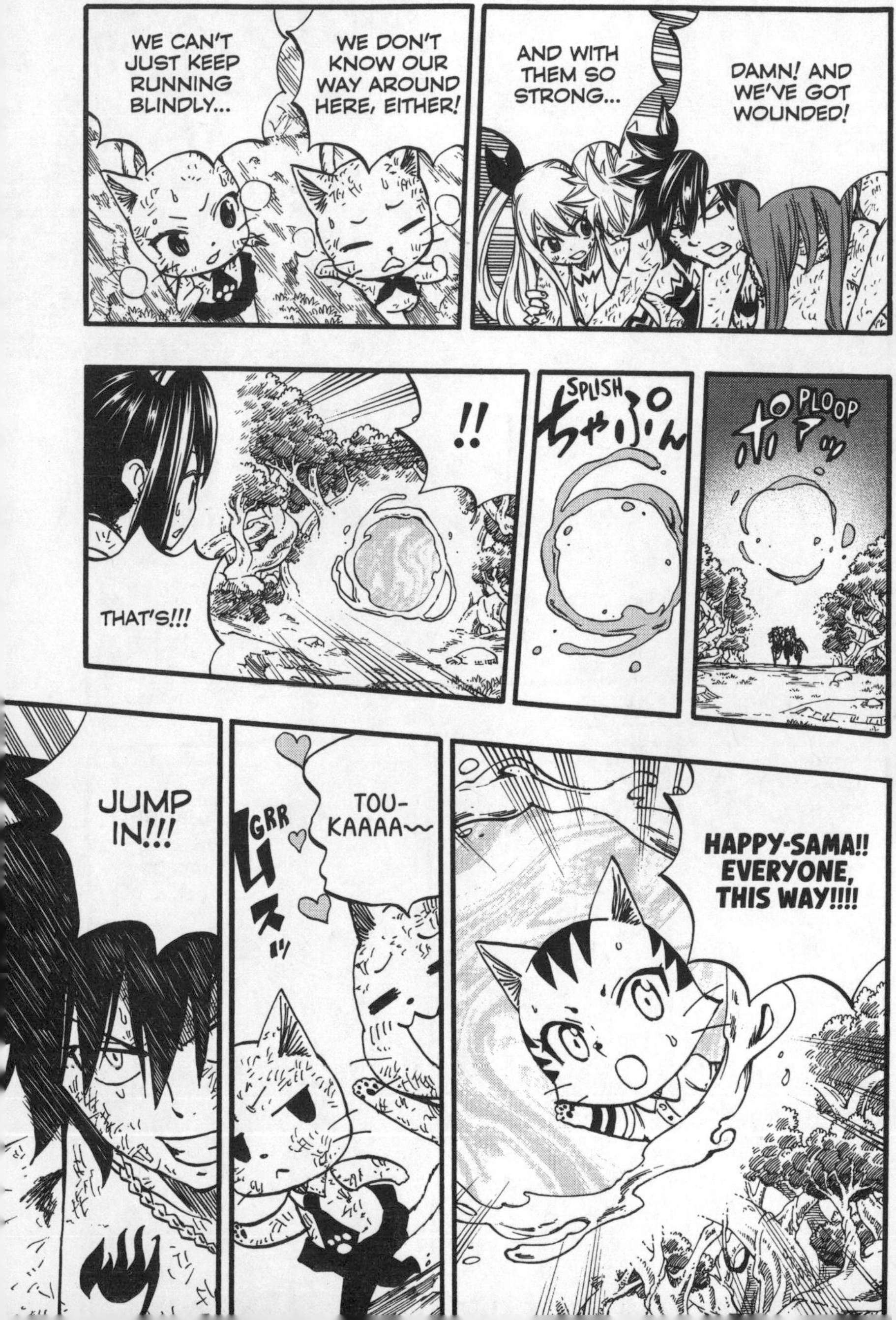
DAMN! AND WE'VE GOT WOUNDED!
AND WITH THEM SO STRONG...
WE DON'T KNOW OUR WAY AROUND HERE, EITHER!
WE CAN'T JUST KEEP RUNNING BLINDLY...
PLOOP
SPLISH
ちゃぷん
!!
THAT'S!!!
HAPPY-SAMA!! EVERYONE, THIS WAY!!!!
TOU-KAAAA~~
GRR
JUMP IN!!!

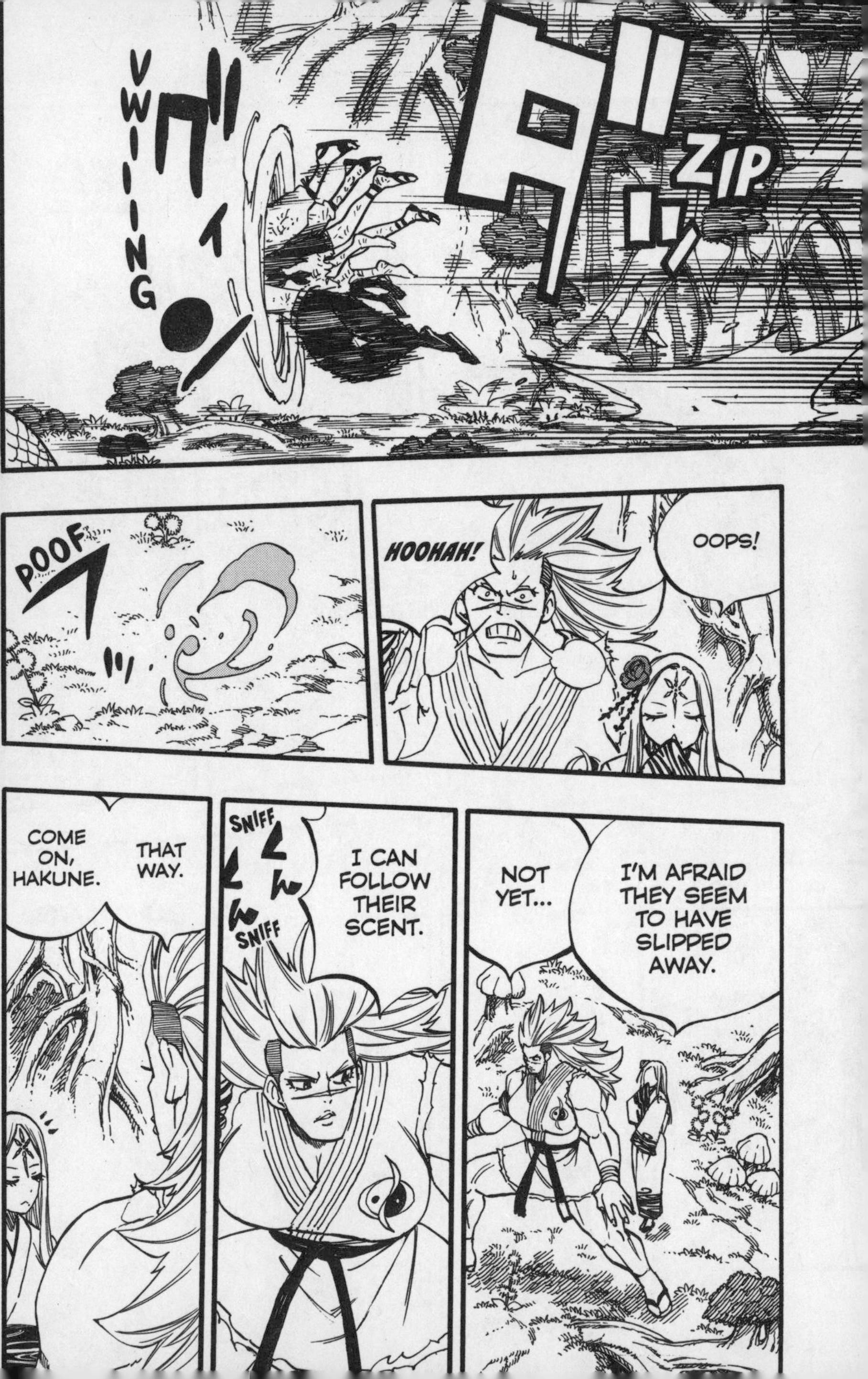
ZIP
VWIIING
OOPS!
HOOHAH!
POOF
I'M AFRAID THEY SEEM TO HAVE SLIPPED AWAY.
NOT YET...
I CAN FOLLOW THEIR SCENT.
SNIFF
SNIFF
THAT WAY.
COME ON, HAKUNE.

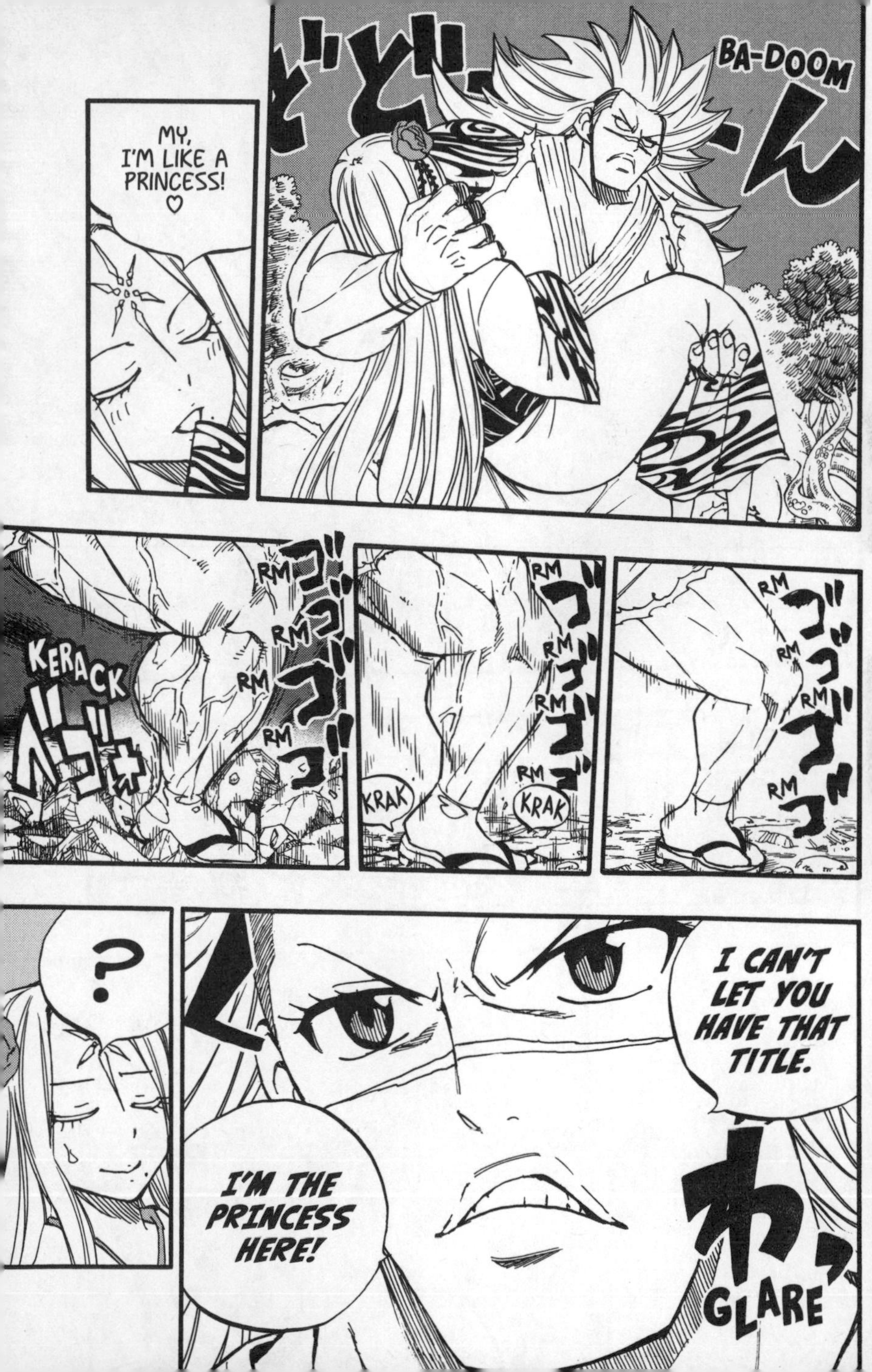
BA-DOOM
MY, I'M LIKE A PRINCESS! ♡
RM
RM
RM
RM
RM
RM
RM
RM
KRAK
KRAK
KERACK
RM
RM
RM
RM
I CAN'T LET YOU HAVE THAT TITLE.
I'M THE PRINCESS HERE!
GLARE
?

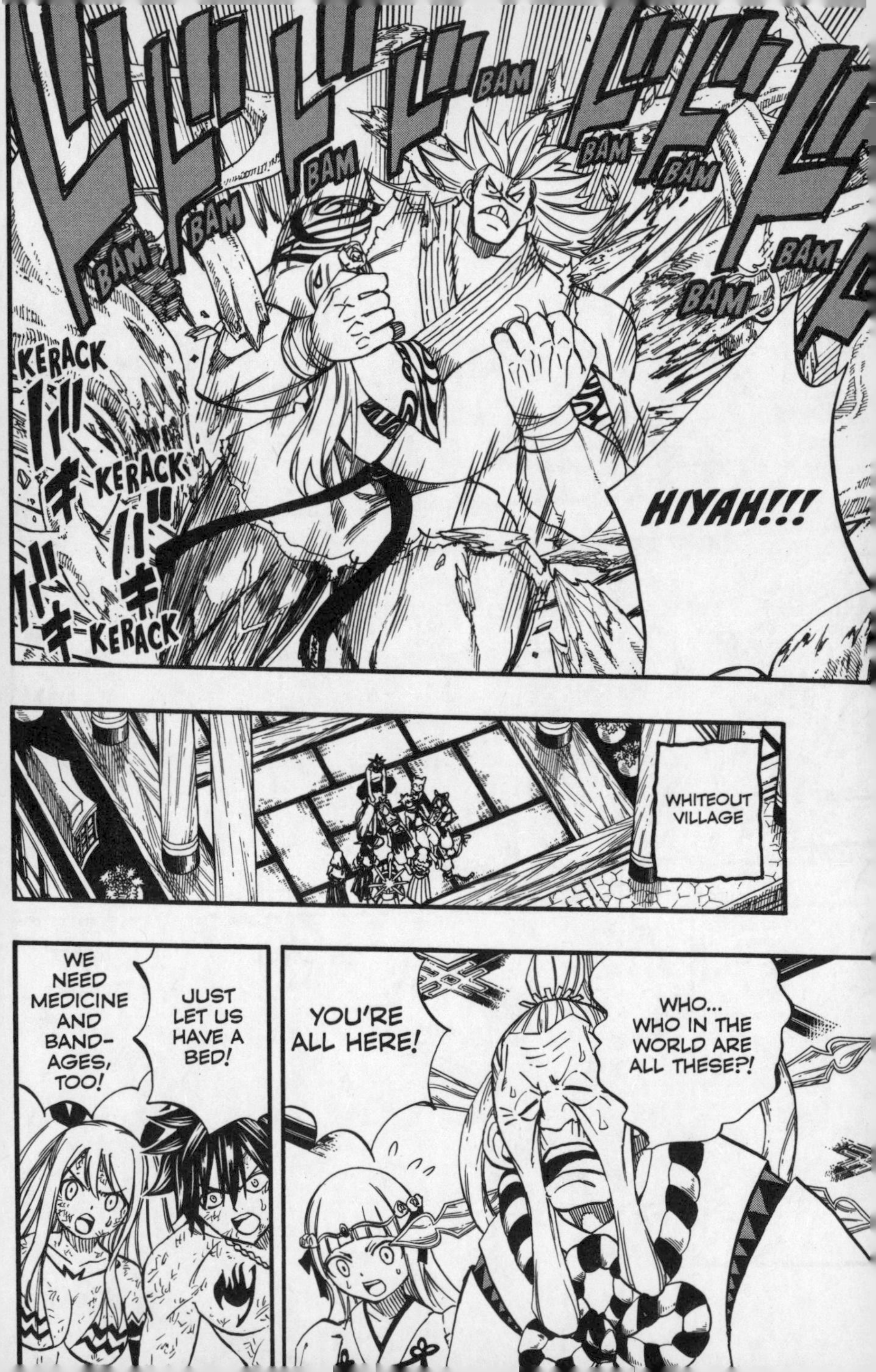

BAM BAM BAM BAM BAM BAM BAM BAM BAM
HIYAH!!!
KERACK
KERACK
KERACK
WHITEOUT VILLAGE
WHO... WHO IN THE WORLD ARE ALL THESE?!
YOU'RE ALL HERE!
JUST LET US HAVE A BED!
WE NEED MEDICINE AND BAND-AGES, TOO!

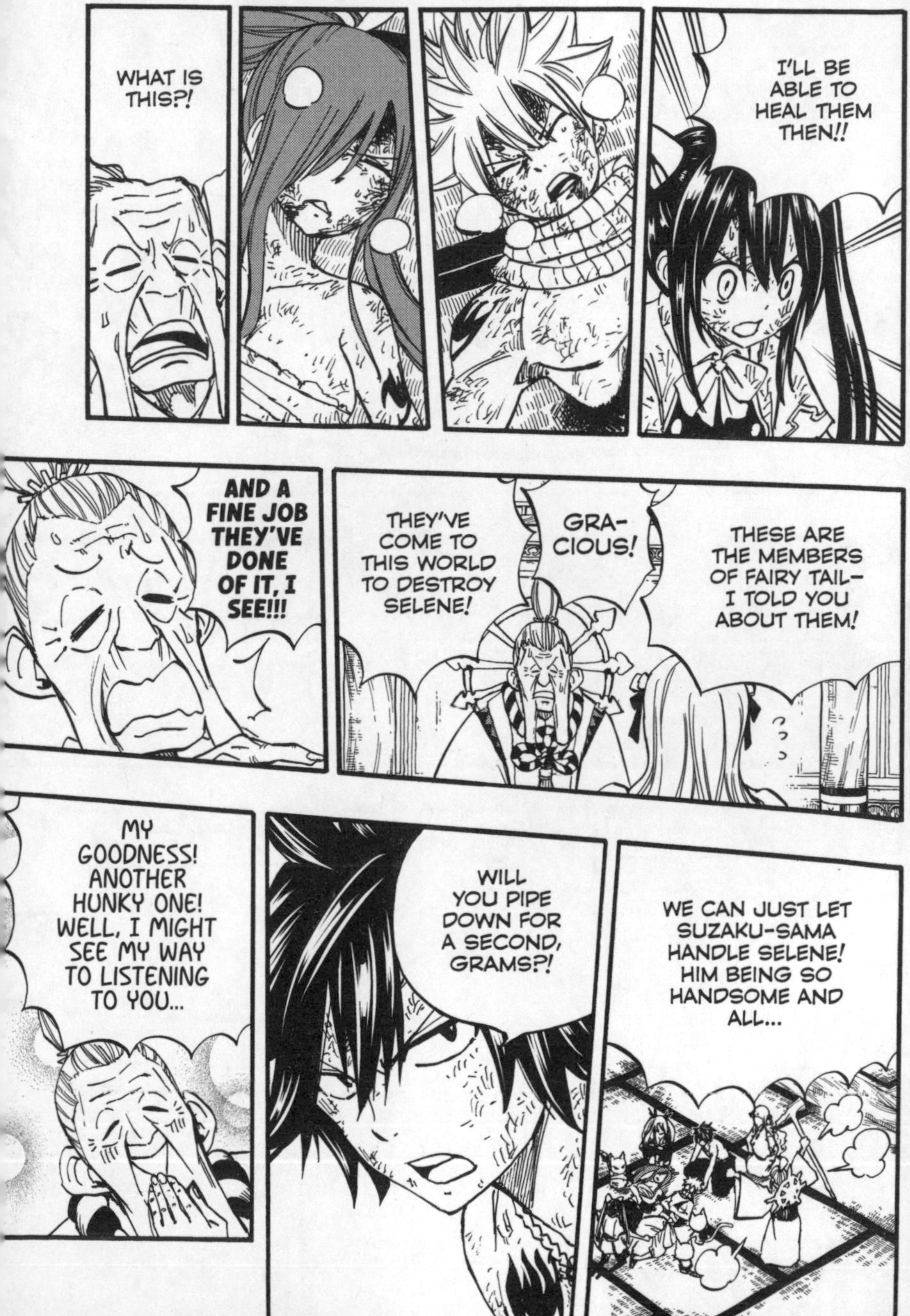
I'LL BE ABLE TO HEAL THEM THEN!!
WHAT IS THIS?!
THESE ARE THE MEMBERS OF FAIRY TAIL— I TOLD YOU ABOUT THEM!
GRA-CIOUS!
THEY'VE COME TO THIS WORLD TO DESTROY SELENE!
AND A FINE JOB THEY'VE DONE OF IT, I SEE!!!
WE CAN JUST LET SUZAKU-SAMA HANDLE SELENE! HIM BEING SO HANDSOME AND ALL...
WILL YOU PIPE DOWN FOR A SECOND, GRAMS?!
MY GOODNESS! ANOTHER HUNKY ONE! WELL, I MIGHT SEE MY WAY TO LISTENING TO YOU...

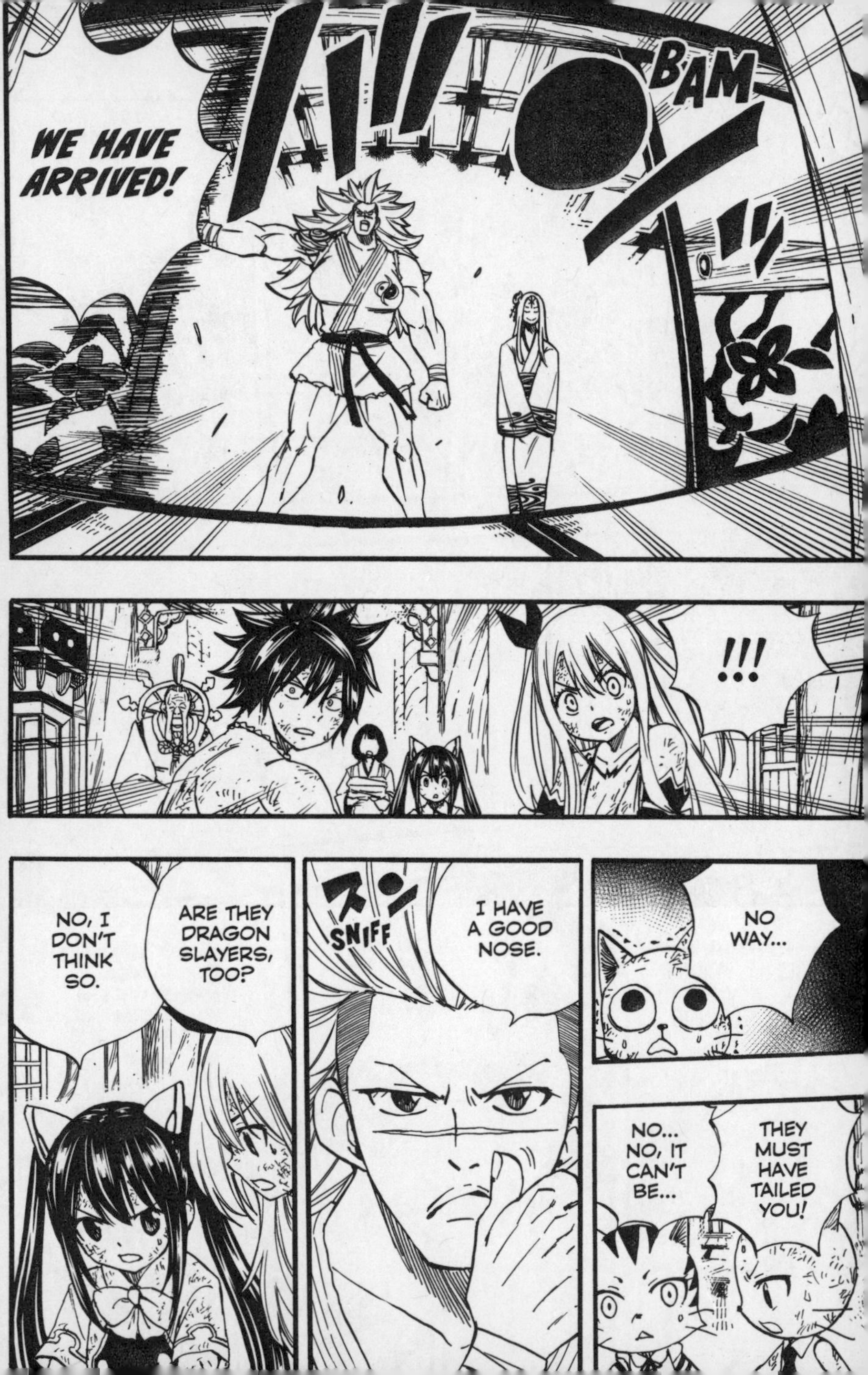
BAM
WE HAVE ARRIVED!
!!!
NO WAY...
THEY MUST HAVE TAILED YOU!
NO... NO, IT CAN'T BE...
I HAVE A GOOD NOSE.
SNIFF
ARE THEY DRAGON SLAYERS, TOO?
NO, I DON'T THINK SO.

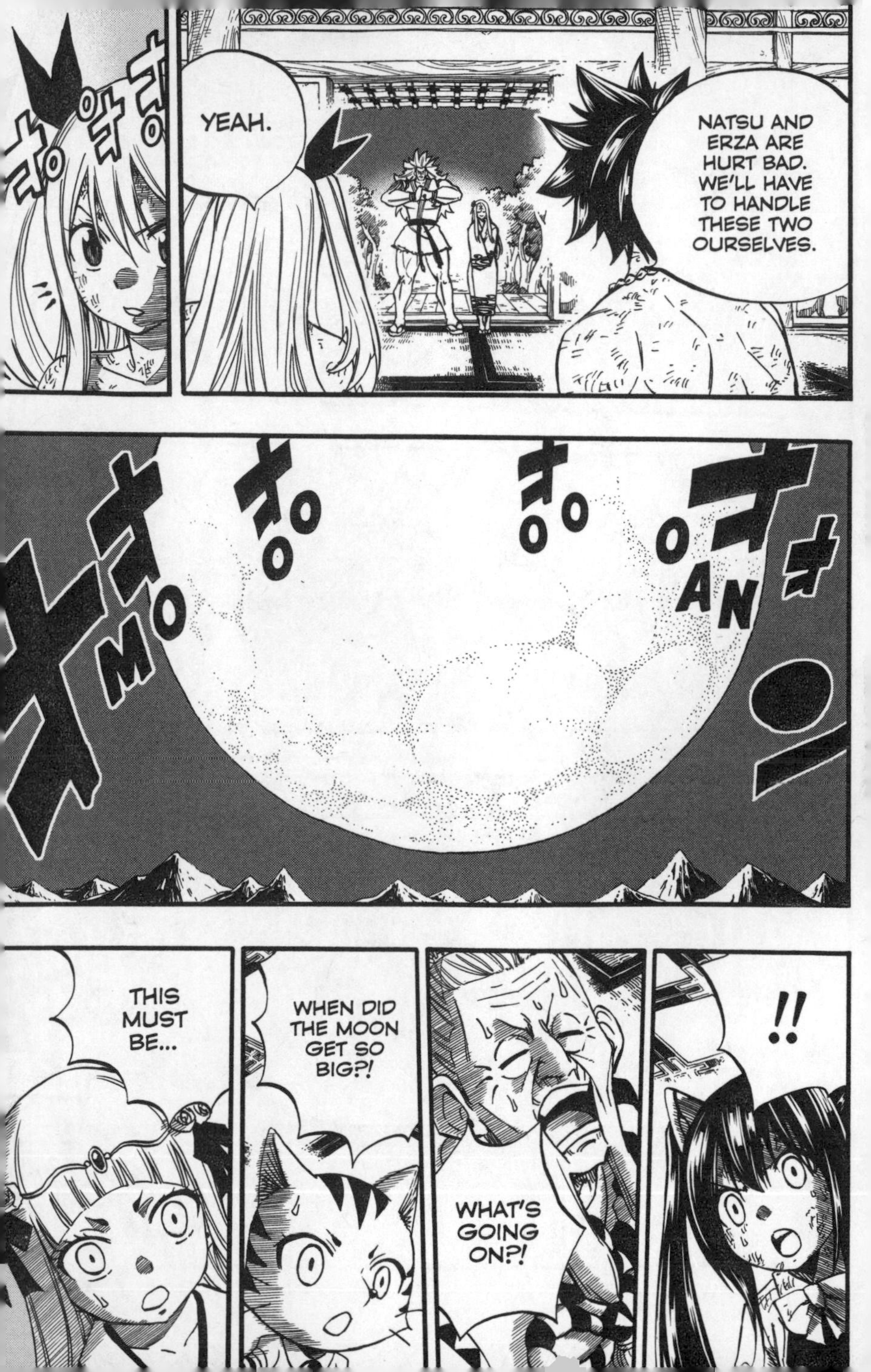
NATSU AND ERZA ARE HURT BAD. WE'LL HAVE TO HANDLE THESE TWO OURSELVES.
YEAH.
MO
OAN
!!
WHAT'S GOING ON?!
WHEN DID THE MOON GET SO BIG?!
THIS MUST BE...

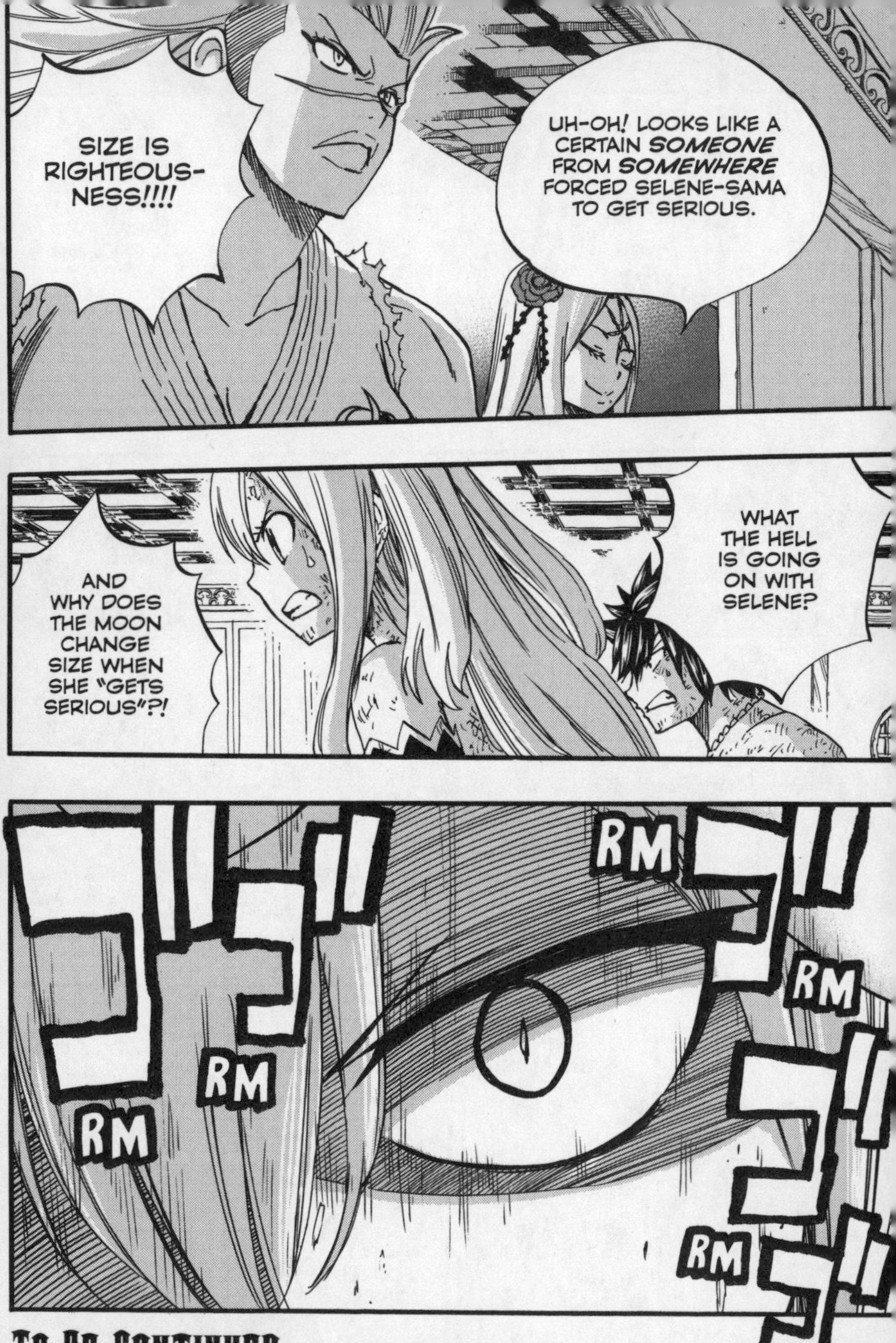
UH-OH! LOOKS LIKE A CERTAIN *SOMEONE* FROM *SOMEWHERE* FORCED SELENE-SAMA TO GET SERIOUS.
SIZE IS RIGHTEOUS-NESS!!!!
WHAT THE HELL IS GOING ON WITH SELENE?
AND WHY DOES THE MOON CHANGE SIZE WHEN SHE "GETS SERIOUS"?!
RM
RM
RM
RM
RM

TO BE CONTINUED

BONUS COMIC
SLOPPY, SOPPY JUVIA

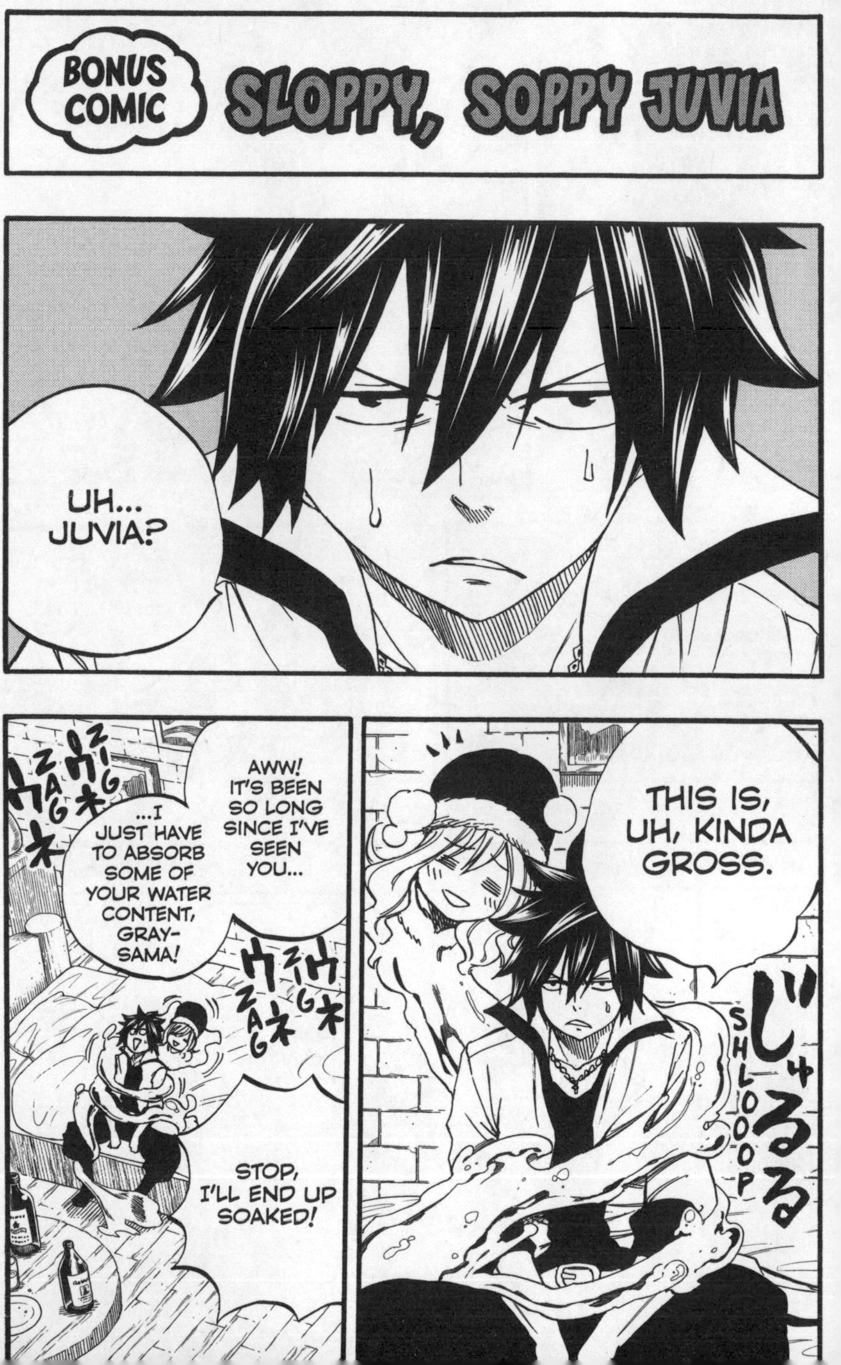
UH... JUVIA?
THIS IS, UH, KINDA GROSS.
じゅるる
SHLOOOOP
AWW! IT'S BEEN SO LONG SINCE I'VE SEEN YOU...
...I JUST HAVE TO ABSORB SOME OF YOUR WATER CONTENT, GRAY-SAMA!
ZIGZAG
ZIGZAG
STOP, I'LL END UP SOAKED!

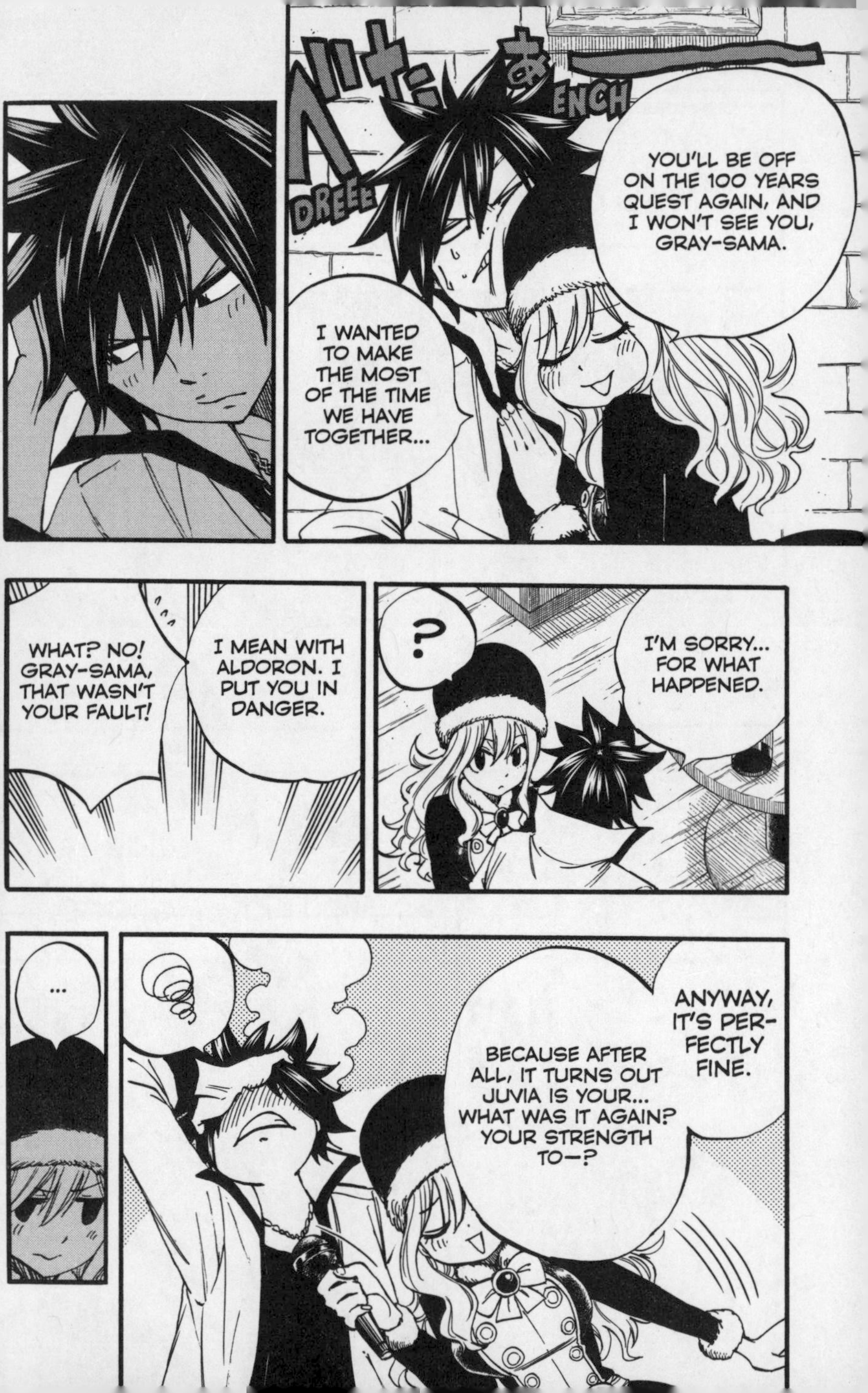
ENCH
DREEE
YOU'LL BE OFF ON THE 100 YEARS QUEST AGAIN, AND I WON'T SEE YOU, GRAY-SAMA.
I WANTED TO MAKE THE MOST OF THE TIME WE HAVE TOGETHER...
I'M SORRY... FOR WHAT HAPPENED.
?
I MEAN WITH ALDORON. I PUT YOU IN DANGER.
WHAT? NO! GRAY-SAMA, THAT WASN'T YOUR FAULT!
ANYWAY, IT'S PER-FECTLY FINE.
BECAUSE AFTER ALL, IT TURNS OUT JUVIA IS YOUR... WHAT WAS IT AGAIN? YOUR STRENGTH TO—?
...

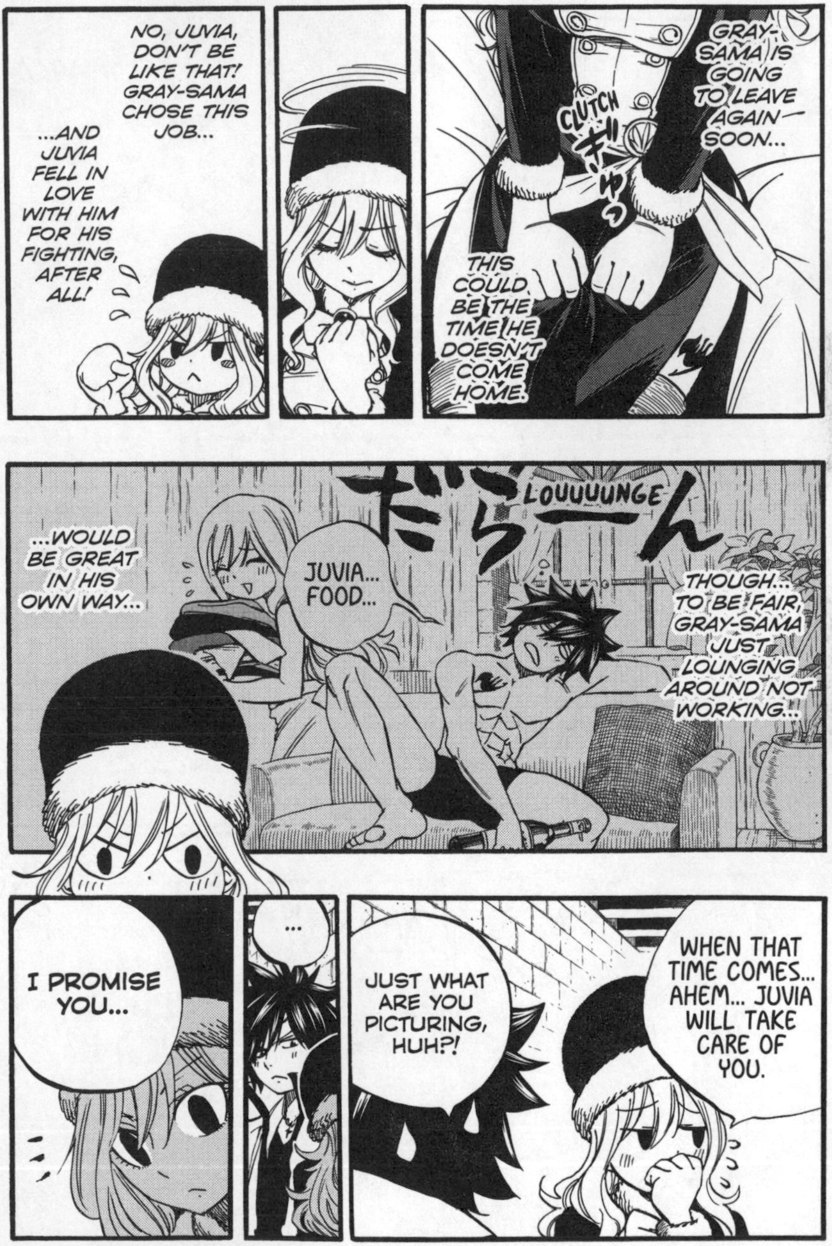
GRAY-SAMA IS GOING TO LEAVE AGAIN SOON...
CLUTCH
ぎゅっ
THIS COULD BE THE TIME HE DOESN'T COME HOME.
NO, JUVIA, DON'T BE LIKE THAT! GRAY-SAMA CHOSE THIS JOB...
...AND JUVIA FELL IN LOVE WITH HIM FOR HIS FIGHTING, AFTER ALL!
だらーん
LOUUUUNGE
THOUGH... TO BE FAIR, GRAY-SAMA JUST LOUNGING AROUND NOT WORKING...
JUVIA... FOOD...
...WOULD BE GREAT IN HIS OWN WAY...
WHEN THAT TIME COMES... AHEM... JUVIA WILL TAKE CARE OF YOU.
JUST WHAT ARE YOU PICTURING, HUH?!
...
I PROMISE YOU...

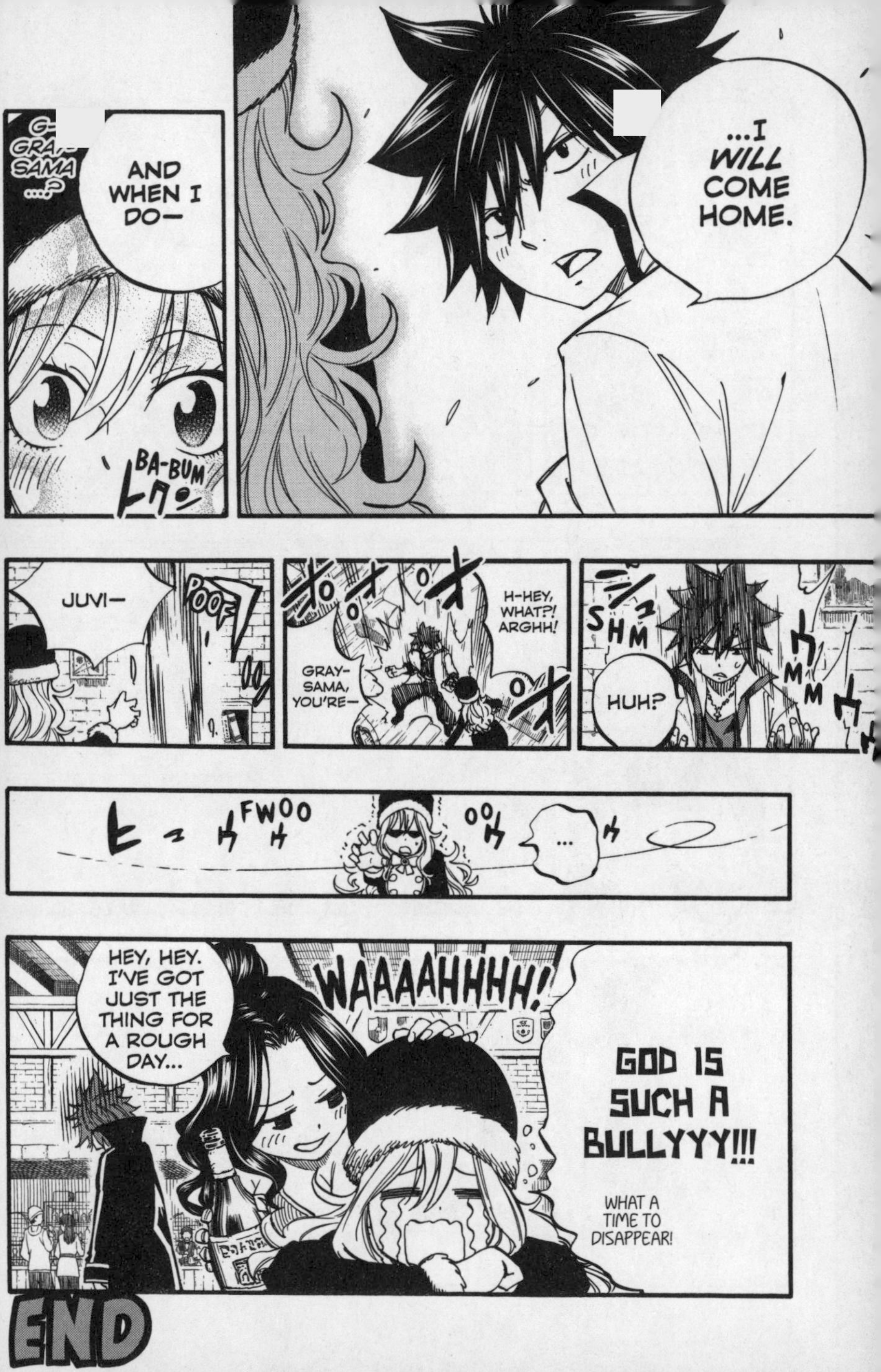
...I WILL COME HOME.
AND WHEN I DO—
G-GRAY-SAMA...?
BA-BUM
SHM
HUH?
H-HEY, WHAT?! ARGHH!
GRAY-SAMA, YOU'RE—
JUVI—
POOF
FWOO
...
HEY, HEY. I'VE GOT JUST THE THING FOR A ROUGH DAY...
WAAAAHHHH!
GOD IS SUCH A BULLYYY!!!
WHAT A TIME TO DISAPPEAR!
END

FAIRY TAIL
100 YEARS QUEST

DE ART RETURNS

(KYOTO PREFECTURE MII)

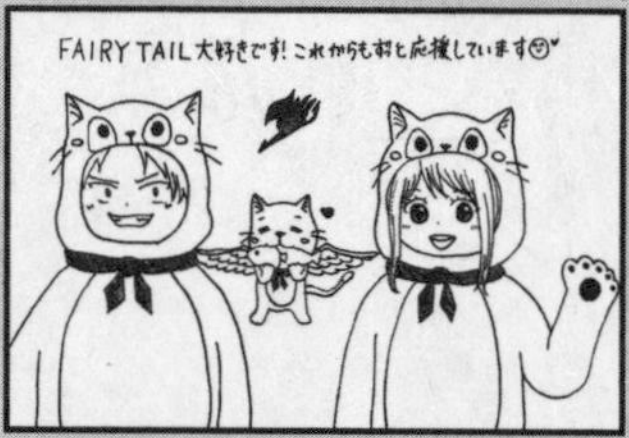
FAIRY TAIL大好きです! これからもずっと応援しています

▲ THOSE COSTUMES ARE ADORABLE!

(SHIGA PREFECTURE MK)

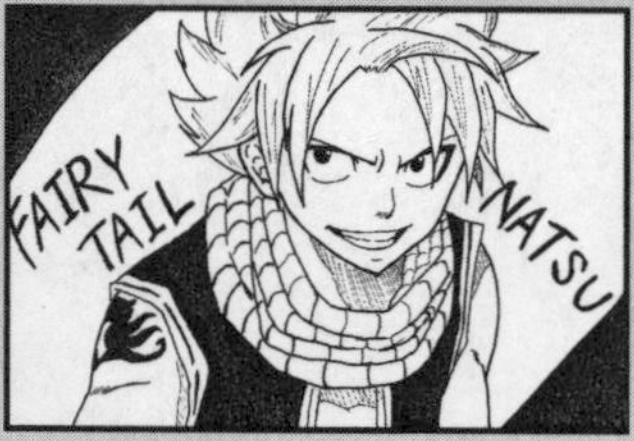
FAIRY TAIL
NATSU

▲ SO COOL!
ALL THREE OF YOUR DRAWINGS WERE FANTASTIC!

(IWATE PREFECTURE SOPHIE KITAKUNI)

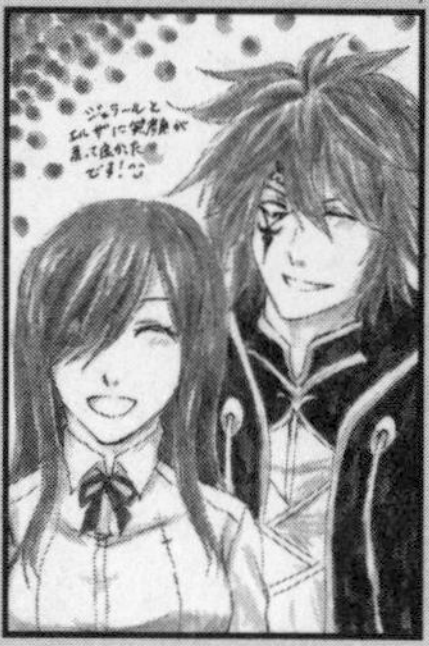
ジェラールとエルザに笑顔が戻って良かったです!

▲ THOSE SMILES ARE HEARTWARMING.

(HOKKAIDO PREFECTURE YUKOKO)

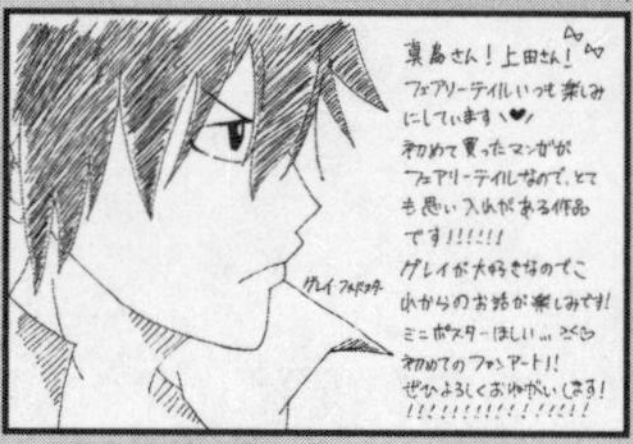
真島さん!上田さん!
フェアリーテイルいつも楽しみにしています
初めて買ったマンガがフェアリーテイルなので、とても思い入れがある作品です!!!!!!
グレイが大好きなのでこれからのお話が楽しみです!
ミニポスターほしい…
初めてのファンアート!!
ぜひよろしくおねがいします!
!!!!!!!!!!!!!!!!

▲ IN PROFILE – SEXY!

(KAGOSHIMA PREFECTURE MUU MUU)

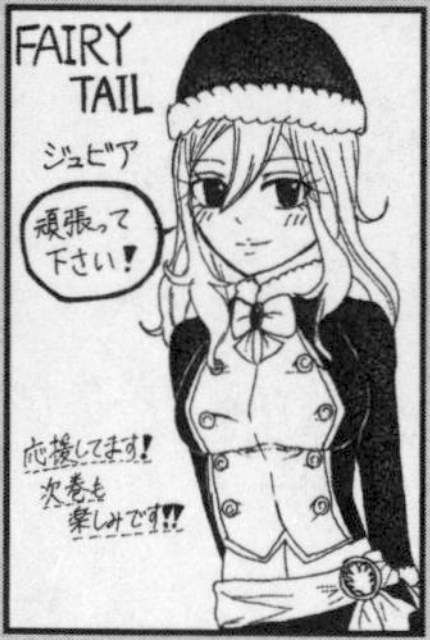
FAIRY TAIL
ジュビア
頑張って下さい!
応援してます!
次巻も楽しみです!!

▲ THINK SHE'S STILL WAITING FOR GRAY TO GET HOME?

FAIRY TAIL 100 YEARS QUEST GUILD

(IWATE PREFECTURE YUKIWI)

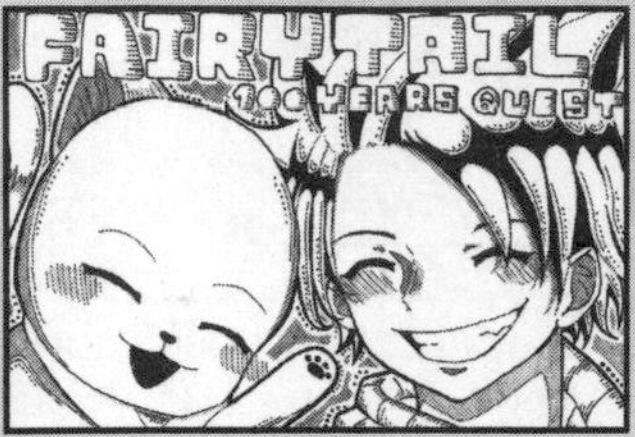
FAIRY TAIL
100 YEARS QUEST

(MIYAGI PREFECTURE KOHARU♪)

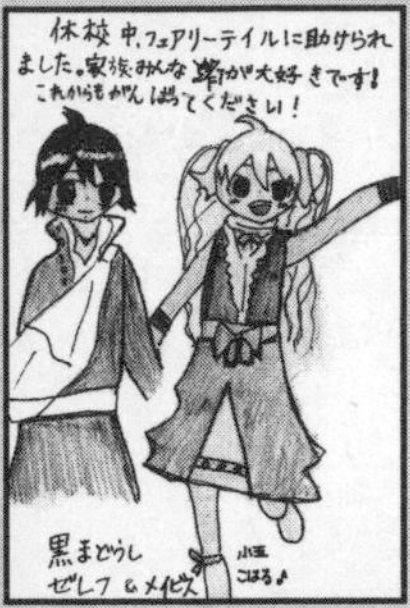
休校中、フェアリーテイルに助けられました。
これからもがんばってください!
黒まどうし ゼレフ & メイビス
小五 こはる♪

▲ HAPPY THEY'RE HAVING FUN TOGETHER – GOOD!

(FUKUSHIMA PREFECTURE RINKA WATANABE)

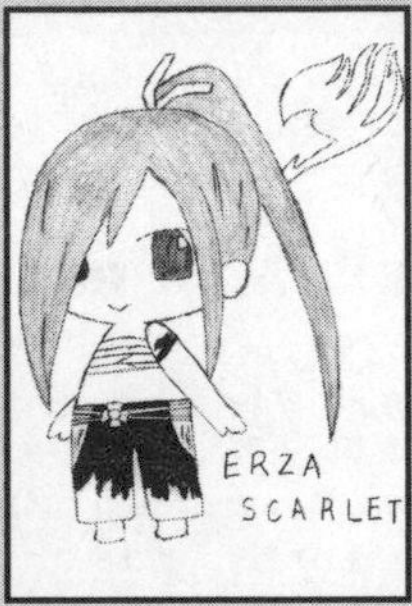
ERZA SCARLET

▲ I LOVE SD ERZA, SHE'S ADORABLE.

(NAGANO PREFECTURE MAI TAKEI)

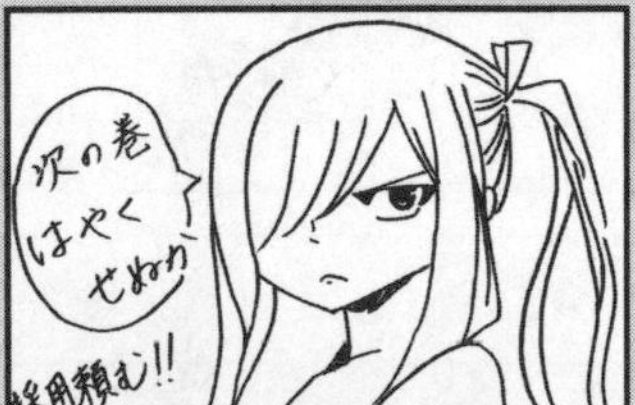
次の巻はやくせぬか
採用頼む!!

▲ I'LL GET IT DONE AS FAST AS I CAN… (GRIN)

(SAITAMA PREFECTURE TANABE KOBAYASHI)

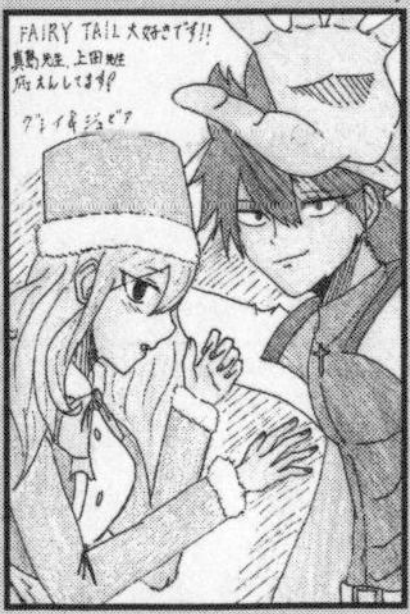
FAIRY TAIL 大好きです!!

▲ ABOUT TO TAKE A NAP?! LOVE HOW HAPPY THEY LOOK!

(WAKAYAMA PREFECTURE RUKI)

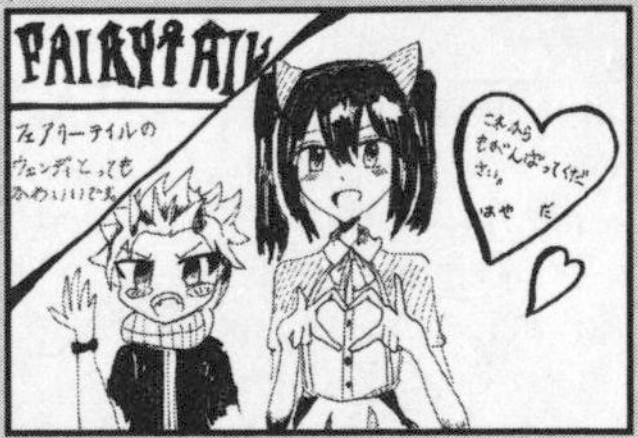
FAIRY TAIL
フェアリーテイルのウェンディとってもかわいいです

▲ THANKS FOR THE CUTE POSE!

TRANSLATION NOTES

Oni-ga-Tsuki, page 16

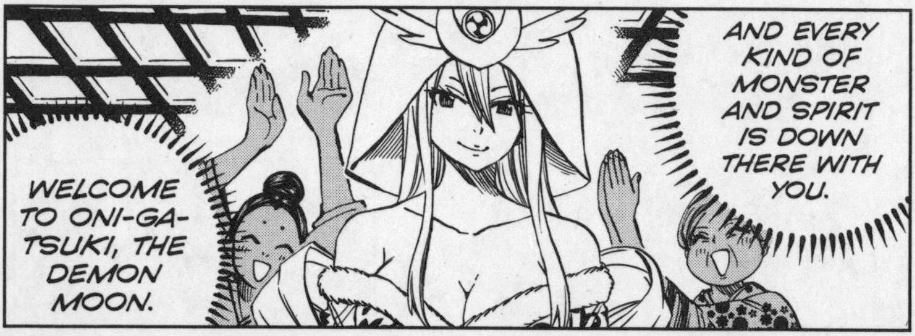
AND EVERY KIND OF MONSTER AND SPIRIT IS DOWN THERE WITH YOU.
WELCOME TO ONI-GA-TSUKI, THE DEMON MOON.

The name of this location seems to recall *oni-ga-shima*, "demon island," the land where Momotaro and his band of loyal animals travel.

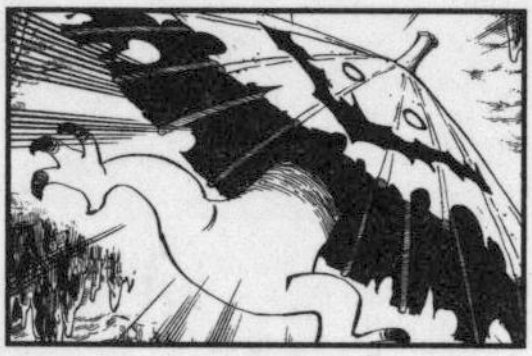

Umbrella Monster, page 18

The first creature Natsu encounters on Blackmoon Mountain might be considered a kind of *kasa-obake* or "umbrella ghost." Although such creatures are most commonly depicted with just one eye and one leg, they may sometimes be seen with two eyes or two legs.

Nuré-onna, page 22

The name of this yokai literally means "wet woman" (*nureru* means "to soak"), but it refers to a creature with the body of a snake and the head of a woman.

Baké-neko, page 32

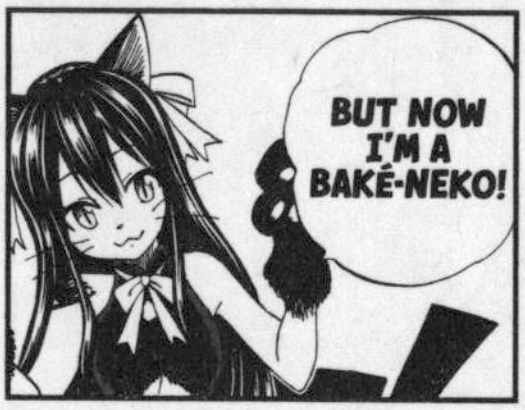
BUT NOW I'M A BAKÉ-NEKO!

Literally meaning "transformed cat" or more figuratively "monster cat," the *baké-neko* is a cat yokai. In her feline form, Wendy frequently includes the sound *nya* or *nyan* in her dialogue, both equivalent to "meow." This is what inspired us to include variations on "meow," "mew," and so forth in her English dialogue.

Suiko, page 35

Also known by the Chinese pronunciation of the characters, shuihu, the *suiko* (literally, "water tiger") is usually believed to be a child-sized, quasi-human creature who lives in or near water, similar to a kappa. In this case, the manga departs from traditional depictions of the yokai, running with the "tiger" part of the name to create these imposing new forms for Carla and Happy. (This might be what inspires Hakune's comment that Yoko's *suiko* are "bigger and stronger than usual.")

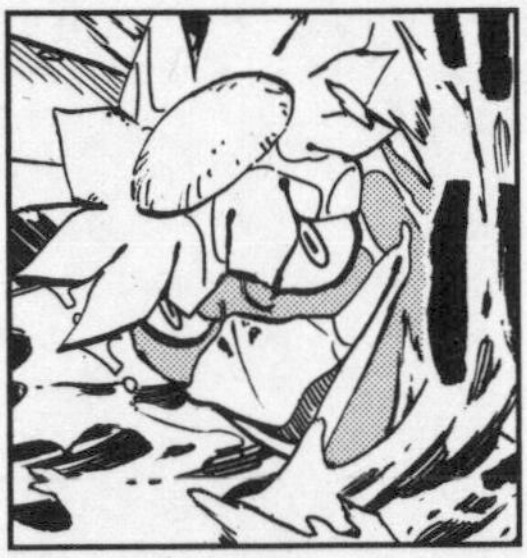

Kappa, page 109

The monster in the middle of this panel appears to be a *kappa*, a Japanese river spirit. They're sometimes mischievous and sometimes downright dangerous, but the point is that this creature would be impervious to Lucy's water attacks.

Ohmagatoki, page 130

Ohmagatoki, literally "the time of meeting evil spirits," is an old word for twilight, from the time when people believed that the transition between day and night was when spirits were likely to be encountered. Yoko refers to it as *gehou*, literally meaning "outside the dharma," or teaching of the Buddha. This can imply the meaning of "immoral," but can also refer to magic arts. The translation draws on the closely related word *gedou*, which means "off the path (of morality or humanity)."

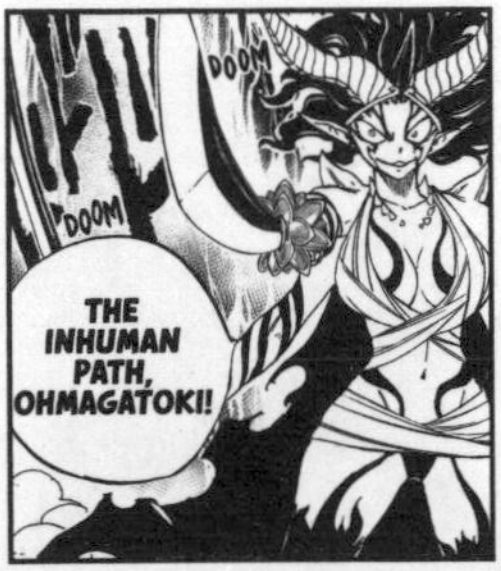
DOOM
DOOM
THE INHUMAN PATH, OHMAGATOKI!

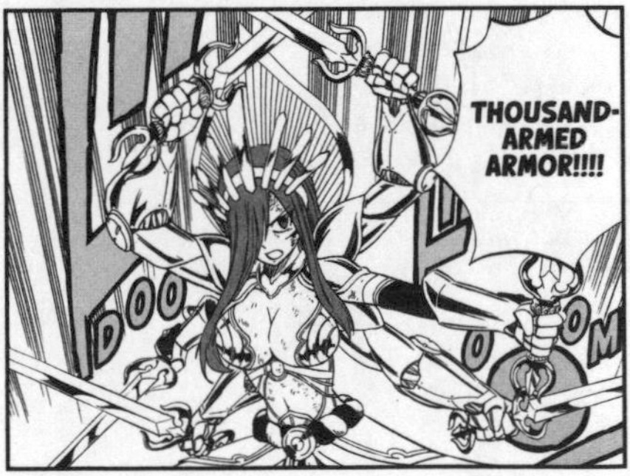
THOUSAND-ARMED ARMOR!!!!

Thousand-Armed Armor, page 133

The term *senju* (thousand-armed) is somewhat figurative in the case of Erza's armor, which appears to have six arms, but it evokes *senju kannon*, "thousand-armed Kannon," a Buddhist deity of mercy and compassion.

Battou-jutsu, page 165

Battou-jutsu (literally, "sword-drawing art") is the skill of drawing and striking with a sword in a single fluid motion.

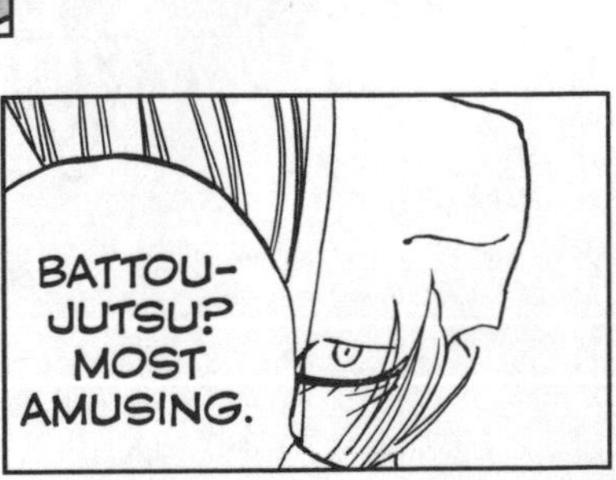
BATTOU-JUTSU? MOST AMUSING.

A Kodansha Comics Trade Paperback Original

FAIRY TAIL: 100 Years Quest 9 copyright © 2021 Hiro Mashima/Atsuo Ueda
English translation copyright © 2021 Hiro Mashima/Atsuo Ueda

All rights reserved.

Published in the United States by Kodansha Comics, an imprint of Kodansha USA Publishing, LLC, New York.

Publication rights for this English edition arranged through Kodansha Ltd., Tokyo.

First published in Japan in 2021 by Kodansha Ltd., Tokyo.

ISBN 978-1-64651-306-2

Original cover design by Hisao Ogawa (Blue in Green)

Printed in the United States of America.

www.kodansha.us

1st Printing
Translation: Kevin Steinbach
Lettering: Phil Christie
Editing: David Yoo
Kodansha Comics edition cover design by Phil Balsman

Publisher: Kiichiro Sugawara

Director of publishing services: Ben Applegate
Associate director, publishing operations: Stephen Pakula
Publishing services managing editorial: Madison Salters, Alanna Ruse
Production managers: Emi Lotto, Angela Zurlo